From Swamp to Wetland

environmental
history
and the
american
south

SERIES EDITORS

James C. Giesen, Mississippi State University

Erin Stewart Mauldin, University of South Florida

ADVISORY BOARD

Judith Carney, University of California–Los Angeles

S. Max Edelson, University of Virginia

Robbie Ethridge, University of Mississippi

Ari Kelman, University of California–Davis

Shepard Krech III, Brown University

Megan Kate Nelson, www.historista.com

Tim Silver, Appalachian State University

Mart Stewart, Western Washington University

Paul S. Sutter, founding editor, University of Colorado Boulder

From Swamp to Wetland

THE CREATION OF
EVERGLADES NATIONAL PARK

Chris Wilhelm

The University of Georgia Press
Athens

© 2022 by the University of Georgia Press
Athens, Georgia 30602
www.ugapress.org
All rights reserved
Set in 10.5/13.5 Garamond Premier Pro by Kaelin Chappell Broaddus

Most University of Georgia Press titles are
available from popular e-book vendors.

Printed digitally

Library of Congress Cataloging-in-Publication Data

Names: Wilhelm, Chris, 1978– author.
Title: From swamp to wetland : the creation of Everglades National Park /
    Chris Wilhelm.
Other titles: Creation of Everglades National Park | Environmental history and
    the American South.
Description: Athens : The University of Georgia Press, [2022] | Series: Environmental
    history and the American South | Includes bibliographical references and index.
Identifiers: LCCN 2021059117 | ISBN 9780820362380 (hardback) |
    ISBN 9780820362397 (paperback) | ISBN 9780820362403 (ebook)
Subjects: LCSH: National parks and reserves—Florida—History—20th century. |
    Environmentalism—Florida—History—20th century. | Tourism—Florida—
    History—20th century. | Real estate development—Florida—History—
    20th century. | Everglades National Park (Fla.)—History—20th century. |
    Everglades (Fla.)—History—20th century. | Everglades (Fla.)—
    Environmental conditions.
Classification: LCC F317.E9 W48 2022 | DDC 975.9/39—dc23/eng/20211214
LC record available at https://lccn.loc.gov/2021059117

For Mom and Dad

CONTENTS

FOREWORD

A decade before the creation of Everglades National Park in 1947, the U.S. Department of the Interior produced a short film on the area of South Florida earmarked for preservation. The production does little to promote the Everglades as a destination for tourists. The camera pans across cabbage palms drooping over slivers of sand and impenetrable banks of mangroves. Water stretches toward a horizon marred by black clouds; long-necked waterfowl pick through stagnant pools and marshy grass. Seven minutes of soundless, flickering black-and-white footage captures no soaring vista, no Edenic oasis—nothing that could be described as awe inspiring or even charming. Twenty years later, a slickly produced pamphlet advertising the "south Florida experience" ran into a similar problem. Despite leaning heavily on stereotypes of Florida as an exotic paradise, the booklet struggled to characterize the appeal of Everglades National Park for tourists. "There is no single point of dramatic focus in the Everglades National Park," the writer admits, no "bold prospect" suitable for a postcard. "No other national park demands more perception and patience of the visitor," for the beauty of the Everglades is not immediately obvious. It is a "mysterious" and "ageless" landscape that requires an appreciation of nature's subtleties.[1]

As federal agencies' attempts at boosterism in the 1930s and 1950s demonstrate, the Everglades National Park fits poorly alongside the purple mountains' majesty of Yosemite and Yellowstone. It was a place carved from neither water nor land but somewhere in between, a place devoid of obvious economic or aesthetic value. Why protect it? *From Swamp to Wetland* argues that changing views of what "nature" meant in the twentieth century and the growing influence of ecology on the post–Progressive Era National Park Service motivated the creation of Everglades National Park. Advocates made it clear that preserving the Everglades from development safeguarded unique flora and fauna and the ecosystems that supported them. At the same time, supporters hoped that the space, its wildlife, and its landscape—whether or not it was suitable for a postcard—could be a potential source of profit through tourism. Like the Everglades themselves, the park's origin is a story full of contradictions and, as Chris Wilhelm argues, a story essential to understanding the history of nature in the American imagination.

Placing the Everglades at the center of debates over the value of wilderness, nature protection, and ecology in the twentieth century challenges environmental historians' habit of looking to the West, rather than the South, for those developments. Although most places in the United States could never claim a truly "wilderness" past, the idea of the wild western frontier has long permeated much of the environmental history of conservation and preservation. In the South, one can rarely take the humans out of nature, thanks to the region's long connection to large-scale agriculture and millennia of human settlement. It takes a certain audacity to imagine a national park in such a place. Thus, southern environmental history lacks the dynamic scholarship on national parks that the American West possesses. *From Swamp to Wetland*, then, not only reorients the scholarly conversation about nature protection toward the South and away from the West but also gives much-needed attention to national parks in a region that cannot hide the continuous presence of humans.

From Swamp to Wetland resurrects the stories and actions of the men and women who both spearheaded and opposed the park's creation, introducing Floridian counterparts to the Muirs and Pinchots of other conservation narratives. Although once the site of vibrant indigenous communities, the Everglades encountered by Europeans was a landscape drained of its people. It was a derelict swamp, an unwanted expanse of land deemed suitable only for the Seminole refugees fleeing American expansionism in the nineteenth century. Later Floridians hoped to drain the Everglades of water, dreaming of an agricultural paradise, and when that failed, to use oil drilling as a shortcut to prosperity in Florida's wild interior. Only in the early twentieth century, thanks to the efforts of the devoted Yankee transplant Ernest Coe, did protecting—rather than eradicating—the Everglades become a viable outcome. Creating a national park took decades, however, and faced both local and federal hostility. Landowners, politicians, and even some Park Service employees pushed back against an Everglades National Park, and Wilhelm argues that their opposition foreshadowed modern conservatism's aversion to environmental regulation.

This book does not, however, have a happy ending. Although advocates succeeded in creating a national park in the Everglades by drawing attention to its wildlife and complex hydraulic systems, only a fraction of the Everglades is protected from agriculture and other development. Even within park boundaries, wildlife has declined precipitously; past and present drainage initiatives—and other "water conservation" efforts—further threaten the area's ecosystems. As Wilhelm shows, the very ecological dependencies that the Park Service sought to preserve has made the area more vulnerable to change, for Everglades ecosystems cannot be preserved as the landscape outside its boundaries diminishes. With this book as our guide, we are in a better place to understand whether Everglades National Park continues to protect a wilderness or creates a new one.

Erin Stewart Mauldin and James C. Giesen
Series Editors

ACKNOWLEDGMENTS

Researching, writing, editing, and publishing this book has been a long journey and I've accrued many debts along the way, far more than I can address in this space. This book began as a dissertation at Florida State University that I completed in 2010. I started at FSU in 2003 under the mentorship of Elna Green, an incredible scholar, teacher, and advisor. Elna took a chance on me as a first-year graduate student and shaped me as an historian, writer, and thinker. I hope this book meets her high bar for historiographical relevancy and clear writing. Fritz Davis graciously agreed to oversee the dissertation to its completion in 2010 and helped orient me in the field of environmental history. I also owe Darden Pyron a debt of thanks. Darden was the most important professor I had as an undergraduate at Florida International University, and he played an enormous role in my own intellectual awakening. An inspiring lecturer, he took an interest in developing the critical thinking and writing skills of students.

The editors at the UGA Press, Mick Gusinde-Duffy, Erin Mauldin, and James Giesen, also were enormously helpful and patient with me throughout the review process. Erin Maudlin especially put an incredible amount of time into reading early manuscript versions, making wonderful suggestions that strengthened the structure and flow of this book. I owe her an enormous debt, and I truly appreciate her sacrifice of time and effort. I was lucky to have Deborah Oliver copyedit this manuscript. Her focus on detail and consistency improved this book greatly.

My research took me to numerous archives and libraries over the years. Some of these were so long ago that I've forgotten the names of the people who aided that early research. I made repeated trips to two archives in particular, and I came to know several archivists well. I spent countless hours at the State Archives of Florida in Tallahassee, both as a graduate research assistant and as an historian working on my own projects. Thanks to Mariam, Boyd Murphree, Dave Nelson, Hendry Miller, and Josh Youngblood. I also spent significant time at the P. K. Younge Library of Florida History at the University of Florida. As a graduate student, I greatly benefitted from the Cecilia L. Johnson Grant for Visiting Graduate Scholars, and I am indebted to Jim Cusick for his continued support and interest in my work.

My friends and family have provided moral, financial, and intellectual support over the years. My parents, Jim and Margann, to whom this book is dedicated, have always been supportive and understanding. This book has been a long time in the making, and I know they're happy to see it in print. My wife, Althea, has likewise been a consistent supporter. As a marsh ecologist, she has also been a great sounding board for ideas, and a great intellectual partner. My oldest and best friends, Marton Cavani and Fabian Kahn, also deserve thanks, and they helped this project along in various ways. In the twenty years I've known them, they've helped shape me as a person, as an intellectual, and as a writer. Another old friend to whom I owe thanks is Cindy Ermus, who in a crazy twist of fate also earned a PhD from Florida State. I don't think we ever thought we'd both follow similar paths—but here we are. My colleagues in the Department of Social Sciences at the College of Coastal Georgia offered tremendous moral support and comradery as well since 2012.

I also need to thank all the students I've had over the years. Their desire for education is what pays my bills. I've had many, many terrific students over the years, and many have been interested in my own research and ideas. It has been a privilege to teach so many students over the years. I hope to continue to grow as a teacher and researcher as I carry on this interesting adventure in academia. Finally, there are countless other people throughout the years—teachers, colleagues, family, friends, baristas, bartenders, and fellow students—who have supported and shaped me throughout the years as well. We all live in a tangled ecosystem of people, and no one creates anything by themselves—thanks to everyone who has crossed my path over the years.

From Swamp to Wetland

INTRODUCTION

On December 6, 1947, Harry Truman took a break from a working vacation at the Little White House in Key West to dedicate Everglades National Park (ENP). The park had been created on June 20, 1947, but park supporters wisely delayed holding the dedication ceremony until the winter, when the Everglades was cool and dry. The ceremony took place on the west coast of Florida in Everglades City, a small town that residents hoped would become a center of park tourism. Park supporters and local residents treated Truman to a Florida experience. He received gifts from Seminoles and Greek immigrant sponge fishers, toured the local Rod and Gun Club, and ate a lunch that showcased Florida foods like stone crabs, Key lime pie, and a dish called Okalaocooche cup, consisting of crushed fruit inside a halved coconut.[1]

After lunch, Truman delivered the keynote address at the park's dedication ceremony. His speech reflected the nation's confused and changing ideas about nature and placed the park in the context of these transitions. Truman's speech harked back to older ideas about the spiritual values of nature, the economic value of tourism, and the conservation of natural resources. Yet he also referenced new ideas concerning the inherent worth of species, the value of wilderness, and the science of ecology.

Truman explained that in the Everglades there were "no lofty peaks seeking the sky, no mighty glaciers or rushing streams wearing away the uplifted land. Here is land, tranquil in its quiet beauty, serving not as the source of water, but as the last receiver of it." While previous parks had protected the geological monuments of the West, this park would instead protect a flat wetland at the southern tip of Florida and the area's "spectacular plant and animal life." Truman outlined the park's biological rationales and noted that if not for the park, "hundreds of kinds of wildlife . . . might otherwise be extinct." Aside from these stirring sentiments, Truman centered most of his speech on the "wise use of our natural resources" and the need for more efficient mining, forestry, and farming practices.[2]

Truman celebrated the park as a wilderness area but also promoted park tourism. The ENP was an "irreplaceable primitive area" that puzzlingly would soon be visited by millions of tourists. Rather than simply being a nature preserve, its "great value" lay in the "enrichment of the human spirit." These tourists would also enrich the economy of Florida, an important factor to the state's business and political communities. Finally, Truman connected the park to the Everglades' water supply. Foreshadowing efforts to restore the area's historic flow of water, he noted that "we need to prevent [the] further dropping of the water table" in the Everglades. At the same time, though, he celebrated human efforts to control water and lamented the "failure to build hydroelectric dams."[3]

Truman's speech, like the park it celebrated, was contradictory. These contradictions reflected the nation's changing attitudes toward nature in the 1930s, 1940s, and 1950s. In the interwar and postwar periods, Americans questioned their relationships with nature: Was nature something humans could control, or were we just another species, albeit a very powerful one, acting within ecosystems? Did nature exist for our spiritual and economic benefit, or did it have inherent value and worth? Should we seek to control nature or protect it for its own sake? For most of its history, the United States embraced an anthropocentric view of nature: humans controlled a pliant environment, which only had worth in the context of human value systems. These ideas were challenged in the interwar period by new ecological ideas that decentered humans from the environment and by a rising sense of biocentrism that posited all life forms had inherent worth.[4]

This book examines the creation of Everglades National Park, a campaign that reflected these transitions in American environmental thought. The park's creation drew on new biocentric and ecological ideas but was also grounded in older, anthropocentric ideas about the preservation of nature's beauty and the conservation of natural resources. Park advocates, National Park Service (NPS) officials, and Florida politicians embraced these new ecological ideas to varying degrees. Park advocates advanced new ecological and biocentric rationales for preservation, yet also touted the park's economic and inspirational values. NPS officials celebrated this park as the best expression of new conservation ideas concerning wilderness and biological preservation. Yet the service had long prioritized preserving nature's beauty for tourists and sought to open the Everglades to tourism. Florida politicians, eager to grow the state's economy during the Great Depression and after World War II, supported the park as an economic venture. Yet they understood that Florida tourism was dependent on the environment. They saw the Everglades' biology as a foundation on which to build a tourism empire. Additionally, they saw the park, and its biological focus, as part of a larger effort to transform the state's identity. This park would help Florida position itself as a modern Sunbelt state at the forefront of the nation's cultural and scientific trends.

The Everglades itself was fertile ground for these new ecological and biocentric ideas. Park supporters found that their traditional conceptions of nature and preservation were inapplicable in these wetlands. Just as the park's creation was a transitional campaign, wetlands are transitional landscapes. Wetlands challenged America's basic ideas about nature. To Americans, both in the past and present, nature means temperate forests, grasslands, hills, and mountains. Nature is the seasons, oscillating between the poles of winter and summer. Nature is terra firma, the solid earth, the dry land. The Everglades is none of these things. It is a subtropical wetland, composed of vast freshwater marshes, mangrove swamps, coastal estuaries, and bays. It is always summer in the Everglades—the seasons are wet and dry, not cold and hot. Most important, the Everglades is not land, nor is it water—it is both land and water. It is marsh and swamp. It is bays, estuaries, tidal creeks, and sloughs. The region's ambiguous wetness, just as much as human action, shaped the region's history and this park's creation. Park supporters faced with the Everglades' wetness had to rethink their ideas about tourism, wilderness, national parks, and nature itself. The unique nature of the Glades influenced the course of this history. Although this is a book about the politics of the ENP's creation, the Everglades itself is also the subject of this work and an actor in this story.

Much has been written about the Everglades, which has become a much-loved landscape, particularly by Floridians (who mostly express this love from a distance). Yet little attention has been paid to Everglades National Park itself; the park's creation has been overshadowed by other aspects of the Everglades' history, like drainage, flood control, and Everglades restoration. Understanding the park, though, is essential. Its creation was a key moment in the emergence of modern environmentalism and marked the beginning of Florida's efforts to protect its environment. The park continues to be central to flood control and restoration efforts in the Everglades today and serves as a larger symbol of the nation's relationship with nature.[5]

The fight for the ENP was an important event in the history of U.S. environmental politics, the environmental history of the American South, and the history of the national parks. The nation's national parks are central elements of its environmental regulatory state; the creation of these parks was likewise central to America's broader efforts to protect its natural environment.[6] Many studies of the U.S. national parks have paid close attention to the parks as cultural creations, as wilderness preserves, and as agents of Native American removal.[7] This book looks at these themes in the ENP but also connects the park's creation to the larger history of American environmental thought and environmental politics. This park was the central agent of the construction of Florida's environmental regulatory state and was perhaps the strongest expression of a new environmental view of nature that first emerged in the 1930s before becoming widely adopted in the 1970s.

Additionally, this work expressly tells the story of a southern wetland. U.S. environmental historians, like past conservationists, have largely thought about nature in the context of temperate, terrestrial landscapes. Traditionally, forests, mountains, plains, and rivers have been more studied than wetlands, deserts, and oceans, although these trends have been challenged by recent works.[8] Similarly, many environmental histories have been situated in the American West. Other regions, like the South, have received less attention, although over the last two decades, southern environmental history has grown tremendously.[9] Given the region's history, agricultural studies have appropriately dominated the field.[10] More recently, scholars have published works that examine Appalachia's environment, the South's forests, and the South's relationship with water.[11]

Other topics central to environmental history, like environmental politics and the creation of the environmental regulatory state, have remained understudied in the South.[12] This is partly due to the South's suppression of democracy and citizen activism and to its history of resisting federal power and the creation of strong regulatory structures. Yet, during the Great Depression and especially after World War II, tremendous change came to the South. Many southern states, including Florida, sought to protect landscapes and ecosystems. This work seeks to integrate the history of environmental politics and environmental state building into the history of the South's environment. Just as it centers wetlands, it centers the politics of park making in the South. This political-environmental approach illustrates the important role of nature in the emergence of the modern South. The ENP was central to Florida's efforts at modernization between the Great Depression and the late 1950s. Important economic sectors in post–World War II Florida, like tourism and retirement, directly relied on state power and on the protection of pristine environments like the Everglades. The ENP's creation was part of a larger historical dynamic, wherein Florida re-created its identity, reshaped its economy, and both exploited and protected the state's natural bounty and beauty.

The fight for the ENP began in 1928. At the start of their campaign, park advocates prioritized reimagining the Everglades. Today the Everglades is a cherished national treasure, a jewel in the National Park System, a symbol of Florida's nature, and an ecosystem with ardent and passionate defenders. Yet before the 1930s it was a dreary, dank swamp—a poisonous, miasmatic wasteland. It was a decried and derelict landscape, ignored and vilified. By the late nineteenth century, only Seminoles lived there, driven by war into that watery region. For most of the state's history, Floridians dreamed of draining the Everglades; their fervent desire was to destroy it and raise an agrarian paradise out of the muck.[13] The Everglades was a swamp, and today it is a wetland.[14] Ernest Coe, the park's most important advocate, redefined the Everglades. He presented this region as an aquatic, tropical, and biological wonderland and tied the Everglades' identity to its fantastic and unique flora and fauna. Coe's rebranded Everglades was drawn from scientific views of the region and reflected new ecological ideas. Yet it also served a political purpose and was explicitly crafted to ensure the region measured up to prevailing national parks standards and to the expectations of national conservationists.

Park advocates next created new rationales for the Everglades' preservation. Both this process and the region's redefinition reflected larger changes in how Americans thought about nature. Those changing ideas can most clearly be seen through the dynamics of U.S. environmental politics. The park's rationales straddled the divide between the conservation of the Progressive Era (1890–1920) and the modern environmentalism of the late twentieth century. Progressive conservation was divided into two camps. Utilitarian conservationists saw nature as a set of resources that needed to be used efficiently. They supported the sustainable use of trees, wildlife, and minerals to ensure a continued supply of natural resources. These ideas were enshrined in the U.S. Forest Service (USFS). Aesthetic preservationists saw nature through a spiritual and aesthetic lens and saw their ideas institutionalized in the NPS. Nature was beautiful, and that beauty uplifted and rejuvenated the human spirit. These scenic values were clearly seen in the western valleys, mountains, and canyons protected as national parks. Yet these two varieties of Progressive conservation overlapped considerably. Both reflected the desires and concerns of elites and both viewed nature in anthropocentric terms. Whether used efficiently or preserved, nature existed for humans to use.[15]

In contrast, modern environmentalism was informed by biological views of nature, was biocentric, and often relied on grassroots campaigns. Informed by the science of ecology, environmentalists saw species, including humans, in the context of ecosystems. These activists addressed new global concerns as well. Pollution was a major focus for environmentalists in the 1970s; the ozone layer, climate change, and ocean plastics have become major concerns since. Environmentalists often saw wilderness as central to preservation, and by the 1980s connected this concern for wilderness to the fate of species. Environmentalism focused on quality of life issues as well. As Americans experienced rising standards of living after World War II, they came to expect and demand clean water, clean air, a healthy environment, and natural beauty.[16]

The fight for the ENP was grounded in Progressive conservation but pointed the way forward to modern environmentalism. Park advocates built on and expanded the concerns of conservationists using ecological and biocentric ideas. For example, Florida preservationists had fought to save the region's wading birds from destruction. These charismatic and beautiful species had obvious value to Progressive conservationists. ENP advocates expanded this impulse to include all species, including predators and reptiles. The park's creation was one of the earliest efforts to protect marine species, and it was the strongest expression in U.S. history of a desire to protect nonwoody plants. Rather than just valuing nature for its beauty, park advocates believed all life had inherent value. Likewise, ENP advocates saw landscapes through an ecological lens. Progressive preservationists saw landscapes in terms of their aesthetic and spiritual values, while ENP advocates saw the Everglades as habitats. Instead of just protecting scenery, ENP advocates sought a park that would protect the habitats and ranges of the Everglades' flora and fauna.

These ecological trends challenged the NPS traditions and policies; the ENP was at the forefront of broader changes within the park service. While most parks protected stunning mountains and valleys for the benefit of tourists, this wetland park would protect the Everglades' biota and would mostly be preserved as wilderness. Before the 1930s, national parks protected the geology of the West. Lacking a long history and a shared cultural tradition, these western geological monuments in turn were symbols of the nation's identity.[17] These western monuments represented manifest destiny, a sense of rugged individualism, and American expansion. These jagged peaks and dramatic valleys also displayed God's fearsome and magnificent power.[18] As sublime symbols of American identity, they likewise signaled God's approval for the new nation. National parks were not just nature preserves or tourist attractions but were cultural artifacts infused with political and cultural meaning. Yet, the Everglades lies only mere feet above sea level. It is eminently flat and has no dramatic geological formations or scenic vistas. Rather than holding geological interest, this park protects biology. The NPS history of geological monumentalism was supplanted in the Everglades by a sense of biological monumentalism. This park's alligators and roseate spoonbills symbolized the nation's embrace of science and biodiversity. While other national parks harkened to a mythic past, this one embraced a scientific future.

America's geological parks were primarily tourist attractions. Two factors in the 1930s challenged the NPS's focus on tourism; both found their furthest expression in the ENP. During the 1920s and 1930s, the NPS was on the receiving end of a barrage of criticism regarding the overcommercialization and overuse of America's parks. Modern wilderness advocates, who in 1935 founded the Wilderness Society, criticized the NPS and influenced the ENP's creation.[19] These activists sought to protect the recreational and spiritual values of wilderness, quickly concluding that banning roads would be the surest way to protect wilderness. In the 1930s, a group of NPS wildlife biologists challenged the service's focus on tourism from a different perspective.[20] Believing that tourism negatively impacted park wildlife, they advocated for new park policies to protect predators and other animals. They also drew attention to the inadequate boundaries in most parks and argued for park boundaries that conformed to the ranges of species.

In response to these criticisms, the NPS altered its policies regarding park wildlife and highlighted the wilderness values of existing national parks. It also sought new parks that centered both wilderness and biological preservation. The ENP was the strongest expression of these developments in the NPS. This park's 1934 authorization was the first time wilderness was enshrined in federal law. This wilderness, though, was biocentric in purpose and would serve to further protect the Everglades' biology.[21] This park's boundaries and future management policies were likewise shaped by biological priorities. Although after World War II the NPS resumed its focus on tourism at the expense of wilderness and biological preservation, the ENP continued to carry the torch for these causes. This park kept the flames of biological preservation and wilderness alive within the NPS until the modern environmentalism of the 1970s rekindled them. At the same time, it remained open to tourists who visited the region's mysterious mangroves, uncanny orchids, exotic wading birds, and fearsome alligators.

These biological and ecological arguments enormously impacted the first phase of the park's creation. From 1928 to 1937, Ernest Coe, a New England nursery owner who had recently moved to Miami, led the fight for the ENP. Coe was a zealous and uncompromising advocate and embodied the larger transitions in American environmental thought during the interwar period. He was a prophet, possessed with a rapturous love of the Everglades' biota; he was also a shameless booster, hawking the prospects of park tourism to Florida's business and political elites. His years in New England were marked by Progressive conservation, but in the Everglades he embraced many of the ideas that underpinned modern environmentalism. Coe was animated by a desire to protect the Everglades' biota, but he spoke rapturously of the Everglades' scenic and spiritual values. He promoted park tourism and the park's economic benefits, but also celebrated the Everglades' wilderness.

Coe publicized the park's value to important national and local constituencies, created the intellectual justifications for the park's creation, and oversaw the park's authorization in 1934. After 1934, Coe failed to move the park forward, in part because he refused to compromise the park's enormous boundaries, which he saw as central to the parks' biocentric mission. Coe's sense of ecological preservation found support within the New Deal and was influenced by the liberalism of the 1930s. Both the ENP and the New Deal represented an expansion of the environmental regulatory state and the power of the federal government. By 1937 the New Deal was waning in power; that year Coe also ceased to be an effective advocate.

The park project lay dormant after 1937 but was revived in 1941 by Florida governor Spessard Holland. Holland was a conservative southern Democrat who facilitated Florida's economic growth and modernization during and after World War II.[22] His support for the park, which encompasses the second phase of the park's creation, was shaped by the moderate consensus politics of the post–World War II era, Holland's own conservative views, and a pragmatic approach to politics. Holland espoused a Sunbelt environmentalism. He accepted Coe's ideas about the need to protect the area's biota from destruction, but he prioritized the park's economic and anthropocentric values. Holland and his political allies sought the economic growth a tourism industry would bring to Florida, but they also understood that Florida tourism was dependent on a pristine and healthy environment. This Sunbelt environmentalism was not just a sense of environmentalism that emerged in the Sunbelt; rather this environmentalism would facilitate the Sunbelt's emergence.

Many Sunbelt states in the South and West experienced rapid industrialization and urbanization during World War II.[23] This growth was federally subsidized, and after the war these Sunbelt states continued to draw on federal resources to further their economic modernization. Although most Sunbelt states sought growth in industrial, resource extraction, and high-tech industries, Florida sought to grow its service industries, especially its tourism sector.[24] To attract tourists, Florida needed to transform its identity. The state could no longer be seen as a backwater southern state, tainted by the legacies of secession, slavery, and racism. National parks had played a role in the creation of U.S. identity in the nineteenth century, and they would likewise help redefine Florida.[25] The ENP was a scientific park built on new environmental rationales. It protected biodiversity and signaled Florida's embrace of modernity. This park, at the forefront of the nation's environmental and scientific trends, signaled that Florida was now firmly at the center of America's mainstream and ready to cater to the desires of tourists, snowbirds, and retirees. Florida would no longer be a backwater state in a backwater region. Instead it was transformed into the Sunshine State, the country's premier tourist destination and retirement location.

Holland shepherded the park to its creation in 1947. This small nucleus of a park then expanded until its boundaries were formally set in 1958. The park represented an enormous growth of federal power in the state. Although Holland and other powerful Florida politicians were political conservatives who typically opposed federal intervention in economic and social affairs, the park's creation was too good an economic deal to pass up.[26]

Another group of political conservatives opposed the park after 1947. Landowners who were connected to the oil industry fought the park's expansion and touted oil drilling in the Everglades.[27] They were led by the McDougal-Axelson family, a politically connected family who had previously made a fortune in the

Oklahoma oil boom. These landowners argued that the federal government, by acquiring Everglades lands, was violating their property rights and behaving dictatorially. These concerns about rights and their attacks on the federal government placed them at the center of a nascent modern conservative movement. Similar rhetoric regarding the federal government's violation of individual rights was a key component of conservative opposition to the civil rights movement in the 1950s.[28] The activism of Everglades landowners, and much of their rhetoric regarding property rights and other issues, foreshadowed later antienvironmental groups and modern conservativism's later opposition to the environmental regulatory state. Using these rights-based arguments, landowners successfully limited the park's expansion and land acquisition efforts in the late 1940s and 1950s. In response to their activism, the NPS significantly reduced the size of the park's final boundaries. Additionally, landowners retained mineral rights on their lands until 1967 and rights to oil royalties until 1985.

The ENP's creation in 1947 reflected an environmental view of the natural world. Rather than destroying or controlling nature, humans protected nature. Inspired by the insights of ecology, park advocates understood that humans existed within ecosystems, and embraced the inherent value of flora and fauna. Floridians had sought to drain and destroy the Everglades, but the ENP would protect this watery wilderness. At the same time, other events in 1947 illustrate how Floridians embraced the opposite view. That year, Florida embarked on a new plan to control the Everglades' water through dams, canals, locks, and levees. In 1947, the state embraced the park's creation, but it also initiated new efforts to control the Everglades' water through a comprehensive system of flood control. These contradictions were consistent with America's changing ideas about nature during the interwar and postwar periods. Although the interwar period was characterized by an increased concern for ecological and biocentric ideas, the decades after World War II were defined by political consensus, economic growth, cultural conservativism, and atomic-age science. Ecological and biological ideas remained important after the war, but this new postwar consensus was also defined by a renewed confidence in humans' ability to control nature.

These new flood control projects were prompted by massive hurricanes that swept through South Florida in 1947. Similar hurricanes in the late 1920s led to the end of Everglades drainage. The park's creation was bookended by disastrous hurricanes, both of which prompted Floridians to reconsider their relationship with the Everglades. These storms were some of the most dramatic ways that nature altered the history of the Everglades. Yet these hurricanes and other natural forces did not dictate history. Rather, entwined together, humans and nature created historical change. Hurricanes in 1926, 1928, and 1947 were all disasters for South Florida's human populations and caused immense flooding throughout the region.[29] Yet Floridians reacted to these storms in different ways as they interpreted the meaning of this destruction through their own cultural and political lenses. The storms in the 1920s came amid an economic depression in Florida's agricultural sector; the Great Depression soon followed in 1929. These events severely damaged the nation's optimism and confidence; Floridians interpreted these storms through this lens of economic decline. These hurricanes exposed the failures of Everglades drainage and led to the end of the Florida land boom.

Just months after the park's creation, two storms similar to those in the 1920s struck Florida. In September 1947, a disastrous hurricane made landfall at Fort Lauderdale and blasted across the Everglades. A second storm in October hit near Cape Sable and cut west across the state. South Florida had already seen record rainfall in 1947; these hurricanes inundated the Everglades and South Florida's agricultural and urban areas. While the 1926 and 1928 storms caused Florida to abandon its efforts to control the region's water, those in 1947 had the opposite effect. By 1947, buoyed by a massive military victory in 1945 and a vibrant postwar economic prosperity, the nation's confidence had returned. Humans had split the atom and created new chemical compounds like DDT—surely they could control the Everglades' water and force it to flow as they pleased.

In 1947, the state of Florida and the U.S. Army Corps of Engineers (USACE) embarked on a comprehensive flood control project in the Glades. Although the goals of this project were less ambitious than previous drainage efforts, flood control and drainage reflected the same belief that humans could control nature. Approved in 1948, the Central and Southern Florida (C&SF) Project sought to control flooding and to provide water to agricultural areas, urban areas, and the new national park. In 1947, Florida's embraced the biocentric rationales for the park's creation, and the C&SF Project's anthropocentric efforts to control nature. Both would play important, and often conflicting, roles in the Everglades' future.

Like Everglades drainage, the C&SF Project dramatically reduced water flow into the lower Everglades and damaged the region's biota and ecosystems. Although the project pledged to deliver water to the park, those promises were often broken and ignored, and instead the C&SF Project diverted water east and west to benefit agricultural and urban interests. By the 1960s, with the Everglades' water increasingly under threat, the NPS and Everglades advocates successfully fought to require the USACE to increase water deliveries to the park. Those efforts have continued into the present day and are central to current restoration efforts in the Everglades.

Since the advent of modern environmentalism, the dearth of water in the Everglades has become an important concern to Floridians. The Everglades, once a maligned swamp, has become a symbol of a fragile nature, destroyed by humans, now under repair. Efforts to restore the Everglades are seen as a test of the nation's environmental and ethical compass. The park is at the center of these efforts. The ENP protected the last great bastion of the undeveloped Everglades. This park was also a catalyst for subsequent environmental campaigns in Florida and for the creation of additional preserves and environmental regulations that protect Florida's environment. Its creation directly led to other preserves in this region, including John Pennekamp Coral Reef State Park and Big Cypress National Preserve. Perhaps most importantly, the park has been a key political factor in ongoing efforts to restore the Everglades' sheet flow. Subsequent generations of activists have used the park as a tool to pry open floodgates, to demolish levees, and to let water flow.

CHAPTER I

The Everglades and a
New England Nurseryman

Today the Everglades is acknowledged as a renowned biosphere, a keystone in America's national park system, and a World Heritage Site. Yet, for most of U.S. history, the region was reviled as a wasteland. Florida sought to drain what people saw as a dark, oppressive swamp in order to convert this wetland into dry farmland. Those efforts failed, but Florida and the federal government today continue to exert control over the Everglades' water through a complex system of flood control. Both drainage and those flood control efforts altered the Everglades' water flow—the water flow that defines the Everglades. The subtle relationships between water flow and elevation make the region unique and diverse. The Everglades is flat, especially compared with the nation's other geological national parks. Yet this flatness is not uniform. Minute changes in elevation cause differences in water levels and in turn give rise to different ecosystems. Sawgrass prairies, pine rocklands, cypress forests, freshwater sloughs, and mangrove forests are marked by difference of just feet or even mere inches in elevation. The Everglades' freshwater runs through these ecosystems until it slowly merges with salt water amid a maze of mangrove islands and shallow bays.

Efforts to create Everglades National Park went hand in hand with efforts to redefine the Everglades. The Everglades' redefinition was consistent with larger developments in U.S. environmental thought. In the interwar period, Americans reconsidered the value and identity of wetlands as part of a larger change in how they thought about nature. The 1930s in particular saw the emergence of many ideas that would later become central to modern environmentalism. The ENP's creation illustrates how modern environmental ideas emerged from Progressive Era ideas about conservation and preservation. Those transitions were mirrored in the life of Ernest Coe, the important park advocate in the 1930s. Coe was a New England nursery owner who in 1925 moved to Florida to start a new life. Before 1925, Coe shared the Progressive Era's confidence in the nation's ability to control nature. Just as Florida sought to drain the Everglades, Coe shaped nature through his nursery. After 1925, Coe was transformed by the Everglades. Over the course of a decade he reconsidered his anthropocentric ideas about nature and embraced an ecological and biocentric view of the environment. In 1928, he embarked on a crusade to protect the Everglades as a national park. Inspired by the wonders of the Everglades, Coe sloughed off his old life as a Progressive nurseryman and became a forerunner of environmentalism and the prophet of the Glades.

The Everglades' most celebrated chronicler, Marjory Stoneman Douglas, wrote that "there are no other Everglades in the world. They are, they have always been, one of the unique regions of the earth."[1] In such a large and diverse world, an ecosystem's claim to uniqueness is often little but hyperbolic praise, but this is not the case with the Everglades. The region is truly unique. That uniqueness is due to two factors: the Everglades' sheet flow and its diverse and fantastic mix of temperate and tropical life.

The historic Everglades was not a large sawgrass marsh filled with stagnant water; rather it was a vast, slow-flowing sheet of water. That water flowed through a diverse number of marsh ecosystems; drier patches of land were occupied by wetland tree islands, hardwood hammocks, or pine rocklands. At the end of its journey, that water flowed through labyrinthine mangrove forests before making its way into some of the most productive and rich marine ecosystems in the world. All of these diverse ecosystems were home to an even more diverse range of tropical and temperate species.[2]

This Everglades existed from about five thousand years ago, until the 1880s. Its existence was due to a complex confluence of geological, hydrological, and climatological factors. Peninsular southern Florida is only just above sea level. It is exceeding flat but almost imperceptibly tilts toward the south. The highest average elevation in the ENP only reaches eight feet above sea level, and the region's average downward slope is about two inches per mile. Water flows south down this slight decline at the barely perceptible rate of one meter an hour.[3] Geological factors prevent this water from seeping into the ground, thus ensuring this slow flow of water. Although the limestone rock underlying the Everglades is as porous as a sieve, its permeability recharges the ground water and helps maintain a very high water table in the region. This high water table is additionally maintained by the Everglades' low elevation and by the dense salt water that surrounds the Florida peninsula on three sides. Due to these factors, for most of the year, there is no difference between groundwater and surface water. The Everglades' water has nowhere to go but slowly south through the region's sloughs and marshes down to bay, gulf, and ocean.[4]

And there is a surfeit of water in this system. The Glades is just one part of the much larger KOE watershed, which encompasses the Kissimmee River, Lake Okeechobee, and the Everglades. Historically, water flowed down the Kissimmee

River and accumulated in Lake Okeechobee. During the wet season (between May and September) water spilled over the lake and flowed through the Everglades. Much of this hydrological system is dependent on rainfall. Rather than the four seasons, South Florida has only two: wet and dry. Average annual rainfall is between fifty to sixty inches, about forty inches of which fall during the wet season. That water collects throughout Central and South Florida and slowly trickles through the Everglades. This flow of water is the lifeblood of the Everglades and today serves as a defining symbol for the region.

Water also determines and defines the Everglades' diversity of ecosystems. Despite its mostly uniform flatness, minor changes in elevation create differences in water levels and salinity that in turn create spectacularly diverse ecosystems. As Thomas Lodge put it in *The Everglades Handbook*, "differences of a few inches in elevation caused large responses in vegetation types." These "variations added intriguing dimensions to the landscapes of the region" and is what accounts for the area's surprising diversity of ecosystems.[5]

The Everglades most well-known biome is undoubtedly the area's vast sawgrass marshes. Today, these marshes compose about 70 percent of the remaining Everglades. They are dominated by sawgrass, a sedge that can grow up to nine feet tall. Although she labeled the Everglades the river of grass, Marjory Stoneman Douglas pointed out that sawgrass is not a grass but a "fierce, ancient, cutting sedge."[6] These marshes are flooded for about ten months each year, and sawgrass is adapted to the fires that often burn these prairies during the dry season. Alligators often nest amid these watery prairies, but species diversity is low and these regions are dominated by sawgrass and periphyton, a strange floating mat of various algae.

Changes in elevation and water level provide the conditions for other freshwater marsh ecosystems in the Glades. Marl or mixed prairies are at a slightly higher elevation than sawgrass prairies and are hence inundated from between three and seven months a year. Different varieties of these mixed prairies occur based on differing soil composition and elevation. These mixed marshes are incredibly diverse and contain about a hundred species of flora. They are important feeding grounds for wading birds and are habitats for fish, amphibians, and invertebrates. The deepest and wettest marshes in the Everglades are the region's sloughs, which are the primary conduits for the Everglades' waterflow. Sloughs are inundated for at least eleven months a year and may experience years without waters subsiding. The average depth of the sloughs is a foot, but in the wet season they may contain over three feet of water. Sloughs contain diverse freshwater marine species and marsh plants.

At higher elevations, wetland tree islands rise from the sloughs and prairies. These biomes, which are inundated for shorter periods, are often named according to their dominant tree species, but they support a multiplicity of flora. Bay heads,

dominated by red bay and sweet bay, are the most common. Bay head[s]
one to three feet above the marsh and are only flooded two to six month[s]
Willow heads (dominated by coastal-plain willows) are often lower and [wetter]
while cypress heads are the lowest. Cypress heads have been often celebrated [for]
their eerie beauty, especially those composed of dwarf cypress. These tree islan[ds]
vary in size from one acre to hundreds.

Many of the flora species found in these wetland tree islands are temperate, but
hardwood hammocks are dominated by tropical species. These hammocks occur
throughout the Everglades on even higher ground than that of wetland tree islands, and they rarely flood. Tropical trees, like gumbo limbo, Florida royal palms,
and stranger figs grow here, as well the temperate live oak. Many hammocks and
wetland tree islands are surrounded by moats or fringed by saw palmettos. The
hardwood canopy blocks much of the sun, cooling the hammocks, while solution
holes and sinks in the oolitic limestone expose ground water, making them more
humid. These conditions create habitats for tropical flora and epiphytic plants like
mosses, air plants, resurrection ferns, and orchids. Fifteen species of bromeliads, a
hundred species of orchids, and about a hundred species of fern grow in the Everglades; most can be found in hardwood hammocks.

The Everglades' pine rocklands are also found at higher and drier elevations.
Tropical and temperate hardwoods grow in these biomes as well, but their numbers are limited by the fires that periodically sweep through these forests. The
dominant species in these forests—slash pine, saw palmetto, and cabbage palm—
are in turn dependent on fire. In the dry season, fires may burn these forests, but
they can tolerate up to three months of flooding in the wet season, and some pine
rocklands thrive only inches above the marsh. These forests contain some of the
most unique flora in the Everglades; twenty different endemic species grow here.

Toward the coast, the Everglades' low slope gradually sinks into salt water. That
line between salt water and land is almost impossible to define. The coast is dominated by five hundred square miles of mangrove forest, the largest such area in
the Western Hemisphere. These trees live in salt water and slowly build up the
soil around them. Three types of mangroves—red, black, and white—as well as
the buttonwood, a plant commonly confused with mangroves, grow in the Everglades. Red and black mangroves are highly salt tolerant; red mangroves have
enormous prop roots that arc feet into the air, while black mangroves sprout small
rootlike structures up through the muck called pneumatophores. Both adaptions
play a role in gas exchange, an important priority for trees whose roots lie in salt-
inundated soil. White mangroves often grow upland of black and red mangroves
and are less salt tolerant, while buttonwoods are even less tolerant of salt and water and often grow in small forests called buttonwood embankments. These forests are about one and a half feet above sea level and act as natural levees for fresh-

All these mangroves play important roles in maintaining
'mportant habitats and nursery grounds to myriad fish,
pecies.

es are a variety of coastal salt marshes, strange coastal
alt marsh plants like black rush (juncus) and spar-
but in much smaller concentrations than in a typ-
rsh. A variety of other salt-tolerant plants, like succu-
ants, grow in these diverse salt marshes and coastal prairies.
ades also contains diverse marine ecosystems. In fact, about one-
the park is covered by salt water. The ENP was the first major effort in the
United States to preserve marine environments. The area's estuaries and bays are
the final destination for the Everglades' freshwater sheet flow. Here, fresh and salt
water intermingle, creating ideal conditions for marine flora and fauna. The Florida Bay is the largest aquatic feature in the Everglades, and it is one of the most remarkable and unique marine environments in the world. This thousand-acre bay
is actually a series of shallow basins separate by mudbanks, each containing its own
discrete environment. The bay was historically fed by the Shark and Taylor River
sloughs, but freshwater flow has decreased due to human alterations, and much of
the sea grass in the Bay has died off as a result. These areas, as well other marine areas like Whitewater Bay and the Ten Thousand Islands are productive marine ecosystems that also provide habitat to wading birds and fish, as well as marine
mammals.

All these habitats, from the sawgrass prairies in the north to the Florida Bay
and Ten Thousand Islands in the south, are home to a mix of temperate species
from North America, and tropical plants and animals from the West Indies. The
heat and humidity limit those temperate species' southern range, while frost limits those tropical species' northern limits. This surprising and fantastic mix of
species is part of makes the Everglades so unique and intriguing. Botanist John
Kunkel Small expressed some of this sentiment in 1937 when he wrote that the Everglades was "a strange country, a land of anomalies and the grotesque. Here fish
sing; snakes often live in trees; epiphytes grow as terrestrials; terrestrials grow as
epiphytes; giant oak trees are arbors for aerial plants and ferns; cacti grow in water; oysters grow on trees and broad-leaved trees grow on rocks lacking soil."[7]

The Everglades' wildlife has often been celebrated for its magnificent variety.
The Everglades is the only place in the world with both alligators and crocodiles.
The region is home to the iconic Florida panther, a subspecies of the American
mountain lion. Familiar temperate mammals, like bear, deer, possum, and rac-
coons, also thrive in the Glades. The area's marine waters contain over a thousand
species of fish. These waters were celebrated by sportfishers throughout the twentieth century as a mecca for sportfishing and angling.[8] Fishing and boating remain

popular activities in the park today. Threatened tropical marine mammals, like the Atlantic bottlenose dolphin and the West Indian manatee, as well as marine reptiles, live in these waters. Eleven species of turtle, including five varieties of sea turtle, and sixteen different snakes can be found in the Everglades.

The most renowned species in the region are undoubtedly the Everglades' birds. These species have long fascinated birders and conservationists. There are almost four hundred bird species in southern Florida; about 60 percent of these are northern species that migrate to the area in the winter. The most magnificent are the region's wading birds. Roseate spoonbills, wood storks, and thirteen varieties of ibis and heron all feed and breed in the Everglades. The iconic flamingo visits the area to feed as well, and likely nested in the area in the past. Before the region's flow of water was altered, these species thrived amid this mix of water and land.

Although today the Everglades is celebrated, for most of Western history wetlands were decried spaces. They were dangerous, pestilent, and worthless. Wetlands were filled with hostile flora and fauna like mosquitos, snakes, alligators, spartina, and sawgrass. The very wetness of wetlands made these spaces wild and hostile to humans. Wetlands resisted human development, and, as a consequence, humans recoiled in fear of these unknown and uncontrollable regions. Throughout Western history, swamps were seen as dangerous and supernatural places. They have been seen as the haunt of ghosts and witches, and throughout U.S. history have been refuges for Native Americans, escaped slaves, and other oppressed peoples.

Because Americans could not control or domesticate wetland, they instead tried to destroy them by draining them and turning them into dry land.[9] The Everglades' history was no different. The first White explorers of Florida's interior recoiled at the Everglades. In the 1840s, soldiers in the Second Seminole War, like army surgeon Jacob Motte, explored and described these marshes. Motte wrote that the Everglades was "the most dreary and pandemonium-like region I ever visited; nothing but barren wastes, where no grateful verdure quickened, and no generous plant took root."[10] Buckingham Smith, a native Floridian who first investigated draining the region in 1847, concluded that "the utter worthlessness to civilized man, in its present condition," made drainage a necessity. The area was "suitable only for the haunt of noxious vermin, or the resort of pestilent reptiles."[11]

Progressive conservationists in the 1920s and 1930s perpetuated these negative views. Zoologist William T. Hornaday insisted that "a swamp is a swamp," and thought the Glades nothing but a wasteland filled with "water moccasins and rattle-snakes." Robert Sterling Yard, a founding member of both the National Parks Association and the Wilderness Society, repeatedly attacked the Everglades as unworthy of national park status. In a letter to Henry Isaac Ward, the president of the American Forestry Association, Yard wrote that one expert he had spoken to called the Everglades a series of "flat uninteresting swamps," while another called it "melancholy and depressing." Even NPS director Horace Albright, who became an enthusiastic ENP supporter, admitted that he had originally subscribed to these negative ideas. Albright wrote that after he had actually visited the area, his "old idea of an Everglades with dense swamps and lagoons festooned with lianas, and miasmatic swamps full of alligators and crocodiles and venomous snakes was entirely shattered."[12]

These views were consistent with U.S. attitudes toward nature during the Progressive Era. The Progressive Era was one the great periods of American reform. After the Civil War, the country began to industrialize, urbanize, and modernize. Enormous corporations were formed by enterprising and often dishonest businesspeople who sought profit and security through the destruction of competition. Their enormous economic power was built on their control and exploitation of America's workers, the country's political systems, and the nation's resources. That economic power translated into political and social power. As these corporations grew, the nation changed dramatically. Americans questioned what these economic, political, and social changes meant for the country's identity and future. The Progressive Era arose from these conditions. Beginning in 1890 and continuing through the end of World War I, Americans sought to address the complex and myriad problems that arose from this new industrial, urban, and modern order. Many Progressives were pragmatic reformers who sought practical solutions to America's problems. Others were passionate ideologues, committed to addressing social problems and economic injustice. In general, Progressives advocated for more government involvement and regulation in the economy, and embraced a wide variety of reforms that touched almost every aspect of American life.[13]

One set of problems the United States confronted was the depletion of the country's natural resources, the destruction of nature, and fears concerning the impacts of urbanization on the spirit and health of American citizens. True to the Progressive Era's diffuse nature, different groups of activists and experts advocated for different solutions to these problems. Utilitarian conservationists were concerned about the depletion of the nation's resources and advocated for the efficient use of trees, water, minerals, soil, and wildlife. Experts armed with scientific knowledge could ensure a steady supply of resources and prevent corporations from destroying the very raw materials on which they depended. These ideas were enshrined in the USFS and quickly spread to the field of game management. Hunters, fishers, and sportsmen embraced these ideas; by protecting game, conservationists could ensure a steady supply of animals to kill. The underlying character of conservation—its focus on expertise and efficiency—was a key component of the Progressive Era.[14]

Progressives also feared the broader destruction of nature and the deleterious effects of urban life. Aesthetic preservationists sought to protect the most magnificent and dramatic landscapes in the United States. These parks and preserves could rejuvenate the spirit of urbanites, provide recreational opportunities, and inspire Americans reconsider their relationships with nature and the divine. These ideas found expression in the nation's national parks, which initially protected the dramatic scenery of the U.S. West for eastern tourists.

These two movements overlapped considerably, both ideologically and in terms of membership. Both sought to address industrialization's impacts on the natural world, and both sought to protect nature. Conservationists and preservationists were both distinctly anthropocentric in their attitudes toward nature. They never doubted that humans could control nature and in fact only sought to protect nature for humans to use. Despite their common causes, conflict over the fate of the Hetch Hetchy Valley in Yosemite National Park drove a wedge between these two camps and has been used by historians to illustrate the differences between preservationists and conservationists. Conservationists sought to dam the valley to provide water and electricity to San Francisco, while preservationists defended the valley's beauty, as well as the integrity and sanctity of Yosemite National Park. Ultimately, conservationists won. This dam was constructed and the valley was removed from Yosemite National Park.

This Progressive Era belief that humans could control nature, as well as prevailing negative ideas about wetlands, paved the way for Everglades drainage. Beginning in 1881, Floridians began to drain the Everglades. They sought to convert this ostensibly worthless swamp into valuable farm land. This region's resources, both its water and land, could be put to use. Hamilton Disston, an industrialist and land speculator, launched a scheme in 1881 to drain large portions of the KOE watershed both north and south of Lake Okeechobee. Disston reclaimed fewer than a hundred thousand acres of land, most of which was north of the lake in the Kissimmee River watershed. His ambitious plans failed, yet these efforts reshaped and disrupted the Everglades' waterflow.[15]

Disston's scheme was abandoned by 1896, but drainage was restarted in 1903 and then greatly expanded in 1905 when Napoleon Bonaparte Broward began his term as Florida governor. Broward was a Progressive politician. He sought to use the government to benefit the common man, and he believed humans could shape and control nature. Drainage would convert this useless swamp into an agrarian utopia populated by small independent farmers. These ambitious plans for drainage became the centerpiece of his 1904 gubernatorial campaign. His slogan, "water will run downhill," reflected his belief that the Everglades would be quickly and easily drained. Broward's arrogance would be his undoing. On becoming governor, Broward funded his drainage program through land sales to speculative real estate interests, not small farmers. Soon after, the state began dredging canals in accordance with a comically incompetent plan dubbed the Wright Report.[16]

Written by James Wright, a former midlevel USDA engineer who served as Florida's chief drainage engineer, the report claimed that 1,850,000 acres could be reclaimed at the cost of just one dollar an acre by digging only eight canals through the Everglades. It dismissed the need for a dike around Lake Okeechobee, and contained gross errors concerning rainfall, runoff, evaporation, and other factors related to drainage. Although Wright's own supervisor sought to delay and amend the report, it was endorsed by the state legislature and quickly became a key piece of propaganda that real estate companies used to promote Everglades land sales. These booming land sales made fortunes, but buyers quickly realized they had been hoodwinked. Rather than an agrarian paradise, their lands were swampy and inaccessible. By 1912, the U.S. House of Representatives investigated the matter and savaged the Wright report. They found, for example, that Wright had calculated the monthly rate of evaporation at nine inches. Because there were only two months in which more than nine inches of rainfall occurred, this actually meant that drainage was not even needed, since according to Wright the entire area would be dried out just by mere evaporation.[17]

Broward and Wright's drainage schemes failed, but the larger dream of draining the Everglades persisted. Just a year after the 1912 House investigation, Florida issued a revised plan for drainage: the Randolph Report. This report recommended a much more robust canal system then Wright's and included the new St. Lucie Canal that aimed to control water levels in Lake Okeechobee. In 1921, construction began on a dike around Lake Okeechobee that would limit flooding south of the lake during the wet season. As a result of these actions, large numbers of farms, which were periodically flooded, did indeed spring up out of the muck lands around the southern rim of the Lake. Yet, many of the Randolph Report's recommendations were never enacted due to funding issues. Drainage efforts under both the Wright and Randolph Reports bore the same underlying flaws. They reflected an arrogance in the ability of human engineering and an ignorance concerning the workings of the Everglades. Drainage certainly benefited the greedy desires of Florida real estate investors but failed to fulfill the agrarian dreams of ordinary Floridians.[18]

Everglades drainage was fatally exposed and finally abandoned after hurricanes smashed into the Everglades in 1926 and 1928. These storms breached the dike around Lake Okeechobee, their rain- and floodwaters overflowed the region's drainage canals, and the entire human-built system was inundated twice in quick succession. Although some minor infrastructure projects were conducted during the Great Depression, the 1929 economic crash meant drainage was dead.[19] Yet Floridians never abandoned the underlying ideas behind drainage and continued to believe that humans could control the Everglades' water and nature itself. By 1947, after the park's creation, the state embarked on a new plan to prevent flooding in South Florida, a venture full of just as much folly and hubris as drainage. In 1948, the federal government and the state of Florida created the Central and Southern Florida (C&SF) Project to control flooding. The C&SF Project created the water control system that exists in the Everglades today, consisting largely of canals, levees, and dikes, as well as water conservation areas that aim to store and clean the Everglades' waters. Although drainage and flood control had different goals, they both sought to control the area's water through the creation of canals, dikes, and levees, and they both negatively impacted the Everglades' hydrological systems and ecological health.

The fight for Everglades National Park occurred between 1928, which marked the end of drainage, and 1947, when plans for the current flood control regime were initiated. Everglades advocates used this pause in human efforts to control the Everglades to advocate for a different human relationship with the region. Rather than controlling the Everglades, a national park could protect the region's ecosystems from further destruction.

Their plans for a park did not, however, prioritize the protection of the Everglades' waterflow, largely because the region's hydrology was not well understood. No serious studies of the Everglades' water flow had been conducted before 1940, and almost none of the scientists and experts who studied the Everglades before the 1930s characterized the Everglades as flowing.[20] Not until the mid-1940s did scientists uncover the precise workings of the Everglades' hydrological systems. Garald Parker, a geologist with the U.S. Geological Service, undertook the first scientific studies of the Everglades sheet flow in that period. Parker's ideas were popularized by Marjory Stoneman Douglas's *The Everglades: River of Grass*, which was published in the fall of 1947, just months after the park's creation. In fact, Douglas and park advocates were actually hopeful that flood control would help secure water for the park.[21] Legislation authorizing the C&SF Project directed the USACE to provide water to the park. The Corps did not follow through on this promise, though.

Not until the 1960s did public concern for the Everglades' waterflow become pronounced. At least four forces in the 1960s and 1970s converged to bring greater and sustained attention toward the Everglades' hydrological problems. A disastrous drought struck in the late 1960s, parching the Everglades. Compounding that problem was the culmination of several flood controls projects that further diverted water from the Everglades. The construction of an enormous jetport just north of the park focused public attention on the Everglades, just as the environmental movement became a mainstream force in U.S. politics.

In the 1920s, 1930s, and 1940s, ENP advocates were instead reacting to the decline of Everglades species. A variety of efforts to commodify the Everglades' biota had severely reduced flora and fauna populations and harmed the region's ecosystems. The plight of the Everglades' wading birds had already been widely publicized, and some minor actions had been taken to curtail plume hunting. According to the American Ornithologists Union, by 1886 more than five million birds were being killed annually to feed fashion trends in women's hats.[22] Wading birds, like those found in the Everglades, possessed some of the most desired feathers. These species' breeding grounds were in the Glades, and entire bird rookeries could easily be shot out. Everglades hunters made fortunes. Ornithologist William T. Hornaday estimated that between 1881 and 1894, Florida's bird population declined by 77 percent due to this trade.[23] State and federal laws were passed to curtail the hunting of plume birds, and ornithologists hired private game wardens to patrol the Everglades, yet these actions had little impact. The laws were full of loopholes and were unenforceable, while wardens had little real power in these frontier regions. The most famous Everglades warden, Guy Bradley, became a martyr for birds when poachers murdered him in 1905. Demand for plumes lessened in the 1920s, but the hunting of plume birds continued into the 1940s.[24]

ENP advocates tapped into this concern for plume birds, but their goals were broader than just protecting charismatic bird species. They were more broadly concerned with all the region's flora and fauna, not just species with obvious value to humans. Additionally, they understood that protecting habitats was essential to protecting species, and therefore sought to create a large park in the Everglades. As the market for bird plumes declined in the 1920s, many hunters shifted their focus to alligator hides. According to one government report, hunters killed over 2.5 million gators in Florida between 1880 and 1894.[25] Hunters also targeted mammals like possum, raccoon, otter, and mink. A variety of collectors—bird egg and snail collectors were the most notorious—also caused great damage to the Everglades. Snail collectors often burned entire hammocks to the ground and then sifted through the ashes for snails. Crocodile and gator eggs were valuable commodities as well. The region's flora was also under threat. Cypress forests, and to a lesser extent pine forests, were threatened by timber operations. Nursery owners and landscape architects took orchids, palm trees, and other exotic and tropical plants out of the Everglades by the truckload. Royal palms were almost extirpated from the Glades, while orchid populations declined precipitously.

Ironically, Ernest Coe, who had owned a nursery in New England, was particularly concerned about the damage his fellow nursery owners were inflicting on the region. Coe and his wife Anna's concerns for the region's orchids was an early impetus to Ernest Coe's Everglades advocacy.[26] Coe was a recent transplant to Miami; he moved to the city in 1925 at the age of fifty-eight, after spending a life in New England as the owner and president of a successful nursery. Coe's first life as a New England nurseryman prepared him for his second career as an environmental preservationist, just as his new life in the Everglades required him to reevaluate his Progressive ideas about the natural world.

Ernest Francis Coe, who sometimes went by "Tom," was born in New Haven, Connecticut, on March 21, 1867.[27] Coe loved nature, and as a young boy "preferred to roam in the woods instead of going to school."[28] In fact, he only attended one year of high school due to "frail health," but he later pursued his artistic passions as a student at Yale. He never matriculated but studied fine arts between 1885 and 1887, taking courses in "anatomy, perspective, drawing, composition, [and] painting."[29] Coe worked briefly as a traveling salesman in 1889 and the next year started working for the Elm City Nursery.[30] He quickly proved his worth as an employee and in 1893 became part owner. By 1901 Coe was president. Although Coe's time and energy were primarily occupied with running the business, he never lost sight of his artistic passions and dabbled in landscape architecture on the side. From at least 1901 on, he was listed as the head of the nursery's landscape department.[31]

Under Coe's management, Elm City Nursery expanded rapidly. In 1896, the nursery "purchased a very desirable tract of land for nursery purposes" in Edgewood, an area just west of New Haven.[32] In 1905, the nursery erected a "large new frame building" at that site and constructed a water tower.[33] By 1915 they outgrew that tract of land, and secured a $200,000 loan to purchase land and construct new facilities in nearby Woodmont. Here, next to a railroad station, Coe set aside twenty-five acres where he designed "an attractive commercial park, where the nursery's products were displayed."[34] Coe also designed the nursery's voluminous catalogs in an art deco style that one trade described as "very artistic" and "interesting."[35] The seventy-two-page catalog for 1916 boasted of "our plantings of some half million of Fruit and Ornamental plants" and "several acres of Roses, more Fruit and Ornamental Trees, Evergreens, Shrubs, [and] Small Fruits."[36] Although once he moved to Miami Coe claimed that he had always been a landscape architect, it is clear he spent much of his time in Connecticut running a large and successful nursery.

Coe sought out exotic plants to sell at the nursey; he was particular enamored with Japanese flora. Along with his wife, Anna, he traveled to Japan and Europe in 1910 and 1911 to study horticulture and to tour other nurseries.[37] As early as 1901, Coe procured "a quantity of this most desirable Japanese Holly" to sell at the nursery.[38] He wrote in the 1907 catalog that he had been busy "ransacking the entire world for the many country's most beautiful trees and plants. Japan alone furnishes a most fascinating collection, and all the temperate zones, both north and south, have contributed their full share."[39] Although in Florida Coe would condemn nursery owners who plundered the Everglades for orchids, in New England he profited from similar activities. Coe introduced at least two new species of ornamental plants to the United States: the ibolium privet and the box-barberry, which he marketed in trade publications and popular magazines in the 1910s and 1920s.[40] Coe also brought the first private collection of bonsai trees to the United States in 1911. He displayed this collection at the nursery, promoted the planting of bonsais in the United States, and in 1925 on his relocation to Florida donated his collection of thirty-two plants to the Brooklyn Botanical Garden. This gift formed the basis of the garden's C. V. Starr Bonsai Museum, and several of Coe's plants remain on display today.[41]

Coe's importation of exotic and foreign plants was consistent with wider horticultural trends during the Progressive Era. Americans imported thousands of new ornamental and agricultural plant species into the United States as part of what historian Philip Pauley called a second phase of U.S. ecological imperialism. Botanist David Fairchild, whom Coe would form a close relationship with in Miami, was one of the central figures in this effort. From his post in the U.S. Department of Agriculture and as a private citizen, Fairchild was responsible for bringing tens of thousands of new plant species into the United States. Even after he retired from the department, he sought to enhance Miami's tropicality by transplanting tropical flora from around the world to the city. Coe's and Fairchild's efforts reflected a belief that humans could control nature and revealed a lack of ecological knowledge concerning the effects of invasive species. Although Coe, and to some extent Fairchild, would later reject this ecological imperialism, this love of exotic flora formed the basis of Coe's love of the Everglades. In Miami, Coe would no longer need to look oversees to find exotic flora. Now it was in his own backyard. In Florida, Coe's ecological imperialism and his "ransacking of the world" would be transformed into a sense of ecological independence and a desire to protect the native flora of the United States from destruction.[42]

Coe's activities as a member of professional nursery organizations gave him practical experiences he would later draw on in his fight for the ENP.[43] Coe presented papers at the annual meetings of the Connecticut Nurserymen and the New England Nurserymen Associations.[44] He served on the legislative committees for these regional associations for many years, and served on the legislative committee and the market development committee for the American Association of Nurserymen.[45] In his role as president of the Elm City nursery, Coe authored articles for trade publications, and wrote the nursery's catalog.[46] These writings provide a window into Coe's early ideas about nature.

Coe believed that humans, through activities like gardening and landscaping, could control the environment and enhance nature's beauty. In the 1906 Elm City catalog, Coe wrote that "the whole country has awakened to realize what great opportunities abound on every side for the creation of greater beauty." Coe applauded the "progressive movements" in America that prompted cities to develop "parks and parkways," and praised individuals who took "an active interest in evolving beautiful gardens."[47] By planting trees, nursery customers would experience "keen personal pleasure knowing that one has added to the sum total of the noble trees which develop into greater beauty from year to year." Trees had utilitarian value as well; they enhanced "the practical economy and beauty of our surroundings."[48] Fruit trees "are not only beautiful, but [are] sure to delight the palate and contribute to the true economy of the household."[49]

Coe's love of bonsai trees further illustrates his Progressive views of the natural world. Popular tastes in the 1910s and 1920s disapproved of these trees, and many found them to be starved, tortured, and unnatural.[50] In a 1923 article in *Garden Magazine*, Coe acknowledged these criticisms, writing that some people might "disapprove of encouraging a plant to grow other than as nature wills" or would not appreciate plants "so very much curtailed in their natural development." To such views, Coe responded with the claim that "practically all the trees and plants deliberately used for either utility or beauty show definite restraints imposed by the human hand." Bonsai were not some unnatural aberration. Rather, it was "perfectly consistent to cultivate and take pleasure" in plants that had so much beauty and "expressive individuality."[51]

In 1925 Coe moved to Miami, a rapidly growing city in the midst of a massive real estate boom, to pursue a second career in landscape architecture. The Florida land boom, and its inevitable bust, was one of the most important events in the history of modern Florida. The boom started in the late 1910s, reaching a fevered pitch in the mid-1920s before its collapse in 1925 and 1926. Miami was the center of the boom, but the frenzy touched the entire state. The skyrocketing land values had many causes. The boom was inextricably linked to the promises of Everglades drainage, and it was made possible due to the construction of transportation networks that opened Florida to the rest of the country. At its core, though, the Florida land boom was simply the most extreme manifestation of the wild, speculative economic logic of the 1920s.[52]

Uninhibited real estate promoters and ambitious developers marketed Florida land throughout the country as a surefire economic asset. Lands were sold and resold, often unseen, throughout the 1920s, increasing in value with each sale until the boom's bust. From 1918 to 1923 (before the boom's 1925 peak), property values increased in the state by 1,000 percent. In 1925, Coral Gables, an ostentatious Mediterranean-themed development planned by George Merrick, recorded $100 million in land sales. The same year, $75 million worth of property was sold in Miami Shores, another subdivision. The greater Miami area saw $60 million worth of construction activity in 1925. Lots in downtown Miami that sold for $1,000 at the beginning of the century sold from $400,000 to $1 million in 1925. The logic of the boom seemed to get more extreme and ridiculous as it headed for bust in 1925. In Miami Beach, lots that sold for $7,000 in June 1925 rose in value to $35,000 in just six weeks.[53]

A market correction was inevitable, but there were many other reasons for the boom's bust in 1925. Transportation problems led to greater scrutiny of the Florida real estate market. The IRS, multiple state governments, and the Better Business Bureau all investigated the market. Increased scrutiny prompted a crash, while a hurricane in 1926 finished it off for good. This destructive storm exposed the lies of real estate promoters; much of the land they sold was underwater, inaccessible, and worthless. Another hurricane in 1928, as well as the onset of the Great Depression in 1929, furthered the downward spiral in Florida land values. The industry would not recover until after World War II.

The boom was not only an important economic and demographic event but also shaped the history of Florida and the Everglades. The bust facilitated the creation of the ENP and altered the course of Ernest Coe's life. In 1925, Coe, along with his wife, Anna, and two nieces they were raising, moved from New England to Miami. Coe hoped to follow his passion for landscape architecture amid the sprawling estates and planned subdivisions that proliferated in Miami during the Florida land boom. Like so many other Florida transplants, Coe jettisoned his former life to chase his dreams. Coe even obscured his own past and perpetuated a myth that he had always been a landscape architect.[54] Soon after Coe's arrival, though, the land boom went bust. Like those of so many others seeking fortune in Florida, Coe's dreams were busted. There would be no fabulous estates or new developments for Coe to design. Yet his desire for a new life in Florida did come true. In Miami, Coe became the prophet of the Glades and the papa of Everglades National Park. If not for the boom, Coe never would have come to Miami; if not for the bust, he would have never fallen in love with the Everglades. The boom had been reliant on Everglades drainage; its bust meant the end of that project. Now, the Everglades could be reconsidered, and perhaps even protected and cherished.

The Everglades transformed Ernest Coe and completely altered the trajectory of his life. This ecosystem, as well as other factors, helped transform Coe from a Progressive nurseryman into an interwar proto-environmentalist. The Everglades awoke in Coe a zealous love for the area and drove him to protect it as a national park. The region also forced Coe to rethink his anthropocentric ideas about the natural world and pushed him to embrace an ecological view of nature. Coe's ecological views formed the park's intellectual foundation, while his zealous love of the Everglades and prophetic style of activism shaped the early fight for Everglades National Park.

As soon as Coe arrived in Miami, he sought out the Everglades. His neighbor Orville Rigby recalled first taking Coe to Cape Sable to see this "strange and unknown" area full of "wild plant life." Rigby noted that Coe soon became "enthusiastic over the wonders of the Everglades" and "with the flora and fauna and the newness of it all to him."[55] Harold H. Bailey was an early guide for Coe's Everglades excursions. In the early 1930s, botanist David Fairchild traveled through the area with Coe as well. On U.S. Senate and NPS inspection trips, Coe and Fairchild sailed through the Florida Bay and Ten Thousands Islands and flew over the Glades' sawgrass prairies in a blimp. Profiling Coe in 1947, journalist Theodore Pratt wrote that, after land boom went bust, Coe "had plenty of time on his hands to take up his habit of wandering through the woods." "Even at eighty," Coe continued "his habit of walking about, alone, in the southernmost tip of the mainland United States." According to Marjory Stoneman Douglas, Coe "tramped everywhere" in the Everglades, "often alone, wearing khaki trousers and a cotton shirt, a canvas hat and sneakers, carrying only a heavy stick." Douglas wrote that Coe "spent nights and days learning and delighting," in the lower Glades and that "he could sleep comfortably anywhere he found himself, on the warm sand beach, on a grassy rise over a slow river with the bull alligators roaring, or on a pile of leaves among logs in a jungle hammock." Coe was not some armchair environmentalist; he knew the Everglades intimately, and his activism was shaped by the region.[56]

The Everglades challenged Coe's very definitions of nature. The subtropical wetlands of the Everglades were nothing like the temperate forests and rocky coasts that Coe was familiar with in New England. Likewise, the region's flora was radically different from the domesticated temperate plants Coe sold at his Connecticut nursery. The changes he experienced in climate and seasonality must have likewise been startling. Coe, like previous Europeans travelers to the tropics such as Alexander von Humboldt and Charles Darwin, became intoxicated with the lure of the tropics. In the same way Yosemite and the Sierra Nevada mountains changed John Muir, the Everglades changed Ernest Coe. The region's biota, particularly its exotic and tropical flora, awoke in Coe a zeal for the Glades and a realization of its value. That value was directly connected to the region's biodiversity and its ecological values.

Coe saw how the Everglades' subtropical wetlands made natural processes and ecological principles visible to humans. For example, in the Everglades, minute changes in elevation and water levels result in entirely different plant associations, neatly illustrating these relationships and shedding light on the dynamics of plant succession. Food webs were more obviously on display in these wetlands than in temperate terrestrial ecosystems. Predation events involving mammals are often hidden from human view, but predation involving insects, fish, reptiles, and birds were common sights in the Everglades. The region's reputation as a breeding and feeding ground for wading birds reflected this dynamic as well. The Everglades' aquatic areas were also noted fish breeding grounds. Alligator holes were other important communities where humans could view ecological processes. Coe wrote that the Everglades was "a land preeminently outstanding as depicting examples of nature processes actually at work. It becomes a great nature university whose lessons open wide the opportunity for the average person to grasp fundamental principles with clear understanding."[57]

The Everglades' incredible biodiversity opened Coe's eyes to the wonders of the natural world. David Fairchild and botanist John Kunkel Small claimed the region contained "more species than any other area of similar size in America." Whereas visitors to a temperate forest may walk for miles and only see "a dozen species," in the Everglades "there are a hundred species there to one in the north."[58] The region's aquatic areas likewise teemed with life. According to one expert, the Everglades had "a greater number of species of fish ... than at any other known place in the world." The park would be "a land of eternal delight to students of aquatic biology."[59]

The hurricanes Coe experienced in 1926 and 1928 further challenged his old ideas about a compliant and submissive natural world. These storms violently displayed nature's power and destroyed human lives and property. They remain two of the most destructive and powerful hurricanes to ever make landfall in the United States. To Coe and other observers, they belied the notion that humans could control nature.[60] Coe experienced the first of these storms within a year of his relocation to Miami. The 1926 hurricane destroyed much of the city, seriously damaged the state's citrus industry, and caused massive flooding around Lake Okeechobee. The 1928 storm made landfall at West Palm Beach, destroying much of that town, and made a similar path toward the lake. That storm ruptured the Okeechobee dike, flooding most of the farming communities south of Lake Okeechobee. These floods killed an estimated 2,500 people. About 75 percent of them were poor Black migrant farmers; their bodies were burned or deposited in mass unmarked graves.[61] This natural disaster, like most in U.S. history, disproportionally affected the oppressed and poor.[62] Coe wrote in 1930 that "tolls and lessons" from these storms were "quite obvious," and represented "a fund of striking examples of nature's hand ... in this region."[63] He wrote extensively about the Labor Day hurricane in 1935 and experienced 1947's storms, which massively flooded South Florida and prompted enormous changes in federal and state water policy in Florida.

When Coe moved to Miami in 1925, he was a Progressive conservationist who believed that humans could control nature. Yet by the early 1930s, he could more accurately be described as a proto-environmentalist. Over the course of a decade, Coe embraced a biocentric ethic and an ecological view of nature, while still holding onto older ideas about the spiritual values of nature. The Everglades was the most important factor in Coe's transition, but human experts also impacted Coe's views of nature. Everglades naturalists, especially those Coe met through his involvement in the Florida Society of Natural History, gave Coe a scientific lens and a body of knowledge that he used to interpret the Everglades. Scientists like Harold H. Bailey, David Fairchild, John Kunkel Small, and Charles Torrey Simpson gave Coe a first-class education on the Everglades' biota and expanded his valuation of nature to include all species, not just those with obvious aesthetic or utilitarian value. In the early 1930s, Robert Sterling Yard and other wilderness advocates forced Coe to think more deeply about the intertwined relationships between tourism, wildlife, and wilderness. Finally, NPS wildlife biologists deepened Coe's ecological views through their criticisms of NPS management practices. George Wright and other scientists pushed Coe to view species in the context of their habitats.[64]

Coe's transitions embodied the larger transitions in U.S. environmental politics during the interwar period. As many historians have noted, the decades between the two world wars were marked by an increased concern for fauna, the emergence of the modern American wilderness movement, and the rise of ecology as a scientific field. Coe's efforts and the broader fight for Everglades National Park were some of the strongest expressions of these new ideas.[65] Ecological views of nature were central to the emergence of modern environmentalism, and to Coe's transformation. Many historians have noted the crucial importance of ecology to modern environmentalism. Ecology reveals the interconnectedness of species and habitats, and places humans and human activity in the context of ecosystems. These ideas have undergirded many of the actions of the environmental regulatory state and the goals of environmentalist organizations.

Coe's understanding of ecology was consistent with the state of the science in the 1930s, when ecology was still an emerging scientific field. By that decade, ecology's pioneers had created a framework for ecological inquiry, established the first graduate schools in ecology, and published a number of foundational works. Ecology in the 1930s—particularly plant ecology—was dominated by the ideas of Frederic Clements. Although today many of these ideas have been rejected, Clements identified some of the central problems of ecological study and set the field's research agenda.[66] Clements argues in *Methods of Ecology* (1905) and *Plant Succession* (1916) that ecosystems are governed by a process known as succession. According to this theory, as plant species colonize an ecosystem, they alter the area's ecology, creating habitats for other plants that in turn alter this ecosystem again. This process of change continues until the area reaches a climax: a balanced community that is the end result of this teleological process. This climax is in "equilibrium with its physical environment," and according to Clements it is "permanent because of its entire harmony with a stable habitat."[67]

Clements's ideas reflected a long-held belief that nature is naturally in balance with itself. Biologist John Kricher called the idea of the balance of nature "one of the most deep-seated assumptions about the natural world," arguing that this paradigm exerted a strong influence on the development of ecology.[68] Coe's concern for the Everglades' ecological balance reflected the state of the field in the 1930s.[69]

To Coe, the park would protect the Everglades' "natural balance, so that biological features not rivaled in the world for interest may remain inviolate."[70] Coe often defended the Everglades' value as a national park in ecological terms. He explained to NPS official Harold Bryant that there had been "virtually no disturbance of an ecologic balance" in the Everglades.[71] In a letter to NPS superintendent Arno Cammerer, Coe wrote the Everglades had "an ecological balance which is perhaps nearer the national park ideal" than any other U.S. park.[72] He thought that, "if left to its own devices," the wildlife of the Everglades "will remain in a numerical balance which will automatically care for itself."[73]

Coe believed that predators, fires, and hurricanes maintained this balance and were critical parts of the Everglades' ecosystems. In contrast, prevailing attitudes toward those forces in the 1930s were mostly negative. Although some of these attitudes were in flux as scientists began to study these forces through an ecological lens, most Americans in the 1930s, including many conservationists, saw fires, hurricanes, and predators as forces that destroyed nature.[74]

Coe's embrace of the Everglades' predators was influenced by the efforts of an iconoclastic group of NPS wildlife biologists. These scientists challenged the NPS's traditional focus on tourism and eventually overturned many long-standing NPS policies that called for the elimination of predators from the parks.[75] Coe and these scientists argued that predators helped maintain the populations of other species. They functioned within ecosystems, and removing them would disrupt the balance of those systems. Coe explained to Arno Cammerer that "cougars, bear, and other normal predators can be expected to continue to do their share in maintaining a normal balance of animal life within" the Everglades.[76] Throughout Coe's correspondence he frequently touted the value of wading birds alongside other species like alligators and panthers. He did not discriminate against predators but rather celebrated all the Everglades' wildlife.

Similarly, Coe came to see hurricanes as forces that shaped the ecology and landscape of the Everglades. In the midst of Coe's Everglades advocacy, the 1935 Labor Day hurricane, a category 5 storm, smashed through the Florida Keys. It destroyed much of the Keys' infrastructure and killed over two hundred World War I Bonus Army veterans employed by the Works Progress Administration. Less dramatically, the storm plowed through Cape Sable's mangrove forests and prairies.[77] Coe toured the destruction at Cape Sable by both boat and plane with a *Miami Herald* reporter, and he wrote extensively about the hurricane's ecological impacts. These writings reflected Coe's belief that hurricanes were natural forces that shaped the Everglades' landscapes, his Clementsian view of ecosystems, and his belief in the balance of nature. They were also a public relations ploy. National park standards dictated that parks be pristine exemplars of America's nature. A Cape Sable that had been destroyed by a hurricane might fail to meet these standards. However, if forces like hurricanes were merely natural phenomenon that helped create these landscapes, then their potential political harm to the park's establishment could be neutralized. Throughout his career as an ENP advocate, Coe repeatedly put his ecological insights to use in his promotional work.

By 1935, Coe thought that hurricanes were one of the many "natural forces" that shaped the Everglades. Coe compared these storms to landscape architects, writing that they were "one of the principle factors in the creating and sustaining of much of the present unique physical, biological, and broadly human interest characters of this region." Coe argued these storms gave Cape Sable "much of its distinctive character" and were "among the agents which carve individuality" into areas worthy of national park status. Hurricanes created the "complicated labyrinths of tidal bays, lakes, [and] connecting waterways" that gave the region its scenic and inspirational value. Connecting hurricanes to the geological tradition in the NPS, Coe explained to NPS official Arthur Demaray that hurricanes had "as much to do with the unique character of the region in this instance, as has the sum total of the erosion which has carved the Grand Canyon."[78]

Coe believed that both destruction and creation were essential to maintain nature's balance. Hurricanes were a necessary destructive force that kept constructive natural forces—which in Cape Sable meant the mangrove—in check. Coe noted that mangroves created islands and helped build up coastlines. He argued that "most of the tree growth on the island[s] in this region owes its initial start" to the mangrove. Red mangroves in particular were "one of the leading agents in the vanguard of this land building process." This species "has a spreading habit and once it gains a strong root-hold, is not easily dislodged." If left undisturbed, the "the process of land building continues on and on, further and further in to the Gulf and Bay waters."[79]

Hurricanes checked these land building processes and brought balance to nature by destroying mangroves. Because of hurricanes,

> new channels are formed and old ones disappear in the shallow waters of the Gulf and bays. New bars and great shallows come into being. The shape and size of outlying islands change, some are washed away and other appear. New beaches are thrown up. Some beaches are augmented, while others disappear. Much of the aquatic growth and accumulated sediment in the bays are washed out and carried inland, and where deposited enrich the ground.

The fringes of trees and shrubs along the waterways and shore lines get a sever trimming. Trees and even whole forests are partially broken down and in instances almost annihilated.[80]

Unknowingly, Coe was actually describing the next paradigm of the ecological sciences. Although he typically thought about ecosystems as being in balance with each other, his writings on both hurricanes and fire implicitly point to the importance of disturbance in ecosystems. Beginning in the mid-1970s, ecologists began to view disturbance, rather than balance, as a central force in the maintenance of ecosystems.[81]

Fire, according to Coe, also shaped the Everglades' ecosystems and landscapes. This reflected Coe's ecological thinking but also allowed him to present the Everglades as a pristine landscape untouched by human destruction. In contrast to Coe's attitudes, the USFS was waging a war on forest fires in the 1930s. Likewise, conservationists and organizations like the American Forestry Association had warned about fires destroying the Everglades.

Coe wrote that fire was "one of the agencies" that created "scenery" in the Everglades and gave the area "much of its charm."[82] Fires, along with hurricanes, were "expert architects" that nature used "in the shaping of her wild spaces." They were "agencies at work in creating and maintaining primeval wonderlands of scenic interests" and deserved "much of the credit for the outstanding individual landscape charm of this region."[83] In a letter to Everglades botanist John Kunkel Small, Coe wrote that "fire is one of the modifying influences that help to keep our Cape Sables unique and the ecological values distinctive."[84] Coe wrote to future ENP superintendent Daniel Beard in 1938 that "fires are a natural phenomenon. They have always swept the Everglades and they are going to continue to do it. It is because of fires that we have pinelands. It is because of fires that the Everglades remain open with grasses and sedges."[85]

Yet Coe condemned the muck fires that burned over much of the Everglades in the 1920s and 1930s. These fires, which were caused by the area's lowered water table, which was in turn a by-product of Everglades drainage, were seen by Coe as an unnatural force that needed to be stopped. He wrote "that some effective means must be found and put into action by which the burning of this peat muck . . . can be stopped." Coe blamed these muck fires on "the putting in of drainage canals through which the waters of these areas escape more rapidly than under natural conditions, and the water table becomes lower than would otherwise be the case, exposing vast amount of vegetable matter to drying out."[86]

Drainage was not only causing muck fires, it was altering the entire Everglades. Yet throughout his Everglades advocacy, Coe avoided all almost all discussion of Everglades drainage. In order to ensure the region measured up to prevailing NPS standards, Coe presented the region as a pristine landscape, unaltered by humans. The same impulse that led Coe to defend fires and hurricanes as natural forces, led him ignore the issue of drainage. It is also likely that at least early in the park fight, Coe did not fully understand the Everglades' hydrology. Scientific studies of the area's hydrology were still in their infancy in the 1940s. Daniel Beard in 1938 and, to a greater extent, Garald Parker in the 1940s, examined how drainage of the northern Glades led to lowered water levels throughout the entire watershed. Only with the publication of Marjory Stoneman Douglas's 1947 book *The Everglades: River of Grass* was the general populace able to develop an understanding of these process.[87] Some Florida naturalists and scientists, among them Harold H. Bailey, Charles Torrey Simpson, and John Kunkel Small, had briefly mentioned drainage as a threat in the 1930s, but none of these authors connected the drainage of the northern Everglades to changing water levels in the southern Everglades, nor did they elaborate on the topic.[88]

Coe occasionally criticized drainage, but it wasn't until the late 1940s that he argued that drainage in the upper Everglades damaged the lower Everglades that were slated for inclusion in the park. However, given his close connection to Everglades scientists, and his statements on drainage, it is possible he was aware of drainage's impacts before then. Many of his early discussions of drainage begin by accurately describing the area's sheet flow but end with baffling conclusions that Coe likely knew to be false. These statements were designed to show that that the southern Everglades had not been adversely affected by drainage and still met national park standards.

In 1930, Coe wrote that the Everglades was "a slightly tilted plain extending from the Gulf level to some four feet elevation along its northern boundary. Drainage is from the north to south, and is slightly inclined toward the west." This statement reflects an accurate understanding of the Everglades' sheet flow. A few sentences later though, Coe incorrectly and comically claimed that "the water table underlying practically the entire south half of this area is influenced by and maintained . . . by the level of the Gulf waters" and that the water level in the southern Glades was not influenced by drainage.[89] In 1931 he wrote a similar letter to the NPS. Here he acknowledged that "the water table underlying the northern portions of this area have no doubt been modified by the lowering of the water level of Lake Okeechobee." However, he argued that the southern Everglades slated for inclusion in the park was "practically unmodified in this respect. This unchanged water table over a great portion of this area is owing to its being governed almost wholly by its relation to the waters of the Gulf of Mexico."[90] In 1934, Coe tried to feed the NPS another line regarding park water levels. Now "the water table within the park area [was] influenced by rainfall" rather than proximity to the Gulf of Mexico.[91]

By the late 1940s, after the park had been established and Douglas's *The Everglades* published, Coe admitted what he may have known all along: drainage in the upper Glades lowered the water table in the lower Glades and caused immense damage to the area's ecology. After the park's establishment, Coe urged the NPS to address the issue of decreased water flow to the park. He suggested that the park gain control of the water conservation areas planned by the USACE in the northern Everglades. Coe argued that "water control within the [water conservation] area" would mean that the park service could "influence the water factor within the Everglades park area" and "assure the water's natural flow."[92] These areas had been altered by human activity and did not measure up to park standards. Yet Coe was willing to sacrifice these standards for the greater ecological health of the region. The park service quickly rejected these suggestions. NPS director Newton Drury noted that the construction of levees, dikes, canals, and pumping stations, would destroy "the natural features of the area" and "remove it from all consideration for national park status."[93]

Coe's ecological views provided the basis for the park's intellectual justifications. Yet Coe was no intellectual. Rather he was a prophet. Possessed with a deep zealous love of the Everglades, Coe proselytized the virtues of the region to all. He embraced an ambitious vision for a national park that would protect the Everglades' habitats and biota for all time. He converted others to embrace these views and built support for the park's creation. More broadly, Coe was a herald for ecological values and forerunner of modern environmentalism. His Everglades activism did not just lead to the ENP's creation but challenged others to rethink their ideas about nature itself. Marjory Stoneman Douglas was the first to note Coe's prophetic nature. She wrote that he had been "possessed" by the idea of saving the Everglades, and that a "blaze that had been lighted in him" that "would dominate his every moment for the rest of his life."[94] Journalist Michael Grunwald used similar language in *The Swamp*. He wrote that Coe was possessed with a "moral fervor." He was "single-minded" and contained "boundless energy."[95] Coe's prophetic and strident style of activism served him exceedingly well in the early fight for the park, when he mostly focused on promoting his specific vision for the ENP. Coe effectively promoted the park, gained the support of important national and state constituents, overturned negative perceptions of the Everglades, and built support for the park's rationales.

CHAPTER 2

Redefining National Parks, Redefining the Everglades

National parks traditionally protected the geological wonders of the American West. These parks catered to tourism; they existed for humans to use and enjoy. New trends in American conservation challenged these traditions. During the interwar period, biological preservation and ecological ideas became more important, as did the concept of wilderness. The NPS sought to keep abreast of these trends but also saw many of these ideas as threatening to its own culture and traditions. Conservationists increasingly criticized the NPS as overly focused on tourism at the expense of wilderness and biological values. The NPS responded to these criticism by altering park policies and by embedding biological values and wilderness in new parks created and planned in the 1930s.

The ENP was at the forefront of these trends and the furthest expression of these new values in the service. This park challenged many of the service's central traditions and pointed the way forward to a new type of national park. Everglades National Park was a biological park in a system full of geological wonders and a wilderness park in an agency that catered to tourism. This park protected a tropical wetland, whereas traditionally, parks preserved temperate mountains and forests. While most national parks were in the West, this park was located at the southern tip of Florida.

Ernest Coe understood that the ENP would be controversial and misunderstood. Not only did this park challenge NPS traditions, but the Everglades challenged America's very ideas about nature. Swamps and marshes had been almost universally reviled by Americans. To create the park, it was essential that Coe replace negative perceptions of the Everglades with positive ideas. Coe's imagined Everglades was defined by its flora and fauna, its tropicality, and its aquatic qualities. This Everglades centered biological values and was informed by the work of biologists who studied the region. Yet it was also explicitly crafted to meet NPS standards and designed to show how the Everglades possessed the scenic and spiritual values expected in all national parks. Coe's redefined Everglades reflected new biological ideas, just as it harked back to the traditions of the NPS.

Although Yellowstone, the nation's first national park, was created in 1872, the National Park Service (NPS) did not exist until 1916. Before this date, the parks were under the purview of whichever federal agency controlled those lands at the time of the park's creation. This meant that, for example, in 1911 thirteen parks were controlled by the USFS, while fifteen fell under the umbrella of the Department of the Interior. Additionally, before 1916, the U.S. Army served as a ranger force in some parks, and the USACE constructed park roads and had additional authority in national parks.[1]

On its creation in 1916, the NPS gained control over all the national parks. Yet the agency remained small, weak, and underfunded. Its first superintendent, Stephan Mather, a publicity-savvy industrialist, quickly moved to expand the NPS portfolio, popularity, and power. Mather pursued new parks, which were carved out of western federal lands.[2] This often embroiled him in conflict with other government agencies, especially the USFS. Mather also prioritized park tourism. Many national parks had been explicitly created as tourist attractions. Their creations were supported by railroad companies and concessioners who saw parks as ways to boost their businesses. Mather likewise supported tourism and saw it as a way to boost public support and federal appropriations for the new agency.[3]

Tourism helped create the parks, but so too did the ideas of John Muir and other Progressive Era aesthetic preservationists. Muir embodied a spiritual view of nature. Places like Yosemite and the Sierra Nevada Mountains were temples of nature where humans could find god and experience the sublime. While ideas concerning the efficient use of resources animated the USFS, the NPS reflected Muir's beliefs. Some areas were so beautiful and exceptional that they should be preserved untouched, for all time. Human tourists could experience those wonders and leave the parks rejuvenated and enlightened.

In 1929 Mather was succeeded by Horace Albright, who had been Mather's right-hand man. Albright was a "Mather man" through and through and supported the park's dual goals of preserving sublime scenery and catering to tourists. Yet, he also accommodated new environmental ideas in the NPS. In the 1930s, the NPS worked to protect wilderness, partly due to criticisms that parks were overcrowded and overdeveloped, but also as a front in a long-running rivalry with the USFS. Albright also supported the work of NPS wildlife biologists who sought to protect wildlife. Most notably, he worked to end predator control policies in the parks.[4]

Albright also helped expand the service in new directions. In 1933, President Franklin Roosevelt transferred the nation's national monuments, battlefield sites, and cemeteries to the NPS, a move that solidified the agency's power and broadened its mandate.[5] The agency sought to create new parks in the 1930s as well. Two desires influenced this expansion. First, the NPS wanted parks in the eastern United States. Most parks were in the remote West, far from eastern population centers. Eastern parks would bring geographical balance to the system, but would also help build political support for the NPS. The agency also sought to include new types of landscapes in the parks. Rather than just protecting temperate mountains and forests, they sought to protect a representative portion of all of the nation's environments. As they pursued these expansions, the NPS also reconsidered the purposes of national parks. Although tourism remained central, the agency altered park management policies to protect wilderness and wildlife. Several new parks, including Isle Royale, Big Bend, and Everglades, were explicitly seen as wilderness parks and represented new ecological ideas.[6]

The creation of new parks posed new challenges. While western parks were carved from federal landholdings, eastern parks were created from privately held or state-owned lands, which the federal government refused to purchase.[7] The responsibility for acquiring parks lands fell to local communities and state governments. Creating these eastern parks required a very high degree of local and state support. To build this support, park advocates created private associations to promote these proposed parks and lobby federal and state governments for needed legislation. Typically, the U.S. Department of the Interior (DOI) and the NPS investigated the areas in question to determine if they met park standards. If they were up to snuff, the DOI recommended federal legislation authorizing the park's creation. A plethora of proposed parks in the 1920s and 1930s were dismissed as substandard, yet the park's federal authorization was only the first step in this process. For the park to be created, state governments next needed to acquire all lands in the park's proposed boundaries and deliver them to the federal government. State governments either appropriated monies for this purpose or created public commissions to raise funds and acquire park lands. Only after the federal government received these lands would the DOI then establish the park. It is worth noting two distinctions with this process: federal governments *authorized* the creation of parks and then *established* them once they possessed the needed lands; private *associations* publicized parks, while public *commissions* engaged in land acquisition.

National parks that were established via this method included Acadia, Shenandoah, Great Smoky Mountains, Isle Royale, Mammoth Cave, Big Bend, and Everglades. Established in 1919, Acadia National Park in Maine was the first national park east of the Mississippi and set precedents concerning the creation of eastern parks. New England elites like Harvard University president Charles W. Eliot and wealthy conservationist George Dorr promoted Acadia and worked for its creation. Dorr convinced John D. Rockefeller Jr. and other philanthropists to donate money for the purchase of park lands; Rockefeller funded the majority of this park and designed its extensive carriage road system. These lands were then deeded to the federal government, which created a national monument in 1916 and then a national park in 1919. Although Rockefeller funded the park's creation, Dorr was this park's motivating force and had much in common with Ernest Coe. Dorr and Coe were both captivated and transformed by the natural wonders of these regions and dedicated their lives to protecting nature.[8]

Coe also had much in common with another important figure in the history of these eastern national parks: Harlan P. Kelsey. Like Coe, Kelsey was a nurseryman, but while Coe promoted Asian and tropical plants, Kelsey promoted native plants. Coe was a New Englander who moved to the South practice to landscape architecture, while Kelsey was a native Southerner who moved to Boston in 1897 to open his landscape architecture firm. Both were active in New England nurseryman associations, and likely knew each other from those groups. Kelsey became involved in conservation issues in Boston, and due his familiarity with the Southern Appalachians was asked to serve on a NPS committee to evaluate the prospect of establishing national parks in the region. In 1924 that group recommended the creation of Shenandoah and Great Smoky National Parks. Kelsey promoted these parks and helped finalize their boundaries. The NPS continued to call on Kelsey in the following decades to help investigate potential park sites, including the Everglades.[9]

The federal government authorized Shenandoah, Great Smoky, and Mammoth Cave National Parks in 1926. Their creations followed paths similar to Acadia's creation. The Shenandoah National Park Association publicized that park and worked to raise the $2 million needed to purchase private lands in the region. They found little success, and the responsibility for raising money was soon transferred to a state commission under the control of Virginia's governor, who quickly determined that $6 million would be needed. In response, the size of the park was reduced, and the state government appropriated $1 million for land purchases in 1928. By 1934, the state deeded park lands to the federal government, which created Shenandoah National Park in 1935.[10]

Great Smoky's creation followed a similar procedure. The Appalachian National Park Association and the Great Smoky Conservation Association publicized the park, and gained support from political and business interests who saw it as an effective way to promote tourism to Appalachia. Park promoters raised $1 million, while the governments of Tennessee and North Carolina each appropriated $2 million. This was about half the money needed for land acquisition. John D. Rockefeller Jr. again played a pivotal role in this park's creation by donating $5 million to the cause. The North Carolina Park Commission and the Tennessee Park Commission used these monies to acquire the lands in their states, sometimes using the power eminent domain, and the park was created in 1934.[11] Mammoth Cave likewise had its Mammoth Cave National Park Association to promote the park. Park lands were donated to the NPS, which created the park in 1941.

The creations of Isle Royale National Park in Lake Superior, and Big Bend National Park in Texas, likewise fit this pattern. These two parks, along with the ENP, were wilderness parks created to protect flora and fauna.[12] Big Bend was established in 1944 largely due to the work of local Texas boosters and politicians who, beginning in 1933, sought to turn this foreboding desert landscape into a tourist attraction. The state of Texas appropriated $1.5 million for land acquisition in the park area in 1941, and the NPS created the park in 1944.[13] Isle Royale was authorized by Congress in 1931 with the familiar stipulation that no federal funds could be used to acquire these lands. The Isle Royale National Park Association publicized the park, but the Isle Royale National Park Commission failed to acquire park lands. Instead, the federal appropriated $705,000 for land purchase on the island in 1933. To get around the 1931 law, these lands were technically used to create Civilian Conservation Corps camps on the island. In 1938, that 1931 law was amended to allow for the use of federal funds and all private lands were acquired by 1940. The NPS established the park that year. In the end, the federal government provided seven-eighths of the needed monies for Isle Royale land acquisition.[14]

The creation of these eastern parks required high degrees of public support because, with the exception of Isle Royale, private citizens and state governments funded their creations. Park advocates often touted the economic value of park tourism to convince local landowners, business groups, sporting groups, conservationists, and politicians to support these parks. Many traditional conservationists looked aghast at these promotional campaigns. They feared these parks would become commercialized amusement resorts and not temples of nature. The fact that eastern parks lacked the scenic grandeur and geological monumentalism of western parks reinforced this suspicion. NPS watchdogs—including Robert Sterling Yard, who helped torpedo a number of substandard park proposals in the 1920s—feared that local populations, greedy for tourist dollars, would steamroll Congress and the NPS into creating substandard parks that would degrade the entire National Park System. Yard was particularly suspicious of those parks in the South, a region he saw as economically desperate and politically powerful.

Yard's concerns were part of larger debate in the 1920s and 1930s concerning the purposes and goals of national parks. Although the first national park was created in 1872, no larger legal framework for defining parks existed before the NPS was founded in 1916. That year, Congress passed the notoriously vague and contradictory National Park Service Organic Act. This short law directed the NPS to both "conserve the scenery and the natural and historic objects and the wild life" in the parks but also "to provide for the enjoyment of the same." The contra-

diction between tourism and preservation was embedded in the NPS legal framework and became a major source of debate during the interwar period. Furthermore, this law did not define what a national park was, nor did it lay out a set
of criteria for national parks status. Boosters, politicians, and local communities
wanted national parks, which created economic growth and brought prestige to
their regions. Conservationists acted as watchdogs over the NPS, making sure
only exemplary regions were granted national park status. The NPS was caught
in the middle. This dynamic was particularly pronounced in the 1920s, as controversy erupted over the Wind Cave, Sullys Hill, and Platt park proposals.[15]

To prevent future controversy, the NPS, the Campfire Club of America, and
almost a hundred other conservationist organizations came together in 1929 to
write new park standards. These standards reflected the transitional attitudes toward nature that characterized the interwar period. They embraced the preservation of flora and fauna and the protection of wilderness but were also firmly
grounded in traditional park values like scenery, tourism, and the spiritual qualities of nature. These standards stated that parks needed to "be of national interest" and needed to possess "scenic magnificence." Yet each park also needed to be
"a sanctuary for the scientific care, study and preservation of all wild plant and animal life within its limits." All "wilderness features" in parks needed to "be kept
absolutely unmodified." Most significantly for the Everglades' wetlands, they
mandated that the park system needed to include representative and unique landscapes that exemplified all of the nation's nature.[16]

The ENP's creation followed the same pattern as these eastern parks, yet its creation was significantly more complicated. This park directly challenged many of
the central traditions of the park system. The ENP pushed the envelope of what
a park could be. Rather than jagged mountains reaching into the sky, this park
would protect flat marshes and swamps, and even marine ecosystems below sea
level. Rather than a geological park, this would be a biological park. Ernest Coe
understood the park's potential to cause controversy; to blunt these potential criticisms, he sought to center the park's rationales and the Everglades' very identity in
the context of new NPS park standards. Coe's redefinition of the Everglades hence
reflected both the political task of creating the park and the centrality of biology
to the Everglades' preservation.

Redefining the Everglades was Coe's first task. Throughout history, Americans
viewed swamps as wastelands. The Everglades had long been seen as "a series of
vast, miasmic swamps, poisonous lagoons, [and] huge dismal marshes."[17] Replacing these negative tropes with more positive ideas about the region was a prerequi-
site to the park's creation. This was a major focus of Coe's early advocacy and dove-
tailed with larger trends. During the interwar period, a larger reconsideration of

swamps of marshes was underway.[18] The fight for the ENP and Coe's redefinition of the Everglades were perhaps clearest manifestations of this larger dynamic.

Coe presented the Everglades as a biological treasure trove, a tropical paradise, and an aquatic wonderland defined by its myriad expressions of water. He drew on three sources to construct this new Everglades. The first were his own experiences in the area. The second were scientists, among them John Kunkel Small, Charles Torrey Simpson, and David Fairchild. These experts challenged Coe's anthropocentric views of nature, educated Coe about the Everglades, and provided Coe with specific ideas about the Everglades that he used to redefine the region. Finally, new park standards influenced Coe's redefinition of the Everglades. Coe's Everglades, especially its tropical and aquatic qualities, were explicitly crafted to meet these new park standards.[19] Coe's Everglades was derived from a specific scientific context, but it was also a political device, engineered to meet a specific political goal. Just as negative views of the region justified and enabled drainage, Coe's Everglades facilitated the region's preservation as a national park.[20]

The most important element of this new Everglades was the region's biota. The Everglades did not just contain fantastic, exotic, and unique flora and fauna—to Coe and his allies, the Everglades *was* its biota. If Yosemite was El Capitan and the Sentinel Dome, then the Everglades was mangrove forests, sawgrass marshes, alligators, and manatees. This emphasis drew on existing concerns about the area—conservationists had tried to protect the area's bird species—but Coe expanded that narrow concerns for wading birds to include all the region's fauna and flora.

Coe's knowledge of the Everglades' flora was greatly informed by John Kunkel Small. Small was a botanist at the New York Botanical Garden and the foremost expert on the Everglades' plant life.[21] He first visited the area in 1901 and returned to the Everglades yearly. Throughout his life, Small published over 450 works, mostly articles in the *Journal of the New York Botanical Garden*, and is credited with naming over two thousand species of flora.[22] His 1903 dissertation, *Flora of the Southeastern United States*, remains an authority on the topic.[23] In 1929, Small published *From Eden to Sahara* for popular audiences. This book was based on Small's 1922 expedition into the Everglades and included many vivid and scientifically informed descriptions of the region's flora. It also railed against the diverse human activities that were destroying the Everglades and its flora. Small wrote that Florida was "yesterday a botanical paradise! Tomorrow, the desert!" He urged that "as much as possible of this natural history museum should be preserved."[24] Coe praised Small's *From Eden to Sahara* and promoted it in his wider correspondence. Coe told Small in 1929 that he had read the book "last night . . . from cover to cover" and hoped that the book would "awaken every loyal reader to action."[25]

Coe had read many of Small's other works and corresponded frequently with the botanist, often connecting his own trips in the Everglades to Small's writings. In 1932, Coe wrote concerning Small's descriptions of the Turner River, an area in the northwest corner of the Everglades that Coe fought to include in the park. There Coe had seen "that interesting and seemingly rare lip-fern (Cheilanthes microphylla) growing on the heaps of oyster shells on Turner Island," as well as orchids and other varieties of flora.[26] Coe wrote to Small again in 1932 about another trip where Coe encountered a stand of "the silk-top thatch palm (Thrinax parviflora)." This "dainty, graceful palm" had "glossy bright green leaves" and trunks that were "generally quite slender, smooth as the royal palm and attractively patterned." Coe had learned about this tree from one of Small's articles that Coe quoted in this letter. Making connections between species and their habitats, Coe described the "deep marl in which these palms are growing." Finally, Coe lamented that these plants could easily be "collected and transported," by some enterprising nurseryman who could "use these trees for gardening purposes." Although in New England Coe had touted his own ransacking of the world, in 1932 he hoped that "through federal protection, these palms and other equally choice features" would be preserved.[27]

Coe often extolled the beauty and value of the region's flora. He wrote that the Everglades had "the greatest variety of plant forms. Palms, orchids and mangroves, typical of the southland are here neighbors with the oak, maple, magnolia and ash."[28] Coe called the "majestic mangrove forest . . . one of the wonders of the world."[29] In a lecture delivered at the Cosmos Club in Washington, D.C., in 1929, Coe rhapsodized about the "dense almost impenetrable tropic forest, [and] jungles where many types of orchids, other air plants and ferns festoon the trees." Visitors to the Everglades would find "tall Royal Palms, towering well above the jungle roof waving their glossy green fronds triumphantly in the breeze."[30]

Small and Coe expanded Progressive concerns for charismatic species of fauna to include all species of flora. They believed these plants had scientific value but also aesthetic value and inherent worth. In contrast, conservationists had rarely sought to preserve flora, unless it was either an economic resource like timber or a scenically significant species like the sequoias in California's redwood forests. This concern for nontimber species of flora marked a radically new avenue for preservation in the United States.[31] Although historians have examined shifting attitudes toward animals in the 1930s, they have not cataloged efforts to protect flora or studied the changing ethical relationships between humans and plants.[32] Coe was at the forefront of these trends and made the protection of plants central to his campaign.

Coe also tapped into existing concerns for the Everglades' birdlife and wrote about these charismatic species. In a letter to conservationist John Merriam, Coe described the "great bevies of herons, ibis, curlews, and egrets shown out with dazzling whiteness, forming in flight, veritable clouds of graceful motion."[33] On a car trip along the Tamiami Trail, Coe saw "white ibis and wood ibis, egrets and other native birds . . . occasionally flying overhead; singly, in two's and three's and frequently a whole flock of them at a time."[34] In 1931 he traveled through the Everglades with a group of Seminoles and reported on the trip via a Miami radio program. The group saw "wood and white ibis, little blue heron, snowy and great American egret." They "came upon an area where many thousands of these were feeding," when "suddenly, and almost with one accord, they took flight." The air above the group "was fairly filled with these strangely beautiful birds, for a while whirling about in great white clouds."[35]

The second element of Coe's Everglades was its tropicality. By painting the Everglades as tropical, Coe sought to show that it was exotic and unique and that it possessed aesthetic value. These traits were important elements of new NPS park standards; a tropical Everglades would ensure that the region met these standards.

Coe's understanding of the tropics and his insistence that the Everglades was tropical were drawn directly from David Fairchild, the most important influence on Coe's early thinking about the Everglades. Fairchild was a world-renowned botanist and an expert on tropical flora. He was married to Marian Hubbard Bell, the daughter of Alexander Graham Bell, and he was very well-connected to conservationists and well-heeled business elites. As the head of the Section of Systematic Seed and Plant Introduction for the U.S. Department of Agriculture (USDA), Fairchild was responsible for the importation of tens of thousands of plant species into the United States. Many of them were tropical, and most were for agricultural purposes. Coe's own experience in ransacking the world paled in comparison to Fairchild's. Their experiences and their love of exotic plants forged a bond and friendship between the two.[36]

Fairchild saw the Everglades through the lens of an established discourse on tropical landscapes that stretched back to the writings of Alexander von Humboldt, Charles Darwin, and Alfred Russel Wallace. Through their travelogues and other writings about the tropics, these scientists—along with visual artists who painted these areas—established a coherent set of ideas about the identity of the tropics that developed in parallel to European ideas about the region they referred to as the Orient, which included the Middle East and Asia. Although the concept of Orientalism has received much scholarly attention, the imagined geography of the tropics has been less studied. Both concepts examine the ways Europeans constructed these foreign places as the "other." Asia, the Middle East, and the tropics were culturally constructed as places that the West was not. The Othering of these areas was not just a way of defining and delineating them but also justified the imperialist conquest of these areas and the oppression of native peoples.[37]

Imperialism shaped the West's social construction of the tropics, but so too did a specific scientific context. The archetypal description of the tropics was Alexander von Humboldt's *Personal Narrative*, which described his journey through tropical South America between 1799 and 1804.[38] Humboldt was a German polymath who laid the foundation for a number of scientific fields. His masterpiece, *Cosmos*, presented nature as a unified whole bound by natural laws. Here, Humboldt essentially created the modern concept of nature. He influenced countless numbers of scientists, writers, and artists, and he remains one of the most important figures in the history of science.[39] According to historian Nancy Stepan, Humboldt's writings on South America "provided a model for writing about and viewing the tropics that influenced naturalists and artists for decades."[40] Two of those scientists were Charles Darwin and Alfred Russel Wallace, whose contributions to this discourse on tropicality were entwined with their work on the development of the theory of natural selection.[41] Ideas about tropical nature were thus bound to some of the most important attempts to understand how the natural world functioned.

According to this discourse, the tropics were superabundant, Edenic, sublime, and exotic. They were also dangerous, pestilent, and unsuited for human habitation. Tropical peoples were cast in a negative light. They were lazy, unindustrious, and often stricken by exotic and dangerous diseases. Justifications for the conquest of these peoples were thus baked into this discourse. Although the concept of tropicality contained both negative and positive ideas, Everglades advocates focused on the positive ones and downplayed or ignored these negative associations.

David Fairchild was inspired by these ideas about the tropics. As a young man, he read Wallace's *The Malay Archipelago* and soon dedicated his life to the study of tropical flora. As he imported thousands of tropical plants into the United States, Fairchild likewise promoted these ideas about the tropics. After spending a career in the USDA working to import tropical plants to the United States, Fairchild relocated to Miami in the 1920s and embarked on a crusade to enhance Miami's tropicality by planting strange and exotic flora throughout the city.[42]

Fairchild saw the Everglades through a global lens, arguing that the region was an American paragon of the tropics. The Everglades was a unique tropical landscape when contrasted with the temperate landscapes of much of the United States and, according to Fairchild, was more impressive and more beautiful than other tropical areas in Asia and Latin America. Fairchild expounded on these themes in a 1929 speech at the annual meeting of the American Forestry Association (AFA). Prominent AFA members were skeptical of the Everglades' value and invited Fairchild to discuss the proposed park. Fairchild presented the Everglades as a slice of the global tropics that was fortuitously located in the United States. He argued that the Everglades contained "the most magnificent mangrove forests in the world." Although Fairchild had "just returned from the table lands of North

Sumatra," he claimed that "nowhere in all my experience have I seen greater numbers of orchids, or more magnificent specimens, than abound in the hammocks of Southern Florida." Likewise, the beaches at Cape Sable "with their groves of coconut palms" reminded Fairchild "of beaches in Samoa and the Fiji Islands and Amboina and the other islands in the Java sea." He compared the Everglades hammocks to those of the "Winneba Plains of the African Gold Coasts" but found that these African hammocks "lacked much of the beauty that characterizes the hammocks of Florida."[43]

Ernest Coe wholeheartedly adopted Fairchild's ideas about the tropics as his own. The Everglades' tropicality was central to Coe's early promotional work. In fact, the word "tropic" can be found in almost every piece of his early correspondence. The initial name of the park, which Coe used between 1928 and 1931, was the Tropic Everglades National Park. Likewise, the original name of Coe's organization was the Tropical Everglades National Park Association. In 1931, when the word "tropic" was removed from the park's name, Coe protested. He explained to NPS director Horace Albright that the word "tropic" differentiated the ENP from other parks and communicated uniqueness. Coe thought the word "tropic" was as important to the ENP's name "as the word 'Caverns' was to the Carlsbad Caverns National Park; 'Volcanic' to Lassen Volcanic National Park and 'Great Smoky' to Great Smoky National Park."[44]

The tropical nature of the Everglades communicated uniqueness, an essential trait for national parks, according to prevailing park standards. In 1929 Coe wrote that the Everglades "is America's only tropic area within the bounds of the States." After the park's authorization in 1934, Coe dashed off a press release stating that the park's "tropical landscape," its flora and fauna, and its "delightful climate at all seasons of the year are features different from those found in other national parks." The Everglades would be "the only National Park located in the true Tropics," giving it "a distinction," and making it "a substantial perpetual asset."[45]

The fact that the Everglades is not in the tropics was irrelevant to Coe. The Everglades was its biota, and since that biota was tropical, the Everglades was therefore tropical. In an article published in the June 1931 edition of *All Florida Magazine*, Coe acknowledged that, geographically speaking, the Everglades was "just outside the tropics, fifty miles north of Tropic of Cancer." Yet, the Everglades was "endowed with plant, animal, and other features characteristic of the tropics." According to Coe, the Glades even rivaled "the Amazon and the East Indies in tropical luxuriance" with its "many square mile of impenetrable tropical jungle within whose fastnesses are many lovely orchids, buttonball and other tropical trees." The Everglades was "truly tropical in both its flora and fauna."[46]

The tropics were a sublime and wondrous place; by labeling the Everglades "tropical," Coe hoped to show that the Everglades possessed the spiritual values required of all national parks. Coe often called the Everglades a "wonderland" or a "jungleland-fairyland" and often wrote about the "the lure of the tropics." In a speech at a recreational convention, Coe proclaimed that, when the ENP was established, tourists "may visit a tropic land and drink in that mysterious lure distinctly characteristic of the jungle land." Tourists visiting the Everglades would realize "the true spirit of this tropic land and its mysterious wonder features."[47]

The last element of the Everglades' new identity was its aquatic character. Other national parks were defined by their rocks; this park would be defined by its water. While subsequent generations of Everglades advocates would focus on the freshwater sawgrass marshes of the northern Glades, Coe emphasized the marine areas at the southern end of the Everglades. These places—Cape Sable, the Florida Bay, Whitewater Bay, and the Ten Thousand Islands—possessed incredible biological diversity and richness. Coe particularly highlighted the spiritual and sublime qualities of these aquatic areas. Coe's use of these aquatic qualities, like his use of tropical tropes, illustrated how the ENP's creation was consistent with traditional park rationales.

Coe frequently contrasted the ENP's aquatic identity to the geological identities of other national parks. In a press release announcing the park's 1934 federal authorization, Coe conceded that the Everglades had none of the geological wonders found in other parks. Instead, it was composed of "azure seas, emerald isles, lakes, rivers, and beaches." He wrote that "about half the area is made up of thousands of wooded islands and other thousands of lakes, bays and interlocking waterways."[48] By casting the Everglades as aquatic, Coe deemphasized the Everglades as a dreary, swampy morass, replacing those negative ideas with more positive cultural concepts about lakes, seas, and rivers—just as Marjory Stoneman Douglas would later do with *The Everglades: River of Grass*.

Coe could never neatly encapsulate his vision of the Everglades in one phrase like "river of grass," but Coe's descriptions of the Everglades as different expressions of water came close to embodying a slogan that conveyed Coe's identity for the Everglades. He commonly called the region a "labyrinth of waterways" or some variation on that phrase. In a 1930 report to the NPS, he called the Everglades a "labyrinth of ramifying waterways." In a letter to Charles Burke, a bureaucrat at the Bureau of Indian Affairs, Coe described the Everglades as "a labyrinth of interlocking bays, rivers, lakes and thousands of islands, creating a nature Venice of tropic loveliness." Coe wrote that this "vast labyrinth of scenic waterways the ENP area contains will no doubt make boating one of its outstanding attractions."[49]

Coe drew this phrase and many of his ideas about the Everglades' aquatic character from Charles Torrey Simpson. Simpson, known in Miami as the Sage of Biscayne Bay, was a conchologist and botanist who by 1930 had lived in South Florida for over twenty years. He authored multiple books on the regions' environments.

In Lower Florida Wilds, his most popular work, recounted Simpson's experiences in the Everglades and influenced Coe's ideas about these wetlands.[50] In some ways, Simpson was similar to William Bartram, a botanist who explored Florida in the late eighteenth century. Both examined flora and fauna through a scientific lens while simultaneously writing about the sublime power of the natural world. Just as Bartram marked the eighteenth-century transition from romanticism to empiricism, Simpson represented changes in science related to the decline of the amateur-naturalist and the rise of the professional scientist. Simpson never graduated high school and was self-trained yet was one of the world's leading authorities on mollusks and worked for the Smithsonian Institution. Simpson effusively wrote about the spiritual values and mystery of the natural world, but he could also "identify some ten thousand shells by sight and give their Latin names."[51]

In Lower Florida Wilds celebrated the uniqueness and strangeness of the Everglades' flora and the sublime value of the Everglades. Paddling through the Ten Thousand Islands, Simpson found channels where

> great mangroves arch, dimming the sun's glare to soft twilight beneath. Air roots everywhere descend into the channels so completely obstructing the passage that we had frequently to chop our way through. Immense orchids (Cyrtopodium punctatum) were in bloom among the trees, and a world of air pines and Catopsis cling to the branches. On the ground are gigantic ferns (Acrostichum), forming the densest thickets, and a monster vine (Ecastophyllum) sprawls over everything. Here and there a great courida (Avicennia) towers above the mangroves; the ground beneath being thickly covered with erect quills or pneumatophores, the curious growth from the roots of this tree.[52]

Simpson wrote that Ten Thousand Islands' "very name savors of mystery, [and] of the joys of exploration and discovery." This was "a region of mystery and loneliness, gloomy, monotonous, weird, and strange, yet possessing a decided fascination." Simpson, like Coe, was particularly enamored with "labyrinthine" marine estuaries of the lower Glades. At Cape Sable, Simpson got lost in an "interminable maze of brackish lakes and passages" and wondered how anyone could possibly find their way "through this labyrinth."[53]

Coe often praised Simpson's writings and acknowledged their influence on him. At the dedication of Simpson Park in Miami, the only preserved hardwood hammock in the city, Coe stated that *In Lower Florida Wilds* "held me spellbound." "No one has painted the picture of this wonderland region as has Dr. Simpson." His writings "greatly stimulated" the fight to preserve the Everglades "forever in its primitive state [as] a haven for its native wild life."[54] While addressing the Cosmos Club in Washington, D.C., in 1929, Coe argued that Simpson knew the Everglades like few others: "[he] has penetrated its jungle lands, navigated its tortuous waterways, visited obscure rookeries where few white men have set foot, slept on its beaches where under the canopy of the clear tropic night he communed with the stars. Dr. Simpson has brought to us the realization of the true spirit of this tropic land and its mysterious wonder features."[55]

Coe used Simpson's ideas to highlight how the Everglades possessed spiritual and scenic values and hence measured up to national park standards. Coe was a clever propagandist and an often extravagant booster for the ENP. Yet he truly believed the Everglades possessed the scenic beauty and sublime power that Americans expected from their national parks. Coe was inspired by the Everglades and saw beauty and wonder throughout the Glades. Like Henry David Thoreau and John Muir, Coe embraced a romantic view of nature. However, Coe's ideas were deepened and informed by his scientific knowledge about the Everglades. Coe connected biological knowledge to nature's beauty, just as Muir connected geological knowledge to the sublime. Coe and other park advocates often acknowledged that scientific knowledge about the Everglades and a strong interpretative program focusing on the region's biology would be needed to help tourists uncover this beauty.[56]

Coe often used Cape Sable, a large cape at the southern tip of the Everglades, as a stand-in for the entire Everglades. This area epitomized the region's aquatic identity, and it possessed the essential scenic and inspirational values required of all national parks. In fact, early in the park fight, Coe rarely even used the word "Everglades" but instead promoted "a Tropic National Park in the Cape Sable section of Florida."[57] In a 1929 speech, Coe declared that Cape Sable was "composed of a great diversity of physical features, including as it does miles of firm, white sand beaches, hundreds of miles of interlocking waterways, lakes and bays, thousands of islands, open everglades, coastal prairies, and broken gulf coast lines with many outlying islands."[58] Coe argued that the Cape was endowed with "scenic interests quite unfamiliar to the average northerner." Tourists would have the opportunity "to rest under the swaying palms, pick up shells along the shore, take a plunge in the waters of the Gulf, and otherwise experience the many distinctive tropic lures these Cape Sables in themselves offer."[59] The Cape had "an almost unending series of panoramic expressions rich in lovely scenic values and spiritual appeal."[60]

Coe's construction of a biological, tropical, and aquatic Everglades would be used by park advocates, legislators, NPS officials, and conservationists into the 1940s. Although Coe was a propagandist and not an intellectual, he built the park's intellectual foundations by relying on ecological and biological insights. This Everglades reflected a political goal: the park's creation. After the park was created, Coe's ideas receded and were supplanted by a new identity for the region.

In 1947, just a few months after the park's creation, Marjory Stoneman Douglas redefined the Everglades as a river of grass with her landmark *The Everglades: River of Grass*. Now the Everglades was a slow-moving sheet of water that flowed through sawgrass marshes and tree islands. While Coe focused on the estuaries and mangrove forests of lower Glades, Douglas emphasized the flow of water through the sawgrass prairies of the upper Glades. Coe's version of the Everglades facilitated the park's creation; Douglas's river of grass likewise had a political purpose: she sought to draw attention to the region's threatened water supply, an issue that remains central to current restoration efforts in the Everglades.[61] These ideas remain central to Everglades' identity because that supply of water is still under dire threat. Yet the Everglades as a river of grass has had too much influence over how Americans think about the Everglades. The ubiquity of these ideas has obscured the true diversity of the Everglades in a way that Douglas never intended. The area is far more than just sawgrass marshes—a fact Douglas's own writings eloquently illustrate. Reexamining Coe's ideas about the Everglades helps reveal and bring attention to the region's diverse landscapes and stunning biodiversity.[62]

There was a final, implicit element of Coe's Everglades: it was devoid of humans. Coe's promotion of a biological, tropical, and aquatic Everglades erased human history from the region. This was an unspoken, yet essential, element of his narrative and reflected important ideas about national parks. Parks were meant to preserve, in the words of George Wright, a "primitive America" that existed before it was colonized by Europeans.[63] Yet all national parks, and especially those in the eastern United States like the ENP, were constructed wildernesses. The creation of all parks entailed the removal of humans and the destruction of roads, houses, and farms. The NPS physically removed humans and their artifacts and imprints from these landscapes. At the same time, park advocates and the NPS erased human histories from the narratives of these natural places in order to present them as untouched wilderness.[64]

The Everglades had been extensively used by humans throughout its history before the park's creation. Permanent settlements were typically located on the edges of the Everglades, along the coasts, on coastal islands, or at the outlets of rivers. Few humans ever permanently lived in the marshes and swamps of the region's deep interior, but hammocks throughout the Everglades were used as temporary sites. The Calusa and Tequesta were among the pre-Columbian Native American groups that clustered along Florida's coasts, hunting and fishing throughout the entire Everglades. These groups were destroyed by European diseases and had mostly ceased to exist by the early 1700s. The remnants of these tribes likely joined the Seminoles, who were relative latecomers to South Florida. They moved to the Everglades in the early 1800s out of necessity. Driven south by the U.S. Army, they found refuge in these swamps and marshes, but only lived on the edges of what would become the ENP. Major Seminole settlements were clustered around Lake Okeechobee and later just north of the Tamiami Trail.[65]

White and Black settlers likewise made their homesteads along the edges of the Glades. Farming settlements sprung up around Lake Okeechobee. Other settlements grew along the southern rim of the Glades. Villages were established at Everglades City, Chokoloskee, and Flamingo, while scattered farms, fishing outposts, and hunting shacks were spread throughout the Ten Thousands Islands, Cape Sable, and Florida Bay. Like Native Americans, they hunted and fished throughout the Glades. These frontier settlements, on the edges of the law, had shady reputations and were often refuges for a colorful assortment of White criminals and outlaws in the early twentieth century. Legendary outlaw Ed Watson lived at the outlet of Lost Man's River, in the Ten Thousand Islands. After he committed a string of murders in the area, Chokoloskee residents killed him in 1910. Another group of outlaws, the notorious Ashley Gang, retreated to a number of hideouts in the Glades between bank heists in the 1910s and 1920s.[66]

Archaeological evidence of these all these human activities is scattered throughout the Everglades. Humans have always used the region, but Coe and other park advocates obscured these activities with their rhetoric about an untouched and impenetrable Everglades. At the same time, these wetlands hid the artifacts and imprints of human settlements. A plethora of natural forces like hurricanes, tides, water, salinity, tropical flora like strangler figs, heat, and humidity effectively destroyed villages, roads, boat landings, canoe trails, fishing and hunting camps, and any other human artifice. Even homesites and larger settlements like Flamingo were precarious and transitory. Hurricanes frequently destroyed these isolated residences, and by the 1935 Labor Day hurricane, most if not all of the White settlements along Cape Sable and the Ten Thousand Islands were gone, as was most of Flamingo.[67]

Coe never directly discussed the history of White and Black settlement in the area. His rhetoric about an untouched Everglades effectively obscured the presence of these individuals. In contrast, Coe celebrated the Seminoles as an inherent part of the Everglades. Drawing from the views of White Seminole rights activists like Minnie Moore-Willson, Coe presented the Seminoles as a people who lived in harmony with the Everglades. Hence, they left no impact or imprint. Coe often suggested Seminoles work in the park as tour guides, or sell souvenirs in the park. His views were extremely condescending and paternalistic. Rather than see the Seminoles as humans with their own agency, Coe saw them more as elements of a museum exhibit, on display for the benefit of tourists.

Coe's imagined wilderness was at its most contradictory in Cape Sable. Coe thought the Cape epitomized the Everglades' natural qualities, yet this was the section of the future park most altered by White settlers. Coe thought the Cape would be the epicenter of tourism in the park, and in fact, the fishing village of Flamingo was eventually converted into the park's primary visitor center. The NPS directly placed their interpretation facilities on the site of the largest settlement in the Glades, effectively erasing its presence and history.

A prominent feature of many of Coe's rhapsodic discussions of Cape Sable was the great mass of coconut palms that lay just behind the beach along the cape. In a 1930 report on the park, Coe described the Cape Sable beaches as enjoying "a background of great groves of tall, graceful cocoanut palms extending for many miles." These beaches with their "swaying palms" were one of the region's "distinctive tropic lures," that gave the ENP its appeal.[68]

Yet these coconut palms were not a natural feature, but rather the remnants of an agricultural venture. In the 1890s, the Waddell brothers planted these trees with plans to sell their fruit in Miami. A caretaker oversaw the grove until it was destroyed by the 1935 Labor Day hurricane. Coe erased the human history of these trees and presented them as part of the Everglades' tropical nature and exotic flora. In one speech he celebrated the "wild state of beaches and waving palms" found at Cape Sable. He acknowledged that cattle ranching and agriculture had been tried in the region but stated that, "owing to its peculiar physical make-up," these activities failed." These failures meant that the cape was now in a "practically untrammeled primitive state."[69]

Coe's imagined Everglades advanced the park's creation. Its tropical and aquatic qualities ensure the Everglades fulfilled park standards, and its biological characteristics reflected the central rationales for the park. While other parks protected geological monuments and inspiring scenery, this park would protect the Everglades' biological contents from destructive human activities. Coe used biological ideas to redefine the Everglades and to craft the park's central justification. He believed the region's flora and fauna had inherent value, and he argued that the park would protect the Everglades' biota. The park's creation would outlaw the destruction commodification and commercial exploitation of those species. More significantly, the park would explicitly protect these species' habitats. These biological rationales for preservation represented a new line of thinking for American preservationists and would later become important elements of modern environmentalism.

CHAPTER 3

Promoting the Park

The creation of any national park is a convoluted and intricate political endeavor. The ENP's creation was further complicated by its biological focus, its wetland nature, and its location in the eastern United States. As we saw in the previous chapter, while western parks were carved out of federal lands, eastern parks were composed of privately owned and state-owned lands. To make these parks, state governments had to acquire these private lands and then deed all park lands to the federal government. Hence, eastern parks like the ENP required a very high degree of support from local political and economic elites. Additionally, because the ENP was a biological, wetland park, it challenged many of the central traditions of American conservation and faced skepticism and even opposition from national conservationists.

Coe led the political effort to create the park through the Everglades National Park Association (ENPA). Through this group, he publicized the park and his new identity for the Everglades. He also crafted a set of new rationales for the park's creation and used these to convince important constituencies to support the ENP. The park's rationales both broke new ground in the history of environmental preservation, and hewed to NPS traditions. Biology was, not surprisingly, central. Coe argued that park would protect the Everglades' flora and fauna, and these species' habitats. This was a departure from traditional rationales for preservation and foreshadowed the emergence of modern environmental ideas. Yet at the same time, Coe touted park tourism and the park's economic benefits. These economic ideas were consistent with NPS traditions and the approaches of Progressive preservationists. These arguments were particularly important to Florida's business and political elites, who cared much more about economics than protecting nature. Just as the Everglades was a blend of land and water, this park's rationales were a mix of old ideas related to tourism and new impulses that sought to protect biology, species, and habitats.

Before he embarked on his own quest for the park's creation in 1928, Coe had been involved in Everglades preservation as a member of the Florida Society of Natural History. Coe headed the group's park committee, which had endorsed the idea of a small park or botanical preserve in the Everglades. Coe's vision was much more expansive and ambitious, though, and in May 1928 he traveled to Washington, D.C., to present NPS officials with his plans for the creation of a "South Everglades Tropic National Park."[1] This six-page proposal contained embryonic versions of many Coe's central ideas about the ENP. The report opened with a celebration of the region's plant life, its tropicality, and its aquatic vistas. Even at this early date, Coe saw the park as a way to protect the area's biology. Much of the proposal aimed to show how the Everglades fulfilled national park standards. Here Coe promoted the region's sublime beauty and inspirational value as a national park. Although this biological wetland park would break new ground in the NPS, Coe still had to show how it conformed to NPS expectations and norms.[2]

Coe's report was met with immediate support and dove-tailed with the agency's desire to expand into the eastern and southern United States. In fact, the NPS had previously discussed the desirability of a national park in southern Florida. After recruiting Florida legislators, the agency moved forward with Coe's proposal. First, the NPS needed to officially investigate the Everglades and determine whether the area met NPS standards. Florida senator Duncan Fletcher oversaw the passage of legislation authorizing such an investigation, which was later conducted in February 1930. The investigatory committee, composed of both NPS administrators and independent conservationists, concluded that the Everglades qualified as a national park and recommended it be protected as such.[3]

On returning to Miami in 1928, Coe outlined the course of action park advocates would follow over the next two decades to establish the ENP. The creation of eastern parks, like Shenandoah and Great Smoky, provided Coe and his allies with a proven blueprint for the ENP's creation. First, Coe would create an association to publicize the park and lobby for needed state and federal legislation, including most importantly the park's federal authorization. Next, the state government would create a state commission to raise funds and acquire the privately owned lands within the park's boundaries. Once the needed land was acquired, the commission would deed those lands to the federal government, which would then create the park. All these actions required public and political support for the park; Coe's promotional work aimed to build that support.[4]

In December 1928, on his return to Miami from D.C., Ernest Coe created "an Association to be known as the Tropic Everglade Park Association." This group, soon renamed the Everglades National Park Association (ENPA), was a single-issue organization. It coordinated with other national and local conservationist groups, but it was exclusively devoted to one goal: the creation of Everglades National Park.[5] The group's first meeting was held on December 11, 1928, at the Nautilus Hotel in Miami Beach. Coe was named the executive secretary, a position he held until the organization ceased to exist, and the only real position of power within the association. David Fairchild was named the first president. He reluctantly took on this position to help the project off its feet, intending to serve only for a short period. He explained to Henry Ward of the Izaak Walton League of America that "I gave my name to this small provisional Association . . . because it seemed a duty of mine to help put the matter before the Intellectuals of the country."[6] Fairchild utilized his extensive connections in U.S. conservationist, scientific, political, and business circles to publicize and build support for the park. He resigned in 1930 but continued to advise Coe and work for the park until 1934.[7]

The ENPA was a top-down organization that supported Coe's activities. In this way, it was similar to other Progressive Era conservationist groups that were run by elites in an undemocratic fashion. The other founding officers of the association were important Floridians who used their connections to raise money for the ENPA. They included Clayton Sedgwick Cooper, the publisher of the *Miami Tribune* and the founder of the Committee of One Hundred, a Miami philanthropic organization; John Shares, a hotel owner from Sebring, Florida; David Sholtz, the president of the Florida Chamber Commerce who would be elected Florida governor in 1932; Thomas Pancoast, a Miami Beach hotel owner and the son-in-law of John Collins, the founder of Miami Beach; and Claude Matlack, a noted Miami photographer. All worked to support Coe's activities and raised money for the Association. Subsequent officers, like Miami judge Halstead Ritter, and U.S. representative J. Mark Wilcox, played similar roles.[8] Coe held all the power in this organization, and association meetings were mere formalities. They mostly consisted of Coe's reports on his recent activities or an educational lecture on the Everglades.

Other members of the ENPA facilitated Coe's activities. They raised substantial funds but could never keep up with Coe's ability to spend money.[9] An audit of association finances in June 1932 found that it had raised almost $12,000 since 1928. More than $5,000 had been raised from popular subscription, while the City of Miami and Dade County had each given the association $3,000. The City of Miami had also given Coe a free office. Yet, the association was $619.63 in the red.[10] Coe freely spent his own money for the cause as well, and by the late 1940s he bankrupted himself fighting for the park. In 1933 in response to a disagreement within the ENPA over fundraising, Coe bluntly and angrily stated how he saw his relationship to the organization. In a letter addressed to the executive council, he wrote that "this Association was organized, if I understand rightly, to afford me the assistance necessary for going ahead, that the Park project, originated by me, might be brought effectively before the public and official bodies."[11]

Just as the park's rationales drew from both Progressive conservation and modern environmentalism, Coe's organization also had characteristics in common with modern environmentalist groups. Although the ENPA's structure was dictatorial, its goals were democratic.[12] The association sought to inform and influence public opinion. Through wide publicity campaigns that relied on multiple forms of media, Coe sought to alter public perceptions of the Everglades and build support for the park. He particularly focused on national and state conservationists and on Florida's political and business communities. Coe also sought to influence popular opinion more broadly through Florida newspapers, radio broadcasts, lecture tours, and national periodicals.

Coe's voluminous correspondence was the most important element of his publicity work. To say that Coe was a prolific letter writer would be a gross understatement. He wasn't merely a dedicated correspondent—he was obsessive. Between 1928 and 1937, Coe's office sent out an unremitting stream of letters, bulletins, copies of previous correspondence, magazine excerpts, reports, and copies of park legislation. Coe's correspondence slackened somewhat after 1937, but he continued to publicize the park until his death in 1951.[13]

Coe aimed to transport the reader to the Everglades through his correspondence. He had spent countless hours exploring the wonders of the region, but he knew most of his readers would never see the region except from an improved road. Many of his letters were written soon after Coe returned home for the Everglades, when his experiences were still fresh in his mind.

After a journey to the Turner River on Florida's west coast, Coe wrote that "the butterfly orchid (epimedium) in abundant bloom, nodded gracefully in the gentlest of breezes. . . . Never were the forests more sparkling green or the open stretches of the glades more restful to the beholder. Never were the lichens and mosses on the tree trunks fashioned into more vivid patterns or more effective coloring." Coe described great flocks of wading birds "flying overhead," on their way back to their rookies. He described the anhinga, which "was occasionally flushed and rose from the water along our way," and the limpkin, which was "a recluse" with a "shrill call . . . [that] pierces the quiet night hour."[14]

Coe had an enormous circle of correspondents. He was on a first-name basis with high-ranking NPS officials, important Florida politicians (including every governor and U.S. senator who served in the 1930s and 1940s), national and state conservationists, and many of Florida's economic elites. Coe used a number of creative epistolary tactics to contact his audiences. He mass-mailed ENPA bulletins to a large list of correspondents. These bulletins contained updates about the park's progress, descriptions of the Everglades' biota, examinations of the park's economic benefits, and copies of previous correspondence. Coe also carbon-copied many of his letters to additional correspondents and stuffed his letters with enclosures. These consisted of reports on the Everglades, the texts of passed or proposed bills, copies of other letters, and other materials.

For example, a 1935 letter Coe sent to the ENPA Executive Council was also mailed to twenty-two other individuals: NPS director Arno Cammerer, Florida governor David Sholtz, conservationist Robert Sterling Yard, the mayors of Miami and Miami Beach, the chair of the Dade County Commission, *Nature Magazine*, the National Audubon Society, President Roosevelt, Secretary of the Interior Harold Ickes, and eleven others.[15] Coe's use of enclosures can be seen in a 1936 letter he wrote to Governor Sholtz concerning park boundaries. This letter, which was also sent to six others, included copies of four other letters on the same topic written by Harold Ickes, NPS director Arno Cammerer, Florida Representative J. Mark Wilcox, and Everglades National Park Commission (ENPC) member D. Graham Copeland. It also included an NPS report on the park's boundaries.[16] This behavior was typical. Marjory Stoneman Douglas remembered that "everyone received letters from him [Coe] constantly, and his long envelopes were crammed with carbon copies of letters he had written to everyone else."[17]

Coe regularly sent ENPA bulletins to a large mailing list. These bulletins allowed Coe to keep in touch with his entire circle of correspondents. A typical bulletin was titled "The Proposed Tropic Everglades National Park," dated April 1929, and labeled "Bulletin no. 7." Although Coe's numerical system usually made little sense, bulletin number 8 was mailed the next day and included copies of correspondence between Coe and Florida senator Duncan Fletcher.[18] Some of Coe's bulletins were simply copies of older letters Coe had received from prominent individuals. Letters from scientists like John Kunkel Small, Victor Shelford, and Ales Hrdlicka, or from conservationists like George Wright, Ding Darling, and Harlan P. Kelsey, were used by Coe to bolster his own statements about the Everglades.[19]

The volume of Coe's correspondence often infuriated his enemies and sometimes even annoyed his allies. *Miami Herald* editor and founder Frank Stoneman was an early park supporter, but according to his daughter, Marjory Stoneman Douglas, "every time Mr. Coe came into the office his [Stoneman's] heart would sink, because he knew Mr. Coe would read him all the letters he'd gotten and all the letters he'd written." Conservationist Henry Ward, who opposed the park in the early 1930s, wrote that he been "flooded with correspondence from Mr. Ernest Coe, regarding the proposed Everglades National Park." ENPC member D. Graham Copeland, who feuded with Coe in the mid-1930s, also complained about how Coe had "flooded" Collier county with "propaganda and publicity" about the park.[20]

Coe reached an even larger audience through the mass media. He cultivated relationships with many Florida newspapers, especially those in Miami. The city's two major papers, the *Miami News* and the *Miami Herald*, favorably and generously covered park matters and editorialized in the park's favor. Coe had a particularly close relationship with the *Herald*, where Frank Stoneman was editor until the early 1930s. Stoneman had long been concerned about the Everglades; he editorialized against Everglades drainage in the 1910s, and after his retirement he served on the ENPA Executive Council.[21] The *Herald* often published Coe's letters to the editors as well. On occasion, they even transformed Coe's bulletins into *Herald* editorials, even as late as 1940, after Coe had ceased to be central to the park project. A bulletin Coe mailed on September 20, 1940, titled "Herein Lies a Danger," was cleaned up and published in the September 23, 1940, edition of the paper.[22]

The *Herald*'s coverage of the park in December 1930 was typical. That month it published eight articles on the ENP. Seven were on the front page, and most were multiple pages long and included photos. These articles covered a DOI report on the Everglades, U.S. House of Representative hearings on the park, and the arrival of a U.S. Senate investigatory delegation in the Everglades.[23] Marjory Stoneman Douglas accompanied this Senate delegation as a special reporter for the *Miami Herald* and wrote a number of articles covering this trip.[24] According to Douglas biographer Jack Davis, this was Douglas's first foray into the Everglades beyond "an improved road."[25] This 1930 trip began her long association with the Everglades and helped transform her from a writer of short stories into the Everglades' most famous advocate. This reporting was Douglas's only contribution to the park's creation, and these articles illustrate how Coe influenced her early ideas about the Everglades. This trip and these articles directly inspired a number of subsequently published pieces, including her short story "Plumes," a nonfiction piece "Wings," and the young-adult novel *Alligator Crossing*.[26]

Florida newspapers outside of Miami also reported on the park's progress. In 1936, the ENPA employed Hester Scott, a press secretary "with a background of many years in newspapers and magazine writing." Scott was extremely successful in placing her press releases in Florida newspapers. Through data gleaned from clipping services, Scott calculated that between July and December 1936, 118 Florida newspapers ran 521 stories about the Everglades National Park. Of these, 387 originated from Scott's own press releases.[27]

Coe also utilized the radio to reach local audiences. In April 1931, Coe organized a weeklong lecture series on station WIOD. Florida naturalists Charles Torrey Simpson, Harold H. Bailey, and John P. Gifford were among the panelists who discussed various aspects of the Everglades. Coe also commented on Florida politics on the local airwaves. In 1937 he attacked Governor Fred Cone's inaction regarding the park and in 1941 praised the election of Spessard Holland to governor.[28]

Coe leveraged his connections with local and national organizations, including Rotary clubs, garden clubs, and conservationist organizations, to promote the park. In 1930 he traveled to Washington, D.C., Philadelphia, New York, and Boston delivering lectures to various "important organizations which have influence in National Park matters." These lectures were accompanied by over a hundred lantern slides of Everglades scenery and biota, many of which were made by ENPA member and Miami photographer Claude Matlack, or by botanist John Kunkel Small. Coe and his wife, Anna, were involved in Miami's social, garden, and women's clubs as well. Marjory Stoneman Douglas recalled that Coe "talked before women's clubs, garden clubs, Rotary clubs, civic meetings, or groups of neighbors. He gave lectures everywhere, illustrated with slides."[29]

National periodicals gave Coe his widest audience. David Fairchild greatly facilitated this effort, and utilized his extensive connections with editors and authors on behalf of the ENPA. For example, in January 1930, *National Geographic* (then edited by Fairchild's brother-in-law, Gilbert Grosvenor) published a ninety-four-page article on Florida written by Associate Editor John Oliver La Gorce. It paid special attention to the Everglades, which La Gorce described as an "extraordinary region" that was "never was the dark, equatorial swamp with boa constrictors dangling from trees." Rather, it was a "rock-bottom shallow basin," that was "really a lake and not a mammoth swamp." The area was "a naturalist's delight," with "virgin forests," "unique flora," and abundant wildlife. La Gorce wrote that "were this area set aside as a national park, the wild life could be protected." In 1940, the magazine published an article exclusively about efforts to create the ENP.[30]

Coe often wrote directly to magazine editors, urging them to publish articles on the Everglades. In 1935 Coe tried to pique the interest of the *Nature Magazine* editor by connecting the park to an article in the magazine's most recent issue. *Nature Magazine* had already run a small news item in July 1934 about the ENP, but perhaps goaded by Coe's letters, they ran a more substantial piece written by Everglades botanist John Kunkel Small in 1937. *Nature Magazine* continued to follow the park's progress with pieces in 1941 and 1947. *Science, Scientific Monthly, Reader's Digest,* the *Review of Reviews, Scientific American,* and other periodicals also published articles on the park in the 1930s and 1940s.[31]

The publications of many national conservationist organizations closely followed the park's progress. The National Audubon Society's journal, *Bird-Lore,* which was renamed *Audubon Magazine* in 1941, paid particular attention to the Everglades and its bird populations. They published yearly updates on the park between 1930 and 1934, and published fourteen stories on the Everglades between 1938 and 1948. *American Forests* (the publication of the American Forestry Association), the *Sierra Club Bulletin, Living Wilderness* (published by the Wilderness Society), and *National Parks Magazine* (the magazine of the National Parks Association) all covered the ENP's progress as well.

These promotional efforts helped build support for the park's creation. Through these efforts, Coe disseminated a new biological identity for the Everglades and new biological rationales for the region's preservation. Existing rationales for preservation revolved around either the efficient use of natural resources or the protection of nature's aesthetic and spiritual values. These rationales were inapplicable in the Everglades. Coe instead drew on his interwar proto-environmentalist to devise new biocentric rationales for the Everglades' preservation. This park would protect the Everglades' flora and fauna, and those species' habitats, from the destructive activities of humans.

These ideas were one of the strongest expressions of a rising sense of biocentric ethics in the 1930s.[32] As historians Thomas Dunlap and Lisa Mighetto show, in that decade scientists, conservationists, and game managers became more convinced that animals had inherent value and a right to exist.[33] Although game conservation had been a core part of Progressive Era conservation, in the 1930s several different intellectual trends converged around the idea that all species had value. Rather than just valuing species for their utilitarian value to humans, conservationists and others began to see that all species had inherent value. This dynamic played out in the NPS as wildlife biologists argued that parks should protect all species of fauna, not just those that had aesthetic or symbolic value. These wildlife biologists exerted a large influence on the ENP. Coe adopted their concerns but expanded them to include flora. Coe was perhaps one of the most committed advocates for flora in U.S. history, and he made protecting the Everglades' herbaceous and woody plant life central to justifications for the ENP's creation.

The science of ecology also shaped the ENP's biocentric rationales. In the 1930s, ecological ideas dramatically altered the profession of game management and management practices in the NPS and the USFS. Adolph and Olaus Murie, Aldo Leopold, Neal Stoddard, George Wright, and other scientists applied ecological precepts to game and land management, upending these fields in the process.[34] While Aldo Leopold advanced a land ethic wherein human ethical systems were extended to the land and soil, George Wright used ecological ideas to challenge NPS management strategies. Wright was the leader of an insurgent group of NPS wildlife biologists who argued that the NPS's overriding focus on tourism was hurting wildlife. They proposed a number of changes to park management norms, including the elimination of predator control programs. Most significantly for the ENP, they argued that parks needed boundaries that reflected the habitats and ranges of species. Coe embraced these ideas and their ecological underpinnings. He connected the protection of these species to their habitats and to the park's boundaries.[35] The ENP was not only the nation's first biological park but also its first ecological one.

Coe's park advocacy was a direct reaction to the exploitation and commodification of the Everglades' biota. He wrote extensively about how commercial hunters, collectors, and other human activities were destroying the regions' flora and fauna.[36] In 1937 Coe noted that the Everglades' "native wild life, both plant and animal, through lack of protection is being decimated by the collector and hunter, both on land and water."[37] He explained to Edward Pou, an important member of the U.S. House of Representatives from North Carolina, that without the park "the native wildlife, both plant and animal, will continue to be ruthlessly destroyed; the flora, by commercial plant collectors, who have already seriously reduced its rare orchids, palms and other plants . . . and the fauna by hunters, trappers and thoughtless tourists who are together destroying the animal life."[38] The park's creation would put a halt to all these activities.

To protect these species, park advocates sought boundaries that conformed to these species' habitats. The habitat concept was central to this park's creation. Although the idea of an ecological balance has been thoroughly examined by ecologists and historians, the scientific and environmental history of the habitat concept is still "one of the great untold stories in American conservation history."[39] Frederic Clements, Victor Shelford, and other early ecologists used the term "habitat" to mean the dwelling place of a species, but the concept had more importance for game managers and wildlife biologists who prioritized the protection of habitats as a means of protecting species.[40] In 1929 Coe described the "partly submerged areas which in turn create uniquely ideal conditions as the habitats for many types of wading birds, water fowl, and is the last stand of the manatee and crocodile in America."[41]

Coe's efforts at promoting the park were incredibly effective. Other conservationists, Florida politicians, and NPS officials embraced Coe's biocentric park rationales and aided Coe in spreading these ideas. In 1931 Florida conservationist Robert T. Morris wrote to ornithologist T. Gilbert Pearson lamenting the destruction that commercial activities were causing in the Everglades. Morris providing the following list of activities caused by "lawless elements" in the Glades: "Egret Rookeries raided for their plumes despite recent policing—Alligators destroyed in great quantities by hide hunters—Deer and turkeys killed in all seasons without any kind of regard for law—Green turtles being exterminated—Brown pelicans slaughtered in their nests—Rare orchids being collected to the point of extermination."[42] John Baker, the president of the National Association of Audubon Societies, supported the park as a way to end the destruction of the region's birdlife. In 1936, Baker fought against the elimination of the Turner River from the park's proposed boundaries. This area included "a magnificent stand of cypress" that teemed "with many forms of spectacular birds and animals, including the rare Swallow-tailed Kite, quantities of wild Turkeys and Deer and great numbers of Egrets, Herons and Ibises." Baker even speculated that "the Ivory-billed Woodpecker, now nearly extinct, may exist in small numbers there."[43]

Even the NPS, which throughout its history had emphasized tourism, saw the

ENP as a biological park. In 1934, the agency sent Harold Bryant and Roger Toll to the Everglades to study the park's potential boundaries. A wildlife biologist, Bryant belonged to a cadre of NPS biologists who challenged the service's focus on tourism and championed the cause of biological preservation in the early 1930s. Additionally, he was one of the founders of park interpretive work and would later serve as the first head of the NPS branch of research and education.[44] Roger Toll had served as the superintendent of multiple parks—including Mount Rainier, Rocky Mountain, and Yellowstone—and was sympathetic to the goals of wildlife biologists.[45] George Wright, the most important of these NPS biologists, accompanied Bryant and Toll. Coe also traveled with the group and helped plan their itinerary.

Bryant and Toll's 1935 report argued that "the strongest argument for the creation of the national park" was "the opportunity to preserve the unique plants and animals of this region for future generations to see and study." In the Everglades they "found extensive primeval conditions and many scientific features that are nationally significant and justify the establishment of this national park." The authors cataloged the wide variety of human activities that were destroying these values, which included hunting, fishing, timbering, and the removal of plants for commercial sale. Due to these actions, the Everglades' species were "not as plentiful as formerly" and several were "in danger of extinction."[46]

Bryant and Toll connected the park's creation to ecological ideas. They noted that the Everglades' "great marsh areas" could serve as an ecological field laboratory. These areas effectively illustrated many of the core concepts in ecology during the 1930s including, "plant and animal inter-relationships," succession, and plant colonization. Bryant and Toll also celebrated the diversity of the Glades' ecosystems. Although at first glance the region looked "monotonous," there was "in reality considerable diversity. Plant associations [such] as palm hammock, coral key, Bay of Florida Key, cypress, saw-grass, mangrove, pine, and grass prairie such as that near Flamingo, should all be represented in this typically biological park." Bryant and Toll noted that protecting these habitats would also mean the protection of "associated animal life."[47]

Daniel Beard's *Wildlife Reconnaissance: Everglades National Park Project* was the NPS's strongest expressions of these new biological rationales. Beard was one of the most important figures in the ENP's history. A wildlife biologist by training, Beard joined the agency in 1934 and held multiple administrative positions throughout his thirty-three-year career. Beard was perhaps predisposed to a life in conservation—his father was Daniel C. Beard, more commonly known as "Uncle Dan," one of the founders of the U.S. scouting movement and an influential nature writer. The NPS sent the younger Beard to the Everglades in 1937 to conduct a wildlife survey, and *Wildlife Reconnaissance* was the result. In 1944 Beard was sent back to the Everglades, this time to oversee a wildlife refuge established in the region. When the park was created in 1947, Beard was the obvious choice to serve as its first superintendent, a position he held until 1958. Beard's work in the Everglades was not just of a biological or administrative nature. He was an adept politician as well. Beard forged compromises with other stakeholders in the Everglades without violating the basic biological principles at stake in the park. Opponents found him likeable and affable; allies gushed at his effectiveness.

Wildlife Reconnaissance outlined the park's biological rationales and celebrated the region's biota. The report also surveyed the different physiographic regions in the Everglades, examined the status of various Everglades species, detailed the destructive human activities threatening the area, and addressed the park's potential boundaries and management problems. It even examined the ecological damages caused by Everglades drainage, making it one the earliest studies of this issue.[48]

Beard opened his report by arguing that "the reasons for even considering the lower tip of Florida as a national park are 90 percent biological ones." These biological features were vulnerable, and Beard feared that, if the park was not created soon, they would vanish. A host of human actions were destroying the Everglades' biota and its "ecological conditions."[49] Because of overhunting, "most game species are losing ground except in the most inaccessible sections of the proposed park." Beard was concerned about "predatory species," which were not protected and were "killed at all times by anyone who has a gun—and everyone does have one." The timber industry was also active, particularly in the Glades' cypress forests. A "big cypress head on Collier property" near the west coast of Florida would "soon be gone." Plant, snail, and egg collectors caused damage. "Lig" hunting, the collecting of "various species of Liggus and Osytyla snails," was "developing into a destructive hobby and precious hammocks are being ruined." Many collectors set fire to entire hammocks and then collected the snails from the ashes. Crocodile and bird eggs were being added to private collections as well. Beard believed the crocodile would soon vanish from the Everglades unless the park was created. Nurseries also damaged the Everglades. "Orchids, palms, and some ferns" were all being removed for landscaping purposes.[50]

Beard was especially concerned with the fate of the alligator. These reptilian predators were almost universally feared and despised by Americans and ruthlessly hunted for their hides. Historian Mark Barrow identified a handful of "bioactivists" who both studied gators and advocated for their protection in the 1930s. These included naturalists Edwards A. McIlhenny and E. Ross Allen and park advocates like David Fairchild, Charles Torrey Simpson, and John Kunkel Small. Coe and Beard can be added to this list.[51]

Beard's desire to protect gators was directly connected to their ecological value. Although he did not use the term, Beard saw alligators as ecosystem engineers that created habitats for an array of other species. Gators constructed alligator holes by clearing muck and vegetation out of depressions in South Florida's limestone bedrock. These gators holes were "concentration points for wildlife during the dry seasons of the year." Beard wrote that "the snail Ampularia lived there and was fed on by Everglade Kites and Limpkins. . . . Fresh water crayfishes were found there and many birds and mammals ate them. There was growth that enabled Florida Ducks, Black-necked Stilts, and other birds to nest." Beard concluded that "these 'gator holes' were little ecological communities of great importance, and *are one of the principal keys to restoring wildlife in the park.*"[52]

Beard blamed the decline of gator populations on commercial hunters. He noted the ease with which gators could be shot, especially at night when hunters used bright lights as lures. Beard wrote that "Seminoles and white hunters are continually working through all of the alligator country every year and the stock is being gradually reduced." Additionally, tourists who happened to see a "gator will almost inevitably pull out a rifle." Alligators had been "common throughout most of the park area," but by 1938 they were rare. Beard reported only seeing four adults and "about one hundred young" gators during the months he spent surveying the park area. Beard believed that with adequate protection "the Everglades Park can eventually be the finest alligator sanctuary in the United States." The park could save this misunderstood and ecologically important species from destruction.[53]

These biological ideas were the central intellectual justifications for the park's creation. Just as important, though, were economic rationales. Coe argued the park would attract tourists to Florida and would create economic growth in the state. Tourism was central to Coe's promotional literature, particularly that directed toward Florida's business and political communities. These groups would be essential to the park's creation and cared much more about money than they did about plants and birds. To some extent, Coe told these groups what he thought they wanted to hear. At the same time, Coe ardently believed in the beauty of the Everglades and in its power to uplift the human spirit. Coe's ideas and actions, as well as the park itself reflected larger changes in how the United States viewed nature. Just as the park's biocentric rationales pointed forward to the rise of environmentalism, the park's creation remained firmly grounded in the traditions of the NPS and of Progressive Era aesthetic preservationists. Tourism would be central to this park's creation, as would claims that the region had spiritual value and inspiring beauty.

Coe claimed millions of tourists would enter the park every year. They would travel the entire length of the state to reach the Everglades and would spend millions of dollars along the way, boosting not just the state's economy but tax receipts as well. Florida already had long tradition of tourism to the state by the 1930s.[54] Coe argued the ENP was one way Florida could cement its reputation as the country's premier tourist destination. These economic arguments had additional salience during the Great Depression and during World War II as the state planned for postwar economic growth.

Coe created detailed arguments about the park's precise economic benefits and touted the unique qualities of Everglades tourism. He commonly repeated the claim that "there will be hundreds of thousands of tourists coming to this National Park annually. They will spend millions of dollars annually while touring the State."[55] In a 1938 fund-raising letter, Coe claimed that the park would "mean an additional influx annually of more than 500,000 visitors and increased expenditures by them within the State of from $75,000,000 to $100,000,000 each year."[56] Coe presented a more detailed estimate in a 1932 ENPA bulletin, calculating that "461,855 tourists visited one National Park during 1931." If that many people came to Florida for an average of twenty days, "spending an average of $10 per day," then tourists would spend "$82,371,000 annually." This would mean that tourists in Florida would spend "$46,185,000" on hotels, "$8,636,694, for gas," and would pay "$273,734" in gasoline taxes. The park would "bring about such a flow of tourist travel that the park will become Florida's great stabilizer."[57]

There were several corollary arguments Coe made concerning tourism. First, since the Everglades occupied the southern tip of Florida, tourists would traverse the entire length of the state to reach the park. In 1936 Coe explained that "this national park will be located in the southernmost extremity of the State. To reach it calls for touring the entire length of the State, giving the tourist an opportunity to see Florida both going and coming."[58] Second, these tourists would pay taxes, enriching the state's coffers. In a letter to Governor Sholtz, Coe noted that the park's "income to the State through gasoline tax alone will amount to many times more in money than would be realized from taxes on lands included in the Park."[59] During the 1936 election, Coe noted that the park would "increase the revenue on the sale of gasoline alone many thousands of dollars annually."[60] Finally, Coe also noted that ENP would remain open year-round and would attract winter tourists; other national parks only attracted tourists in the summer. One ENPA bulletin argued that "the key to Florida's future place in the sun is beyond doubt its superb winter climate."[61] Another bulletin noted that the ENP attract "tourists and nature students traveling south during the winter season."[62]

Coe also touted the larger, intangible benefits of park tourism. He believed that the park would alter Florida's economy and identity, turning it from a backwater agricultural state to the premier tourist destination in the country. Coe made these arguments early in the park fight, but they became more important after World War II as the state modernized.[63] In 1930 Coe wrote "the world wants to make Florida its great winter playground, the place to tour, recreate, and gain health and inspiration. Our own local troubles mean little to it. The world is glad to pay and pay liberally when it is out on a pleasure bent."[64] In a bulletin that reprinted letters between Coe and T. J. Brooks, Florida's assistant state commissioner of agriculture, Coe argued that tourism would displace agriculture as the state's most important industry. Brooks wrote to Coe that the value of tourism "exceeds the value of any one crop or source of income to the state." The ENP would be "a new attraction which will bring thousands" to Florida and "will mean many millions of [of dollars in] revenue."[65]

Coe's ideas about park tourism were more nuanced, though, than this propaganda suggested, especially as his thinking evolved throughout the early 1930s. Coe frequently told his audiences what he thought they wanted to hear and admitted more than once that much of his talk about tourism was designed to elicit local support for the park. In a 1931 letter to the American Civic Association, he stated that "my economic promise that any national park project stimulates is only a means for an end." Coe communicated the same sentiment in 1931 to conservationist and landscape architect Frederick Law Olmsted Jr. Coe wrote that many of the ENPA's bulletins "have been deliberately planned to stimulate local interest," so he stressed "the economic side as it related to local citizens."[66]

Yet, Coe earnestly believed in the positive benefits of Everglades tourism and wanted tourists experience the wonders of the region. He often wrote about the Everglades' "inspirational value as a nature reservation" and touted the region's spiritual value.[67] In a 1929 bulletin, he wrote that visitors to the park "will take away the memories of having realized an ofttime longed for experience and its thrilling sight[s] and unfamiliar wonders."[68] Coe hoped that the Everglades would inspire tourists to rethink their relationships with the natural world and hence further the park's biocentric goals.

Regardless of his true intentions, Coe's aggressive publicity tactics and his discussions of tourism provoked controversy and caused a number of influential traditional conservationists to briefly oppose the park in the early 1930s. This opposition was led by Robert Sterling Yard of the National Parks Association (NPA), and included George Pratt of the American Forestry Association, and Henry Ward of the Izaak Walton League. These organizations, especially the NPA, acted as watchdogs over the NPS and often opposed park proposals that they viewed as substandard. These traditional conservationists wanted parks that possessed scenic magnificence, sublime vistas, and geological monuments. They also believed that unbiased elites, like themselves, were best suited to judge national park standards. They saw public campaigns, like the one Coe embarked on, as damaging to park values. Although parks were created for public enjoyment, they believed the public was destroying the parks and their spiritual and scenic values through overuse. A novice in the field of conservation, Coe unknowingly stepped into these debates concerning park standards, the methods of park creation, the purposes of national parks, and the relationship between tourism and wilderness.[69]

Robert Sterling Yard was one of the most important conservationists and national park advocates of the early twentieth century. He aided in the creation of the NPS in 1916 and the NPA in 1919, and he was of the founders of the Wilderness Society in 1935. Yard was a park purist who believed parks protected scenery and the sublime. To Yard, national parks were synonymous with the dramatic geological landscapes and monuments of the West. Yard spent much of career advocating for park standards and fighting the creation of substandard parks. Although he initially celebrated park tourism, Yard soon became alarmed at the overcommercialization of parks and concerned that the scenic and spiritual values of the national parks were being destroyed by tourism and overuse. In the 1920s, Yard embraced wilderness as a way to protect these values. Although his embrace of wilderness put him at the cutting edge of environmental thought in the interwar period, Yard was in many ways an old-fashioned conservationist committed to Progressive and anthropocentric ideas about nature.

Yard was predisposed to oppose the Everglades. He thought the region was just another swampy, infested morass, with none of the scenic or spiritual qualities he expected in national parks. Coe noted that Yard had "a negative complex" when it came to "any National Park project not featuring high mountains or low valleys, titanic phases of nature."[70] Yard's opposition was also borne out of his commitment to the traditional methods of creating parks. Yard had played a role in the creation of many western parks and recoiled at the methods employed to create eastern parks. Yard believed that experts—making dispassionate decisions, uninfluenced by the vagaries of the public or the economic desires of local interests—should decide what areas became national parks. He was angered that Coe tried to use popular opinion to influence the political process of the park's creation. The fact that Coe touted the park's economic benefits to local communities further incensed Yard. Coe's aggressive publicity tactics and his loose talk about park tourism fed Yard's fears that this park was another boondoggle pork project designed to boost Florida's economy at the expense of both natural values and park standards.

Yard's opposition to the ENP began with Coe's very first attempt to promote the park. In late 1928 or early 1929, Coe and David Fairchild cowrote a letter to prominent scientists, politicians, and conservationists asking them for their opinions about the Everglades. Coe used these replies to promote the park throughout the early 1930s.[71] Yard, Henry Ward, and George Pratt all took exception to this scheme. Yard was particularly incensed, but all saw this effort as an attempt to unduly influence Congress and the NPS. To these conservationists, Coe was circumventing the traditional and proper method of park creation.

Yard immediately attacked Coe's effort in letters to Fairchild, the Secretary of the Interior, and other conservationists. He wrote that "the purpose of these letters and the folder they mention can be no other than to whip into action public expectation and Congressional demand for an area whose national park standards have not been determined by the Interior Department."[72] According to Yard, Coe's letter made it obvious that the ENP was nothing but a "promoter's proposition."[73] Yard opposed the "gathering of the opinions of hundreds of people all over the country who have not seen the Everglades, or who are not familiar with national park standards as to whether it wouldn't be nice to have a park there and using them in nation-wide circulation to create a powerful political argument." Yard thought Coe was engaging in a political tactic that was "of a new and dangerous kind," and he emphasized that Coe was *not playing the game!* According to Yard, "Mr. Coe's clever mind has devised an altogether new way of prejudicing Congress and government in favor of local demand. He plays his trout skillfully giving plenty of line. While declaring that the Park Service is to be fully consulted, he brings to bear on the Interior Department and Congress, in advance thereof, a pressure of 'national demand,' that politicians find very hard to resist."[74]

Yard connected Coe's tactics to those used to create other eastern parks. According to Yard, "the Southern Appalachian park campaigns [for the Great Smoky and the Shenandoah National Parks] proved that the only way money can be got from local publics and state legislatures is by promising the coming of a million motorists to add to the prosperity of the neighborhood and the state tax on gas." Once those promised were made, Yard thought the NPS would be "morally and politically bound to furnish the highways and camps to take care of such an invasion" of tourists.[75] He concluded that "nothing is more damaging to the . . . National Park System than [the] local raising of money to buy [a] park area upon the argument that local profit will result from the motor travel that such a park will bring into the state."[76]

Yard also attacked the Everglades itself, arguing that the area did not meet park standards. In a statement delivered to the House Committee on Public Lands, Yard admitted that the area was "marvelous in its botanic detail and variety" but that, because it was "not scenically valuable," it should not be preserved as a national park.[77] Yard repeated this criticism to NPS director Horace Albright, writing that "several botanists and zoologists" were opposed to the park "because they couldn't believe that the scenery warranted national park status."[78]

Henry Ward also protested. In a letter to Fairchild, he opposed these "efforts to stampede legislative bodies" and insisted that "National Parks are not amusement resorts." Ward explained that the Isaak Walton League "does not propose to support anything merely as a means for the State to get out of the government maintenance costs for Coney Island amusement parks." George Pratt expressed similar concerns. He explained to Fairchild: "I am absolutely opposed to a National park at the end of Florida. I do not believe, judging from the correspondence you have enclosed, that this region measures up the standard required for a National Park. . . . Too many states are trying to secure the cooperation of Congress to have national parks created in their particular States, and I am absolutely opposed to this one."[79]

David Fairchild tried to assuage these concerns. He extolled the Everglades' natural values and explained that the ENPA was only seeking to protect these values. Aware that many conservationists held negative attitudes toward swamps, Fairchild asked them to withhold judgment concerning whether or not the Everglades met national park standards until they had actually seen the area, or until the NPS made its investigation. Ward and Pratt, both of whom knew Fairchild personally, were somewhat swayed. They accepted Fairchild's word that the ENPA was not a gang of selfish boosters trying to extract pork-barrel spending from the federal government, and both agreed to hold off judgment on the Everglades' value.

Although the NPS had investigated the Everglades in 1930 and determined that the region met park standards, Yard and Ward sponsored their own investigation into the region. This independent investigation would be free of Coe's influence and could objectively determine the Everglades' value. In January 1932 William P. Wharton, a member of the Audubon Society and of the NPA, and Fredrick Law Olmsted Jr., a landscape architect like his father before him, investigated the Everglades. Wharton and Olmsted delivered their results to the NPA and subsequently published their findings in the March 1932 issue of *American Forests*.[80]

Olmsted and Wharton went to the Everglades to determine if the area possessed "scenery—qualities which take and hold the attention of all visitors, impressing and inspiring them with a sense of power and vastness and beauty in nature."[81] While other investigations, like Roger Toll and Harold Bryant's 1934 study of the park's boundaries, examined the area's biological value, Olmsted and Wharton sought the sublime in nature. Ultimately, they found these values in the Everglades' biology. Olmsted and Wharton placed the Everglades' biology in the context of traditional preservationist concerns. They thus bridged the gap between Coe's biocentric views and Yard's desire to protect dramatic and inspiring scenery. Although historian Alfred Runte argued that this report reflected new ideas concerning ecological preservation or, in Runte's words "total preservation," it more accurately reflects the transitional nature of the fight for the ENP. Instead,

NPS studies of the Everglades—like Bryan and Toll's 1934 study or Daniel Beard's *Wildlife Reconnaissance*—embodied Runte's total conservation.[82]

Olmsted and Wharton found the sublime in the mangrove forests of the lower Glades and in the area's bird rookeries. In an effort to connect the Everglades' biology to the geological tradition of the NPS, they described these biological features using geological metaphors. The Everglades' mangroves created an "impression of power." These forests were a "long frontal cliff of columnar trunks" that rose "abruptly out of the Gulf of Mexico . . . bearing the brunt of storm waves that sweep across a thousand miles of water." The mangroves were "picturesque and strange and full of stimulus to observation and thought." Olmsted and Wharton described "the bird life of the region in its relation to the scenic and inspirational qualities of the area." They wrote that "no one who has seen these remarkable birds flying in line against the blue sky can fail to be impressed by their great beauty and interest." These birds created an "impression of sheer beauty . . . no less memorable than the impressions derived from the great mountain and canyon parks of the west." The authors also commented on the geological value of the Everglades. They found shoals "visibly forming and shifting"; mangrove seedlings "forming precarious colonies on hazardous shoals and accelerating their upbuilding into islands"; marine organisms "forming coral-like reefs of nascent limestone over the marl margins of established mangrove-islands"; and storms "breaking and tossing great fragments of these 'reefs' along with shells and mud, to form what might become the fossiliferous conglomerates of some future geologist."[83]

Olmsted and Wharton's report convinced traditional conservationists that the Everglades met park standards. These were not just dreary, miasmatic swamps, but biologically valuable wetlands full of interesting and beautiful plants and animals. Due to these debates, Yard and other conservationists began to broaden their ideas about the purposes of parks and the value of wetlands.[84] Yet the ENP remained controversial, and Coe remained a lightning rod for criticism. As the park's authorization wound its way through Congress in 1931, new debates erupted over the related issues of tourism and wilderness in the Everglades. Once again, Coe's exaggerated promotional tactics instigated controversy. His rosy projections regarding millions of tourist flocking to this new park infuriated activists like Yard. Yard was not only a NPS watchdog but also a member of new burgeoning wilderness movement that sought to prevent the construction of roads and other facilities in the nation's protected areas.

CHAPTER 4

Authorizing a Wilderness Park

Coe's promotional work built support for the state and federal laws needed for the park's creation. State legislators bought into the park's economic value early and passed several state laws in the early and mid-1930s that facilitated the park's creation. Attaining federal legislation, especially authorization for the park, was a more difficult and important task. Coe was involved in these efforts but often relied on allies to lobby legislators. His own prophetic style of activism made him an effective promoter, but as a poor politician, Coe often stoked controversy and even fought with other park advocates. During 1931, Coe and Robert Sterling Yard again came into conflict. This time they clashed over the Everglades' wilderness values. Yard feared that the ENP would be overdeveloped and that tourists would destroy the region's wilderness values. As a result, Coe, Yard, and the NPS agreed to amend the authorization for the ENP to outlaw all new road construction in the park and to explicitly protect the region as a wilderness. The park authorization bill was finally passed in 1934 after years of effort. This law was the first time the federal government protected wilderness through legislative action.

More importantly, this wilderness challenged conventional ideas about wilderness and prioritized biological preservation. Yard and other wilderness advocates defined wilderness as roadlessness, and they valued wilderness as a recreational and scenic resource. These ideas, which were shared by the nascent U.S. wilderness movement, had been formed in the context of temperate mountains and forests. ENP advocates, in contrast, saw wilderness in the context of the Everglades' wetland and aquatic environments. Park advocates argued that roadlessness had little meaning in these watery landscapes and suggested new ways of defining wilderness. Rather than seeing wilderness as a recreational resource, ENP advocates saw it as a management strategy that would protect the Everglades' biota and habitats. While Yard embraced an anthropocentric, resource-driven view of wilderness, ENP advocates saw wilderness through a biocentric lens.

Creating any national park is an inherently political and legal process, and indeed a substantial number of state and federal laws were needed to create the ENP. Although Coe often directed efforts to pass these laws, he mostly relied on allies to work more closely with legislatures. One needed state law would enable the creation of a state commission empowered to acquire park lands. In 1929 Coe spent five weeks in Tallahassee "acquainting the members of both houses with the real merits of the Project" and working for legislation, which was approved in May 1929. This commission, named the Everglades National Park Commission (ENPC), would not be formed until 1935.[1] A complementary bill enabled Florida's Internal Improvement Fund (IIF), a state agency that owned large swaths of the Everglades, to deed land to the ENPC. This bill was passed in 1931, mostly due to the efforts of May Mann Jennings.

Jennings was one the most important Florida reformers of the first half of the twentieth century. She was the longtime president of the Florida Federation of Women's Clubs and held leadership roles in numerous other organizations. Through these groups she fought for women's suffrage, prohibition, education reform, child welfare reform, and other causes. She was also an important conservationist. Known as the mother of Florida forestry, she played a key role in creating the Florida State Board of Forestry. Although she supported Everglades drainage, she also fought to protect the Everglades. She was largely responsible for the creation of Royal Palm State Park in 1916, which was absorbed into the ENP in 1947, and she served twice on the ENPC. Exceedingly well connected in Florida, Jennings used these connections to further her political goals. Her father was a state legislator, and her husband, William Jennings—cousin to frequent presidential candidate William Jennings Bryan—served as governor from 1901 to 1905.[2]

In 1931, Jennings worked for a state law that would allow the IIF to deed up to 325,000 acres of land to the ENPC. When Jennings updated Coe on the status of the bill, he angrily demanded that this cap on acreage be eliminated. Coe even threatened to travel to Florida's capital, Tallahassee, to make this demand personally. Jennings wrote back explaining that altering the bill so late in the legislative process would jeopardize its passage and alienate sympathetic legislators. Jennings informed Coe that "things are very tense up at Tallahassee and I really think it would be fine for those in charge of the bills to have you and others write them and thank them."[3] In the words of her biographer, Jennings was a "genteel activist."[4] She had extensive personal connections within the Florida legislature and worked to create change from within the political system, often relying on compromise measures. Her style of activism clashed spectacularly with Coe's uncompromising, impatient, and zealous personality. Coe and Jennings's relationship continued to deteriorate after 1931, and the two clashed repeatedly between 1935 and 1937 when they both served on the ENPC. Ultimately, this bill passed and Coe worked later to remove this cap on acreage.

Coe relied on his close friend and ally David Sholtz to help pass other minor state laws. Sholtz was a founding member of the ENPA and was Florida's governor from 1933 to 1937. In May 1935, Coe asked "Governor Dave" to support three pieces of legislation needed for the park's creation.[5] The first amended Jennings's 1931 law to eliminate that acreage cap. The second was a toothless law that banned hunting and collecting in the park area, while the third bill appropriated $25,000 for the ENPC operating budget.[6] Larger appropriations were passed by the Florida legislature every two years between 1935 and 1947.[7] These three minor bills were quickly approved by the legislature and signed into law.

The most important law needed for the park's creation was a federal law that would authorize the parks' creation. Gaining passage of this law proved to be a difficult task. Federal legislators were often totally unacquainted with the project or its supporters, and many saw the Everglades as a swampy morass, unfit for national park status. ENP advocates were closely connected with state lawmakers but lacked support at the federal level. Between 1931 and 1934, the ENPA deployed a variety of strategies to build that support.

On such tactic was to take federal legislators and bureaucrats into the Everglades itself. In February 1930, the NPS conducted its official investigation to determine whether the Everglades met park standards. That trip was led by Coe and Fairchild and not only recommended the park's creation, but gave park supporters an opportunity to hobnob with important federal officials.[8] Between December 28, 1930, and January 2, 1931, Coe led six members of the U.S. Senate and their families through the Everglades. After the trip, one senator remarked that he "was sold on the park idea for the Everglades" and that he hoped legislation "can be expedited to the point where we can obtain early designation of the area." Another important trip occurred in January 1933 when David Fairchild took Ray Lyman Wilbur, the Secretary of the Interior, into the Everglades.[9]

These trips revealed to important lawmakers and bureaucrats the wondrous sights and biological value of the Everglades. Horace Albright, testifying before a House committee spoke at length about how his February 1930 trip opened his eyes to the true nature of the Glades. The area was wholly unlike other national parks. It was "quite flat" and had a "unique topography" defined not by rocks but by its "water and plant life." Albright described the "long sweeping beach" of Cape Sable and called the mangrove forests of the region "spectacular." Instead of having roots in the ground, these trees' roots "start out of the tree 10 or 15 feet in the area and spread out in all direction." Albright talked at length about the Glades' bird rookeries and testified that "there is nothing more spectacular and thrilling than to see those tens of thousands of enormous birds in the trees. You can see them for miles before you get to them, just as far as your eyes can reach, trees laden with great birds."[10]

Park allies also held congressional hearings on the park. The most notable of these was held in December 1930 by Miami's U.S. representative, Ruth Bryan Owen. Owen was a groundbreaking figure in American political history. She was the South's first female member of Congress, the nation's first female ambassador, a pioneering female filmmaker, and a successful writer. Owen was the daughter of William Jennings Bryan, making her cousins by marriage to May Mann Jennings. Like her father, Owen was a gifted public speaker who pursued a political career. She served in the U.S. House of Representatives from 1929 to 1933 and during her tenure worked for the ENP's creation.[11]

Owen's congressional hearing was mostly a stolid and routine affair, but her gift for the dramatic made headlines across the country. To convince skeptical representatives to support the park, the ENPA had arranged for a panel of experts to testify on the Everglades' flora and fauna. Representatives asked pointed questions concerning the purposes of this park, the identity of the Everglades, and the park's cost to the federal government. On the second day of the hearing, Dr. Howard Kelly, a retired physician from John Hopkins University and an amateur herpetologist, testified on the value of the Everglades' snakes. Although most Americans held negative attitudes toward these reptiles, Kelley argued that most snakes were harmless. In the midst of his testimony, Kelly suddenly pulled a king snake out of his bag. Owen "boldly picked" it up, and to show it was harmless, "coiled it about her neck to the amazement of startled male members" of the committee, some of whom had treated Owen in a condescending and rude manner. According to a United Press story carried by newspapers throughout the country, Owen proved to be a snake charmer and a Congress charmer who saved the hearings with her showmanship and ingenuity.[12]

Despite this hearing's success, the ENP's authorization was blocked by House Republicans in 1931, although it passed easily in the Senate. In fact, House Republicans blocked the bill from coming to the floor in 1931, 1932, and 1933.[13] The Senate, meanwhile, authorized the park every year between 1931 and 1934, often unanimously and without debate. In the House, the bill fell prey to partisan antics and, after 1933, to opposition to federal New Deal spending.

In 1931, Ernest Coe blamed Ruth Bryan Owen for the bill's delay. She had placed the bill on the House Calendar, which was reserved for bills that would require no federal appropriations. According to Horace Albright, this was the only way to ensure that the bill would come up for vote that session.[14] House Republicans argued, though, that because the park would eventually require federal spending, it belonged on the Union Calendar. They removed the bill from the House Calendar and prevented it from coming to a vote.[15] According to Albright,

Coe charged that "had it not been for Mrs. Owen the Everglades Park bill would have passed the House. He is entirely wrong." Albright urged Fairchild to make sure that Coe "not to say anything that would embarrass the authors of the bill because they must be depended upon to promote the measure next winter."[16]

A year later, Coe offered a weak apology to Owen.[17] He continually created controversy; this was not the last apology he would write to a park ally. The park bill was blocked again in 1932, and later that year, Owen lost her reelection bid. Rumors spread throughout South Florida and in the House that Coe orchestrated her removal as punishment for her failure to deliver the park bill. Her loss was actually due to her support of Prohibition.

Coe provoked another controversy in 1931, just as the park bill was awaiting a vote in the House. In 1930, Coe had circulated a fifteen-page report on tourism in the ENP. This document included a park map showing an ambitious road network and substantial tourist facilities. Yet it also contained vast wilderness areas and large park boundaries that encompassed the habitats of threatened species. This map reflected Coe's desire to promote the park to Florida's business interests and his willingness to cater his advocacy to fit his audience, yet it also was borne from Coe's naive belief that large numbers of tourists could visit the park without damaging the Everglades' biological values. Although Coe later disavowed this map as propaganda and his thoughts concerning tourism and wilderness in the park continued to evolve throughout the 1930s, this report nonetheless represented his early ideas about tourism in the ENP. In early 1931, as the bill authorizing the park was awaiting a vote in the House, Robert Sterling Yard got hold of this map. It reignited his opposition to the park, which entered a second phase that revolved around the issues of tourism and wilderness.[18]

Coe's 1930 map included three major roads in the ENP. The first was the Ingraham Highway, which connected Miami and Flamingo, a fishing village at the southern tip of the Glades on the eastern edge of Cape Sable. The road, which had been poorly constructed in the 1920s, was frequently flooded during the wet season. The NPS consistently stated it would repair this road after the park's creation and maintain it for tourists. Today, parts of this road comprise the primary road in the park (SR 9336).[19] Coe's expansive park boundaries encompassed a second road, the Tamiami Trail. Completed in 1928, this major thoroughfare ran across the Everglades and connected Tampa to Miami. In the late 1940s, the NPS eliminated all lands north of this road from the park's proposed boundaries, and no sections of this road were ever included in the ENP.

The map's third road was an entirely new highway that would branch off from the Tamiami Trail on the west coast of Florida and then loop south through Cape Sable before connecting to U.S. Route 1 near the Florida Keys. According to author Bruce Epperson, this road appeared on Dade County maps for decades but was never constructed.[20] Coe, who never passed up an opportunity to sell the park, incorporated this road into this 1930 promotional map. He wrote that this "Trunk Park Highway" would be "a means of access to a great variety of the park interests." It would "bring before the traveler opportunities to contact with many of the most attractive features of the entire park area." In the midst of this ambitious program of park development, Coe audaciously claimed that these three roads would actually help protect the Everglades' wilderness values. This highway "would accommodate . . . auto touring and economic transportation acceptably and economically, leaving the rest of the great area practically in its primitive wildness."[21]

This trunk park highway would bring tourists to Cape Sable, which Coe believed would be the primary center of tourist activity in the park. Coe knew that the Everglades would defy the expectations of national park tourists who expected sweeping vistas and geological monuments. He believed Cape Sable possessed some of those scenic values and could be one of the few real tourist attractions in the park. Here the NPS could construct "over-night-stopping facilities," as well as a more isolated "tenting colony" and a "thatch-roof hut colony" at Northwest Cape. Although Coe promoted park roads, he though most tourists would travel through the park's "literally hundreds of miles of waterways." This report outlined several possible boating itineraries embarking from the Cape.[22]

Despite these proposed developments, Coe believed the vast majority of the ENP would remain roadless wilderness. Included on this map were "great primeval nature areas" that would protect "the same primeval physical conditions which prevailed there before the advent of white men." Coe's ideas about wilderness, even in the early 1930s, were connected to a biocentric ethic. Rather than providing humans with spiritual and recreational benefits, these wilderness areas meant that "wildlife could continue on in its normal balance."[23] Astoundingly, Coe prefigured some of the same arguments conservation biologists made about wilderness and biological preservation forty and fifty years later. In the 1970s and 1980s, Reed Noss and other conservation biologists, and Dave Foreman and other activists, criticized wilderness as too anthropocentric a concept. They called for wilderness areas to be converted to wildlife refuges and noted that many of the characteristics of wilderness, especially roadlessness and sufficient size, were essential to the integrity of wildlife refuges, which needed to be large, contiguous, and free of roads. Size was a particularly important quality: healthy ecosystems needed top predators, which in turn needed large ranges to maintain healthy populations. In 1930, Coe made a similar point. He wrote that because the Everglades' wilderness areas were so large that there would be "sufficient freedom of range to give life forms the normal conditions whereby it can maintain that virility from generation to generation essential to continued vigor of a species."[24]

Despite this emphasis on wilderness, Coe's road network infuriated Yard and reignited Yard's opposition to the ENP. In early 1931, Yard angrily explained in a letter to the NPS that, although he was no longer opposed to the park in principle, he did "oppose including the big business highway [the Tamiami Trail] carrying every kind of traffic" in the park's boundaries. Yard proposed cutting that highway and all land north of the road from the park's boundaries, leaving an ENP that would only contain "the magnificent primitive" area in the southwest corner of the Everglades. Yard connected these roads to Coe's publicity efforts as well. He reiterated his previous concerns about the "policy of local people raising the purchase money" for the park.[25] Yard explained to Horace Albright that although the NPS would "cut out the gulf highway" to Cape Sable, he lamented the public "already expects it" due to Coe's efforts.[26]

Yard's new criticisms of the park's inclusion of the Tamiami Trail underscore his views about national parks and wilderness. Yard was not only a park purist, but one of the founders of the Wilderness Society. In 1935, Yard and seven other important environmental activists, including Aldo Leopold, Bob Marshall, and Benton McKaye, helped establish the organization. Wilderness was a relatively new concern for conservationists. Alarmed at the overuse and overdevelopment of the nation's natural areas, conservationists embraced the concept of roadless wilderness in the 1920s and 1930s as an antidote. Wilderness advocates identified roads as the central force that facilitated the destruction of these areas. Roads "literally paved the way for all other threats to wilderness."[27] Roads allowed civilization to enter the nation's national parks and forests, and they destroyed the spiritual and recreational values of these natural areas. To these activists, wilderness would help protect these important recreational and anthropocentric resources. They sought to prevent road building on federal lands and laid the intellectual groundwork for the wilderness system that exists in the United States today.[28] Robert Sterling Yard, as Paul Sutter explains in *Driven Wild*, was a unique figure in the Wilderness Society. He was the only member of the group to come from the NPS, and in many ways he was the most conservative and traditional member of the society. Yard embraced wilderness as a way to protect the scenic and spiritual values of national parks. The inclusion of the Tamiami Trail in the park would destroy those values. Yard wrote that including this road was "a new, undesirable, and dangerous precedent" that would damage national park standards and cause a "loss of prestige to the park system."[29] While ENP advocates wanted to protect important species and habitats north of the Trail, Yard was willing to sacrifice the protection of these habitats on the altar of roadlessness.

Coe and the NPS worked to defuse Yard's criticisms and sought to compromise. Coe, once again, apologized to Yard and defended his promotional materials as simply propaganda designed to build support for the park in Florida. According to Yard, when confronted with his map of the park, Coe called his trunk highway to Cape Sable "nothing." It was "merely an inspirational line that I [Coe] sketched in there myself." The road "does not mean a thing" but was only "a practical location" for a road "if the Park Service *should* want a west-side highway." Coe informed Henry Ward that this road was "the suggestion of an outside party and not of any significance."[30]

NPS officials also addressed Yard's criticisms. Horace Albright argued that "there has almost never been a park set aside that is more of a true wilderness area that the Everglades." Once the park was created, "the major portion ... [of the park] will have to remain in its primitive condition."[31] Coe's highway to Cape Sable was never considered by the NPS, but Albright admitted that he would "advocate the reconstruction of the road to Cape Sable." This "would mean making perhaps 25 percent of the proposed park accessible," leaving the other 75 percent "closed to all but those who could afford to make the trip by boat, or to those who are hardy enough to tramp through a region which must be about the worst in the world from the standpoint of a pedestrian."[32] Albright chided Coe, not for the first or last time, about his troublesome promotional activities and warned him to be more careful with "propaganda" that "will be embarrassing to the National Park Service." He urged Coe "above all don't use any maps showing that highway around Cape Sable."[33]

Ultimately, Yard's concerns were put to bed when ENP advocates and the NPS enshrined the protection of wilderness in the ENP's authorization. In February 1931, Coe met with Robert Sterling Yard, Ruth Bryan Owen, and Gilbert Pearson of the National Audubon Society at the Cosmos Club in Washington, D.C. They discussed a variety of amendments to the park bill, the most important of which would secure the Everglades as a wilderness and outlaw any road construction in the park. Coe enthusiastically embraced this proposal. According to Yard, "Mr. Coe is so enthusiastic over these provisos that he said positively that he would rather see the bill go over to the next Congress so as to have their ideas embodied in the text than to let the present bill pass without them." Yard was likewise satisfied. He assured Ray Lyman Wilbur that this amendment would "satisfy all objectors to the present bill." Four years before Yard helped found the Wilderness Society in the Cosmos Club, Coe and the NPS pledged to protect the Everglades as a wilderness.[34]

This bill authorizing the ENP was blocked by House Republicans in 1931 and then again in 1932. That year, Owen lost her reelection bid and was succeed by J. Mark Wilcox, a Democrat who worked closely with Coe into the late 1940s. Wilcox served three terms in the House and worked diligently to secure funding for civic projects in South Florida during the Depression. He broke with FDR in 1938 as a result of the president's court packing scheme and unsuccessfully ran for the

Senate that year as an anti–New Deal Democrat. After this loss, Wilcox retired from politics but continued to serve West Palm Beach as a devoted public servant and booster. He likewise continued to aid Coe throughout the 1940s as an executive officer on the ENPA.[35] Like Owen, Wilcox failed to bring the park bill to the House floor in 1933, but park advocates redoubled their efforts in 1934. Coe stayed in Washington from February 18 to June 30 that year. He met with legislators and NPS officials and continued to write letters. One letter emphasized to spending-conscious legislators that no federal monies would be used to create the park.[36] Another boasted of the park's support among twenty national conservationist organizations.[37]

On May 24, 1934, Wilcox finally succeeded in bringing the ENP's authorization to the House floor, despite what one Democrat called "a Republican filibuster pure and simple."[38] Even though the issue had been delayed for four years, the House spent just one hour debating the park. Even that minimal debate was largely irrelevant to the actual merits of the park. Instead, it reflected partisanship, opposition to the New Deal, and a conservative desire to reduce spending amid the Great Depression. Republican park opponents attacked the Everglades' natural values, argued the park's creation would increase federal spending, and tied the park project to wealthy Florida Democrats. House Republicans subscribed to traditional ideas about the purposes of national parks: parks were tourist destinations that offered visitors spiritual uplift and sublime experiences. Swamps, like the Everglades, were wastelands and had none of these inviting qualities. Therefore, enormous amounts of federal spending would be required to create a tourist destination in this foreboding swamp. To these ENP opponents, the park was obviously just another scheme concocted by Florida real estate interests to extract money and investment from the federal government.

Anti-park Republicans mocked the notion that anyone would willingly travel into this mosquito-infested swamp. One representative described the ENP as "a snake swamp park on perfectly worthless land in the State of Florida." Another claimed that the Everglades was "a great snake country." In Florida "they are canning rattlesnake meat. There rattlesnakes grow to great dimensions, some of them weighting as much as 40 pounds." Massachusetts Republican Alan Treadway, who had for years successfully blocked the bill from coming to a vote, stated that to get into the Everglades, "you would have to swim . . . and if you did you would be eaten by crocodiles or bitten by snakes." Treadway mocked the "fine language and unadulterated adjectives" found in some of Coe's writing about turtles hatching at Cape Sable. Treadway sarcastically exclaimed "my Lord, is not that a wonderful proposition! We will get a great crop of little turtles." To House Republicans, biological preservation was not a reason to create a national park.[39]

Park opponents argued that because this park was so foreboding, the federal government would need to spend millions of dollars to make it accessible to tourists. Representative Fredrick Lehlback argued that real estate interests were pushing the park. The New Jersey Republican argued the federal government would be forced to build "a road at a cost of 1 million dollars" per mile in the Everglades. The park was scheme to force the government to "pour countless millions into that swamp" that would in turn add value "to the surrounding real estate of Florida." The ENP was "the most perfect example of supersalesmanship of Florida real estate [...] that has ever been made public."[40]

Republicans argued that Democratic donors, who were invested in Florida real estate, were using the park to get rich. Their attacks targeted Barron Collier, a park advocate who owned most of the eponymous Collier County, and Judge Halstead Ritter, a member of the ENPA. Republicans saved most of their vitriol, though, for Henry L. Doherty, a hotel owner, financier, and Democratic fund-raiser who had recently bought the famous Biltmore hotel in Coral Gables. Doherty was only tangentially involved in the park's creation (he had donated money to the ENPA), but he was under investigation by the Federal Trade Commission for matters totally unrelated to the ENP.[41]

Democrats defended the Everglades and promoted several amendments that addressed Republican concerns about spending. The first mandated that no federal funds could be used in the park for the next five years. Representative Edward Cox, a conservative anti–New Deal Democrat of Georgia, explained that "the bill provides that no expenditure whatever shall be made by the Government on the development of the park for 5 years after the adoption of the bill." Additionally, "the Government is not expected to expend one dime in the acquisition of property," in the park area. Coe managed to repeal this amendment in 1937. Another amendment severely limited road construction in the ENP and mandated that the park remain a wilderness. These provisions had little effect on attitudes toward the bill.[42]

After an hour of debate, the bill came to a vote and passed the House, with 222 yeas, 145 nays, and 64 abstentions. Voting for the park were 22 Republicans and 200 Democrats; 76 Republicans and 69 Democrats voted against; and 17 Republicans and 47 Democrats abstained. Although the bill had been delayed for four years, there was little doubt it would easily pass the House. This bill of course only authorized the park. For it to be created, the State of the Florida would need to deed all lands in the park's boundaries to the federal government.

Coe had caused a great deal controversy on the path to the park's authorization, yet he also deserves credit for promoting the park, for directing state and federal legislative efforts, and for creating the intellectual foundation for the park. When

J. Mark Wilcox defended the ENP from Republican attacks, he had an armory of arguments for the park's creation. Using Coe's language, Wilcox argued the Everglades was "unique and distinctive." It was "the only natural tropical growth in the continental United States." The park would protect the Everglades' biota, which included "certain species of bird and animal life" that were "rapidly becoming extinct" and species of trees and plants that were "being rapidly exploited by commercial interests." The park would "preserve this area in its primitive state," and road construction and development would be minimal.[43]

This bill was a major stepping-stone toward the park's creation, but it is even more historically significant for another reason. This law included an amendment that required the park to be preserved a wilderness, making this law the first time wilderness was enshrined in federal law.[44] This so-called wilderness amendment stated: "Said area or areas shall be permanently preserved as a wilderness and no development of the project or plan for the entertainment of visitors shall be undertaken which will interfere with the preservation intact of the unique flora and fauna and the essential primitive natural conditions now prevailing in this area."[45]

This wilderness amendment, and the ENP more broadly, were the fullest expression of the NPS's larger turn to wilderness in the 1930s. John C. Miles, in *Wilderness in National Parks*, examines how Isle Royale, Kings Canyon, and Grand Teton National Parks were all created and planned as wilderness parks in the 1930s. The ENP was the most important of these wilderness parks. These wilderness parks were partly a response to criticisms made in the 1920s and 1930s regarding the overuse and overdevelopment of parks. They were also another front in the NPS's long-running rivalry with the USFS, which had first protected wilderness in 1924 in Gila National Forest and had already written regulations limiting human activity in "primitive areas" in the national forests. Perhaps more importantly, wilderness in the NPS was influenced by the efforts of George Wright and other NPS wildlife biologists. These biologists saw wilderness through a biocentric lens and thought it could be used to limit tourism and protect park wildlife. These ideas found their fullest expression in the Everglades.[46]

The events that led to the wilderness amendment also forced Coe and the NPS to think more deeply about the entwined issues of tourism, wilderness, and biological protection in the Everglades. A neophyte in the field of conservation, Coe knew little about the underlying issues before the 1930s, while the NPS's history of catering to tourism meant that it too was only just beginning to think about parks as wilderness. Traditional wilderness advocates thought about the concept in the context of temperate mountains and forests and defined wilderness as roadlessness. They saw wilderness as a recreational and spiritual resource that delivered benefits to humans. ENP advocates, though, situated the concept of wilderness in the Everglades' subtropical wetlands and marine ecosystems. They deemphasized the importance of roadlessness, due to the terrain of the Everglades, and saw wilderness as a way to protect the Everglades' biology. The ENP's wilderness was not only the first congressionally mandated wilderness area, it was the nation's first biocentric wilderness and challenged prevailing ideas about wilderness as roadlessness. These ideas were an important but overlooked factor in the history of the U.S. wilderness movement.

Especially after 1931, Coe connected wilderness to the protection of the Everglades' biology. In a 1934 press release, he announced that the Everglades was the "last remaining great primitive wild-life region in America."[47] In a 1935 speech he declared that the ENP was "practically one great primeval wilderness, wherein still remain many of the wild life native to this region."[48] In 1941 Coe wrote to Aldo Leopold, one of the founders of the Wilderness Society. Coe explained to Leopold that preserving the ENP as a wilderness would "maintain the ecologic balance so important in the maintenance of species, and this with the minimum of interference by man."[49]

NPS officials were more even forceful about this wilderness's biocentric purpose. Horace Albright defended the park from Yard's attacks using biological arguments. He insisted the park's creation would not entail "destroying or impairing the biological conditions" found in the Glades but would rather ensure that region would "remain in its primitive condition . . . as a wild-life refuge."[50] Arno Cammerer, who succeeded Albright as NPS director, also saw the park as way to protect habitats. During discussions over the park's boundaries in 1935, he weighed the benefits and drawbacks of including in the park sections of land north of the Tamiami Trail. Cammerer wrote that these lands were important due to "the fine wilderness character of the cypress hammocks to be found there and their importance as winter feeding grounds for birds." He explained that "we have plenty of trouble administering areas where animal life migrates outside park boundaries and are anxious to avoid similar conditions in new parks." Although including this area carried "with it the disadvantage of including a main highway," Cammerer ultimately concluded that protecting habitats north of the Tamiami Trail outweighed excluding this road from the park.[51]

Other NPS officials likewise saw protecting these habitats as more important that protecting wilderness for wilderness's sake. In his boundary report, Harold Bryant argued that the area north of the Tamiami Trail was "extensively utilized as winter feeding grounds by birds" and that it was the "nesting grounds of at least two rare species—the swallowtailed kite and the limpkin." Bryant wrote that, since the purpose of the park was to preserve sensitive biota, "this area should be included within the boundaries." Excluding it "would destroy its efficiency as a wildlife refuge and prevent [the] proper protection and administration of the park."[52] In the late 1930s, Daniel Beard advocated for the area's inclusion in the park as a way to secure the flow of water into the southern Glades. He wrote that "any deflection of flow north of the Trail would cause profound ecological changes throughout much of the park area."[53]

Daniel Beard was the most vocal, important, and thorough defender of the ENP's biocentric wilderness values. His 1938 study of the park's biology, *Wildlife Reconnaissance*, argues that this park's wilderness would protect biology rather than scenery or the sublime:

> The southern Florida wilderness scenery is a study in halftones, not bright, bold strokes of a full brush as in the case of most of our other national parks. There are no knife-edged mountains protruding up into the sky. There are no valleys of any kind. No glaciers exist, no gaudy canyons, no geysers, no mighty trees unless we except the few royal palms, not even a rockbound coast with the spray of ocean waves—none of the things we are used to seeing in our parks. Instead, there are lonely distances, intricate and monotonous waterways, birds, sky, and water. To put it crudely, there is nothing (and we include the bird rookeries) in the Everglades that will make Mr. Jonnie Q. Public suck in his breath. This is not an indictment against the Everglades as a national park, because "breath sucking" is still not the thing we are striving for in preserving wilderness areas.[54]

Beard argued that wilderness in this park was a management strategy designed to protect the area's biota, not a recreational resource for humans to use. He wrote that "recreation is strictly limited" in the Everglades. Rather, the justifications for the park were "90 percent biological ones." In a 1942 memo to the NPS, Beard argued that "the biota *is* the park. If plants and animal life are irreparably destroyed we can have no park."[55]

Park backers also challenged contemporary definitions of wilderness. Their ideas reflected the transitional qualities of wetlands and illuminate the complex ways that humans and wetlands have interacted with each other throughout history. To state the matter simply, wetlands are wet. This wetness made them hostile to humans. Humans are terrestrial; the species evolved on the savanna, not in the water or in wetlands. Humans are biologically ill-suited to spending large amounts of time in waterlogged and inundated environments. The Everglades' flora and fauna is also hostile. In the Everglades, sawgrass, which Marjory Stoneman Douglas described as a "fierce, ancient, cutting sedge," is aptly named and ubiquitous; mosquitos and a panoply of biting insects are a constant irritant; alligators and snakes—species that humans find frightening and threatening—often lay just out of sight.[56]

Because they are wet, wetlands elude human control. In contrast to forests and plains, wetlands are not easily domesticated. These wet landscapes often remain outside of human society. Because of this, humans have historically seen wetlands as melancholy, dangerous, and supernatural places. In the United States, wetlands have often been refuges for Native Americans, escaped slaves, and criminals. This ability to resist human society imbues wetlands with more wildness then other landscapes. Unlike in forests or grasslands, it is incredibly difficult to build roads, buildings, fences, or other structures in wetlands. Humans can easily and unintentionally carve a trail into a forest simply by force of habit. Henry David Thoreau, in a memorable passage from Walden describing why he left the woods, noted that he "had not lived there a week before my feet wore a path from my door to the pondside; and though it is five or six years since I trod it, it is still quite distinct."[57] In contrast, wetlands are trackless and quickly overtake evidence of human artifice. The only way to domesticate a wetland is to drain it, and even this is just a fleeting exercise of human power that often dramatically backfires.

Everglades advocates thought about the region's wilderness in the context of these hostile and wet landscapes. Ernest Coe immediately saw how he could use these ideas to promote the park's biocentric purpose to conservationists and promote park tourism to Florida boosters. He thought the Everglades itself would restrict tourists to the few developed areas in the park. The park could thus accommodate large numbers of tourists without harm to the area's biological values. Coe wrote that ENP could "preserve its integrity as a wilderness area, nature reservation, bird sanctuary[,] and at the same time have a portion of it open to the touring public."[58] Coe explained to Arno Cammerer in 1935 that the park could be opened up to tourism without "appreciatively intruding upon the primitive character of the area as a whole," due to the Everglades "vast regions of almost impenetrable jungles" that were "difficult of access."[59]

Although there was a loud note of booster enthusiasm in Coe's writings about wilderness, NPS wildlife biologist George Wright endorsed these basic views in both *Fauna* and in his private correspondence. In 1931 Wright wrote that in the Everglades "the usually opposing functions of pleasure ground and game sanctuary could both be developed without prejudice of one cause or the other." Small areas in the Everglades "could be opened up" to tourists while the vast majority of the park would remain roadless and undeveloped for the "conservation of the unique flora and fauna" of the area. This was "due to the terrain of the Everglades themselves. The visitor cannot wander at will over the landscape. He will be absolutely confined to the roads and development areas."[60] Although in most national parks roads opened up forests and other landscapes to hikers and campers, the Everglades' hostility and wetness would constrain tourists to the roads.

Daniel Beard pushed these ideas even further as he studied the Everglades.

He argued that, because of its wetness, this wilderness needed to be defined differently than traditional terrestrial wildernesses. Prevailing definitions of wilderness were dependent on a certain number of acres being roadless, but according to Beard "the so-many-acres-makes-a-wilderness angle means little in southern Florida" because "there will be always be places where one can be completely isolated in the Everglades." Beard thought that "five miles from a highway in this country is real wilderness and there is not one person in a hundred who will go even a few hundred feet from the beaten path." The Everglades itself would limit recreation. Beard wrote that "hiking is practically out of the question except for the very hardy few who can brave the sawgrass." Beard was unworried about "dudes trampling it [this wilderness] out of existence." Likewise, "camping will be more restricted than in most [National Park] Service areas." Beard, perhaps unconsciously, also connected this wilderness to tropes about the superabundance and lushness of tropical landscapes. Beard wrote that the Everglades would "always be a wilderness capable of overwhelming the puny efforts of mankind by the sheer exuberance of its own life."[61] This region was simply wetter and wilder, and more exotic and strange than any other wilderness in the United States.

The Everglades' aquatic areas challenged roadlessness wilderness in another way. The future park would include not just wetlands, but vast aquatic areas like Florida Bay and the Ten Thousand Islands. This park, as well as other protected areas in South Florida—including John Pennekamp State Park (established in 1959), and Biscayne National Park (established as Biscayne National Monument in 1968)—were some of the first marine protected areas in the United States.[62] Wilderness activists saw wilderness as roadlessness, but this concept was completely useless in marine ecosystems. Park advocates and NPS officials maintained that these aquatic areas would still qualify as wilderness even as they were extensively used by tourists.[63] They believed that boating, especially guided boat tours, would be the primary tourist activity in these areas. In contrast to automobiles, boats required less infrastructure, caused less of an impact on these landscapes, and limited tourist activity.[64]

Boating was central to Coe's ideas about tourism in the ENP. Boat tours would allow tourists to see the aquatic wonders of the region without the construction of roads or other intrusive infrastructure. Tourists could thus enter this wilderness without damaging it. Coe wrote that "boats carrying large number of tourists" would travel "through a labyrinth of interlocking bays and river ways."[65] Coe outlined itineraries that would take tourists by boat throughout Florida Bay, along the Cape Sable beaches, into "the lakes, rivers and bays of the entrancing Whitewater Bay region," "up the coast to the Shark and Harney Rivers," and through the Ten Thousand Islands.[66]

NPS wildlife biologists endorsed the centrality of boating in the ENP. In *Fauna of the National Parks*, George Wright wrote that, in the Everglades,

> the physical characteristics of the terrain are in favor of the wild life. People can not wander at will over the landscape. On land, their movements will be circumscribed by the limits of the development areas. In boats they will only be able to go where guides are licensed to take them. A stranger might soon be lost on these trackless waterways. Thus, though it would seem to be an anomaly at first glance, large numbers of people can be admitted to the area without disturbing the great rookeries. This will require a certain amount of precaution in locating a few roads and utility areas and in marking the water lanes, plus a few reasonable restrictions upon visitors in some critical areas.[67]

Wright's biocentric criticisms of national parks became central to the fight for the ENP. George Melendez Wright and his fellow NPS wildlife biologists, among them Joseph Dixon and Ben Thompson, received doctorates from UC-Berkeley under the direction of Joseph Grinnell. A groundbreaking ornithologist and mammologist, Grinnell developed many of the techniques of those disciplines. He was also a noted conservationist who studied park wildlife and criticized NPS wildlife management strategies. Grinnell's studies and criticisms influenced NPS policies about park wildlife; his students continued and furthered these studies and critiques.[68] Wright, Grinnell's most important student, joined the park service in 1927 as an assistant park naturalist at Yosemite. In 1929 he proposed that the agency conduct a wildlife survey and establish a wildlife office; Wright, who was independently wealthy, funded both. Wright led this study, and in 1933 the NPS published its results as *Fauna of the National Parks* (often referred to as *Fauna*), the first publication in a series of works on the topic.[69]

As historian Richard Sellars shows in *Preserving Nature in the National Parks*, Wright and his fellow biologists challenged the NPS focus on tourism and argued that parks should protect wildlife. According to Sellars, 1933's *Fauna* was "a landmark document" that "proposed a truly radical departure" from NPS management strategies. Wright and his cadre of biologists "promoted an ecological awareness in the Service and questioned the utilitarian and recreational focus that dominated" the NPS.[70] *Fauna* surveyed the current conditions of wildlife in the parks, identified threats to park wildlife, and laid out strategies to restore wildlife to its pre-Columbian state. Wright and his coauthors paid particular emphasis to the myriad conflicts between humans and wildlife inside the parks and proposed solutions to these complicated problems.[71]

Fauna especially criticized the failure of park boundaries to conform to the ranges of wildlife. Wright argued that most parks failed to protect wildlife due to their incomplete boundaries, and he recommended that boundaries of future parks be drawn in accordance with the habitats of species:. Wright wrote: "A park is an artificial unit, not an independent biological unit with natural boundaries (unless it happens to be an island). The boundaries, as drawn, frequently fail to include terrain which is vital to the park animals during some part of their annual cycles. The smaller the total area of a park the more its animal life may be endangered by external influences. Problems caused by the failure of parks as biological entities have to do with their geographical aspects, such as size and boundary location. It is easy to think of them as problems of geographical origin." Wright argued that park boundaries "must be drafted to meet the needs of their wildlife" and drafted in accordance with "natural boundaries."[72] Yet all parks to this point had been established with borders that had been dictated by political and economic considerations. Coe quixotically sought to remedy that with the ENP. Wright's broader ideas about park boundaries became central to Coe's own thinking about the shape of the ENP.

Wright also cataloged the myriad ways that tourists and tourism infrastructure negatively impacted wildlife. Wright argued that it was "obvious that numbers of people can not dwell in the park without displacing the fauna from human centers and otherwise disrupting the sensitive ecological relationships of nature." The solution though was not to ban tourism but to plan developments and park boundaries "in such a way as to minimize the disturbance of the biota as much as possible."[73] Wright essentially called for parks to be zoned. Tourism could be restricted to certain sections of the parks through farsighted planning, and sensitive habitats could be closed to tourists.

As a result of *Fauna*, the NPS established a wildlife division. More publications in the *Fauna* series followed, and the agency altered many of its practices concerning wildlife. Most notably, Wright's work led to the end of predator control policies in the parks. Yet Wright's influence was short lived; he died in a car accident in 1936. Without his leadership, the influence of these biologists declined. In 1940 the wildlife division was closed and its staff transferred to the U.S. Fish and Wildlife Service. Increased demands for park tourism after World War II further hampered Wright's agenda. Not until the 1960s would the fate of wildlife again become important in the NPS. In 1963, the NPS published *Wildlife Management in National Parks* (more commonly known as the Leopold Report), a document that set the NPS agenda for the coming decades and largely reiterated *Fauna's* own prescriptions. Historians have lauded Starker Leopold's report as groundbreaking and reflective of new environmental ideas, and in contrast they have ignored George Wright's immense contributions to the history of U.S. environmentalism.[74]

Although Wright's work is relatively unknown, he was in many ways a companion figure to Aldo Leopold, Starker's father. Aldo Leopold worked for the U.S.

Forest Service, criticized that agency's practices and tried to push the USFS to protect wilderness and wildlife. Wright followed a similar path within the NPS. Leopold's magnum opus, *Sand County Almanac*, was published posthumously and enormously influenced how Americans thought about nature. Leopold died in 1948 at age of sixty-one, his life unfinished; Wright's life had barely started when he died in 1936 at the age of thirty-one. He never had the opportunity to write a great meditation on nature. One of the great what-ifs of U.S. environmental history revolves around Wright's premature death. In 1936, Wright and Roger Toll—another rising star in the park service—died in a car accident while on an NPS trip examining the possibilities of wildlife refuges and parks along the United States–Mexico border. Had he lived, Toll could have been a leading figure in the NPS, while Wright's voice could have made immense contributions to modern environmentalism. He would have been sixty-six years old in 1970 on the first Earth Day. Wright's ecological and biocentric vision for preservation could have altered the nation's environmental history.

Despite their short-lived influence over the NPS, the ideas of Wright's cadre of biologists had an enormous impact over the fight for the ENP. More than any other national park, Everglades National Park was truly a biological park dedicated to the preservation of the area's flora and fauna. Wright's ideas found their fullest expression in this new park and were enshrined in ENP management and operations after its creation. Wright enormously influenced Coe as well. Their association begin in February 1931 when Wright, as part of a NPS group, toured the Everglades.[75] In their 1931 and 1932 correspondence, Coe and Wright discussed many of the issues *Fauna* tackled in 1933. Coe celebrated *Fauna*'s publication, distributed it to his allies, and republished Coe and Wright's letters as ENPA bulletins.[76] Wright's work further deepened Coe's understanding of ecology and had an enormous influence on the way Coe and the NPS thought about the ENP's boundaries.

In accordance with Wright's prescriptions, Coe advocated for park boundaries that would both protect habitats and regulate tourism. His initial vision for the park was enormous. The 1934 law authorizing the park noted it would encompass around 1.3 million acres, but Coe's vision was closer to 2 million acres.[77] These boundaries encompassed important habitats such as the feeding grounds of wading and migratory birds north of the Tamiami Trail; the Florida Bay, which included bird rookeries and crocodile habitats; large sections of what is now Big Cypress National Preserve, home to most of the Florida panther population; large swaths of the mangrove swamps of the Ten Thousand Islands; immense sections of the sawgrass prairies; sections of Key Largo that contained coral reefs; and a section of land around the Turner River that contained cypress forests and other rare flora.

In addition to large boundaries, Coe proposed zoning the ENP. By corral-ling tourists to specific areas, the rest of the park's biological and wilderness val-ues could be protected. Park zoning via the development of park master plans was a new NPS development in the early 1930s. Led by Thomas Vint and other land-scape architects, this effort sought to create comprehensive plans for the construc-tion of roads and tourist facilities.[78] Coe picked up on this trend and highlighted how zoning could restrict tourism and protect wilderness.[79]

Coe foresaw substantial tourism development in two areas of the park: Cape Sable and Key Largo. Both were geographically isolated from the rest of the park and were along important waterways that would facilitate boating. Coe had al-ways seen Cape Sable as a tourist center in the park. At the southern tip of the Glades, the cape was relatively isolated from the rest of the region. Placing tour-ist facilities there, especially those that revolved around boating, would effectively limit tourism. In the mid-1930s, Key Largo and its coral reefs became particularly important to Coe. These coral reefs were on the eastern side of the island, far re-moved from the rest of the park. Coe thought developing this remote area for tourism would help protect the rest of the Glades from tourism. He believed that both the cape and Key Largo also possessed the spiritual and scenic values tourists expected in national parks. He argued that the beauty and inspirational value of these reefs were "equal to the lure of the geysers of Yellowstone, the titanic eroded valley of the Grand Canyon and the majestic bold cliffs and waterfalls of Yosem-ite." Tourism in the area would require "boating facilities for cruising and fishing on so large a scale as to be almost beyond the pale of imagination" and would ne-cessitate "business activities all along down the Keys." Coe also touted the area's bi-ological value. This section of the park would protect not only coral reefs but also hardwood hammocks on the island. Coe noted those forests were "very beauti-ful" and bore fruit that provided food for birds and other species.[80] This area's in-clusion in the park was extremely controversial, particularly in Monroe County, which saw Key Largo as central to the county's economic development. In fact, the NPS never seriously considered the area for inclusion in the park. Yet, Coe continued to push for the area's protection into the late 1940s, even after the park's 1947 creation. Through the efforts of ENP advocate John Pennekamp, the area was protected in 1959 as a state park that now bears his name: John Pennekamp Coral Reef State Park.

Coe's vision for the ENP seemed contradictory: large numbers of tourists would experience the Everglades, but without infringing on its biological integrity or wil-derness character. These contradictions reflected the dualities of the Everglades: the region was both water and land. That duality itself would limit the harmful impacts of tourism in the park. Coe's vision seems overly enthusiastic but was intellectually consistent with the ideas of George Wright and followed from an ecological view of nature. Coe's vision, however, was also impractical. Key to his vision for the park were enormous park boundaries that included many controversial sections of South Florida. These large boundaries, which explicitly included the habitats and ranges of species, were directly influenced by George Wright's prescriptions in *Fauna*. Yet, Coe's unwillingness to compromise his vision doomed Florida's efforts to acquire Everglades lands after the park's 1934 authorization. His refusal to adjust the park's boundaries angered many of this allies in the mid-1930s and made the park's quick creation unlikely. Coe's ambitious vision had a far-reaching impact, though. It set an agenda for the preservation of South Florida's natural landscapes that guided and fueled subsequent generations of activist. Those regions cut from the ENP over Coe's objections were subsequently protected through other means. Those parks, preserves, and refuges continue to shape the landscape of South Florida and reflect Coe's biocentric vision.

Plate 1. Ernest Coe in the Everglades, 1929. Photograph by Claude Matlack, member of the ENPA. HistoryMiami Museum.

Plate 2. David Fairchild (far left), Mariam Fairchild (second from left), and Ernest Coe (second from right) with three unidentified men in 1931. Photograph by Claude Matlack. HistoryMiami Museum.

Plate 3. Department of Interior inspection in Miami. The group boarded the Goodyear blimp in the photo and viewed the Everglades from above before also traveling through the area via boat. Miami, February 11, 1930. From left to right: Dr. T. Gilbert Pearson, president of the Audubon Societies of America; J. B. Semple, Miami naturalist and collector for the Pittsburg Museum; Arno. S. Cammerer, associate director of the NPS; C. H. Redder, mayor of Miami; U.S. Representative Ruth Bryan Owen; David Fairchild; Horace M. Albright, director of the NPS; Ernest Coe; Roger Toll, superintendent of Yellowstone National Park; Herman C. Bumpus, expert on park education and former head of the American Museum of Natural History in New York; Harlan P. Kelsey, botanist and member of the Southern Appalachian Park Commission. HistoryMiami Museum.

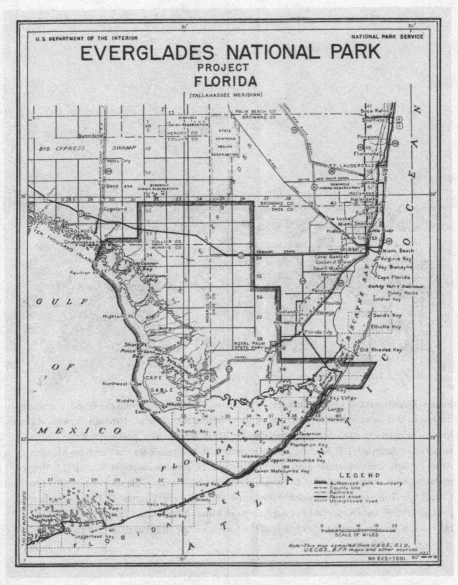

Plate 4. Maximum park boundaries as Ernest Coe advocated for them. These were codified into law by the 1934 bill authorizing the park. Spessard Holland Papers, P. K. Younge Library, University of Florida, Gainesville.

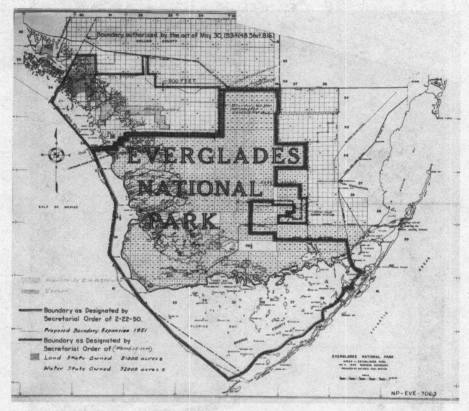

Plate 5. Map of the 1951 proposed boundary expansion. March 12, 1954. LeRoy Collins Papers, State Archives of Florida.

Plate 6. Spessard Holland (left) and Millard Caldwell (right), August 21, 1947. State Archives of Florida, Florida Memory database.

Plate 7. Harry Truman (left) and John Pennekamp (right) at the ENP dedication ceremony, December 6, 1947. State Archives of Florida, Florida Memory database.

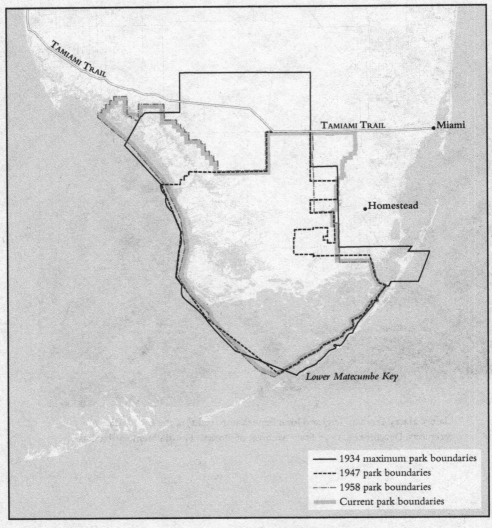

Plate 8. Changing boundaries of Everglades National Park. Mapping Specialists.

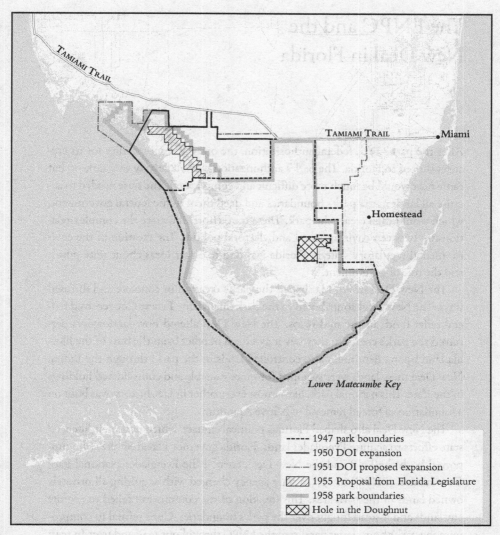

Plate 9. Park boundary proposals of the 1950s. Mapping Specialists.

TAMIAMI TRAIL

TAMIAMI TRAIL • Miami

• Homestead

Lower Matecumbe Key

----- 1947 park boundaries
——— 1950 DOI expansion
—·—·— 1951 DOI proposed expansion
1955 Proposal from Florida Legislature
1958 park boundaries
Hole in the Doughnut

CHAPTER 5

The ENPC and the
New Deal in Florida

After the park's 1934 federal authorization, the onus of responsibility for its cre-ation shifted to Florida. The park's authorization was a relatively easy task—what came next would be much more difficult and complicated. The state needed to ac-quire all lands in the park's boundaries and deed them to the federal government, which would then create the park. These state efforts illustrate the complex rela-tionship between environmental and electoral politics. The creation of the envi-ronmental regulatory state in Florida was tied to larger ideas about state power and the role of government.

The New Deal in Florida shaped the park's creation in concrete and diffused ways. The New Deal contributed to the park financially; Ernest Coe received fed-eral relief funds in the mid-1930s. The New Deal altered how landowners per-ceived the park's creation: they saw it as a form of relief from the bust of the Flor-ida land boom. Seminoles also controlled lands in the park; through the Indian New Deal these lands were swapped for more valuable and consolidated holdings in the state. This national park, like almost every other in U.S. history, was built on a foundation of forced removal of Native Americans.

The New Deal also shaped Florida's political climate, which in turn, influenced state efforts to acquire Everglades lands. Florida governor David Sholtz, who sup-ported both the ENP and the New Deal, created the Everglades National Park Commission (ENPC) in 1935, a state agency charged with acquiring all privately owned lands in the park area. This iteration of the commission failed to acquire any lands and instead fought over the park's boundaries. Coe's refusal to compro-mise the park's boundaries paralyzed the ENPC throughout 1936 and 1937. In 1937, a new governor took office. Fred Cone opposed the park's creation and the New Deal. He prioritized spending cuts and defunded and disbanded the ENPC. The park project lay dormant throughout his gubernatorial term. Yet the NPS contin-ued to work to protect the Everglades. While they awaited a new governor, the agency conducted important scientific studies of the Everglades' biota and began examining the Everglades' sheet flow.

෨

The New Deal had a transformative effect on many facets of U.S. life, but it espe-cially changed the U.S. South and rural America.[1] Many of its initiatives sought to rejuvenate rural life and farming, and many of its conservationist efforts focused on protecting soil and forest resources. This focus on the efficient use of resources made the New Deal's "new conservation" quite similar to the old conservation of the Progressive Era.[2] The Civilian Conservation Corp's (CCC) focus on rec-reation and tourism reinforced this link. The CCC and other relief agencies built new state parks and constructed tourist facilities in many state and national parks. Many conservationists criticized the New Deal's emphasis on resources and tour-ism as inadequate to the nation's environmental problems or as downright harm-ful to nature.[3]

Yet the New Deal did support much that was new about conservation. Histo-rians have noted how criticisms of the CCC and other New Deal initiatives dove-tailed with existing debates concerning wilderness and tourism, and provoked conservationist to think more seriously about these issues. Those debates, in turn, contributed to a growing proto-environmentalism during the interwar period.[4] The New Deal bolstered this interwar proto-environmentalism in concrete ways as well. It helped create an institutional framework and funding source for some of these environmental causes. For example, a number of relief agencies supported the fight for the ENP. Most importantly, the New Deal altered how Americans perceived the government and laid the groundwork for the later expansion of the environmental regulatory state.

Although Ernest Coe had been a Republican in New England, he enthusias-tically embraced the New Deal and sought financial and political support from FDR's new government programs. He likewise viewed Franklin Roosevelt as a po-tential ally in the fight for the park. This made sense, as FDR was an unabashed supporter of the national parks. He made headlines in 1934, 1937, and 1938 when he visited national parks and gave an important radio address in 1934 that cele-brated the NPS slogan "1934—A National Park Year."[5] Coe repeatedly and unsuc-cessfully tried to pull the president into the fight for the ENP. He sent FDR car-bon copies of correspondence on the park, mailed him most ENPA bulletins, and even asked the president to join the ENPA in 1938.[6] Coe often used a Roosevelt quote about the park in his promotional work, although one of Roosevelt's secre-taries insisted that Coe note that FDR delivered the quote while he was the gov-ernor of New York. Coe also used intermediaries to try to reach the president. He repeatedly urged Governor Sholtz to set up a meetings or deliver messages to the president.[7] Somewhat comically, Coe even dredged up a distant relative of Roo-sevelt's living in Miami. Coe found Grace Lyman, whose grandfather was a first cousin of FDR's great-grandfather, and convinced Lyman to write a letter to the president—a letter that Coe typed, edited, and mailed. This 1934 letter, which included Coe's address as the return address, urged the president to use "your direct influence" to "overcome opposition" and "assure the passage of the [Everglades] park bill in the House."[8]

Despite Coe's efforts, Roosevelt did little to directly advance the establishment of Everglades National Park. He did sign an executive order in October 1934 withdrawing all federal lands in the ENP area from sale or other use, but he never spoke publicly in favor of the park.[9] In 1934 Harold Ickes asked FDR to support the ENP's authorization. FDR only directed one of his aids to "let some of the people in the House know I am in favor of this bill, if they want to pass it without any particular trouble."[10]

Although Roosevelt kept his distance from the ENP, New Deal agencies supported the park's creation. Although the CCC may have seemed like an obvious place for Coe to find support, the agency played no role in the park's creation. The CCC had a camp in Royal Palm State Park (RPSP), an area that would be included in the ENP, but Coe was not involved in the project. The RPSP was a manicured tourist attraction that contradicted much of Coe's rhetoric about the Everglades' wilderness qualities. The CCC further developed Royal Palm, dynamiting holes in the limestone rock, constructing an artificial lily pond, and building a deer park.[11] The NPS undid some of these developments but largely maintained the site as a center of tourist activity. The former state park became the site of the Anhinga Trail, one of the most popular tourist attractions in the ENP.

Two other New Deal programs directly contributed to the park's creation. Between 1934 and 1937, Coe received about $8,800 from the Federal Emergency Relief Administration (FERA) and the Works Progress Administration (WPA).[12] These federal monies were used to create property abstracts for Everglades lands. These abstracts were a collection of all legal documents that affected a piece of land and included records of all sales, debts, and taxes. According to Coe, FERA funds allowed the ENPA to employ "three attorneys, three abstractors, two stenographers, and one supervisor," as well as other office staff in 1935.[13] Abstracts for Everglades' lands were difficult to compile, as much of this land had been bought and sold multiple times throughout the Florida land boom. Many of these lands had never been surveyed, and due to the Depression most of them had accrued unpaid back taxes. According to Coe much of the land "was sold in a speculative way many times during the 'Florida boom.'" Coe's team found instances where "the same piece of property has been deeded out two or three times by the same individual" and instances where the property had been sold "in which the person selling did not and never had had title to the property."[14]

Coe attached great importance to this project. He believed (quite rightly) that many landowners had an inflated sense of what their lands were worth. He thought (incorrectly) that these abstracts would disabuse them of these notions.

He wrote that "it is safe to say that little real understanding of present values exists among many property owners" and that these owners were unaware of "the amount of tax accumulations and other obligations" on their property. Coe argued that these abstract records would enable the state "to negotiate with owners of land within the Park project area, fully informed as to the status of the records involved." Coe even hoped that, when presented these document, landowners would donate their property to the park.[15]

Everglades landowners also looked to the New Deal for aid. They saw the establishment of the park as a way to recover from the bust of the Florida land boom. Owners of small holdings, who often experienced economic suffering during the Depression, saw the park as a form of relief and looked to sell their meager lands to the federal government for badly needed cash. Many of these landowners held small plots in the planned, but never fully developed, subdivisions of Pinecrest and Poinciana.[16] Their letters to Coe and Governor Sholtz were very similar to those that Depression-stricken Americans wrote to Franklin Roosevelt and other politicians begging for aid and assistance.[17]

For example, Mrs. Raphie Adams of Tampa wrote to Coe in 1935 about her lands in Poinciana. She bought a lot there "in boom time and certainly at top price." Since then she had "lost everything I owned and have been without work for a long time." Another Poinciana landowner, Mrs. G. A. Ginger of New York, inquired "what the chances of getting rid of" her lands in Poinciana were, and what, if any money she could receive from their sale. She wrote that "we have so far put 1,000 dollars in them and owe a little back taxes." Mrs. J. H. Hill of Texas wrote a similar letter. She explained that "I need this money very much and will certainly appreciate any information you might give me in regards to whether or not I can sell now." Other landowners were more demanding. Dr. Ella X. Quinn wrote to Governor Sholtz about land her sister, Miss Erma Quinn, purchased in Pinecrest in 1923. This piece of property had been purchased for $500, and Quinn desired "to be reimbursed for this lot." Her sister wrote that Erma "is now 70 years of age [and] worked laboriously for that $500 and the taxes which are paid to date." Unfortunately, most of the lands in Poinciana were worthless. According to Coe, they were worth "less than 50 cents per lot."[18]

Large landowners likewise looked to the federal government. Rather than a form a relief, they saw the park as a bailout that would let them recoup capital from bad real estate investments. Although some later opposed the park, these landowners were initially enthusiastic about the government purchasing their lands. Ivar Axelson and his father-in-law D. A. McDougal, eagerly discussed selling their lands to the NPS in the 1930s. Their family controlled the Chevelier land company, owned large portions of land in Cape Sable, and were responsible for the partially developed Pinecrest subdivision. Later, in the 1940s and the 1950s they led opposition to the park's creation and expansion. However, in 1934, Ivar claimed that he could "deliver this land at a nominal price."[19] According to NPS official Harold Bryant, McDougal had "payed [*sic*] the taxes for several years, sinking his personal fortune" into the Chevelier company as other stockholders ignored their responsibilities. Since 1935, "the taxes had remained unpaid." McDougal "was anxious to know if the park project would help him salvage the wreck." McDougal had indicated to Bryant that "his company would be glad to sell out at a small fraction of original values."[20]

Landowners supported the park, but only because they had failed to profit from Everglades real estate. Florida had failed to drain the Everglades, and the region's persistent wetness forced landowners to abandon their efforts to develop the Everglades for farming or urban development. The region could not be converted into private property. The Everglades would remain wetlands and would be turned back into public property. As Ann Vilesis shows in *Discovering the Unknown Landscape*, wetlands have been viewed ambiguously as private property throughout U.S. history. Land can be private property, but water is often a public resource. Wetlands, because they are both land and water, have never fit neatly into these categories.[21] In 1850, the Swamp Land Act gave the Everglades to the state of Florida, on the condition that the state drain the region and convert it to dry land. As these lands were drained (or as promoters claimed they were drained), they were converted to private property. When hurricanes smashed into Florida in the mid-1920s, landowners found that they owned not dry land but rather inundated marsh. One real estate speculator reportedly remarked that "I have bought land by the acre, I have bought land by the foot, but I have never before bought land by the bucket."[22] The Everglades was revealed as wet and the real estate boom went bust. A private property regime had failed in these wetlands. Creating a national park in the region would make these wetlands public property once again. These sawgrass prairies, tree islands, and mangrove swamps would continue to be inundated by flowing water, rather than bulldozed to make way for farms and subdivisions.[23]

Seminoles were also impacted by the New Deal and by the park's creation. In 1917 the state of Florida created a 99,000-acre Seminole reservation in the southwestern corner of the Glades. This land was within the park's proposed boundaries and would need to be acquired by the state before the park could be established. The creation of the ENP, like the creation of most national parks, entailed the forced removal of Native Americans.[24] Ironically, in the case of the Seminoles, this removal was part of an effort by the federal government to improve the lives of Native Americans. The Indian New Deal, an effort led by reformer John Collier, sought to restore lands and sovereignty to Native Americans. This 99,000-acre reservation had never been widely used by the Seminoles and was seen by them and by their White allies as a substandard piece of land. Through the Indian New Deal and the ENP's creation, this parcel was swapped for more valuable and accessible lands that were contiguous to other Seminole holdings. This new reservation lay on the western edge of Broward and Palm Beach Counties on the east coast of Florida just north of Miami and became one of the primary Seminole reservations in Florida.

The unique history of the Seminole tribes affected their relationships with the Indian New Deal and the park's creation.[25] The paradoxical wetland nature of the Everglades also influenced the contours of this history. The Seminoles did not originally live in the Everglades, but rather formed in northern Florida in the 1700s as Creeks from Georgia and members of other tribes fled warfare and destruction. Even before Florida was acquired by the United States in 1819, White settlers came into conflict with the Seminoles; the First Seminole War occurred in 1817–18. After Florida became a territory in 1822, many Seminoles were moved to a reservation in central Florida north of Lake Okeechobee in 1823. With the passage of the Indian Removal Act in 1830, the U.S. government endeavored to remove the Seminoles to Oklahoma. Although many relocated, some resisted. Between 1835 and 1842, three thousand Seminoles waged war against thirty thousand U.S. troops. The Second Seminole War was the longest and most expensive war with Native Americans in U.S. history. During this war, the Seminoles migrated south into the Everglades, and by the war's end only a few hundred of the tribe were left in the area.[26]

Seminoles isolated themselves in the Everglades, using the hostile nature of these wetlands to protect themselves from further White encroachment and violence. The Seminoles maintained some relationships with White settlers who ran nearby trading posts. In 1917, White activists who advocated for the tribe convinced the state government to create a 99,000-acre reservation in the far southwest corner of the Everglades. These lands were remote and unsuited for cattle ranching, the primary economic activity of many Seminoles. No members of the tribe actually lived on this land, although it was used for hunting.[27] The Seminoles had acquired other small tracts of land via federal action as well. These other holdings, which amounted to about 26,000 acres, were widely scattered throughout South Florida. Most of this land was likewise unsuitable for farming and grazing and also provided poor hunting grounds.[28]

By the 1930s, the Seminoles were fractured, disorganized, and spread across numerous camps in the Everglades. They were largely isolated from modern U.S. culture and had little contact with government entities. Although most Native American tribes had been subjected to government policies like the Indian Removal Act or the Dawes Act, the Florida Seminoles had successfully resisted the imposition of these policies by isolating themselves in these hostile wetlands.[29]

The Indian New Deal was thus the first time the federal government interacted with the Seminoles on a peaceful basis. The Indian Reorganization Act (IRA), passed in 1934, attempted to strengthen tribal cultures and worked to create and recognize tribal governments. It also ended the allotment provisions of the Dawes Act that eliminated tribal lands. The IRA even tried to restore lands and resources to tribal groups. The IRA's goals were ambitious: it aimed to reverse a century of government removal and assimilation policies. Its successes were mixed.[30]

The architect of the IRA was John Collier, a sociologist and Native American–rights advocate who led the Bureau of Indian Affairs under FDR from 1933 to 1945.[31] Collier's record was also mixed. Although he sought to improve the lives of Native Americans, his efforts reflected his own romantic views of Native peoples. Collier tried to protect Native American cultures, but he also supported some assimilationist polices as practical and necessary. His efforts to overturn more than a century of harmful government policies were not an absolute success, but he did fundamentally alter the government's relationship with Native Americans.

Collier paid particular attention to the Florida Seminole. In his 1922 article "The Red Atlantis," Collier laid out his vision for Native American–U.S. relations. He argued that modern industrial societies could learn from the close-knit tribal communities of Native Americans.[32] Collier found his ideal and romanticized group of Natives in the Everglades. He visited the Seminoles in 1935 and was struck by the extent to which the group had maintained its traditional culture. Collier wrote that the tribe's status in the 1930s as having never been subjected to federal control or the reservation system was "unique among that of all Indians."[33] According to Seminole historian Harry Kersey, Collier thought that any assimilative efforts among the Seminoles should be limited and undertaken slowly and cautiously. They needed to be protected from modern America and needed to receive more political power and more lands that would allow them to continue their traditional lifestyles.[34]

Collier's desire to improve, consolidate, and expand the land holdings of Seminoles coincided with the creation of the ENP. From the very start of the park fight, Ernest Coe and other advocates had argued that the Seminole reservation in the Everglades would be included in the park. Coe proposed that the state of Florida swap Seminole lands inside the park area for other, more valuable, lands outside the park. Sensitive to the plight of the Seminoles and to the park's political implications for both Seminoles and their White allies, Coe even argued that the park would benefit the tribe. In 1929, Coe explained that Seminoles would lose their hunting grounds in the park but could work as "guides through the tortuous waterways" of the ENP and produce souvenirs for tourists, an activity in which they were already engaging.[35]

Repeatedly throughout the 1930s, Coe communicated similar sentiments to

John Collier and used these letters in his broader correspondence. Coe argued that the park would be "a solution to the whole Seminole problem both economic and social." Seminoles could work as park guides and sell souvenirs, but Coe also thought that they would be "attractions" in the park with their "costumes" that Coe described as "colorful to the extreme and unique." Despite this condescending and dehumanizing view, Coe also echoed Collier's muddled ideas about the Seminoles' traditional culture. Coe thought the park's creation would give Seminoles time and space to decide their own relationship with modern U.S. culture. The park would allow the Seminole's "social life" to be "relieved of the many pitfalls now assailing him on every hand," and would let the Seminole "work out his own destiny."[36]

Despite this rosy propaganda, Coe proposed the removal of Native Americans from their lands to facilitate the park's creation. This was a common dynamic in the history of national parks and in the larger history of preservation in the United States. As many historians have noted, preservation efforts in U.S. history were often driven by White elites and were often undertaken at the expense of Native Americans, other minority groups, and subsistence hunters and farmers. National parks in particular have been deeply marked by this dynamic. The creation of every national park has entailed the removal of humans.

Due to the Indian New Deal and to the Seminoles' own unique history, this process took on a different tone and dynamic in the Everglades. Ironically, the removal of Seminoles from the park was part of an effort to give Seminoles more political power and a unified structure of landownership that would facilitate their own economic success and self-sufficiency. While park advocates worked to swap the Seminoles' park lands, Seminoles' rights advocates and the Bureau of Indian Affairs worked to consolidate Seminole landholding more broadly. They wanted to transform the Seminole's scattered plots of substandard land into a few large blocks of land that could be used for cattle ranching, an activity many Seminoles saw as consistent with their historical traditions.[37] The Indian New Deal also sought to organize the tribe politically, a task made difficult by the highly fractured nature of the Seminole peoples. Historian Harry Kersey cataloged these divisions: the Seminoles typically spoke either Creek or Mikasuki; some were "progressives," willing to engage in government efforts, while others were "traditionalists" who refused all government aid; they were divided into "at least three major socioeconomic factions"; and they were further divided by geography and political loyalties.[38] In the words of one government employee, the Indian Reorganization Act was "not a 'reorganization' in Florida. It is rather an organization."[39]

In 1935 and 1936 John Collier worked with Secretary of the Interior Harold Ickes and Governor Sholtz to facilitate these land exchanges, the largest of which facilitated the park's creation. Collier, Ickes, and Sholtz consulted with Seminoles during this process, but they never took Seminole demands seriously. Instead, they sought paternalistic solutions that they believed would benefit Seminoles, without limiting the park's creation or Florida's economic development.

In March 1935, when a group of Muskogee-speaking Seminoles from the Cow Creek band asked Collier and Ickes for three million acres of land, Ickes brushed off the request and instead focused on other efforts.[40] Likewise, when a group of Seminoles met with Governor Sholtz in 1936, they asked the government to simply "pohann checkish" (just let us alone).[41] Sholtz joked that, in the midst of the Great Depression, he "wished everybody who needed state aid would be that easy" on him.[42] Sholtz explained to Ickes that what the Seminoles really meant was that they wanted "to range anywhere over the present Everglades territory without being confined to a reservation."[43] Ickes and Sholtz agreed this was not possible and instead focused on delivering more lands to the tribes. They focused on tracts "they can farm." Their ancient tradition," according to Ickes, "was in part a farming tradition."[44] Ickes also wrote in support of Seminole hunting and fishing rights in the ENP and preferential hiring for park employment, although these benefits never materialized.[45]

In March 1935, Ickes worked with legislators to pass a federal law that facilitated land swaps on federal lands in the Everglades.[46] That same month, Sholtz worked on passing a state law that would enable the swap of the Seminoles' 99,000-acre reservation in the park area for a similar-sized piece of higher-quality land north of the Tamiami Trail.[47] On December 23, 1936, the IIF Trustees of the exchanged the 99,200-acre Seminole reservation in the southwest Everglades for a 104,800-acre tract of land in the western section of Broward and Palm Beach Counties. According to Harry Kersey, this was "a good trade." The Seminoles received lands that could be "highly cultivated" and were "prime grazing lands." The consolidation of Seminole lands "provided an isolated, secure haven in which the Indian people could determine their own rate and extent of acculturation."[48] As a result of this and other land exchanges, by 1936 the Seminoles controlled 180,000 acres of land across just three reservations.[49]

The removal of Seminoles from the park area was thus part of the larger Seminole experience during the Indian New Deal. Although this experience may have had long-term positive benefits for the tribes, it also meant the eventual end of Seminole hunting and land usage in the ENP. When the park was finally created in 1947, Seminoles were informed that hunting was now banned in the park area. Additionally, those preferential rights for Seminoles in the ENP that Coe and Ickes touted never materialized.

In 1947, ENP superintendent Daniel Beard only found three Seminoles who still used lands in the park. On May 30, 1947, Beard met with the three men—William McKinley Osceola, John Jumper, and Jim Tiger—to discuss the park's policies. Jumper explained that he had crops in a hammock in the park, and that the water was too low to move his other goods out of the area. Beard responded that "the government is in no great hurry and does not wish to impose any hardships on him or his people." Beard gave Jumper a year to clear out of the Everglades and offered to help him move his goods. As Jumper and the other men were only hunting garfish and frogs, Beard also informed them that could continue to hunt for the rest of that year, as Beard was not "particularly worried about what little frogging or garfishing this family does." Beard reached what he called "a gentlemen's agreement" with the group, and he reported to the NPS that the "meeting was entirely cordial and there seemed to be no resentment on the part of the Seminoles over the plan."[50] Beard's assessment could easily have been the result of rose-tinted glasses. After all, the ENP's creation entailed the removal of Native Americans from their lands and was just another chapter of the long history of the forced removal of Native peoples in the United States. Yet this process was also consistent with New Deal efforts to reverse a century of racist federal policies toward Native Americans. Seminoles may have benefitted from the land exchanges that facilitated the park's creation, but forced removal and war with the United States is what pushed Seminoles to the Everglades in the first place. Their late and cursory acquirement of a large tract of arable and contiguous land in the 1930s was a poor consolation for centuries of injustice by the United States.

The New Deal directly impacted Florida's efforts to acquire Everglades lands. Coe received federal funds to facilitate this task, but the New Deal had a broader and more diffused impact as well. The political and intellectual impact of Roosevelt's agenda permeated U.S. politics and culture in the 1930s. Florida's politics and the state government's agenda reflected the rising and falling fortunes of the New Deal. David Sholtz, who served as governor from 1933 to 1937, strongly supported the New Deal and used his office to advance the park's creation. As the New Deal's fortunes waned after 1937, Florida elected Fred Cone, an anti–New Deal conservative Democrat who sought to cut spending and reduce the size of the government. He withdrew all support for the park's creation. Both governors saw the park through the lens of the New Deal and through their larger ideas about the government's duties and actions during the Depression.

David Sholtz was an unlikely figure to guide the southern state of Florida through the Great Depression. Born in Brooklyn to German immigrant parents of Jewish heritage, Sholtz began practicing law in Daytona Beach in 1915. The next year, he was elected to the Florida legislature and began his political career. He ran for governor in 1932 as an outsider candidate and surprised the political establishment by winning the Democratic nomination by what was then the highest margin of votes in history. Wisely, Sholtz hitched his sails to the political fortunes of Franklin Roosevelt; the two bonded after Giuseppe Zangara's assassination attempt on the president in Florida. Sholtz became a vigorous supporter of the New Deal and worked to gain federal funding for the state. Sholtz also strongly supported the ENP's creation. He was a founding member of the ENPA and a longtime ally of Ernest Coe. Sholtz, who had been a leader in the Florida Chamber of Commerce, believed in the park's economic benefits and saw it as a way to alleviate the effects of the Great Depression in Florida.[51]

Sholtz's election was fortuitous for the park's future. After its 1934 federal authorization, the state was now responsible for acquiring all private lands in the park's boundaries. The governor supported this effort and created the ENPC in 1935 to take on this task. The creation of such a commission was a common practice in the campaigns for eastern national parks. Yet in the 1930s, a powerful agency with a large budget, appointed by an executive officer, with a mishmash of letters in its name, was immediately connected to the New Deal in the minds of Florida politicians. The ENPC was an expansion of the state's powers, which if successful, would enlarge the government's power over nature even more through the establishment of a national park. The state appropriated as much as $87,760 biannually to the commission and gave it enormous powers. It could purchase lands within the park's boundaries and was "vested with the power of eminent domain."[52]

The membership of the ENPC and its approach to political action had much in common with the New Deal's corporate reformist liberalism. The commission had liberal goals—it sought to create a large national park that would protect flora and fauna—but it also worked within South Florida's existing power structure. Many historians have argued that Roosevelt's New Deal was often pro-business and pursued conservative means to reach liberal ends.[53] Sholtz's choice of commission members was consistent with Roosevelt's own approach to change. He ensured that powerful interests in the Everglades would have input and a measure of control over those government actions. Consequently, the ENPC included some of the most powerful landowning and political interests in the Everglades.

Shortly after the NPS finalized a study of the park's boundaries in January 1935, Governor Sholtz activated the Commission and appointed its members. Ernest Coe was the obvious choice to lead the ENPC. Although Coe tried to convince Sholtz to keep landowners off the ENPC, this effort failed.[54] After consulting with a diverse group of interested parties, Sholtz made his official appointments in May 1935.[55] The membership of this iteration of the ENPC consisted of ENPA members Coe, Thomas Pancoast, and John Shares; May Mann Jennings and T. V. Moore from the Florida Federation of Women's Clubs; representatives of Everglades landowners, including D. Graham Copeland (representing the Collier interests), J. W. Hoffman (Model Land Company officer), and Norberg Thompson (landowner from Monroe County); and businessmen from various parts of Florida, including William Porter, who served on the Monroe County Commission. Three other businessmen, Lorenzo Wilson, A. L. Cuesta Jr., and Dr. Hamilton Holt, served on the commission but did not play large roles in its activities. As expected by all, Sholtz named Coe as executive chair.[56]

Although Coe experienced great success as the head of the ENPA, his tenure in the ENPC was disastrous. The association's goals were to publicize the park, to which Coe's prophetic nature and uncompromising zeal were well suited. The commission's goals were to acquire land in the park. This process that required cooperation and compromise—skills that Coe lacked. Additionally, Coe ran both organizations in a dictatorial fashion. The association essentially existed to support Coe's activities, and his authoritarianism was tolerated. When Coe tried to run the ENPC in a similar manner, he provoked anger, rancor, and controversy. Compounding these problems was the fact that Coe continued to serve as the head of the ENPA while also running the ENPC. Coe even tried to use the ENPA's publicity machine to impact debates and disagreements inside the ENPC, a strategy that infuriated other members of the commission.[57]

Although the commission had been named in May 1935, Coe delayed calling the first meeting until his New Deal–funded abstracting project was completed. He hoped these abstracts would show how little Everglades lands were worth, which he thought would give him leverage over the commission members who represented landowners. ENPC members quickly protested Coe's lack of action. Lorenzo Wilson, May Mann Jennings, and J. W. Hoffman all wrote to Governor Sholtz, asking that the governor himself call the ENPC's first meeting.[58] Eventually, Coe called a meeting in January 1936, but it was unproductive and accomplished little. Coe's ally, Thomas Pancoast, was named chair of the commission, and four committees were formed: finance, legislative, public relations, and lands and boundaries. There was no substantive discussion concerning the charges of these committees or a plan of action for fundraising or land acquisition. The ENPC never drafted a budget, either, a fact Jennings noted at almost every meeting. Coe was named the treasurer of the commission in addition to being its executive chairman, another decision that Jennings harshly criticized. Just as Coe irresponsibly spent the association's monies, he spent commission funds as he saw fit and with no oversight.[59]

Coe resisted holding commission meetings throughout 1936. Association meetings had never been substantive affairs, and Coe saw no reason why commission members should wield any power or have any responsibilities. At the ENPC's first meeting, Jennings proposed a motion that the commission meet every three months. This motion carried, yet Coe ignored it. During the more than two years that Coe headed the commission, he only ever held five meetings. The first was in January 1936, and the other four were all held between December 1936 and May

1937, as the commission fought over the park's boundaries. In October 1936 Jennings explained to Governor Sholtz that "there are few of us on the Board [of the ENPC] who do not feel that things are moving as fast as they should. We are not satisfied to be figureheads." She accurately stated that Coe was trying "to take over the entire functions of the Commission," and that there was "a growing feeling of dissatisfaction" among many on the Commission.[60]

Despite the ENPC's lack of action, the commission's land and boundaries committee took initiative and began a comprehensive analysis of the park's boundaries. The members of this committee, who served powerful political and real estate interests, had a keen desire to shape the park's boundaries in specific ways. William Porter was a banker and lawyer with extensive real estate holdings in Key West. He represented Monroe County's political and business elite and desired the exclusion of Key Largo from the park. D. Graham Copeland represented Barron Collier's economic interests. An industrialist who owned most of the eponymous Collier County, Collier supported the park's creation but wanted a small area around the Turner River excluded from the park. Collier was currently constructing a sawmill near the river and believed the area had potential value as a port. The last member of the committee was J. W. Hoffman, the vice president of the Model Land Company (MLC); that company wanted to sell the majority of its Everglades lands to the state but wanted valuable agricultural lands in the eastern section of the Everglades near Homestead excluded from the park. Committee members sought to advance their own economic agendas but also rejected other boundary adjustments and largely embraced Coe's expansive park boundaries.

Rather than seeking to compromise with these real estate interests, Coe vehemently opposed these boundary adjustments. This fight plunged the ENPC into chaos throughout 1936 and 1937, and ultimately doomed the group's efforts. Although Coe deserves much of the credit for the park's progress between 1928 and 1935, he also deserves much of the blame for the ENPC's failures between 1935 and 1937. He believed, based on his reading of George Wright's *Fauna of the National Parks*, that park boundaries needed to reflect biological factors and not political and economic considerations. Wright had argued that most parks failed to protect species and habitats because their boundaries were compromised by the political process of a park's creation. Coe insisted that this park's boundaries be dictated by biological concerns.

Coe believed these three areas up for exclusion contained key biological features. Those eastern lands Hoffman wanted excluded from the park contained sawgrass prairies, marl prairies, and most importantly the Taylor Slough. These vast, flat prairies were all important feeding grounds for birds; park advocates would later note that the Taylor Slough was a central conduit for the Everglades' sheet flow. The Turner River contained a key Everglades archaeological site and possessed incredible biodiversity. This cypress forests around the river were some of the magnificent and diverse in Florida. The river was also bordered by wet prairies and its outlet was covered in mangrove forests. Coe was most concerned about the land and waters of Key Largo. Coe wanted to protect the eastern section of the key and a large section of those Atlantic Ocean waters that bordered the key. This area was far removed from the rest of the park, and was not even technically in the Everglades. This site would protect marine ecosystems, spectacular coral reefs, and tropical forests typical of the Keys. Coe in particular would come to obsess over these tropical coral reefs, which were unlike any other ecosystem in the United States. Coe also thought Key Largo could be an important center of tourism in the park.

The starting point for Porter, Copeland, and Hoffman's efforts to reshape the park's boundaries were the maximum park boundaries laid out in 1935 in the Bryant-Toll report. Based on Harold Bryant and Roger Toll's eleven-day trip in the region, the report was heavily influenced by George Wright's ideas about park boundaries. This report mostly adhered to the maximum park boundaries laid out by the NPS in 1930, which in turn were based on Coe's original 1928 recommendations.[61] Bryant and Toll advocated for a large park that would adequately protect the Everglades' flora, fauna and habitats. George Wright, who had traveled with Bryant and Toll on their inspection trip, wrote that the park's "maximum boundaries are the very minimum necessary to make this a national park of standards commensurate with our existing system."[62]

Finding that Coe had created a great deal of controversy concerning the park's boundaries among important groups, Porter, Copeland, and Hoffman also worked to quell that opposition. Sportsmen from the Dade County chapter of the Izaak Walton League (IWL) wanted all land north of the Tamiami Trail excluded from the park and bore animosity toward Coe. Commercial fishers in Monroe County were likewise upset with Coe's intransigence and wanted to eliminate their fishing grounds from the park. Coe's insistence that the park include sections of Key Largo incensed Monroe County's economic and political elite. Coe admitted to Arno Cammerer in 1936 that "there has flared up in Monroe County . . . a vicious opposition to including any of Key Largo within the park."[63]

To address these complaints and to gather input on the park's boundaries, the ENPC Lands and Boundaries Committee held a public meeting on June 27, 1936. This public meeting was inclusive and open, and all parties were given the opportunity to speak. Although Coe had often tried to influence public opinion, he had never held an event as democratic or open as this. This type of public meeting would later become a routine matter in environmental decision-making after the passage of the National Environmental Policy Act in 1970.

Over forty individuals representing a diverse group of interests spoke at this meeting, which lasted six and half hours. William Albury, who spoke on behalf of the Monroe County Commission, opposed the inclusion of Key Largo in the park and argued that the county would "be bankrupt if you take our land from us." Commercial fishers and spongers in Monroe County suggested that the park's boundaries be constricted to the "high water mark on the mainland" and argued the park's creation would threaten their industry. E. B. Moylan Jr., speaking for the Dade County IWL, asked that all lands north of the Tamiami Trail be excluded from the park. Other sportsmen concurred, and argued that those lands had no value in a national park as they were only composed of sawgrass prairies. Landowners also spoke. All supported the park's creation, but they had diverse opinions regarding the park's boundaries. Most expressed a concern for how their lands would be acquired, and some insisted on a guarantee that they be paid a fair price for their lands.[64]

NPS employees and local conservationists defended the park's maximum boundaries. Ben Thompson, an NPS wildlife biologist and one of the coauthors of *Fauna of the National Parks*, tried to assure these diverse groups that they would be treated fairly. Other Everglades advocates—including James Stanley from *Natural History* and Jessica Seymour from the Florida Federation of Garden Clubs—advocated for the park's maximum boundaries. Seymour argued that the Everglades' "native plant life is being destroyed every day" and needed to be protected.[65]

The Everglades' sawgrass prairies were an important focus of these debates. Although these sections of the Everglades are today celebrated as a river of grass, they were relatively ignored by ENP advocates and sometimes became the target of attacks. These prairies are unremarkable landscapes. They are scenically monotonous, dominated by just a few common species of plants. Members of the Dade County IWL argued that these sawgrass prairies had "no value" to anyone other than hunters. Copeland seemed to agree and remarked that they added "no material benefit" to the park. Hunters and landowners saw only a vast expanse of grass with no scenic or recreational value. Park advocates, though, urged these sawgrass prairies be included in the ENP. Seymour argued that these prairies were "not just sawgrass—it is something that nature has created." Reflecting the park's biocentric purposes and its emphasis on the preservation of flora, she argued that these prairies were "a portion well worth conserving." Another local conservationist, R. A. Livingston, pointed out that "the areas of sawgrass" are important "feeding grounds for birds" and "must be protected." Livingston saw these ecosystems through an ecological lens, but by the late 1930s ENP advocates saw these prairies through a hydrological lens. They were a key conduit for freshwater through the Everglades.[66]

As this meeting closed, Copeland requested that Coe hold an ENPC meeting on August 29, 1936, so that the lands and boundaries committee could present its report. Instead, Coe delayed the next commission meeting until December 2, 1936. In the intervening period, he ramped up the ENPA's publicity machine to undermine the committee's work and to publicize his own vision for the park. As a result, the ENPC's December 1936 meeting was full of rancor and discord. Coe had spent months criticizing the committee's boundary proposals, and now Porter and Copeland (Hoffman was not present) responded to Coe's attacks. Porter claimed that Coe was a "master in the art of dissemination and of spreading propaganda and publicity." Copeland concurred, complaining that Coe had "literally flooded this country with literature, doing everything in his power to counteract the duties that this Commission has given this Committee." Through the ENPA, Coe had "repeatedly deluged the people with his idea of what the park boundaries should be." Copeland also criticized the way Coe ran the commission. He argued that Coe was "extremely unethical" and that he had "certainly acted improperly." Copeland called on Coe to resign from either the association or the commission and protested that Coe was "running the Commission as he pleases." Yet, at the end of this meeting, Copeland and Porter proffered Coe an olive branch. Copeland amended his motion to approve the lands and boundaries report to make it clear that this report was only "a definite starting point" on the park's boundaries. This would allow the ENPC to move forward with land acquisition while negotiations over the park's boundaries continued. Coe refused to accept this peace offering. Instead, he and his allies voted against this report. The motion passed anyway, and the ENPC sent the boundary report to the NPS for consideration.[67]

Although this report reflected the economic interests of its authors, it also largely embraced Coe's expansive park boundaries and rejected other suggested boundary curtailments. Altogether, the lands and boundaries committee eliminated 188,643 acres from the park. These reductions included 45,799 acres around the Turner River, 27,644 acres in the Florida Bay and in the Key Largo area, and 115,200 acres in Dade County on the eastern edge of the park. The committee rejected the boundary adjustments of other interests, like commercial fishers and sportsmen, finding that those concerns were "motivated by selfishness almost exclusively." They kept lands north of the Tamiami Trail in the park and seemed open to including the waters of Monroe County in the park.[68]

Coe obstinately refused to consider these adjustments because he believed they would harm the park's biological integrity. His refusal to compromise was a lost opportunity to establish the park before the post–World War II economic boom and a speculative market in Everglades oil leases drove up the value of these lands. The compromise park landowners envisioned in 1937 would have been slightly larger than the park's 1947 boundaries and most importantly would have extended the park north of the Tamiami Trail. Instead of compromising, Coe led a crusade against the lands and boundaries report that consumed the ENPC for the rest of its existence. John Shares's attacks on D. Graham Copeland were the most vituperative and reflected the larger dynamic within the commission. Shares owned a hotel in Sebring, Florida, and was a founding member of the ENPA and a close ally of Coe's. Shares called the boundary report a "damning brief" and stated that its only intention was to "protect private holdings from being included in the park area." While Shares announced he was fighting for the public's interest, he condemned Copeland for protecting "special interests" and pursuing "selfish and private aims." Shares threatened to introduce a bill banning landowners from serving on the ENPC and to "arouse" the west coast of Florida "to such a high pitch" over Copeland's selfish behavior.[69] He eventually attacked Copeland's upbringing and education as this correspondence devolved into bitter personal attacks.[70]

These volatile confrontations spilled over into the ENPC's next two meetings, held on January 11 and April 3, 1937. NPS officials Arno Cammerer, Harold Bryant, and Ben Thompson attended the January meeting. They tried to mend fences and stressed the need for compromise but failed in their efforts.[71] Florida Federation of Women's Club members May Mann Jennings and T. V. Moore played peacemaker at the April meeting. They pleaded with the men on the committee to stop fighting and get some work done. Jennings commented that, with "the way we are moving," the park would never be created. Moore suggested that the commission needed more "give and take," more compromise. She suggested that "you can get lots more with sugar than you can with vinegar."[72]

The infighting continued at the final meeting of this iteration of the ENPC, held May 3, 1937. Here, the commission also belatedly discussed the need to lobby for a renewal of the ENPC's biannual appropriation, which expired on June 20, 1937. Jennings was placed in charge of this effort. She traveled to Tallahassee that month to speak to thirty-eight of the thirty-nine state senators and fifty of the ninety-five House members about this issue.[73] Copeland praised Jennings's efforts: "I have never known anyone to work as hard and as faithfully on legislation as Mrs. Jennings has done in this case."[74] Jennings concurred, writing that she had "never worked so hard for anything in my life as I did for that appropriation." Although Jennings encouraged other members of the ENPC and the Florida Federation of Women's Clubs to join in her effort, she insisted that Coe remain on the sidelines. She explained to Thomas Pancoast that "it would only make matters worse if Mr. Coe got to Tallahassee."[75]

Complicating the fate of this appropriation was the fact that Florida had elected a new governor in November 1936. Although Coe was typically active during Florida's elections, he was occupied with both the ENPC's boundary controversy and with personal issues in 1936. His wife Anna had been ill throughout 1936 and in May of that year suffered a cerebral hemorrhage.[76] Coe ignored the 1936 election, and as a consequence Fred Cone began his term unacquainted with Coe and the ENP project. Coe first met with Cone in February 1937. He reported that the governor had a "keen interest in the Everglades National Park" and "looked upon it as one of Florida's most important projects."[77]

Coe's faith in the new governor was deeply misplaced. Fred Cone effectively killed the park project for his entire gubernatorial term. He quickly cut all funds for the ENPC and worked to gain control over the commission. Augustus Houghton, a Miami conservationist who served on the Camp Fire Club Conservation Committee, reported that Cone believed that "a million acres" was "too large for a national park." The governor would "not ask the people of the State to put up the money," nor would he "consent to the State transferring its lands to the federal government." Cone thought that if the federal government wanted the park they should "make the necessary appropriations, so that the park, being a national park, will be created by money from the entire nation." Houghton bluntly informed Arno Cammerer that "you can expect no help from Governor Cone."[78]

Fred Cone's opposition to park was connected to his opposition to the New Deal. Cone was a conservative anti–New Deal Democrat who believed that the best prescription for Florida's depressed economy was drastic cuts in government spending. At the same time, Cone sought to concentrate power in the governor's office and tried to reign in many of Florida's miscellaneous commissions and bureaus.[79] He believed that these agencies, including the ENPC, wasted money and interfered with the free market.[80]

Due to Jennings's efforts, the state legislature passed a $87,760 two-year appropriation for the ENPC in 1937. Yet Cone insisted he would veto any ENPC appropriation over $10,000.[81] Jennings convinced Cone to sign the bill, but he did so only on the condition that every member of the commission resign. Cone had engineered a similar scheme with the State Board of Public Welfare.[82] On July 28, 1937, Cone accepted the resignations of the entire ENPC and approved this appropriation.[83] Coe was one of the last members to resign. He informed Arno Cammerer that this recent development left him "deeply concerned and depressed."[84] In November 1937, Governor Cone appointed a new commission. It was only "a skeleton organization" and spent no state monies. G. O. Palmer, a close friend of Cone's, was named to head this ENPC, which never actually met as a group. Cone explained that this organization would remain in existence so that "when the federal government gets ready to take over the park, if they ever do, we can just turn it over to them, as the state is going to be hard run for money for the next year, and it is my plan not to spend but little of money appropriated by the last legislature."[85]

Though he was one of Cone's political allies, Palmer supported the park's creation and futilely tried to convince Cone to back the project. Echoing much of Coe's writings, Palmer wrote many long letters to the governor extolling the economic virtues of the ENP and describing the area's flora and fauna.[86] Palmer even defended Coe. On assuming control of the commission, Palmer found $6,657.76 in unpaid bills. Yet Palmer argued that Coe "served well and efficiently" and "did not even pay himself." Rather he "let his enthusiasm for the Park outweigh any business judgement that he may or should have exercised."[87] Palmer's ENPC had limited access to funds and was solely occupied on keeping the commission's records of Everglades landownership updated.[88] Palmer oversaw the commission until 1946, when the ENPC was reactivated.

Coe's promotional activities slackened during Cone's administration, and Coe was never truly effective after 1937. Meanwhile the NPS chose to wait out Cone's four-year term in the hopes that the next governor would be more amenable and cooperative. While they bided their time, they conducted several important studies of the Everglades' biology, ecology, and hydrology. These informed NPS efforts to create the park and laid the groundwork for the ENP's management after its 1947 creation.

Although by the mid-1930s Wright and his cadre of biologists lost influence within the NPS, their ideas remained central to the ENP. During Cone's administration, the NPS dispatched Daniel Beard to the Everglades to study the region's flora and fauna. In 1938 the agency published *Wildlife Reconnaissance: Everglades National Park Project*, a 106-page publication that offers one of the earliest and most comprehensive analyses of the Everglades' ecology and biology. Notably, *Wildlife Reconnaissance* examined water levels in the Everglades, a topic that scientists were only just beginning to study. Although the effects of drainage and water control efforts have dominated discussion of the Everglades since the 1947 publication of Marjory Stoneman Douglas's *The Everglades: River of Grass*, before that date knowledge about the Everglades' water flow was severely lacking. Douglas's work was heavily based on research conducted in the late 1930s and early 1940s by Garald Parker of the U.S. Geological Service. Beard and other NPS scientists examined the issue during this period as well.

Wildlife Reconnaissance accurately described the Everglades hydrology, and argued that "restoring water levels" was "the most important problem to be settled before the Everglades Park is established." Beard argued that drainage canals built in the Everglades before the 1930s diverted "water off to the Atlantic" that otherwise would had flowed into the region, thus lowering water levels. The construction of the Herbert Hoover Dike after the 1926 hurricane further contributed to the problem. Beard wrote that although many observers thought that "drainage has not affected water levels in the ... Everglades Park very much," the lowered water table could easily be seen in many places. Beard found evidence for drainage's negative effects in his observations of gator holes, in the upper courses of rivers, and in the locations of feeding grounds and rookeries. While Garald Parker utilized a geological approach to examine the Everglades' hydrology, Beard found ecological evidence that pointed to the Everglades' altered waterflow.[89]

During the late 1930s and early 1940s, the NPS slowly realized that protecting the Everglades' flora and fauna would be a more difficult task than initially thought. Coe's activism in the early 1930s was motivated by a desire to protect the Glades' biota from destruction hunting and collecting practices. He thought that a park would end these practices and protect the Everglades.

Arthur Demaray, another NPS employee, had come to a different conclusion based on *Wildlife Reconnaissance*. He wrote that Beard's study "tends to indicate that changed water levels are in all probability fundamentally responsible for the depletion of characteristic plants and animals" in the Everglades. Demaray noted that rookeries in the Florida Bay were severely depleted despite the fact that plume hunting had ceased in the area. Ornithologists concluded that a "lack of water" was "the reason the great bird rookeries are now gone." According to Demaray, the NPS "believes that restoration of water levels is fundamental and must be accomplished if the area becomes a park." Yet he also noted that it was "impossible" to determine why these water levels had been altered "because of the very serious lack of factual data." Demaray urged that "a comprehensive survey" of the issue be conducted.[90] The NPS was beginning to realize that the Everglades, and nature as a whole, was more complicated and connected than previously thought.

At the same time, Garald Parker, a scientist employed by the U.S. Geological Survey (USGS) began studying the issue of saltwater intrusion into Miami's water supply. Parker connected this issue to Everglades drainage, which had lowered South Florida's water table and allowed salt water to seep into the Biscayne Aquifer. Parker soon began more comprehensive studies of the drainage issue. Representatives of the USGS, USACE officials, state and local politicians, scientists, and NPS bureaucrats called a meeting in June 1939 to discuss this problem and chart a path toward a solution. Their meeting was mainly an information session, but, according to one NPS employee, it gave "enough food for thought to inspire a coordinated plan to meet the real crisis." The attendees agreed to coordinate their resources and conduct a "survey of Florida's water resources."[91] These issues would become central to ENP administration and management after its creation.

These scientific studies continued throughout the late 1930s and early 1940s while the NPS bided its time, awaiting a new governor in the state. It would also need a new generation of park activists. Plagued by health, family, and economic problems after 1937, Coe had ceased to be effective. His wife was ill from 1936 until her in death in 1940 at the age of seventy. Coe, who turned sixty-eight in 1935, was in ill health after that year as well. Additionally, he faced financial troubles, particularly after 1937 when he ceased to receive a salary from the ENPC. Coe spent every dime he had on the park project and it seems that, by the 1930s, the money he had made as a nurseryman finally ran out. In the 1940s, he at least lived partially on charity from family members and from the local Rotary Club.

Coe's achievements were immense. He was one of the great Florida environmentalists and he deserves more attention from historians and from Floridians. He redefined the Everglades and broadcast new biological rationales for its preservation. He built support for the park's creation in Florida and created the intellectual underpinnings for the park's establishment. Coe spread a broader vision for the preservation of South Florida as well, and brought to the fore the important biological and ecological values of the Everglades. He particularly highlighted the region's flora and marine ecosystems. Coe's tenacious and prophetic activism had been immensely successful in the early 1930s but would be replaced in the 1940s by a more sober and moderate group of Everglades activists. Using Coe's ideas and standing on his foundation, they saw the park to its completion in 1947.

CHAPTER 6

The Creation of
Everglades National Park

The fight for the ENP was restarted in 1941 by newly elected governor Spessard Holland, who quickly became the park's most important and effective advocate. The first phase of the park's creation was marked by the Great Depression and the New Deal, and it was shaped by the prophetic zeal of Ernest Coe. This second phase was molded by the economic recovery Florida experienced during World War II, a new postwar political consensus, and the business-minded, conservative pragmatism of Sunbelt politicians and boosters. New park advocates like Holland, his gubernatorial successor Millard Caldwell, and *Miami Herald* editor John Pennekamp compromised with landowners and the NPS to create the park in 1947.

Holland and Caldwell were both conservative politicians who typically opposed federal intervention in state affairs. Yet they vigorously supported a massive expansion of the environmental regulatory state in Florida. The park's enormous tangible and intangible economic benefits were enough to convince these conservatives to compromise their own political views. They thought the park would bring tourists to the state, but more importantly, they believed it would help transform Florida's economy and identity. The park was a key element of Florida's economic modernization; it would help the state slough off its agricultural and southern past and aid in its emergence as the Sunshine State. This park though was a biological park. Holland and Caldwell both supported the biological preservation of the Everglades, which they saw a foundation on which to build a tourism empire. The state's tourism industry, like its modern identity, was dependent on pristine natural environments, crystal clear water, and sandy beaches.

Spessard Holland was one of Florida's most important twentieth-century politicians. His father, Benjamin Franklin Holland, fought in the Civil War, moved to rural Bartow, Florida, in 1890, and became active in the state's two great pre–World War II economic sectors: real estate and citrus farming. Spessard was born in 1892. He left the farm and received a bachelor's degree from Emory University and a law degree from the University of Florida. He served in the Air Service

Signal Corps in World War I, for which he was awarded a Distinguished Service Cross. After the war, he returned to Bartow to practice law and was appointed a county prosecutor in Polk County. In 1920, he was elected county judge in Polk, serving two four-year terms. In 1932, he began the first of his two terms in the Florida Senate, where he strengthened Florida's schools, opposed new taxes, and reformed the state's citrus laws. Holland's conduct in the state senate earned him a statewide reputation as an honest, pragmatic, and effective politician. With the support of Florida's business community, Holland was elected governor in 1940. He ran the state efficiently and prioritized economic growth, education reform, and road construction. Most of his term, though, was spent on matters related to World War II. His successful gubernatorial term catapulted him to the U.S. Senate in 1946, where he served until 1971, the year of his death.[1] Holland had a successful career as a senator and was well regarded in Florida and in the Senate for his integrity, decency, and willingness to compromise. Holland never lost an election and left a huge mark on Florida's history.

Throughout his political career, Holland worked to transform Florida. Before World War II, Florida was a rural, agricultural state with a small and ineffective government. Holland's own family came from an agricultural and rural background. Holland left the citrus farm for a political career, a move that mirrored the changes he pursued at the state level. As governor and as a senator, Holland worked to modernize the state's economy and government. Federal dollars greatly facilitated these efforts. The New Deal injected federal money into Florida, but federal spending during World War II intensified Florida's transformation from a backwater agricultural state to a modern urbanized state.

During the war, federal spending exploded from just $9 billion in 1940 to $98.4 billion in 1945. Florida received more than its fair share of the pork. The federal government placed 172 military installations in the state, including massive bases like Camp Blanding, which became the state's fourth-largest city during the war. The war prompted an agricultural boom as well. Florida had its first $100 million citrus crop in 1942–43. The state's shipbuilding industry was rejuvenated, and even the tourism industry rebounded despite the war. The Great Depression was finally over, thanks to federal wartime spending. By the early 1940s, nine million new jobs were created in the country; at the same time, sixteen million Americans enlisted in the armed forces. Incomes skyrocketed as well. In 1933 Floridians earned just $424 million; by 1943, that number had ballooned to $2 billion.[2]

These economic changes were accompanied by immense demographic change. The state's population grew from 1,915,000 in 1940 to 2,465,000 in 1945, but these census figures missed most the transient and temporary residents who called Florida home during the war. City newspapers and observers during the war noted the enormous additional growth. For example, Pensacola saw an additional 100,000 temporary residents in 1945, while Miami in 1944 absorbed an additional 325,000 residents. In the fall of 1942, for example, 78,000 military personnel were stationed in Miami, busting the seams of the city's numerous hotels.[3]

These trends continued into the postwar era, as Florida and other states in the Sunbelt experienced economic growth and demographic change.[4] Sunbelt states urbanized and industrialized, much of this change was federally subsidized. In some ways these developments allowed southern states to catch up to the rest of the nation. At the same time, many Sunbelt states led the way forward into the post–World War II era. The Sunbelt was suburban and embraced the high-tech and service industries that would be essential to the future of the nation's economy. Florida in particular embraced a postindustrial future. Service sectors—like tourism, retirement, health care, and other consumer-driven service industries—became central to the state's economy, as did high-tech sectors like the aviation and aerospace industries. Many of these sectors greatly benefitted from federal programs. Federal highway spending was key to the state's tourism industry and suburban growth; Social Security checks and later Medicare made the state's retirement industry possible; the federal space program's headquarters at Cape Canaveral directly created the state's aerospace and aviation industries. Florida's population growth continued after the war as well. By 1950, the state's population grew to 2,771,305, and by 1960 it had exploded by 78.7 percent to a population of almost five million.[5]

These economic and demographic changes brought pressure for social change. Many southern states resisted these challenges to the region's White supremacist and patriarchal social and political structure. The rise of modern conservatism in the United States was inextricably linked to these efforts to prevent the social change that accompanied the economic modernization of the South. Florida, likewise, struggled with these issues. The state worked to shed its legacy of slavery, segregation, and racism with mixed success. Much of modern Florida, though, embraced pluralism, particularly cities like Miami that became major destinations for Latin American immigrants.

Spessard Holland was at the forefront of these changes. As governor he worked closely with the federal government to place military and shipbuilding facilities in the state during World War II. He modernized the state's education system and its property tax collections. Holland typically opposed taxes but supported new gasoline taxes that would bolster Florida's program of road construction and indirectly, the state's tourism industry. During the war, Holland lobbied the federal government to ease travel restrictions and gasoline rationing in Florida for the industry's benefit. As a senator, he steered military and highway spending into Florida and worked to place aerospace facilities in the state.

Holland furthered Florida's economic modernization and, like most Sunbelt politicians, welcomed federal intervention in the state when it created economic growth. Like his fellow southern conservatives, though, he resisted the South's social modernization and opposed federal action when it challenged the state's social or racial order. Most southern Sunbelt conservatives were struck from a similar mold. Holland opposed labor unions, was vehemently anticommunist, and espoused a states'-rights philosophy on race. Yet Holland was more willing to embrace true change and less interested in defending the old order than a typical moderate southern conservative.

Holland's record on race illustrates his conflicted ideas about civil rights for African Americans, his fealty to the concept of law and order, and the limits of his own willingness to challenge southern traditions. Holland twice prevented lynch mobs from engaging in acts of terrorism and violence. As a state senator, he personally blocked a lynch mob in Lakeland from lynching two Black men accused of murdering a White police officer. He then prosecuted the two in court; both were found guilty. Holland again preventing a lynching in Tallahassee by ordering Florida State Guard units to protect three suspects from lynch mobs. As a state senator, Holland led to the charge in 1938 to eliminate the state's poll tax. As a U.S. senator, he introduced the Twenty-Fourth Amendment in the Senate in 1962, which made the poll tax unconstitutional in federal elections. Yet Holland also opposed the civil rights movement, voted against the Civil Rights Act of 1964, and signed the Southern Manifesto, which pledged to use all mechanisms at the South's disposal to oppose 1954's *Brown v. Board* decision outlawing segregation in public schools.[6]

The ENP's creation was consistent with Holland's political agenda and with his ideas about nature. Holland supported the park as a way to build Florida's tourism industry, an economic sector that was dependent on a pristine environment. He understood how the park's economic values were derived from the Glades' biological values and hence embraced the cause of environmental preservation. While Coe epitomized an interwar proto-environmentalism, Holland embodied a new Sunbelt environmentalism. Coe touted the park's economic values but prioritized the park's biocentric purposes. Holland embraced the protection of the Everglades' biology, but only because it would create economic growth. Holland's ideas about nature were likewise complicated. Holland grew up hunting and fishing in the still-undeveloped interior of Florida, and due to the influence of his wife, became an ardent bird-watcher. He loved nature, yet he prioritized economic growth and was unlikely to support any conservation causes that would imperil that economic prerogative.

Holland's economic view of the park was influenced by Coe's promotional work. Although he was no longer central to the project after 1937, Coe continued to publicize the park throughout the 1940s. He was particularly active during the 1940 gubernatorial election. In a mailing from that year, Coe noted that the federal government would "expend millions of dollars in developing" the park and argued that more than a half million visitors would enter the park a year.[7] During World War II, Coe connected the park to Florida and to the South's postwar economic future. Many Americans expected large federal public works projects after World War II to prevent an economic recession. Coe wrote that after the war the United States would embark on "a big nation wide scale of new construction and reconstruction." The South would especially be "in for development" to bring it up to northern standards. The park's creation was one project that could facilitate Florida's modernization.[8]

Holland bought into the park's economic appeal early. As a gubernatorial candidate he regarded the park "as the best financial investment the State has now in sight."[9] The park "will bring in many thousands of additional tourists who wouldn't come except for the park. They will see many new things, they will come back, they will stay and invest their money here and help build our state to even greater heights. It will produce many millions of additional dollars in tax revenue. It will bring tremendous revenue to hotels, restaurants, people in private business and to my mind is just about the biggest single business proposition now pending. I speak of it as a business proposition." Additionally, the federal government, not the state, would be responsible for the park's upkeep and development. Holland thought the NPS would "put in an amazing amount of money to make it such that it can be visited." "They will have to do many expensive things, it will be a long and most expensive matter to develop the park."[10]

Holland understood that the park's economic values were derived from the Everglades' biological values. The area's flora and fauna was its tourist attraction, hence they needed to be protected. At a 1946 ENPC meeting, Holland explained that the reason the Everglades was "so desirable as a park is that it has so many things which can't be found anywhere else in the United States and some nowhere else in the world. Such things as the great white heron, the roseate spoonbill; such things as swim in the water, the manatee; such things as the crocodile." Remarkably, Holland emphasized that these reptilian predators were "well worth preserving."[11] Holland particularly understood the value and appeal of the Everglades' birds. Birding would be a major activity in the new park, and Holland worked closely with Audubon president John Baker. They ensured that Audubon wardens could protect birds on private lands before the park's creation, they lobbied the NPS to create tourism and birding opportunities, and they worked together to acquire private lands needed for the park's creation.[12] Unlike Coe, Holland did not think the Everglades' biota had inherent value but rather saw it as foundation on which to build a tourism empire. Holland believed that the park was a "business proposition, one under which the people of the state, by investing a little additional money, can go far toward making a reality of the park."[13]

The creation of the ENP would bring more than just tangible economic benefits, though. National parks have cultural importance and bring diverse intangible benefits to local areas. They can reorient local economies around tourism, prompt the creation of additional tourist attractions, and redefine the cultural identities of states and localities. The meanings of national parks and their roles in facilitating and promoting a specific brand of American nationalistic tourism, were central to U.S. tourism between 1890 and 1940.[14] Holland and his allies believed there were three intangible ways the park would benefit Florida: it would advertise Florida tourism, it would reorient the state's economy around tourism, and, most importantly it would help transform Florida's identity.

Everglades National Park would act as an enormous advertisement for Florida's broader tourism industry. Coe explained to Holland that the park would stand "as a perpetual advertisement of a tropical fairyland, unique and outstanding among the other great national parks of the nation."[15] G. O. Palmer, the head of the moribund ENPC from 1937 to 1946, claimed that the publicity value of the park "would be worth more annually than the entire State expends annually for advertising purposes."[16] In a 1947 speech to the Florida State Retailers Association, park advocate and *Miami Herald* editor John Pennekamp touted the increased publicity the park had generated. According to Pennekamp, Florida's Citrus Commission had spent $2 million on advertising, while the State Advertising Commission had spent another $500,000, yet "they failed to achieve, by direct purchase, even a fraction of the attention which the creation of this Park has accomplished."[17] Additionally, national park status would help legitimize both the Everglades' natural values and Florida tourism more broadly. The Everglades in particular needed this federal approval, as most Americans still viewed swamps in a negative light. Although these attitudes were in flux in the 1930s and 1940s, national park status would go a long way toward destigmatizing a landscape that had been seen as a snake-and-mosquito-infested wasteland.[18]

The park's creation would greatly facilitate the emergence of Florida's "modern identity as a tourist empire."[19] By the 1940s, Florida was already an established tourist destination. Holland and other park supporters hoped the ENP's creation would solidify Florida as the premier tourist destination in the United States. Florida tourism, and tourism in the broader South, had long been connected to the region's natural environment.[20] In the 1890s and 1900s, the proliferation of both Henry Flagler's and Henry Plant's railroads and hotels allowed affluent northern tourists to escape harsh northern winters in the sunny climes of Florida. Miami and Miami Beach became major attractions in the 1920s, and even during the Great Depression and World War II, Florida managed to attract large numbers of tourists. Despite travel restrictions and gasoline rationing, the war probably spurred more tourism to Florida than it prevented. Thousands of servicemen and women stationed in the state during the war later returned as tourists. Holland looked to build on this tradition and thought the creation of a national park would enhance Florida's reputation as a tourist destination throughout the nation. Many supporters believed the ENP would have transformative effect on Florida tourism, similar to the actual impact of the 1971 opening of Disney World. The park did, in fact, prompt the creation of dozens of additional tourist attractions, state parks and preserves, and sightseeing opportunities in southern Florida.[21]

Holland believed the park's creation would also help remake Florida's identity. Since the end of the Reconstruction, the South had tried to refurbish its identity to facilitate economic growth. Southern politicians acted as boosters, luring business to their states by presenting a business-friendly image of the region. Often this meant an embrace of a low wage, nonunionized workforce, and a deregulated business climate. It also entailed at least lip service to harmonious race relations, sectional conciliation, and an embrace of modern values. While these New South boosters employed public relations campaigns to present a favorable image to corporate America, Florida sought to completely remake the state's identity. Rather than just attracting investment from corporate executives, Florida sought to convince millions of U.S. and international tourists of all stripes to visit the state.[22]

The ENP could aid in this redefinition. National parks were important cultural touchstones and had facilitated the creation of an American national identity.[23] In the same way, the ENP could help remake Florida's image in the aftermath of World War II. The cultural values of western parks were derived from their geological monuments, yet, the Everglades had no craggy peaks, deep valleys, or wide canyons. Rather, in a sharp break with NPS history, this park's cultural significance would reflect the ENP's biological rationales.[24] The Everglades' birds, alligators, sawgrass prairies, and mangrove forests became the park's monuments. This biological wonderland became one of the nation's cultural treasures. The ENP signaled an embrace of modernity and science. It allowed Florida to stake a claim at the forefront of American cultural and scientific trends. The park signaled that Florida no longer a backwater state from a backward region, tainted by the legacy of slavery and secession.[25] Rather, Florida was now modern and scientific. It was integrated into the national fabric and was eager to cater to the desires of U.S. tourists.[26]

Holland's embrace of modernity and of the park's biological monumentalism illustrate the dynamic and forward-thinking aspects of southern identity after World War II. This park pointed the way to the future, both for Florida and for the nation. The park's creation signaled the state's social and economic modernization. This new identity was tied to the state's environment and necessitated the protection of that environment. Tourism was not the only new industry in Florida birthed by the state's embrace of modernity, midwifed by the federal government, and dependent on Florida nature. The state's retirement industry also revolutionized the state and greatly altered the state's demographics. Latin American immigrants flocked to modern Florida as well. Just as the ENP signaled an embrace of biodiversity, migration from Latin America reflected Florida's acceptance of pluralism and cultural diversity. Just as the Everglades was a tropical outpost in the temperate United States, South Florida would become a Latin American outpost in the United States.

The park foreshadowed modern environmentalism and prefigured the popular rise of ecology. As southern environmental historians have shown, despite its backward reputation the South was sometimes at the forefront of environmental thinking in the United States. Ecological insights were important to the thinking of other southern scientists and conservationists like George Washington Carver, Herbert Stoddard, and Archie Carr. The science of ecology also found fertile ground in the South. Southerners Eugene and Howard T. Odum were at the center of the development of modern ecology and authored the first textbook on the topic in 1953.[27]

Holland was no ecologist, but throughout his thirty-year political career he reliably and steadfastly supported Everglades National Park. As governor he worked to rebuild support for the park among sportsmen, the commercial fishing industry, and Monroe County after Ernest Coe angered these interests in the 1930s. Holland resolved the indebtedness of the Everglades Drainage District, a state agency that owned much of the land needed for the park's creation. Most importantly, he created the Everglades National Wildlife Refuge (ENWR), a precursor to the park that protected park lands while exploratory oil drilling proceeded in the Everglades. Holland continued to support the park as a Senator. He assisted in the park's creation, sought appropriations for the ENP, and helped finalize the park's boundaries.

Holland wrapped up the Democratic nomination for governor in May 1940 and immediately began preparing for the start of his term in January. He supported the park during his campaign and quickly met with Coe and NPS officials to discuss the steps needed to make the park a reality. He soon found that the primary obstacle to the park's creation was exploratory oil drilling in the Everglades. Holland worked to establish the park between 1941 and 1943, but he also allowed drilling to continue on state and private lands in the park area.[28] He believed that little to no oil would be found in the area and that oil drilling would deliver few economic benefits to the state, especially when compared to the ENP's economic impact. Yet he also wanted to respect the rights of property owners and he wanted to give oil companies a chance to prove him wrong.

In March 1941, Holland met with NPS officials to discuss the park's creation. He noted that "one of the difficulties facing the establishment of the proposed park was" the oil issue. Holland wanted the park created as soon as possible and suggested that the NPS create the park during his term by acquiring only the surface rights to lands in the park's potential boundaries. This proposal would allow private landowners and the state to retain their mineral rights in the park and would presumably permit exploratory oil drilling throughout the park. This proposal was immediately rejected by the NPS. The reservation of mineral rights on park lands was anathema. As Holland learned from Newton Drury, who had recently become NPS director in 1940, national parks required lands "where natural conditions are to remain inviolate." Instead, the NPS suggest an alternative. Lands with mineral reservations could be turned over to the U.S. Fish and Wildlife Service, which could protect the Everglades' biota while oil exploration continued.[29]

A wildlife refuge had little appeal to Holland. According to the governor, "a wildlife refuge tends to keep people out instead of bringing them in." This type of preserve would not bring Florida the economic benefits of a national park. Instead, Holland bided his time. He and other park supporters assumed drilling would soon peter out as oil companies failed to strike. Oil exploration in South Florida had only begun in the late 1930s, and despite the enthusiasm of some landowners, few positive indications of oil had been found. Indeed, many companies soon withdrew from the Everglades after concluding that there was no oil there. D. Graham Copeland reported in 1941 that the Gulf Oil Company had expended $269,000 "in its investigations and had dropped the matter." Likewise, "the Sun Oil Company had made similar investigations somewhat further north with like result."[30]

Between 1942 and early 1943 Holland held three conferences with NPS officials concerning the park's creation. All three dealt with the same issues: the need to set a deadline at which point oil exploration on state lands would cease, the possibility of future oil royalties being delivered to the state, reductions to the park's proposed boundaries, and the possibility of acquiring the Model Land Company's Everglades lands.

At the June 1942 conference, NPS officials agreed to reduce the total park area from 1,454,000 acres to 1,018,000 acres. The park's original maximum boundaries had been enormous and impractical; this was yet another in a long line of boundary reductions made by the NPS. Holland, Drury, and others also discussed the oil situation. Holland again asked the NPS to accept state lands and create the park, but this time, instead of oil rights reserved for the state, Holland inquired about oil royalties. These royalties would mean that "if the Federal Government ever authorized exploration for gas, oil or other minerals therein, and if such gas, oil or other mineral were discovered and produced, that all the usual royalty rights . . . would in such case accrue to the State of Florida."[31]

At the next meeting in August 1942, Holland began pushing for a new strategy for the park's early creation. He wanted the NPS to meet with the Model Land Company (MLC) and acquire its Everglades lands. The MLC was the largest private landowner in the park area and owned much of the southeastern sections of the Glades.[32] Holland wanted the NPS to acquire the MLC lands, combine them with the state's lands, and then create an initial park that would expand later.[33] Holland would advocate for this approach for the next five years. These issues were further discussed at a March 1943 conference. Significantly, by that time the NPS and Holland had agreed on the need to "set a definite time limit for oil and gas explorations." NPS Superintendent Newton Drury suggested putting the date at "12 or 18 months from January 1 of this year (1943)."[34] Holland later set a deadline to terminate oil leases on state lands by May 1, 1944, unless oil had been found. According to Drury, Holland had "taken the position that the [ENP] Project cannot be held up indefinitely by oil prospecting."[35]

Unfortunately, just as Holland and Drury had agreed to halt drilling, oil was found in November 1943 just outside the park area at the Sunniland oil field. This well, the first in the state's history, was drilled by the Humble Oil Company, a subsidiary of Standard Oil. Just as Florida tourism would be subsidized by federal spending, this oil well was subsidized by the state of Florida. In 1939 the state announced a $50,000 prize for the first productive well in the state. The Sunniland well won that prize, yet it only ever produced small amounts of low-quality oil. In practical terms, this well was a failure. Oil companies, geologists, and politicians soon concluded that no oil existed in the Everglades. Yet for real estate interests and oil speculators, the Sunniland well was an enormous success. It dramatically renewed interest in Florida oil and led to a boom in oil leases, land sales, and exploratory drilling in the Everglades. Those activities in turn forced Holland and the NPS to move more decisively to create the park. In December 1943, Drury explained to Holland that he was "somewhat apprehensive over possible damage to park values . . . as a result of the accelerated [oil] exploratory program." Drury urged Holland to create the park as soon as possible to avoid further damage to the area's biological values.[36]

At a series of meetings held between December 30, 1943, and January 1, 1944, Holland and the NPS debated three strategies for the park's creation. Holland's proposal reflected his desire to monetize the Everglades' biota while oil drilling continued in the Everglades. He proposed to "set aside fee simple, without the reservation of mineral rights, several key areas of several thousand acres in order to establish protection for the bird rookeries, feeding grounds, and other important biological features" in the Everglades. While oil drilling continued in other parts of the Glades, the most biologically valuable—and hence economically valuable—sections of the Everglades would be protected and monetized as tourist attractions. When the oil frenzy subsided, the rest of the park could be created.[37]

The NPS rejected this proposal, both for practical and ecological reasons. Ray Vinten, who oversaw two national monuments in St. Augustine, investigated this proposal. Vinten, an NPS employee who became heavily involved in the ENP's creation in the 1940s, found that a park composed of "small key areas can not be established," since rookeries, feeding grounds, and roosts changed from year to year, often "from five to seven and possibly ten miles from the original site."[38] NPS officials also noted that this proposal was really for a series of national monuments, not for one national park.

The NPS offered a counterproposal: break the entire park area into six units and acquire these units one by one free from any mineral reservations. The NPS could protect these areas; then, after a period of years, when "a major portion" of the area was delivered to the NPS free from all mineral reservations, it could establish the park and develop it for tourists.[39] This proposal was unacceptable to Holland. It delayed the economic benefits of park tourism for decades. Holland also objected to this plan because it failed to accommodate oil drilling on private lands. Although Holland sought to end drilling on state lands, he was reluctant to interfere with oil drilling on private lands and resisted any government intrusion on private property rights. He wrote that, until the oil flurry was resolved, deeding lands without mineral reservations was completely unacceptable "to the general public." He also believed that "the size of the first unit of approximately 200,000 acres, which would be required to be conveyed . . . without oil reservations of any kind would preclude our going further in the effort to" create the park.[40]

With these proposals both unworkable, the only remaining option was the previously discussed creation of a wildlife preserve. Under this plan, the state would deed all its Everglades lands to the U.S. Fish and Wildlife Service, which could protect the "natural values" of the Everglades while exploratory oil drilling continued.[41] By August 1944, Holland concluded that this strategy represented the best chance for the park's creation, but he had one concern. Holland wanted to make the authorizing legislation "entirely definite that the whole purpose thereof would be to move toward the establishment of the park." He proposed that if the refuge was not converted into a national park within ten years, the lands within would revert to state ownership. Holland wanted to guarantee that the preservation of the Everglades would bring economic benefits to Florida.[42]

On December 13, 1944, Holland and NPS officials hammered out the final details of this agreement. Most of the discussion centered on the refuge's—and hence the future park's—boundaries. Holland initially presented the NPS with a park map that outlined a much larger area than Holland had ever previously discussed with the agency. Ray Vinten excitedly explained that these areas "included more land than we had hoped for."[43] These boundaries reflected not just Holland's desire to protect bird populations but also an understanding that these birds were dependent on both habitats and waterflow. Holland explained that the Florida Bay was included because "there were many rookeries in that area and thousands of birds nested and fed there, especially the [Roseate] Spoon Bill."[44] He also supported the NPS suggestions to expand the park's boundaries north, which would secure waterflow to the park. John Baker explained that this area was important due to "the relationship of this drainage basin to the Shark River."[45]

The end result of these discussions was a very large area that encompassed approximately one million acres. John H. Davis of the USGS noted that this "larger area had some advantages over the retracted boundaries because wild fowl and animals range over considerable territory in feeding."[46] Vinten noted that this area represented "a much wider variety of land types than have been included in any previous compromise with the State." These boundaries were "a very substantial framework for the building of a national park."[47] In fact, these boundaries became the park's initial boundaries in 1947. (See plate 8.)

The refuge's creation signaled Florida's commitment to the ENP and acted as a deadline for exploratory oil drilling. Holland explicitly tied the requirement that a park be created in ten years to oil drilling. He informed the NPS that the state "could work it out on the basis that leases would not extend beyond that time [the ten-year period] except in the event of commercial production."[48] Holland worked to end oil exploration in other ways. He limited oil exploration on MLC lands in the Florida Bay, on which the state owned half the mineral rights. In 1943 oil companies were "requesting extension of exploration agreement up to ten years" on these lands. According to Holland's secretary, Ralph Davis, the governor "vigorously opposed this on grounds it would be detrimental to park." On Holland's recommendation, drilling was only extended to two additional years, and excluded from all offshore waters in the region.[49]

Throughout his political career, though, Holland typically opposed federal intervention in economic and state affairs and sought to protect individual property rights and free enterprise. For instance, Holland signed the Southern Manifesto in 1956, which decried "the Supreme Court's encroachment on the rights reserved to the States and to the people," and justified his opposition to the Civil Rights Act of 1964 on states'-rights grounds. Holland's actions in the Everglades appear particularly exceptional when compared to the role he played in the Tidelands Controversy. An increase in offshore drilling at the end of World War II led to increased conflict between states and the federal government over the ownership of tidal lands and offshore waters. Holland led a "bipartisan effort to restore state title over offshore submerged lands." He introduced the Submerged Lands Act in the Senate, a bill that returned these offshore lands to the states and protected state oil royalties. President Eisenhower signed the bill, declaring that he would "always resist federal encroachment upon rights and affairs of the states."[50]

One park opponent noted this contradiction. Raymond Parker, a local attorney and pilot, explained to Florida politician Charley Johns that Holland had been "a leader in the fight to restore to the state their mineral rights in the tidelands" but that he was also "a leader in donating to the Federal Government state-owned properties for Park purposes without" reserving mineral rights. Parker wrote that "these inconsistencies are amazing to me."[51] Holland's fight for the ENP was an exception to his consistent desire to limit the power of the federal government and to protect property rights. Holland compromised his conservative ideas about government to protect the environment and to facilitate economic growth in Florida. His pragmatic and economic support for the Everglades' ecological preservation foreshadowed the later emergence of ecotourism and reflected Holland's own enlightened pro-business ideology.

Holland's gubernatorial term ended in 1945; he joined the U.S. Senate the next year. He was succeeded as governor by Millard Caldwell, a close political ally who pursued a similar economic and political agenda. Caldwell was a pro-business conservative who won the Democratic gubernatorial primary by attacking the liberalism of his opponent. As governor, Caldwell worked to modernize and streamline the state's government. His most notable accomplishment was an education reform package that entailed an enormous increase in education funding and brought the state's standards up to the national level. He supported segregation and opposed labor unions in the state, and generally supported the conservative credo of limited government. He also eagerly sought federal spending in the state. After his term expired, he served in the Federal Civil Defense Administration and as a justice on the Florida Supreme Court. Like Holland, Caldwell was a conservative Sunbelt Democrat who supported Jim Crow, facilitated the modernization Florida, and eagerly sought federal spending in his state. He saw the ENP as an important part of Florida's postwar, modern economy and oversaw the park's creation in 1947.[52]

As soon he wrapped up the Democratic primary, Caldwell was brought into the state's efforts to create the ENP. Holland had continued to focus on MLC lands, which he saw as the key to the park's creation. He thought those lands could be combined with the state's holdings in the Everglades to create an initial park that could expand later. Additionally, if MLC lands could be acquired at a reasonable price, a precedent would be set for subsequent land purchase and momentum would build for further purchases. Furthermore, MLC lands were under lease to oil companies; acquiring them would discourage further oil exploration. Caldwell and Holland discussed a state appropriation of $250,000 to purchase these lands but soon realized that the MLC valued its lands much more highly.[53] At a meeting in early 1945, the MLC offered to sell its lands to the state for $365,000 dollars. Holland thought this proposal "was a 'first offer' and subject to a counterproposal and further negotiation."[54] More troubling, though, was the fact that this deal did not include a large portion of lands to which the MLC held disputed title. Holland noted that court action would likely be needed to resolve that issue if the company was not willing to sell these lands outright.[55]

Another hitch in Holland's plans revolved around Ernest Coe. Although Coe was no longer an effective park advocate, he still controlled the ENPA and wielded influence. Holland convinced the NPS to reduce the park's boundaries and throughout his gubernatorial term pushed for a smaller initial park that would expand into its fuller boundaries over time. Coe fought these proposals vigorously. He believed that only a full park that included sections of Key Largo, large areas north of the Tamiami Trail, and areas of the west coast of Florida around the Turner River should be established. He criticized Holland's curtailed park boundaries and undermined Holland both publicly and in correspondence with the NPS. By the end of his term, Holland was fed up with Coe and wrote that he needed to "fall into line." Coe was "confusing the picture and the minds of the general public by continually bringing up and contending for the establishment of the original area."[56]

Caldwell also saw Coe as an obstacle and worked with *Miami Herald* editor John Pennekamp to respectfully, but firmly, deal with Coe. Initially Pennekamp, who would soon become central to the park's creation, suggested making Coe "president emeritus or chairman of the board" of the ENPA in order to get Coe "out of a position of absolute authority," while still showing respect to "him as the man who really originated the idea of the park." Business organizations in Miami, like the local Chamber of Commerce and Rotary Club, could then "absorb the functions of the Association" and raise the funds needed for land acquisition.[57] The Chamber of Commerce was initially supportive of this idea, but its full cooperation never materialized and this plan went nowhere.

Instead, Caldwell publicly issued Coe an ultimatum. If Coe wanted a park that conformed to the original maximum boundaries, then he needed to raise the money to purchase those lands. Caldwell held a press conference on May 23, 1945, and "served notice that he expects more active local support" for the park's creation. Caldwell stated that "unless the local people, particularly the Everglades National Park Association, show some real interest, I'm going to withdraw ... state support." The ENPA needed to start "raising money" for land acquisition, or get out of the state's way.[58] Coe soon admitted defeat and in February 1946 resigned from his position in the ENPA.[59]

With Coe sidelined, John Pennekamp took charge. While Coe's prophetic zeal was essential to the early fight for the park, Pennekamp's pragmatism and professionalism were crucial to the final push for the park's creation. Pennekamp first visited to Miami in 1925 (the same year as Coe) as a Cincinnati journalist covering the Florida real estate boom. He fell in love with the city, took a job at the *Miami Herald*, and soon became the backbone of the paper's editorial team. Pennekamp worked at the *Herald* for over fifty years, and over the course his career became an outspoken advocate for the freedom of the press and supported a variety of social and environmental issues. After the ENP's creation, Pennekamp worked to create John Pennekamp State Park in 1959, which protected those sections of Key Largo that Coe had fought to include in the ENP. Pennekamp served on the board of Florida state park system in the 1950s and 1960s and worked to expand, promote, and modernize the state park system.[60]

Pennekamp's involvement in the ENP was not necessarily borne out of his strong love of the Everglades or deep concern for nature. In fact, previous to his involvement in the ENP, he had never been involved in conservation issues. According to fellow *Herald* journalist Nixon Smiley, "Pennekamp more or less fell into conservation." Pennekamp himself remarked that he was "a conservationist by acclaim."[61] Essentially, Pennekamp was ordered by the *Miami Herald*'s owner, John S. Knight, to support the park's creation. Around 1945, Holland sat next to Knight on an airplane flight from Washington, D.C., to Florida and convinced Knight to support the park's creation. Knight called Pennekamp into his office the next day and Pennekamp "was told to put *The Herald*'s full support behind it and give as much of his personal time as possible."[62]

By October 1945, Pennekamp became Caldwell's point person on the park. That month Pennekamp met with Audubon president John Baker and NPS officials in New York City. Here he declared that Caldwell "wished to move forward with the establishment of the National Park" and endorsed Holland's plans for the park's creation. This entailed the quick creation of a small initial park whose boundaries would expand over time. To facilitate this, Pennekamp "asked the National Park Service to prepare a map" showing the minimum area needed for a park, the size of the current wildlife refuge, and the park's final intended boundaries. C. Kay Davis, the head engineer of the U.S. Soil Service's offices in Florida, next agreed to prepare a report on land values in those areas. Using this information, the state could then determine how much money would be needed to acquire these lands. Pennekamp suggested to Caldwell that he create a committee to negotiate with landowners and a "financing campaign" to raise the needed funds.[63]

Caldwell approved of Pennekamp's plan and instructed the still-skeletal ENPC to cooperate with him in all ways.[64] These swift and direct actions impressed the NPS and Florida officials. In contrast to Coe, Pennekamp was professional, willing to compromise, and clear about his goals. Ray Vinten remarked that Pennekamp added "considerable weight and stability" to the state's efforts.[65]

By December 1945, the NPS had prepared the requested maps. The maximum boundary remained the original maximum boundaries. These had been laid out by Ernest Coe, approved by the federal government in 1934, and then endorsed by the NPS in 1937. The NPS declared the minimum boundaries to be those agreed on by Spessard Holland and the NPS in 1944 and enshrined in the ENWR.[66] (See plate 8.)

Pennekamp also asked Caldwell to appoint a new ENPC charged with promoting the park; coordinating, directing, and participating in fund-raising; and then acquiring park lands.[67] This newly established ENPC first met on April 25, 1946. Chairing the commission was August Burghard, a Fort Lauderdale journalist, advertising executive, booster, and philanthropist originally from Macon, Georgia.[68] Former ENPC members May Mann Jennings, Norberg Thompson, and D. Graham Copeland were reappointed to the commission. The ENPA, which had essentially ceased to exist, was not represented. The rest of the commission members were drawn from the ranks of prominent Floridians, and many were members of local Chambers of Commerce.[69]

As chair, Burghard handled the day-to-day and logistical elements of the commission, while Pennekamp set the ENPC's agenda and worked to enact it. Pennekamp explained to the commission that their job was going to be "to purchase the Park." The ENPC needed to determine "what kind of campaign exactly we shall have to make, and how much money we shall have to raise." He estimated that this amount would be no more than $2 million, but that to get a firmer figure, the commission needed to "find out how many private property owners there are there, and how much, approximately, it is going to take to acquire their property."[70] Burghard later summarized the commission's "ultimate" goals to Governor Caldwell: the ENPC would "acquire the needed land . . . and dedicate this park *during your Administration.*"[71]

At the first meeting of this iteration of the ENPC, Pennekamp and Burghard examined the gritty details of the park's creation and created a detailed plan of action. The commission set a budget for itself, something Coe's ENPC had never done. Finally, they formed committees with delineated responsibilities. The publicity and education committee was directed to work with local Chambers of Commerce and women's clubs "to handle a program on publicity and education." The land acquisition committee contacted landowners and informed them of the park's impending creation. The ENPC also planned their next two meetings and named an executive committee, which included Burghard, Copeland, Jennings, and Pennekamp.[72] After this meeting, Pennekamp secured free legal advice for the commission: Florida Power and Light put one of its lawyers, Will Preston, at the ENPC's disposal. Preston conducted a study of all state and federal laws affecting the park's creation and answered other pertinent legal questions.[73]

NPS officials attended this meeting and praised this new group's efficiency and practicality. T. J. Allen, the NPS Southeast regional director, told this new commission that he was "particularly impressed by the Governor's way of presenting the case to this new Commission." Contrasting this approach with Coe's, Allen stated that "sometimes commissions of this sort can spend a lot of time sitting around making speeches and going into raptures of what's out in the Everglades." Allen thought that "at this stage, we hope you can keep your mind on the important thing, which is to acquire land and get the Park created."[74]

By July 1946, the ENPC contacted all landowners in the park area requesting that they contribute their lands to the state. A short formal letter from the governor, as well as a longer and more detailed letter from the ENPC were both utilized.[75] No donations were forthcoming. Landowners wanted to be paid, although a few requested to exchange their lands for other state lands outside the park. The idea of creating the park via land exchanges had long been discussed but never implemented. In 1931, Florida passed a law giving the Internal Improvement Fund (IIF), a state agency that controlled the state's lands, the authority to exchange privately owned lands inside the park area for state-owned lands outside the park. This power had not been used until 1946, when the ENPC set up thirty-one land exchanges. This efforts were in vain, however, because by this date the IIF had made other plans for those state-owned lands north of the park area.[76] In 1946 and 1947, the IIF transformed its Everglades lands in Palm Beach, Broward, and Dade Counties into water conservation areas.[77] These areas would soon become integral parts of the USACE Central and Southern Florida Project.[78] Daniel Beard and the NPS supported this development and believed that it "would protect the watershed for the national park." Yet it also meant the elimination of "all the exchangeable lands" and would complicate the park's creation.[79]

After this disappointing response from Everglades landowners, in October 1946 park advocates redirected their efforts to acquiring MLC Everglades lands. At Holland's urging, the ENPC met with MLC Vice President Carl Hawkins on November 23, 1946.[80] Hawkins insisted that MLC lands were worth $6 an acre. This unreasonable price caused the ENPC to quickly abandon negotiations.[81]

By the end of 1946, the situation looked bleak. Acquiring lands via donation had failed, land swaps were no longer possible, and the MLC refused to consider a reasonable price for its lands. The ENPC concluded that they would need to raise $2 million to purchase, via eminent domain if needed, all the lands in the minimum park area. Although park advocates had always assumed that they would have raise these funds from private subscription, Pennekamp believed he had found another source of funding. Florida's economy, and its tax receipts, had been booming since the end of World War II. According to Florida's Comptroller's Office, major sources of state revenue in 1944–45 equaled over $65 million. That number had jumped to almost $107 million by 1945–46 and ballooned to $126 million by 1946–47.[82] In short, the state was flush with cash. Pennekamp suggested something that had seemed impossible during the Great Depression and World War II: the state of Florida could simply appropriate money to buy park lands. Pennekamp discussed this idea in a meeting with Florida politicians at the end of December and continued floating the idea to legislators in January.

At an ENPC meeting on January 14, 1947, Pennekamp announced "that the Commission was planning to submit to the State Legislature . . . an appropriation of about $2,000,000 for the acquisition of private lands." In March, the commission presented its case to Caldwell and the cabinet.[83] The ENPC presented the governor with a "$40,000,000 map" showing the park's minimum boundaries and made the argument that the park's creation would bring $40 million a year into the state's economy.[84] According to NPS Southeast Regional director T. J. Allen, the ENPC had "expected Governor Caldwell to object" to the plan. Instead, he "not only agreed to support" the appropriation but also promised "$500,000 immediately from a fund under control of the Governor for the construction of post-war projects of benefit to Florida."[85] Caldwell directly connected the ENP's creation to Florida's postwar economic growth. Gilbert Leach wrote that "you could have knocked all of us down with the same feather when our good old Skipper (Caldwell) responded as he did."[86]

With Caldwell on board, Pennekamp next moved to persuade the legislature. MacGregor Smith, the head of Florida Power and Light, arranged a meeting between Pennekamp and powerful members of the Florida legislature from the northern sections of the state. Dubbed the Pork Choppers or the Pork Chop Gang, these socially conservative, rural legislators dominated the state's politics between the 1930s and the 1960s.[87] Although many South Florida politicians supported the park, these northern areas were less economically and culturally tied to Florida tourism. Gaining their support would ensure the park's creation.

Miami Herald journalist Nixon Smiley later recounted this meeting between the Pork Chop Gang and Pennekamp. The group met at Smith's hunting camp near Ocala a few weeks before April 8, 1947, the start of the new legislative session. Before a traditional North Florida dinner of chicken and rice, Pennekamp had already elicited from the group a promise of $400,000 for the park. Although this story cannot be verified by other sources, Smiley suggested that a particularly lucky run of cards in an after-dinner poker game led to the appropriation of the full $2 million needed for the park's creation. A 1967 *Herald* article by Smiley was even titled "Poker Game Helped Found Everglades Park." Yet, it was more likely that the Pork Choppers, like Holland and Caldwell, understood the park's tangible and intangible economic values. Flush with cash at the end of World War II, they made a practical decision to support the park's creation.[88]

The 1947 session of the Florida legislature opened on April 8. On April 16, the Senate unanimously voted to appropriate $2 million for the acquisition of private lands in the Everglades. The bill passed the House by an 83–6 margin the next day. On April 24, Governor Caldwell signed the bill into law.[89] In an astonishing turn of events, Florida's state government quickly and without debate appropriated these funds and essentially created the park. Buoyed by a vibrant economy, lawmakers invested in future growth through the ENP's creation.

In anticipation of this appropriation, Holland, Caldwell, and Pennekamp opened negotiations with the NPS on the exact terms for the park's creation. The NPS had already reiterated that the boundaries of the ENWR agreed on in 1944 would remain the park's minimum boundaries.[90] By April 1947, the parties agreed on additional terms. First, the state would deliver $2 million to the NPS, which would be used to acquire all privately owned lands within the park's minimum boundaries. The second point related the state's mineral rights on lands formerly owned by the state in the ENWR. The state had retained those rights when it deeded those lands to the federal government in 1944, and it now agreed it to deliver them to the NPS. If active leases were present on those lands a seventy-two-square-mile area had active leases on the "streams"), then the state would cede those mineral rights as the leases expired. The state would receive "customary royalties" on any oil produced on those lands in the future, yet there was essentially no chance the NPS would ever authorize drilling in a national park. Finally, the state would transfer all lands owned by the state board of education in the area to the federal government.[91] The NPS also insisted multiple times in strong language that this park would only be a "park nucleus," which would "be enlarged into the completed park as circumstances permit."[92] Governor Caldwell agreed that these boundaries would not "preclude expansion."[93]

Florida officials moved quickly to comply with this agreement. By June 17, 1947, the NPS received all the paper work on these land transfers and a check for $2 million.[94] On June 20, 1947, Secretary of the Interior Julius Krug officially created Everglades National Park.[95] The boundary of this "nucleus" park encompassed 1,228,488 acres, but only 451,840 of those acres were actually owned by the federal government and included in the park. This temporary boundary would serve as a nucleus for later expansion.[96] The campaign that Ernest Coe had started in 1928 had finally reached its goal. Although it took almost twenty years to create the park, the final push for the park's creation in 1946 and 1947 unfolded remarkably quickly. Due to the enormous economic growth Florida experienced after World War II, and with the promise of even more tourism-fueled growth to come, Millard Caldwell, John Pennekamp, and even Florida's old rural conservative powers quickly mobilized to establish Everglades National Park.

Amid these rapid developments, a group of landowners connected to the oil industry sought to prevent the park's creation. Many of them were profiting from oil leases and land sales in the area and wanted to continue these activities rather than sell their lands to the NPS. They also feared the ENP's inevitable expansion. These landowners were led by the McDougal-Axelsons, a powerful and politically connected landowning and oil family. Joining their cause were other landowners and Florida Attorney General J. Tom Watson. These groups were not organized enough to fight the park's swift creation in 1947, but they later successfully limited the park's expansions in the 1940s and 1950s.

J. Tom Watson took the lead in fighting the park in 1947, but he was mostly ineffective. Watson served as Florida's attorney general and was a member of the IIF Board of Trustees. He supported oil drilling in the region and opposed the park's creation. He hoped these issues would bring him political support and an enhanced profile as he prepared to run for governor in 1948. Watson also personally disliked both Holland and Caldwell. He frequently and futilely opposed their agendas, often by using the office of the attorney general to initiate lawsuits against the state. Watson was disliked by many in the state government and had a reputation for being "irascible" and "belligerent." On one occasion he even physically threatened Holland and challenged him to settle a "dispute outside by more direct means." Holland calmly and professionally ignored this challenge.[97]

On June 13, 1947, Watson refused to sign the deeds handing the state's school lands and mineral rights over to federal government.[98] He wrote that he was "unalterably opposed to the giving of mineral rights to the government."[99] A week later, he prepared a forty-page legal document attacking the park's legality and filed an injunction to halt the state's delivery of these deeds to the federal government.[100] This injunction request was rejected, but Watson quickly appealed to the Florida Supreme Court.[101] On December 16, 1947, the court soundly rejected Watson's suit. Watson argued that the state's appropriation constituted a gift to the federal government from the people of Florida and was thus unconstitutional. The court rejected this logic, noting that "the power of the legislature to appropriate public funds to establish public parks is not open to question" and that it was not the court's job to rule on the "legislative wisdom in creating the park."[102]

Pennekamp took the lead in attacking Watson and his allies in the *Miami Herald*'s editorial pages and in public speeches before Florida groups. On June 19, 1947, Pennekamp wrote that the "only opposition to the park has come from speculators in oil leases. The history of such speculation in the Everglades is a scandalous story of the mulcting of widows and other innocents."[103] Pennekamp flayed Watson and other landowners again in an October 1947 in a speech before the Miami Civilian Club. The *Miami Herald* reported that Pennekamp "denounced 'land pirates' and 'oil lease speculators' who ... sought to profit from the park." For the next decade, Pennekamp used similar rhetoric to defend the park against this faction of landowners.[104]

Watson failed to delay the park or win the Democratic nomination for governor in 1948 and soon faded from Florida politics. Yet before his retreat, Watson, using his campaign's letterhead, lashed out at Pennekamp on May 6, 1948. According to Watson, Pennekamp was the "kind of human cur whose yaps are so caninish as to attract little attention from me, other than because of the noise being made." Watson threatened that "if I ever meet you face to face, where I can do so without giving offense to my surroundings, I intend to try to spit in your face, as this is the only gesture which I can think of that would express my personal feelings toward you." Pennekamp framed this letter and hung it in his office.[105]

Although the ENP was created on June 20, 1947, the park dedication was wisely delayed until the winter. On December 6, 1947, President Harry Truman officially dedicated the park. John Pennekamp, Millard Caldwell, Spessard Holland, and other important figures spoke as well. Ernest Coe, still upset at reductions to the park's boundary, reluctantly attended at the last minute and did not speak.[106] Most of these speeches revolved around the Everglades' anthropocentric benefits, yet Coe's biocentric vision for preservation remained central to the new park. In 1936, at the first meeting of the ENPC, Coe explained that this park would be protected "as a nature sanctuary and breeding ground. It is even against the law to swat a mosquito."[107] In 1947, the new park was immediately the target of criticism involving mosquitos. To control mosquito activity at the park's dedication, the NPS sprayed DDT at the dedication site. Concerned citizens protested NPS use of this chemical, fifteen years before Rachel Carson alerted the general public to the dangers of DDT and other chemical pesticides.

Herman Shuptrine, a Tampa conservationist, complained to Millard Caldwell that the spraying of DDT was "a slap in the face of every conservationist ... in the State of Florida." Shuptrine thought DDT was "hazardous to wild life" and was outraged that this chemical was used in "a place set apart for the protection of our wild life."[108] Herbert Mills, another Tampa conservationist and a noted clinical pathologist, also protested. He claimed that the spraying of DDT was "contrary to the principles of conservation" and noted the negative medical effects of even small amounts of this chemical. Reflecting the park's biocentric rationales, Mills wrote that "insects are just as much an integral part of our wildlife pattern as any other form of life."[109] Daniel Beard, the new park's superintendent, wrote to Shuptrine to set the record straight. DDT had been sprayed only in Everglades City at the airport where a fish fry for the park's dedication was held. It had not actually been used in the park, and Beard pledged that he would do "everything possible to conserve and restore the wildlife of this new national park."[110] Even at this early date, the park was already serving the purposes Ernest Coe intended: the ENP would not only protect the Everglades and its biota, it would further encourage Americans to appreciate and respect the inherent value of all life. This monument to biology could inspire future generations to embrace ecological values.

CHAPTER 7

Finalizing the Park's Boundaries

Everglades National Park in 1947 was only a nucleus park: its incomplete boundaries were intended to serve as a basis for further expansion. It was also a hollow park: the NPS did not own title to all the lands within its boundaries. After 1947, park advocates, Florida politicians, and the NPS sought to address both issues. Just as the park's creation was shaped by the concerns of an embryonic modern environmentalism, the park's expansion was opposed by individuals espousing ideas that would become core components of modern conservativism. A group of landowners who were profiting from oil leases and land sales fought park land acquisition and expansion efforts. They successfully limited park expansion by arguing that the federal government was violating their property rights and curtailing their personal economic freedom. Their focus on property rights and their belief in limited government places these landowners at the center of modern conservative thinking. These conservative ideas won them support and allies and even convinced park advocates, like Spessard Holland, to accommodate their demands.

Efforts to limit park expansion played out between 1947 and 1958 in three phases. The first occurred between 1947 and 1949 as the NPS sought to acquire lands within the 1947 boundaries. Landowners opposed these efforts and in 1949 received protection for their mineral rights on park lands until 1958. Between 1950 and 1954, landowners opposed NPS efforts to expand the park's boundaries. By 1954, they successfully convinced Florida's interim governor Charley Johns and a significant portion of the state's legislature to block the park's expansion. In 1955, Johns was replaced by LeRoy Collins, who worked with the NPS to finalize the ENP boundary between 1955 and 1958. Landowners again influenced this process. They were able to win significant reductions in the park's final boundaries and retained their mineral rights on park lands until 1967. The park's final 1958 boundaries represented significant reductions to the park's 1934 maximum boundaries and included substantial mineral rights inholdings.

&

The park's opponents after 1947 were led by the McDougal-Axelson family, powerful and politically active landowners. They had deep ties to oil companies, real estate investors, and politicians in Florida and Oklahoma, and successfully mobilized these groups to fight the park's expansion. The family owned a controlling stake in the Chevelier land company, one-sixth of the Chatham Bend land company, and large sections of land on Cape Sable. Chevelier was the second-largest land company in the Everglades after the MLC and owned land in the northwest Everglades. The company had been founded by James Jaudon in 1917 and played a role in the construction of the Tamiami Trail. After the bust of the Florida land boom, the company was deeply in debt and financially troubled. D. A. McDougal bought into the company in 1917 and took advantage of its depressed financial situation to consolidate his ownership stake and gain control over the company. McDougal became the company president in 1929.[1]

Daniel A. McDougal, who went by "D.A.," was the respected patriarch of the family. D.A. was a lawyer and judge who had been involved in Democratic Party politics in Oklahoma and was heavily involved in real estate and oil drilling in the state. In 1908 oil was found on his lands and he became a millionaire overnight. McDougal served in the Oklahoma House of Representatives as a Democrat for one term, and even after his move to Florida he maintained his relationships with Oklahoma politicians like U.S. senator Bob Kerr. Although he played a large role in fighting the park, his wife, Myrtle McDougal, had the more notable political career. Myrtle was a Democrat and a leader in Progressive reform politics in Oklahoma. She "founded or headed over forty organizations" in the state, spearheaded the creation of the state's women's clubs, was a leading Oklahoma suffragist, and held multiple positions in the Oklahoma Democratic Party in the early 1920s. The McDougals spent most of their lives in Oklahoma, and both were native southerners; D.A. was from Tennessee, Myrtle was born in Mississippi, and both had lived in Savannah, Georgia. Beginning in the 1910s, they heavily invested in Florida real estate and often wintered in Miami. In 1940 the couple retired to Miami.[2] McDougal and his wife thought of themselves as southern elites who had a responsibly and a natural inclination toward leadership. In the frontier state of Oklahoma, they saw themselves as pioneers who, through their economic, political, and social activities, created a White society. In Oklahoma, Myrtle sought to bring order to the territory through social reform; D.A. sought to convert wilderness into marketable commodities. After their successes on the Oklahoma frontier, the family turned their attention to the Everglades, an area they saw as another frontier ripe for exploitation.

The family inculcated their three daughters with their entrepreneurial zeal, frontier spirt, sense of social responsibility, and political activism. Their household also placed a large emphasis on literature and the arts. Mary McDougal, who like her mother was involved in the Democratic Party, was the most notable daughter and the one most involved in the family's economic affairs. Mary left Oklahoma in the 1910s and moved to Greenwich Village, where she garnered a reputation as a writer and activist. Mary incorporated her Oklahoma frontier upbringing into her new Greenwich Village lifestyle and gained some measure of notoriety in the bohemian community. According to her biographer Marilyn Hoder-Salmon, Mary carried a pistol, made repairs to her automobile, and "earned a reputation for the fiery speaking technique and reform zeal acquired by campaigning in Oklahoma's wild oil-districts for prohibition." Mary was also a successful novelist, playwright, and poet. Her most notable work was the novel and play *Life Begins*, the basis of the "forgotten American film classic" of the same title. Mary wrote dozens of books, including a book of poetry with her sister Violet McDougal, who was Oklahoma's first poet laureate.[3]

Mary's literary career, as well as her family's booming finances, gave her an economic independence that matched her personal independence. She refused to marry until age thirty-three, when she met Ivar Axelson, an aspiring economist who was selling Everglades lands in Miami. The two had a child in 1928, when Mary was thirty-seven. Her childbirth experiences became the basis of *Life Begins*. After they married, Ivar joined D.A. as a principal investor in the Chevelier land company. Their financial independence allowed them to travel extensively. During the 1920s, 1930s, and 1940s, they lived in New York, Washington, D.C., Los Angeles, Oklahoma, and Miami. Axelson was an instructor for a period of time at the University of Oklahoma and worked in Washington at the U.S. Treasury Department's Division of Monetary Research. He eventually received his PhD in economics from Yale in 1944 and later was a lecturer at the University of Miami.[4]

Throughout the 1930s, 1940s, and 1950s, the family applied their independence and rebellious, their experiences in political activism and political service, and their ability to write and communicate, to their fight against Everglades National Park. Just as they had sought to build a White society in the state of Oklahoma, the family sought to incorporate the Everglades into the nation's political, social, and economic mainstream. In their fights with the NPS, they cast themselves as players in a struggle for economic and political freedom. They were the underdogs and protagonists of a drama that unfolded in this wetland wilderness. The federal government was a powerful antagonist who sought to thwart their efforts to tame and transform this wilderness.

The family believed the Chevelier tract to be "the richest land in the world, covered with wonderful timber and underlaid with millions of dollars worth of the most valuable minerals." They sought to drill for oil and planned housing developments in the Everglades. Mary recalled sitting on the floor of her parent's living room with her sister Violet platting out the town of Pinecrest. D.A. "wanted the business district built around a square like the little Southern towns that he loved" complete with "a tree-shaded square and a statue of a Confederate soldier dominat[ing] it all." Mary on the other hand wanted the city to be "modern and efficient." Although in the 1920s a few buildings were constructed, the town soon "reverted back to wilderness" after the bust of the land boom. Like most Everglades landowners, the family supported the park's creation in the 1930s during the depths of the Great Depression. They changed their tune as the economy recovered during World War II. The war not only boosted Florida's real estate market, it also created demand for new domestic oil sources. Despite little evidence that oil existed in the region, landowners with connections to the oil industry, among them William Blanchard, Effie Knowles, and the McDougal-Axelsons, sought to drill for oil in the Everglades, which they saw as virgin territory ripe for exploratory drilling. Not a single well had been drilled in the state before 1926. By 1938 seventy wells had been drilled in Florida, but only forty-five of them reached below a thousand feet, and none of them struck oil. Landowners argued that further drilling would surely be successful. Oil drilling, like Florida's tourism industry, was subsidized by the government. In 1941, Florida offered a $50,000 bounty for a successful oil strike. This award set off a speculative boom in oil leases and increased sales of Everglades lands.[5]

The McDougal-Axelsons employed a number of creative strategies to profit from exploratory oil drilling in the Everglades. Notably, none of them depended on oil being found but guaranteed the family large profits in the event of an oil strike. The foundation of all these strategies were the leases made to oil companies who drilled in the Everglades. In the 1920s and 1930s, the family actually gave free leases to oil companies on the condition that they drilled wells on these lands. These leases and wells led to additional oil leases and future drilling. Reminiscing in 1961, Mary McDougal Axelson wrote that "it is needless for me to tell you how much money the Chevelier owners have taken in since that time [1949] in oil rentals and sales."[6]

These activities drove up demand for Everglades lands, allowing the family to profit from land sales. These sales were often prompted by news of oil leases, newspaper articles about oil, or the drilling of new wells. Mary wrote to her husband about a flurry of land sales in 1949 that were the result of "the new well in Collier County or the *Miami Life* stories or else rumors about other wells to be drilled." She wrote: "wouldn't it be wonderful if we could pull in some cash! . . . You know *me*—I *always* enjoy selling oil land."[7] Land sales further increased the value of these lands, earning the family even more money. Eventually, when the government acquired these lands, they would have to pay these inflated prices to acquire them. In short, the longer the family delayed the park's creation, the more profit they could extract from oil companies, real estate investors, and the federal government.

Significantly, these land sales were not in fee simple. Rather, the family sold surface lands (which they had long regarded as worthless) and only half of the mineral rights to buyers, while they retained the other half. This gave them half of the revenues from oil leases on the lands they had sold, ensuring them enormous profits if oil was found in the Everglades, even on lands they had sold. Ivar Axelson wrote to prospective buyers in 1950 "offering lands in northern Monroe County near the location of the Forty Mile Bend discovery well to be drilled this year" for between $10 and $35 an acre. All these lands were under lease to various oil companies, and annual rentals were "from 10 to 50 cents" an acre. These lands, like others he sold through the Jones Real Estate Company, only conveyed "50% oil, gas and mineral rights," to buyers, leaving the other 50 percent for the McDougal-Axelsons.[8]

Just as Spessard Holland supported the park for economic reasons, the McDougal-Axelsons were motivated by economics. Holland saw the park as a way to boost long-term, broad economic growth for the entire state. The McDougal-Axelsons saw the park as a threat to their own short-term and immediate profits. Although they opposed the park for personal economic reasons, throughout their campaign against the ENP in the late 1940s and 1950s they crafted a number of arguments designed to sway politicians, business interests, and the general public in Florida. They argued that oil drilling would bring untold economic benefits to the state of Florida. They connected drilling to national security during World War II and the Cold War. In the 1950s, they argued that Everglades land should be excluded from the park and used for expanding urban development and agriculture in South Florida. They also attacked the Everglades itself. They argued that this worthless swamp was unworthy of national park status and would never be a successful tourist attraction.

None of these arguments resonated with Florida's business and political elites, and none succeeded in altering the politics of the ENP's creation and expansion. The state had already bought into the prospects of Everglades tourism, and oil was never discovered in profitable quantities in the Everglades. Oil supporters could only ever point to the potential that oil might be found at some indeterminate future date. In contrast, tourism was a sure bet. Before a U.S. House committee in 1947, Ivar Axelson argued that "the large expenditures of oil companies in this area is sufficient evidence that the area has large oil potentialities." Eight years later in 1954, Axelson could still only claim that Everglades lands "are considered very favorably as to oil possibilities and for the most part are now under lease to major oil companies."[9]

Landowners only successfully impacted the politics of the park's creation when they presented themselves as citizens whose property rights were being violated by the federal government. These arguments resonated with Spessard Holland, Millard Caldwell, and the rest of Florida's political community. This focus on property rights was central to the liberal Enlightenment tradition of U.S. intellectual thought and soon became central to modern conservative ideas about economics, rights, and the role of the government. These ideas were particularly important to conservatives who opposed the civil rights movement and became central to the New Right's takeover of the Republican Party.

Western conservatives in the same time period were, in contrast, slow to adopt these new rights-based arguments. As a consequence, they had little success in wresting control over natural resources from the federal government. In the 1940s and early 1950s, western mining and ranching interests sought to gain more power over the vast federal holdings in the West. These interests were allied with western Republican legislators who, between 1945 and 1947, held hearings and introduced fifty-eight separate pieces of legislation addressing federal lands in the West. Some of the more radical bills would deliver the federal lands directly to the states, which could then either more loosely regulate them or divest them to private interests. These ranchers profited enormously from grazing on federal lands but attacked the federal government as "a bunch of Communist-minded bureaucrats." Conservationists opposed these efforts, which they labeled the Western Land Grab. Historian and essayist Bernard DeVoto, who wrote for *Harpers*, led the charge and was joined by other magazine writers, among them Wallace Stegner, and by the leadership of the Izaak Walton League. They painted the land grab as an extreme and radical effort by economic interests to loot the federal government and the public trust. This first land grab quickly failed on being exposed by DeVoto.[10]

A second phase of the Western Land Grab occurred between 1951 and 1954. According to DeVoto, previous efforts "were too crude." This time, ranchers "hired some brains to brush a little suavity and finesse over the steal." They now proposed delivering control over USFS lands to ranching associations and giving lessees additional privileges over federal lands. This second effort gained steam after the 1952 election when Republicans gained control of the presidency, House, and Senate for the first time since the 1920s. The Republican Party platform in 1952 included a plank on public lands that firmly allied the party with these conservative western interests. Everglades landowners likewise allied themselves with Republicans in 1952 and touted the party's plank on public lands. The plank, which was written by Senators Eugene Millikin of Colorado and Richard Nixon of California promoted "legislation to define the rights and privileges of grazer and other cooperators and users." DeVoto and his allies again attacked this effort, and the second land grab failed like the first. In 1954, the strongest land grab advocates lost their reelection campaigns, while those who opposed these bills, including ENP supporter Gracie Pfost, won handily. DeVoto celebrated the 1954 election as a "complete a repudiation of the Administration's resources policy."[11]

These western conservatives failed to create arguments that resonated with the general public, were connected to basic American principles, or were grounded in positive language. In contrast, the McDougal-Axelsons connected their fight against the ENP to their traditional ideas about property rights and achieved success. Although like western land interests they assailed any government interference in the economy as the work of "Communistic New Dealers," the rhetoric of Everglades landowners had more in common with that of anti–civil rights activists in the Sunbelt suburban South. As Joseph Crespino, Matthew Lassiter, Kevin Kruse, and other historians have shown, anti–civil rights activists argued that their property rights and individual freedoms were being violated by an aggressive federal government that was inappropriately intervening in local and state affairs. Kruse argued that Georgians taking part in White flight from urban Atlanta "stressed individual rights over communal responsibilities, privatization over public welfare, and 'free enterprise' above everything else."[12]

Everglades landowners used similar rhetoric, but instead of fighting civil rights legislation their movement was a backlash to the rise of the environmental regulatory state.[13] These Everglades landowners believed they had a right to exploit nature and believed that, in the words of historian Donald Worster, the government "should permit and encourage this continual increase of personal wealth.[14] To landowners, the ENP was an example of an increasingly common and troubling dynamic: the government was acting to protect the broader public good at the expense of their own private enterprise.

Western economic interests saw their relationship with nature in the same way but were slow to embrace the populism and rights-based ideology of modern conservatives. Eventually they found common ground with modern conservatives and anti–civil rights activists, all of whom opposed increased federal intervention in private affairs and sought to roll back the power of the federal government. Between 1978 and 1981, these western conservatives waged the Sagebrush Rebellion, a third Western Land Grab that utilized states'-rights rhetoric. According to historian James Morton Turner, the states'-rights arguments of these groups, and the fact that they were openly funded and supported by corporate interests, made them easy targets. Like their predecessors in the 1940s and 1950s, they were "dismissed as proponents of special interests."[15]

These activists regrouped in the 1980s and 1990s and embraced the rhetoric of modern conservatism. A fourth Western Land Grab, now labeled the wise use movement, presented itself as a grassroots campaign concerned with the property rights of individual citizens. These activists adopted the rhetoric of modern conservatism and altered the Republican Party's approach toward environmental issues.[16] Enlightenment ideas about property rights were used to bolster private interests and profits. By connecting their own economic and social causes to these fundamental American ideas, modern conservatives influenced popular opinion. Business conservatives followed this trend and have likewise used ideas about property rights and personal freedom to bolster their economic and political power.

Although Everglades landowners positioned their protection of property as a traditional American value, the way they defined their property was actually a recent invention. Property owners were willing to part with their surface rights, which they had long seen as worthless, but demanded retaining their mineral rights. The separation of mineral and surface rights can be traced to the creation of broad-form deeds used by coal companies in Appalachia in 1890s. The federal government used a similar mechanism to separate subsurface rights from surface rights in the Stock-Raising Homestead Act of 1916, which created 640-acre homesteads exclusively intended for grazing. The invention of split-estate ownership in both these instances facilitated industrialization and the conversion of nature into commodities.[17]

This practice had particular utility for landowners in the Everglades as they confronted the wetland nature of their lands. The failure of drainage meant that these lands remained wet. This essential wetness prevented landowners from converting these swamps and marshes into private property. They had failed to incorporate the region into a capitalist system and reluctantly conceded that these lands had no value and would return to public ownership through the park's creation. Wetlands have always been problematic and contradictory in Western society. As Ann Vilesis has noted, in the United States, "land has been considered as private property and water as public property," yet because wetlands are both land and water, they have often existed in a sort of economic and legal limbo. Split-estate deeds were a novel way to extract value from wetlands. Split-estate deeds enabled these landowners to salvage some value from the disaster of the Florida land boom and the failure of Everglades drainage. They could retain the ownership of any minerals beneath their lands, while giving up the rights to the surface of their lands, which after all was covered in water for most of the year anyway. The region's sawgrass prairies, its wide sloughs, and its mazy mangrove forests would be protected by the park, while the rights to minerals beneath those lands could be bought and sold as a commodity. The wetland nature of the Everglades thus forced landowners to redefine the very concept of property to make it fit into this contradictory landscape.[18]

The weakness of the environmental regulatory state in the Everglades also impacted landowner's efforts. The ENP in 1947 was a hollow park—the NPS did not own title to all the lands within its boundaries—with incomplete boundaries. To solidify the government's sovereignty over the region, the NPS made land acquisition its immediate priority. The federal government did not unilaterally create a park but rather exercised weak and incomplete control over the park's expansion and land acquisition efforts. Using state monies, the NPS acquired the privately owned lands in this small nucleus park. Then, in negotiations with Florida, it expanded the park's boundaries. This fragmented process gave private citizens and the state government opportunities to influence the park's final shape.

Immediately after the park's creation on June 20, 1947, the NPS established a land acquisition office that used the state's $2 million appropriation to acquire the privately owned lands within the park's 1947 boundaries.[19] This process was entirely novel within the NPS. Older western parks had been carved out of federal holdings, while lands in newer eastern parks had been acquired by state governments or private organizations. Land acquisition in the Everglades, though, would be a herculean task. The Everglades' wetness complicated landownership in the region. The NPS land acquisition team faced a dizzying array of complex problems. Because the area was so wet and hostile, surveying the Everglades had been a practical impossibility. Much of the land bought and sold during the land boom had never been surveyed and lacked clear titles. Additionally, much of it had back taxes owed on it and sometimes a parcel was claimed by more than one individual. Park advocates and state officials noted that the federal government had more resources and expertise than the state in this matter and therefore delivered the state's funds to the federal government, which then oversaw the land acquisition process.

The first major acquisition involved the MLC lands. Spessard Holland had long argued that these lands, which were the largest single privately owned bloc in the region, were the key to the park's creation. Indeed, this purchase would set important precedents for subsequent land purchases by establishing the value and status of mineral rights. These negotiations illustrate the complexity of Everglades landownership and the land acquisition process. They also shed light on the attitudes and goals of landowners and the NPS. While landowners typically overvalued their land and sought to be paid for improvements they had made to those lands, the NPS sought to pay landowners lower prices in order to efficiently use the public's $2 million appropriation. In truth, most of these lands had little value, since they were, after all, covered in water.

In September 1948, Vice President Carl Hawkins of the MLC, the NPS assistant chief counsel Donald Lee, and other members of the NPS land acquisition office opened negotiations on the sale of the MLC lands. The company had divided its lands into three parcels, and began with the sale of "Unit No. 1." This section of land consisted of 127,710 acres of land in and around Whitewater Bay and Cape

Sable and included some lands along the Ingraham Highway near Bear, West, and Cuthbert Lakes. A large portion of this unit consisted of sovereignty lands. Sovereignty lands lie below the mean high water line and are owned by the state by virtue of its sovereignty. The MLC argued that these lands had been included in land grants given to Henry Flagler as subsidies for the construction of his railroad line, but their status was disputed. Complicating this matter further was the fact that these lands, like most of the Everglades, had never been surveyed. The MLC took the position that 41,257 acres in this unit were sovereignty lands, while the NPS argued that 61,068 acres qualified for that designation.[20]

Another disagreement revolved around hiatus lands. This area had not been surveyed, but surveyors had run meander lines, which conformed to shorelines and were used to define township and section lines. Hiatus lands existed in between township and section lines on adjacent properties and were the result of errors in the meander lines. Florida's meander lines were notoriously inaccurate. NPS surveyors found 24,960 acres of hiatus lands in unit 1, in addition to the 127,710 acres of land the MLC clearly owned. The ownership of these hiatus lands was disputed, and a court would need to determine ownership of both the sovereignty and hiatus lands. Instead, both parties compromised and agreed to include all these lands in this sale. As NPS director Newton Drury noted, this meant that "two very vexatious lawsuits will be avoided." Similar problems arising from hiatus and sovereignty lands were commonly faced by the NPS land acquisition office.[21]

Hawkins opened negotiations by stating that he valued these lands in unit 1 at $407,000 but would reduce his asking price to $259,000. This price was far above what NPS land appraisers had valued the land, but Donald Lee soon discovered that much of Hawkins's attitude was due to his belief that a 15,668-acre section of Flamingo lands was suitable for farming and worth at least $10 per acre. Lee and the NPS believed this land was worthless for farming and had found that section of land underwater during the wet season. Throughout the land acquisition process, landowners commonly held misconceptions concerning the condition and value of their Everglades lands. Rather than debating these values, Lee suggested eliminating this parcel from this sale. After smoothing out the parcel's irregular boundaries, Lee and Hawkins eliminated 17,790 acres of land from unit 1, leaving 109,920 acres of land, plus an additional 24,960 acres of hiatus lands under consideration. Hawkins quickly agreed to sell those 134,880 acres to the NPS for $115,000.[22]

The status of the mineral rights beneath these lands was another complication. These lands were all currently under lease to oil companies. The MLC owned half the mineral rights, while the state of Florida retained the other half. Hawkins and Lee allowed the MLC to retain these mineral rights until January 31, 1956, when these oil leases ran out, or as long as oil was being produced on these lands in commercial quantities. Audubon president John Baker criticized this portion of the deal, writing to NPS director Newton Drury that it was "a complete contradiction of a National Park Service policy principle." He feared this sale would set a dangerous precedent in national parks whereby landowners would retain mineral rights. Baker also thought this would mean that the NPS would "not in good conscience deny to other land owners the retention of oil rights."[23]

Drury agreed that "the situation" concerning mineral rights inholdings was "not an ideal one" but also argued that this land purchase was "a good deal" and the best solution available. Drury believed that "the real redeeming feature of our contract with the Model Land Company is the relatively short period of time which the reservation of the Model Land Company has to run . . . and the very low price we have had to pay per acre for the partial rights." Drury correctly believed that oil would not be found in that short period. Furthermore, Drury understood that this deal would set the terms for subsequent land purchases and oil reservations. As Hawkins correctly noted, landowners were sure to criticize this sale, as "landowners have had a far higher estimate of the value of their lands than the figures which we have agreed to accept."[24]

In early 1949, the NPS and the MLC met to discuss the rest of the MLC's lands in the park's 1947 boundaries. These included 73,000 acres of land the MLC labeled units 2 and 3, as well as marl prairie lands that had been excluded from the previous sale.[25] Although Hawkins had given up on the idea that the marl prairies were valuable for agriculture, he insisted that the presence of the Ingraham Highway, which ran through units 2 and 3, made these lands valuable. Hawkins later complained that the MLC had spent $200,000 paving that road and got nothing for it from the NPS. The company had also spent $130,000 digging drainage canals and had paid $200,000 in taxes, meaning they invested at least $530,000 in these lands. In fact, the road was badly in need of repair and was underwater most of the year. One of the NPS's first actions in the park was to reconstruct this road, a project that cost almost $3 million and was completed in 1957. These drainage canals, like other improvements landowners had made, made these lands less valuable to the NPS. Throughout the land acquisition process, landowners often sought to be compensated for such failed efforts to develop Everglades lands.[26]

Ultimately, Hawkins compromised and agreed to sell the 73,000 acres of MLC land remaining in the 1947 boundaries for $180,000. As with the previous sale, the MLC would continue to own its mineral rights until either 1956 or 1958, depending on the length of oil leases on those lands, or as long as oil was produced in commercial quantities. At the end of these negotiations, Hawkins felt that he had done the NPS a great favor by compromising. He noted that, with those two land sales complete, the NPS would own "about fifty percent of all privately-owned lands" in the park's 1947 boundaries. Additionally, "the work of further and future acquisition on the part of the National Park Service will be made much easier."[27] This agreement between the MLC and the NPS set important precedents for land acquisition in the Everglades and indeed facilitated the land acquisition process.

Before land acquisition could proceed, the NPS sought to gain federal authority to condemn lands and acquire property by eminent domain. Although some park advocates, like John Pennekamp, believed the NPS already had this power, the agency noted that, because it was using state funds and because of the complicated nature of the oil situation, it would be wise to err on the side of caution. The McDougal-Axelsons were, in turn, able to use this situation to influence the park's creation. In 1947 they saddled the bill with amendments that would limit the park's expansion and protect the mineral rights of landowners. This bill was quickly pulled, but in 1948 a similar situation developed. According to U.S. Representative J. Hardin Peterson of Florida, landowners had lobbied the House Committee on Public Lands and would likely be able to secure a five-year reservation for mineral rights on park lands. Peterson and Pennekamp let this version of the bill die in committee and sought to reintroduce it next year. Peterson believed that "unless oil is discovered this summer it will be much easier next year," while Pennekamp thought it best to "await the composition of the new Congress."[28]

By 1949 though, the terms of the MLC's land sales altered the political calculus surrounding mineral rights in the park. Rather than a five-year reservation that would expire in 1954, the MLC secured the mineral rights until 1958. This sale set a precedent for subsequent land sales that the DOI felt obliged to respect. Secretary Krug informed Peterson that the NPS intended "to treat all owners on substantially the same basis if they so desire." The McDougal-Axelsons were also aware of the implications of the MLC sale. The two parties had been working together since the early 1930s, and after the 1949 sales Hawkins wrote to Ivar Axelson, explaining that the terms of this sale "have established a precedent" that other landowners would be able to use.[29]

Indeed, the McDougal-Axelsons used this precedent to alter the 1949 park bill. Since the park's creation, they had been fighting to protect their mineral rights using a variety of tactics, many of which foreshadowed future arguments in favor of oil drilling but failed to impact the ENP's creation in the 1940s and 1950s. For example, the family tried to connect oil drilling to national security concerns. In 1947 Ivar Axelson noted that oil rights needed to be protected "more than ever before" due to the "possibility of war with Russia." Testifying before a Senate committee in 1949, D. A. McDougal promoted Everglades oil as a way to "fuel our battleships and planes to defend our country against foreign attack in case of war." At the same hearing, Axelson argued that "the national oil shortage and the danger of war with Soviet Russia require that every effort be made to produce any oil that many underlie this park and not to prevent its production."[30]

When landowners focused on their property rights, they gained political support in both houses of Congress, even from ENP supporters like Florida Senators Spessard Holland and George Smathers. The family and allied landowners, including Arthur Klipstein and Effie Knowles, testified at House and Senate hearings concerning the "effort to prevent the condemnation of mineral rights of private owners within the Park area." As D. A. McDougal explained to a Senate committee, action needed to be taken because "the property rights of the individual citizen are involved."[31]

The McDougal-Axelsons recruited small landowners to their cause and sought to present their case as one that affected a large number of ordinary citizens. In 1947, the family created an organization called the Everglades National Park Landowners Association. This group's stated purpose was to secure "the reservation of oil, gas and mineral rights . . . for a period of at least 25 years and as long thereafter as oil, gas and minerals are produced." Smaller landowners joined this organization and often used formulaic letters to communicate with legislators. Gloria Laswell, a widow who owned 220 acres of land, protested "the taking of my land and mineral and oil rights away from me." Laswell asked her representative "why cannot the mineral and oil rights be retained by their *rightful* owners? At least— permit us to retain these rights for a period of 25 years or while gas and oil are produced." Another small landowner, Ralph Folwell, wrote a similar letter, asking for "a reservation of mineral rights for 25 years and as long thereafter as oil and gas is produced." Folwell added that these twenty-five years were actually too short a period because the Everglades "is a vast and virgin territory" and would require "deep drilling."[32]

Park allies countered these arguments and attended hearings, lobbied legislators, and wrote their own letters. John Pennekamp in particular vocally attacked these landowners throughout the 1940s and 1950s, often from the editorial pages of the *Miami Herald*. Pennekamp stressed to his readers that no oil existed in the Everglades. Although 185 wells had been drilled in Florida since 1901, only one had struck oil, producing only small amounts of inferior crude. Yet dishonest landowners were using these wells "to create an artificially high value for the land." Pennekamp cast the McDougal-Axelsons and their allies as "highly organized, volatile, self-seeking individuals" who were using "devious lobbying tactics to frustrate the will of the people." Pennekamp even dismissed landowners' rights-based arguments as dishonest. He wrote they were just "using oil rights as a smokescreen to conceal other purposes, all of them designed to chisel as much as possible for themselves from what remains of the State's $2,000,000."[33]

Despite Pennekamp's efforts, landowners were successful in 1949. The DOI and Spessard Holland both supported giving all landowners the same deal the MLC had received. Holland, in particular, who was after all a political conservative, was swayed by landowners' arguments concerning their rights. He explained to D. A. McDougal that "I fully agree with you that the property rights of individual citizens are more sacred than the policy of the Department of the Interior in national park matters." Holland proposed a compromise to "preserve the rights of land owners permanently," and thought that "it should be possible to arrive at a reasonable adjustment of the mineral reservation problem." He ensured that the 1949 park bill gave all landowners exactly what the MLC received in 1948: mineral rights for landowners until 1958, or as long as minerals were being produced in commercial quantities. This 1949 law also gave the DOI the authority to use the money appropriated by Florida to acquire lands via eminent domain. According to Interior Secretary Julius Krug, land acquisition in the park would be "speeded up measurably" due to this legislation.[34]

Armed with the clear legal authority to acquire Everglades lands, and with the oil question at least temporarily solved, the NPS began acquiring land in the park's 1947 boundaries. Those boundaries encompassed 1,228,488 acres of land. Florida had already deeded 865,410 acres of its lands to the federal government. The 4,000-acre Royal Palm State Park, which was owned by the Florida Federation of Women's Clubs, was deeded to the NPS on October 29, 1948. The remaining 359,078 acres were privately owned. The MLC's tract comprised 207,880 acres, meaning that the NPS had to acquire an additional 151,198 acres of private lands in the 1947 boundary area.[35]

By September 1950, the NPS had purchased 26,685 of those acres; 124,513 remained in private hands. Five entities owned about 75 percent of this remaining acreage. The largest tract was owned by the Palgrave company, which was owned by Arthur Klipstein, a vocal proponent of oil drilling in the Everglades. In 1950, the NPS began condemnation proceedings on lands belonging to about 165 private individuals or companies, including D. A. McDougal, Ivar Axelson, and Klipstein. All the condemnation lawsuits were combined into one case, which was then tried in five geographical groups. These cases were all completed by the end of 1952. By April 1953, the NPS had acquired all the lands within the 1947 boundary area.[36]

The ENP's second phase of expansion and land acquisition occurred between 1950 and 1954 as the NPS sought to expand the park's boundaries in three areas. These included a northwestern expansion that included parts of the Ten Thousand Islands and connected the park to Everglades City; a northeastern expansion that included sawgrass prairies and freshwater sloughs and would help secure waterflow into the park; and what was referred to as the Hole in the Doughnut, an area in the southeastern section of the Glades that was being used for agriculture and was mostly surrounded by park lands. All were contentious to varying degrees. Although the NPS had insisted that the park would expand beyond its 1947 boundaries, the park's final boundaries had never been agreed on. The McDougal-Axelsons and their allies fought these expansions. They continued to focus on mineral rights but also deepened their criticisms of the government and attacked the park's ecological rationales as an obstacle to Florida's economic growth. The family also gained new allies: agricultural interests opposed the park's expansion into the Hole in the Doughnut, while Monroe County's economic and political elite sought to reduce the park's northwest expansion.

The northwest expansion was prompted by the Collier family, who in February 1948, offered the NPS about 32,000 acres of land near Everglades City. The Collier family supported the park's creation and wanted to connect it to Everglades City, which they hoped would be a center of park tourism. This gift significantly complicated the park's expansion. Because portions of this gift were outside of the park's 1934 maximum boundaries, the DOI did not have the legal authority to accept these lands. Federal legislation would be required to finalize this expansion. The NPS saw this expansion as worth the trouble, mostly because it saw these lands as biologically valuable. This area included sections of the mangrove forests in the Ten Thousand Islands area, as well as a previously controversial tract of land around the Turner River.[37]

Prompted by this donation, the NPS laid out plans for a northwest expansion that included the Collier lands and other state-owned and privately owned lands. Holland, Florida governor Fuller Warren, and the trustees of the Internal Improvement Fund (IIF) endorsed this expansion, as well as a northeast expansion. The IIF, which controlled all state-owned lands, passed a resolution on June 12, 1951, promising to deed all lands in those boundaries to the federal government "without cost." Shortly thereafter, the Collier family deeded 32,000 acres of land to the IIF. The NPS could not actually accept those lands because they were outside the park's 1934 boundaries, so the IIF held those lands for the federal government. Meanwhile, Holland pursued federal legislation to fix these boundaries, while Governor Warren gave the DOI approval to use money from the state's 1947 $2 million appropriation to acquire the lands in the northwest boundary expansion. The largest piece of land needed was the Patten Tract, a 29,873-acre section of land that the NPS acquired for $96,931.25 in 1953. The Patten Tract, the Collier lands, and the state-owned lands compromised three-fourths of the entire northwest expansion. After the purchase of the Patten Tract in 1953, the NPS still had $325,000 left from the $2 million state appropriation, which they sought to use to purchase the additional private lands needed to complete this expansion.[38]

The northwest expansion infuriated the McDougal-Axelsons. The remaining needed lands included those owned by the Chevelier company, in which the McDougal-Axelsons owned a controlling interest. Furthermore, this expansion would jeopardize oil drilling; oil companies were already protesting that the NPS had refused to allow them to drill for oil in the park, despite the fact that private citizens had retained mineral rights on park lands. State officials had their own complaints, noting that the state of Florida had not been given the same protections that private citizens had received for their mineral rights in 1949.

These three issues—the boundary expansion, the inability to drill in the park, and the lack of mineral rights for the state—played out in the IIF between 1950 and 1954. The IIF administered Florida's land holdings and was controlled by the trustees, a body composed of Florida's cabinet members. Florida's cabinet was not appointed by the governor but were rather independently elected positions. The cabinet was hence an independent body composed of individuals with their own political agendas, not appointees committed to the governor's agenda. The governor therefore did not control the cabinet but "was simply one voice among seven."[39]

Oil interests and landowners took advantage of Florida's weak and decentralized executive branch to fight the park's expansion. In 1952 they focused on the state's lack of mineral rights in the park. Although private owners had been allowed to keep their mineral rights, the state of Florida deeded those mineral rights to the NPS in 1947. In 1952, Commonwealth Oil, which was partially owned by J. L. McCord, a close ally of the McDougal-Axelsons, tried to force the NPS to return those mineral rights to the state. McCord convinced the IIF to lease him oil rights on park lands under the stipulation that the lease would only be honored "if and when the Federal Government returns to the Trustees" the state's mineral rights. The IIF complied, but the NPS rejected this lease, noting that it would be "contrary to the agreement" that the IIF entered into "with the Federal Government" when the park was created in 1947.[40] Most of the trustees accepted the NPS assessment; Florida's attorney general concurred, citing the agreements wherein the IIF ceded its mineral rights to the federal government. Yet in August 1952 the trustees voted to award this oil lease to Commonwealth anyway, making it contingent on federal authorization.[41]

This lease was never fulfilled, and instead Commonwealth Oil petitioned the IIF to transfer that lease to another site outside the park in January 1953. The IIF approved this request, and the company began drilling at the forty-mile bend site just outside the park near the Tamiami Trail. This gambit to drill in the park failed, but the McDougal-Axelsons and their allies had made their point: the NPS would not allow drilling in the park. This gave landowners further ammunition against the federal government. As a bonus, Commonwealth Oil opened up a new drilling operation on the ENP's border.[42]

Meanwhile, the McDougal-Axelsons lobbied the state legislature to oppose the NPS's boundary expansions. Ivar Axelson traveled to Tallahassee in June 1953 and prevented the passage of a bill supported by John Pennekamp that endorsed the park's northwest expansion. Axelson convinced the legislature to pass a bill expressly forbidding the park's expansion, even though it violated previous agreements between the state and federal government and was likely unconstitutional. Bernie Papy, a powerful Key West banker, real estate baron, and then a ten-term Florida legislator, led this effort. Papy, the so-called King of the Keys, was allied with the Pork Chop Gang and had enormous influence in the legislature, despite past accusations of bribery and corruption. Papy and other Monroe County interests opposed the park's boundaries in the 1930s and had successfully eliminated Key Largo from the park. Because this northwest expansion included sections of Monroe County, Papy shrewdly labeled it a "local bill." This designation was reserved for bills that applied only to a legislator's district and were almost always passed "as a legislative courtesy." The bill only garnered three nay votes in the Florida House and none in the Florida Senate.[43]

State senator James Franklin from Fort Myers noted an enormous outpouring of support for the Papy bill. Franklin explained to Spessard Holland that he had "received more telegrams and letters in support of the Bill than I have in connection with any other Bill every pending in the legislature." Franklin supported the park's creation and asked Holland for advice about how to handle this delicate situation. Holland informed Franklin that the U.S. Congress would ultimately define the park's boundaries and noted that Governor Dan McCarty opposed the bill. Holland thought it likely to pass and suggested that Franklin could vote for the bill out of loyalty to Papy, and then "Dan could veto it."[44]

This is exactly what happened; Governor McCarty vetoed the bill. According to McCarty's administrative assistant, the bill "was clearly unconstitutional and ... would have nullified an obligation between the Trustees of the Internal Improvement Fund of this State and the United States. It would have brought about a breach of faith of a prior understanding." McCarty, who had been elected in 1952, eagerly supported the park and took a firm stand against oil drilling. Nine months into his term, on September 28, 1953, McCarty died, and state senate president Charley Johns became interim governor. Johns was a powerful member of the Pork Chop Gang and is best remembered as the head of the anti–civil rights and anti–gay rights Florida Legislative Investigation Committee, a red-scare investigatory body commonly known as the Johns Committee. Johns's tenure as governor was marked by discord, charges of corruption and malfeasance, and controversy. Two political opponents he suspended called him "the biggest liar in Florida" and "the worst political despot in the modern history of Florida." Johns vigorously supported oil drilling in the Everglades and allied himself with the McDougal-Axelsons. He had even purchased stock in Everglades oil companies, although on becoming governor he divested himself of those holdings to prevent an obvious conflict of interest.[45]

Johns quickly moved to prevent the park's expansion through the IIF. In a move that would shock park supporters and delight oil interests, on January 19, 1954, the trustees of the IIF rescinded their 1951 resolution that endorsed the park's northwest boundary expansion and revoked their support for those boundaries. The McDougal-Axelsons and their allies placed enormous political pressure on cabinet members to vote against the park's expansion. Fred Elliot, a long-time IIF administrator, reported that the trustees had received "numerous protests . . . in connection with the proposed expansion" of the park. Ivar Axelson later thanked Johns for his support, writing that "the land owners, sportsmen, tax payers, oil and timber developers, agricultural developers, and others whom we represent are most appreciative of the stand you have taken."[46]

Park advocates protested the trustees' actions at the March 22, 1954, IIF meeting. The trustees explained that they revoked this resolution because the federal government had not yet passed legislation fixing the park's boundaries. The NPS and Holland were incredulous. Both complained that they had not even been notified of this issue until after the resolution had been passed. Holland argued that the "State of Florida was not living up to its part of the agreement." Senator George Smathers made similar complaints and noted that, rather than taking brash action, "differences can be worked out by conferences." NPS director Wirth likewise felt that the NPS "should have been consulted before the 1951 resolution had been rescinded," and that "the whole matter could have been ironed out." Nothing concrete came of this meeting, but Johns made his own position clear. He closed this meeting by stating that he was "against any expansion of the Everglades National Park" and that "as long as he is Governor he will do all he can to get these oil rights back in the State and stop expansion of the park boundaries."[47]

The McDougal-Axelsons' already strong political position was bolstered in February 1954 by the second discovery of oil in Florida's history. That month, Commonwealth Oil struck oil at the forty-mile bend site that they had leased from the IIF in January 1953. Just as with the Sunniland field, though, this well produced only small amounts of low-quality oil. During 1954, the well produced an average of just thirty-two barrels of oil a day. Commonwealth drilled a second well two months later at the site, which produced an average of forty barrels a day that year. By September 1955, both wells were abandoned after producing just 32,888 barrels of oil. Despite these meager results, this oil strike, just outside the ENP, caused new excitement and speculation about Everglades oil and temporarily strengthened the position of landowners.[48]

All these events in 1954 gave new energy and purpose to the McDougal-Axelsons, who redoubled their efforts against the park's expansion. Ivar Axelson wrote to a Washington ally in February 1954 that "events have moved very fast here" and cataloged all the positive developments. He noted the IIF's 1954 resolution rescinding its support for larger park boundaries, Governor Johns's position that the ENP "has enough lands and should expand no further," the cabinet's opposition to the park's expansion, the large number of local and state organizations that opposed the park, actions by the Monroe County Commission, and the legislature's passage of the Papy bill.[49]

The McDougal-Axelsons' new energy and confidence was matched by a shift in rhetoric. Beginning in 1954, they drastically escalated their attacks on the federal government. Landowners had gained previous concessions from the federal government by arguing that it was violating their property rights. They extended this logic and now charged federal officials with trampling individual rights, with destroying freedom, and with behaving despotically. Their economic concerns were recast in a militant conservative political rhetoric.

Landowners also shifted their economic rhetoric. Whereas before 1954 they touted an oil industry, they now utilized a broader message of economic growth and attacked the park's ecological rationales. This antigovernment and pro-growth rhetoric foreshadowed the later antienvironmentalism of modern conservatives. Although the McDougal-Axelsons had embraced the reformist zeal of the Progressive Era through the Democratic Party in the South, beginning in the 1950s their opposition to government action pushed them toward the nascent conservative wing of the Republican Party. They increasingly connected the park to conservative attacks on the New Deal as a socialist experiment and to fears that Soviet ideas had infiltrated the U.S. government. They often referenced the metaphor of the iron curtain and argued that the park's creation represented a new iron curtain, or a mangrove curtain, in the Everglades.

In 1954, Mary McDougal Axelson wrote that NPS superintendent Conrad Wirth was "a crook and a liar" and alleged that DOI officials "fought violently against the land owners being permitted to keep their mineral rights." Arthur Klipstein, the president of the Palgrave Company, bitterly complained that "the New Dealers with socialistic ideas who unfortunately still are in command of the NPS . . . have so cleverly engineered the land grab in Southern Florida." Klipstein charged that this land was "confiscated (for that is what it amounted to) by the United States Government under the New Deal."[50]

E. C. Lunsford, an orthodontist who served on the ENPC and owned small portions of land on Cape Sable, made similar criticisms. His vigorous letter-writing crusade against the park reflected a wider conservative backlash against government and a rising fear of communism. Lunsford purchased his Everglades lands in 1945 on the eve of the park's creation and immediately began drawing up plans for "some high-type hotel development." Somehow Lunsford came to believe that, because he had served on the ENPC, the NPS would grant him special privileges to develop the cape as a high-end resort. When the NPS instead acquired his lands via condemnation proceedings, Lunsford attacked the government for violating his rights.[51]

In 1952, Lunsford compared the acquisition of his lands to his experiences working "behind the so-called Iron Curtain" and complained that because of the federal government's actions, his son would "never have the opportunity . . . to work and toil as an individual." Lunsford alleged to Holland that the DOI "absolutely lied to me beyond any shadow of a doubt" regarding the development of the Cape. He argued that the power of the federal government needed to be reduced, spending and taxes needed to be cut, and bureaucrats needed to be fired. In a 1957 statement before a House hearing, Lunsford claimed that his lands now lay behind a "Mangrove Curtain" that the government had erected in the Everglades. He lambasted the DOI for lying about the purposes of the park and urged that an investigation be opened into the park's creation. Lunsford concluded that NPS actions reflected "the lack of respect on the part of some of our Washington officials for the wishes of the people."[52]

This antigovernment rhetoric reached a deafening roar after March 12, 1954, when the DOI issued a secretarial order that enlarged the park boundaries in the northwest section of the park. This unilateral expansion was perfectly legal, as these lands were all in the park's 1934 maximum boundaries, yet it was seen by landowners as arbitrary and unprecedented. On March 15, 1954, sixteen South Florida sportsmen and business organizations protested to Governor Charley Johns and demanded "that he rescind" this order. A few weeks later, on March 27, 1954, Ivar Axelson wrote to Senator Hugh Butler, a Nebraska Republican who served as the chair of the Interior and Insular Affairs Committee. Axelson informed Butler, who was a close ally of the family, that the DOI "continually violated the will of Congress" by preventing oil exploration. Now they seemed bent on subverting the will of the people by expanding the park's boundaries. Axelson argued that "this secretarial order is without parallel, as far as we know, in the history of this country." It was "issued in the most arbitrary fashion without consultation with Florida's state officials" and "without a public hearing." Axelson's onslaught of criticism continued: "The seizure of these lands" was "arbitrary and un-American, and we believe it to be illegal." The DOI's action was "a despotic act and one lacking in common honesty."[53]

As South Florida grew in the 1950s, Axelson and his allies also began to argue that the park was limiting the region's growth, and that park lands were need for farming, ranching, and residential development. These arguments foreshadowed many of the economic arguments of later antienvironmental activists who argued that environmental preservation limited economic growth. Axelson wrote that much of the 271,000 acres added to the park by the 1954 DOI order could be "converted into resort homesites." The area was dominated by coastal mangrove forests, which Axelson called "potentially the most valuable land" in the region. He wanted these forests cleared and the waters of the bays filled so that valuable coastal developments, like those in Miami Beach, could rise out of the mangroves. He also argued these lands could be used for ranching, farming, and timbering. The IIF had leased 16,000 acres of these lands to "Mangrove Products, Inc.," a company that "has spent some $75,000 in experimentation on Mangrove timber." Axelson alleged there were "millions of feet in pine timber" in this area as well. Ironically, Mary McDougal Axelson thought that including these mangrove forests in the park "would shut off the last of South Florida's beautiful inland bays from the living use of her people." Rather than the park opening up the Everglades to tourism, it would in fact "prevent boating, swimming, and resort use" and would result in the "cruel deprivation of the area." She wrote that "God made these bays for all the people!" and that they needed to be kept out of the park so that the public could use them.[54]

An anonymous ally of the McDougal-Axelsons was even more optimistic about future development in the Everglades. Writing to Florida senator George Smathers, this person assailed Park Superintendent Daniel Beard for trying to create a union of "gibbering naturalists and vermin protectors" that would sabotage Florida's 1954 election. Beard had given "false and misleading information" and "should be immediately dismissed and have charges preferred again him for misfeasance in office, and tried." Instead of a national park, this author tried to appeal to Smathers's ego and touted a canal "40 foot wide and 12 miles long, the SMATHERS CANAL." This canal "will dry this country and then there will arise a new city on the shores of the GULF, 'GEORGETOWN' of great tropical beauty."[55]

Although the McDougal-Axelsons had been lifelong Democrats, they increasingly found themselves more at home in the conservative wing of the Republican Party. They cooperated with the Republican Club of Greater Miami and lobbied Eisenhower's Secretary of the Interior Douglas McKay. McKay, whose nickname was "Giveaway" McKay, hailed from the conservative wing of the party and had sought, with a mixed record, to reduce federal landholdings. Axelson met McKay in early 1953 and followed up this meeting with a nine-page letter outlining his attacks on the ENP. Referencing the Republican Party's 1952 platform, which included a plank critical of federal land management, Axelson argued that the park issue involved the question of the "highest use for these lands." While the NPS wanted them kept as "wilderness forever," landowners wanted them "left free to be developed by private enterprise, brought into cultivation and ranching, [and] explored and developed as to oil and other minerals." Rather than worthless lands, Axelson argued that "the threatened land is valuable." Those lands in the park's northwest expansion had "as much potential value as most of Miami Beach had before development reached it."[56]

Buttressing these arguments were landowners' attacks on the Everglades eco-systems. They presented the region as a mosquito-infested wasteland and mocked the NPS's ecological rationales for the park's expansion. These attacks had little impact on the park's boundaries but again foreshadowed the rhetoric of later antien-vironmentalists. These arguments also reflected the McDougal-Axelsons' views of nature. The family subscribed to a capitalist frontier ethos where nature needed to be "improved" by human actions and converted into capital. They believed government and other social institutions existed to facilitate that exploitation, not to protect lands for the broader public or for future generations.[57]

In 1954, Axelson wrote that the park would bring the "unrestricted breeding of mosquitos" and the "unlimited breeding of birds to ravage the farmer's crops." The park protected "rattlesnakes, water moccasins, alligators, and wild boar" and would "endanger the lives of settlers and their children." The McDougal-Axelsons mocked the park's "'ecological'" rationales and argued that park officials were trying to acquire "a vast and valuable gulf front area" in the northwest Everglades "in order to produce 24,000 pounds of frogs and other such foods daily for some wild birds." The family instead wanted "these lands developed, not to produce bird food, but human food, cattle, and farm products." Although Mary McDougal Axelson boasted that she a bird watcher "in heart," she complained that "the Audubon Societies and the Garden Clubs will always be ready to sacrifice everybody's else's rights and property except their own for the alleged benefits of the little birds."[58]

These attacks were in response to NPS ecological and biological justifications for the park's expansions. Daniel Beard, who became park superintendent in 1947, advocated for park boundaries that conformed to the Glades' biological features. George Wright's ideas about biological park boundaries continued to shape the ENP. In January 1948, Beard wrote that "the west coast area... is the most important land acquisition beyond [the] 1944 boundaries." As early as 1949, Beard was already exasperated by the NPS's inability to expand the park northwest and mailed the NPS an egret scalp, "one of several picked up on private lands along the Gulf Coast." Beard explained that "on lands that are still privately owned and being held by oil speculators," there were shacks "used irregularly by fishermen and poachers." The park needed to acquire these lands and protect those bird populations. At a 1953 public meeting held by the McDougal-Axelsons, Beard explained that the park was "really a wilderness wild life preserve [that existed] to maintain representative sections of this area." This northwest expansion contained the nesting sites of "over 60,000 white ibis with lesser numbers of roseate spoonbills, egrets, and herons." Not only was plume hunting still being conducted in the area, but "the alligator population was practically wiped out," in the area, and "every wild orchid we knew of... was stolen last spring."[59]

Beard defended other boundary expansions in biological terms as well. The proposed northeast expansion would protect "the main drainageway" for the park's waterflow. Likewise, Beard explained to Spessard Holland that those agricultural lands in the Hole in the Doughnut were essential because they were "within the Taylor Slough drainage" and were an important source of waterflow through the park. This area also had "importance as a bird feeding ground." According to research sponsored by the Audubon Society, that area was "the most important and essential feeding area for the Cuthbert Lake Rookery" and was "used extensively by the birds that roost at the end of Anhinga Trail."[60]

In early 1956, Beard completed an ecological survey of the northwest expansion, which he labeled "the vital zone." He argued that excluding the "vital zone would knock the ecological props from under the Everglades National park." Throughout 1956 and 1957, attacks on the "the so-called 'vital zone.'" dominated the McDougal-Axelsons' efforts to influence the park boundaries. They claimed that this "'vital zone' is much more 'vital' to the rapid growing population in South Florida, especially in Metropolitan Miami, than to the birds. Human beings have 'ecological' needs as well as the birds. Let us also think about them." They argued that including these lands in the park was akin to "an iron curtain cutting off all of Monroe County's mainland from the Gulf." The family's legislative allies in Florida also attacked the vital zone. William Neblett, a Florida state senator representing Monroe County, dismissed Beard's reports as being "full of 'the ecology of the birds.'" Bernie Papy likewise attacked the vital zone as too large and useless or, as he put it, "for the birds."[61]

The NPS, which had compromised on park boundary numerous times since 1934, held firm to its 1954 order expanding the boundaries, despite Florida governor Charley Johns's opposition. The NPS had faced a hostile Florida governor before and knew it merely had to wait out Johns's term. In any case, Johns was only an interim governor, and a special election was scheduled for January 1955. Although landowners, oil companies, and Monroe County lawmakers opposed the park, it was still popular throughout the state and had earned the support of most of the state's business and political community.

The third phase of the park's expansion began with LeRoy Collins's gubernatorial term. In 1955, LeRoy Collins defeated Johns in the Democratic primary, then defeated park opponent J. Tom Watson, who had switched parties to run as a Republican in the general election. During Collins's two gubernatorial terms, he charted a moderate course for the state on civil rights, supported education, opposed the death penalty, and worked to improve the state's economy. Widely seen as one of the state's most successful governors, he prioritized finalizing the park boundaries and reluctantly agreed to a final compromise boundary.

On February 25, 1955, NPS director Wirth asked Governor Collins to comply with the DOI's 1954 order expanding the park's boundaries and turn over all state lands in the area. In response, Collins called an IIF meeting to discuss the issue. Collins "hoped the boundaries of the park could be established once and for all," yet there was strong disagreement concerning this issue. Most of the IIF Trustees supported a proposal put forth by William Neblett, which entailed a small 20,000-acre corridor expansion that would connect the park to the Collier lands. This proposal had taken the form of a resolution that passed the Florida Senate but failed in the House. In contrast, the NPS's desired boundary expansion in the northwest section of the park entailed 271,000 acres.[62] (See plate 9.)

At the next IIF meeting in May 1955, the NPS made an extraordinary effort to compromise and finalize the park boundaries. It reduced the size of the northwest expansion by eliminating eastern sections of the Patten Tract from the park. It also eliminated the proposed eastern boundary expansion and agreed to delay acquiring lands in the Hole in the Doughnut "as long as they were used for agricultural purposes." Spessard Holland urged the IIF to take this deal, as it was "more liberal in the matter of exclusion" than previous deals. Holland also made the veiled threat that, if the IIF did not agree to these boundaries, he would "feel some obligation to introduce legislation in Congress fixing the permanent boundaries" anyway. Although Collins supported this deal, the rest of the trustees rejected this offer.[63]

In response, Wirth withdrew his compromise offer to Collins, noting that the NPS had already gone "a great deal further than we felt justified" and that "the Park project would have nothing to gain" by "any further compromise." In response, Collins suggested to both Wirth and Holland that they simply ignore the IIF's decision and proceed with federal legislation on the boundary as they saw fit. Collins supported the park but was loath to anger vocal landowners and powerful state legislators, and he was unwilling to go against the wishes of his entire cabinet. One Miami journalist described the boundary issue as a "hot potato," an assessment Collins surely shared.[64]

Debates over this park's boundary became entangled with disagreements concerning the park's commercial development in 1956 and 1957. Although the NPS prioritized the protection of the Everglades' biology, Florida park advocates like Spessard Holland and John Pennekamp prioritized the park's economic impacts. Holland and Pennekamp were frustrated at NPS unwillingness to construct overnight accommodations for tourists at Flamingo, a forming fishing village that would soon become the park's primary tourist attraction. The two had been pushing for development in the park since its creation, but the NPS had insisted on delaying the construction of tourist facilities until it finalized the boundary. Their reasoning was that development would increase land values and thus the amount of money needed for land acquisition.[65]

In 1954, the NPS relented and began plans to develop an interpretive site, hotel, restaurant, gas station, and marina at Flamingo. Yet the following year, in response to a NPS report that criticized these developments as harmful to the park's biology, Director Wirth nixed the hotel. Holland and Pennekamp protested. Pennekamp in particular was exasperated with Wirth. He wrote to Smathers that Wirth's "ability to develop" excuses on the housing issue "seems inexhaustible" and sent Smathers a list of seventeen excuses Wirth had offered for not constructing housing units at Flamingo. Pennekamp urged Governor Collins to use the boundary issue to force the NPS to construct overnight accommodations at Flamingo. Collins agreed and noted that any further discussions with the NPS would have to wait until they kept "their agreement on housing."[66]

Ultimately, the NPS caved. Pennekamp wrote to Collins with inside information, explaining that the NPS negotiator on the boundary issue "has been told to make to you whatever concession is necessary in the overnight housing dispute" to make progress on the boundaries. Consequently, in February 1957, Wirth announced he would authorize the creation of a sixty-room hotel with a swimming pool at Flamingo. The NPS also agreed to further reduce the northwest boundary expansion. It reduced a three-mile wide strip of waters in the Gulf of Mexico to two-mile wide strip. Additionally, it severely reduced the eastern edge of this expansion to conform to the compromise Elliot Line, which connected the park to the Collier lands through the Patten tract. That line excluded much of the Chevelier tract as well as 7,040 acres in the Patten tract, which would be deeded to the state. This settlement also addressed the Hole in the Doughnut, which would be included in the park but would not be acquired by the NPS as long as it was "used for agricultural purposes." Finally, the proposed northeast expansion was eliminated entirely. Wirth and Holland agreed to support federal legislation to finalize these boundaries, and although Governor Collins agreed to support this settlement, he noted that his support "was not binding on the other members of the Cabinet."[67] (See plate 9.)

In fact, his cabinet refused to support this settlement. They did agree, however, that "if Congress passes a bill setting boundaries," the IIF would comply and deed all lands in the boundary to the NPS. Florida's politicians were thus able to have it both ways. They could give the NPS what they wanted, while still covering themselves politically and serving local interests. Collins explained to Pennekamp that "the quieter this matter can rest now the better, so far as Tallahassee is concerned."[68]

Next, Holland and Smathers introduced a bill finalizing the park's boundaries in the U.S. Senate, while Dante Fascell, Dade County's U.S. representative, and Gracie Pfost, a U.S. representative from Idaho and the chair of the Subcommittee on Public Lands, worked to introduce bills in the House.[69] On July 11 and 12,

1957, the House held a public hearing on the boundary bills. John Pennekamp and Kathryn Hanna, the chair of the Florida Board of Parks and Historic Memorials, were among the park supporters defending the park's boundaries. E. C. Lunsford, Bernie Papy, Ivar Axelson, and J. L. McCord were among the steadfast park opponents arguing against park expansion and rehashing their familiar arguments about the mineral rights of landowners.[70]

By 1957, oil had still not been found in the Everglades in profitable quantities, yet the House subcommittee was swayed by these rights-based arguments and extended landowners' mineral rights. The oil rights landowners had been granted in 1949 were set to expire in 1958. As part of this boundary bill, Congress extended those rights until October 9, 1967, and the rights to any oil royalties until 1985. Holland called these provisions "unusually generous" and touted his continued desire to protect individual rights. On June 23, 1958, both the House and Senate approved the ENP boundaries on voice votes without debate. On February 25, 1959, the State of the Florida and the federal government completed the deed exchanges for the recently approved boundaries. Some private lands were still to be acquired using federal funds, but by that date, the story of the park's creation was complete.[71]

Of course, the 1958 boundaries were not the park's final boundaries. In 1989, major additions were made to the park's northeast boundary. Additionally, lands in the Hole in the Doughnut still needed to be acquired when farming ceased in the area. Complicating this matter further, in response to the Cuban missile crisis, the federal government began construction of the HM69 Nike Missile Base in the Hole in the Doughnut, within the park's boundaries. The U.S. Army operated that base from 1965 to 1979. By 1974, the NPS had acquired the other private lands in the hole and integrated them into the park. After the base closed in 1979, it was incorporated into the park, and many of its facilities were converted into park offices. The missile barns and two decommissioned missiles were protected as a historic district and remain on display in the park as a reminder of the Cuban missile crisis, the Cold War, and the continued possibly of nuclear annihilation. The ENP was the nation's first biological and ecological national park, yet it is also a human artifact that bears the mark and history of our species. The ENP is a monument to the Everglades' biology, but also contains this memorial to the destructive powers of humanity.

Managing the Everglades

Creating a national park is more than just acquiring land and drawing boundaries. The NPS had to hire staff, write park regulations, develop sections of the park for tourism, and protect and restore the Everglades' ecosystems and biota. In 1947, the ENP only existed on paper. Daniel Beard, park superintendent from 1947 to 1958, created a functioning national park. Beard had only a small staff and a miniscule budget, but his energy, enthusiasm, and competence made the early ENP successful. During the first few years of the park's existence, park staff were mostly preoccupied with law enforcement, the eviction of squatters and former residents, the regulation of commercial fishing, biological research and restoration, and the creation of facilities and activities for tourists. Over time, issues related to water flow became central to Beard and his staff.

Law enforcement, which primarily meant enforcing the park's boundaries and the ban on hunting in the park, was the first priority in 1947. The U.S. Fish and Wildlife Service had patrolled the ENWR before 1947, but it had few resources and little success. Beard had managed that refuge before being transferred by to the NPS to oversee the park, and had been granted authority over the few remaining Fish and Wildlife rangers in 1947. These rangers supplemented the meager resources Beard had in the park's early years. The ENP slowly acquired equipment and hired park rangers to patrol the park both by car and boat. The wetland nature of the Everglades made policing the area difficult and poaching easier. Stopping hunting along the Tamiami Trail was a key early priority. In 1947, rangers met with sportsmen and hunting groups to inform them of new regulations, posted signage along the park's northern boundary, and policed the area vigorously to set the tone for future behavior.

In November 1947, just six months after the park's creation, rangers found evidence of eighteen airboats in the park hunting frogs (which were a valuable delicacy) and found four rookeries shot out. Beard noted that "ranger personnel are not yet equipped to completely stop this." By February 1949, the situation had not improved. Beard reported that hunters using airboats had caused "a very serious loss of alligators throughout the vital areas of the park." Although rangers had spent "several nights and days on the case," their "lack of comparable equipment" prevented them from stopping the poachers. By January 1950, Beard reported that the situation was "vastly better than last year, but there were still a few holes to plug. That month, rangers patrolled 1,425 miles via boat and 2,327 miles on land.[1]

The next month, Beard declared that although small-scale poaching would likely continue to be a problem, "the regular incursions of market hunters is . . . at an end." Park rangers had "smoked out" the "ringleader of the market hunters for alligators." Those poachers were "swamp wise and army trained" and had become increasing sophisticated in their techniques as rangers harassed them. They hunted "only at night by small boats, burying carcasses so vultures would not congregate, and hiding among the mangroves by day." Air and boat patrols, an equipped and staffed ranger force, as well as cooperation with state authorities, were all essential to securing this victory.[2]

Another major law enforcement priority (and major headache for Beard) was the colorful and lawless fishing village of Flamingo. Although Coe and other park advocates presented the Glades as uninhabited by anyone other than Seminoles, there had been scattered and infrequent White inhabitants in the lower Everglades as far back as the 1870s. Mostly located in the Ten Thousand Islands and Cape Sable, these settlements consisted of precarious farms or fishing outposts that were often threatened by the Everglades' hostile conditions. Most of the houses and farms that still existed into the twentieth century were destroyed by either the 1926 hurricane or the Labor Day hurricane of 1935. At the time of the park's creation, Flamingo was the only substantial settlement, although a few commercial fishers also lived at nearby Snake Bight, and other small homesites still existed along the west coast.

Cape Sable was inhabited by White settlers as early as the 1870s. Farms, cattle ranches, and a coconut plantation were all established in the last three decades of the nineteenth century, but all failed. Flamingo grew into a vibrant village in the 1890s, fueled primarily by the lucrative plume trade. It had around a hundred settlers in 1902 and boasted a post office and school. After that date, the village declined. An attempt to open a two-story hotel at the site in 1915 failed, and although the Ingraham Highway connected Flamingo to Miami in 1922, the village did not attract many residents. In fact, the dredging crew building the road only saw three houses at the site in 1921. Moonshining was probably the most important activity in Flamingo throughout the 1920s. Historian Charlton Tebeau describes "Cape Sable Augerdent" as "a fearsomely powerful brew never forgotten by the uninitiated after the first drink." The 1926 hurricane damaged the village, but the 1935 Labor Day storm wiped it out entirely. Flamingo residents rebuilt their village, and by the early 1940s commercial fishing became the dominant activity at the cape.[3]

Partly due to the park's impeding creation, Flamingo boomed in the 1940s. The village had been occupied by squatters and fishers whom Beard compared to tenant farmers working for commercial fish companies. Many residents, though, soon began catering to tourists. Beard found that, by 1945, there were eight cabins, one dorm, three skiff rentals, one "beer joint," a few places that served fish dinners, and airboat charters in Flamingo, all run by residents, and all criticized by Beard as substandard. Although a hurricane in 1948 destroyed much of Flamingo, residents continued to run these wildcat concessions. After the hurricane, "the famous 'Cootie Roberts' Beer Joint' reopened after being hauled back from the mangroves" and the "House Fish Company at Flamingo" stopped fishing and instead started work on a "wildcat concession" that included "tourist cabins, [a] store, and [a] restaurant."[4]

Part of the village's attraction was its notorious and "lurid" reputation. Flamingoites resisted the new park's authority, and over the years its residents were involved in "several minor skirmishes" with rangers over park regulations.[5] Residents issued death threats against several rangers and at times openly flouted park rules.[6] Beard recounted one incident where residents after "internal applications of the finest products of Milwaukee, . . . gleefully butchered and consumed . . . a large turtle named after the park superintendent."[7] In June 1948, rangers blamed Flamingoites for shooting out the Catfish Key rookery. That month, rangers stopped seven men at Flamingo on their way to the beach at Cape Sable to hunt turtles. One ranger reported that Joe Duthert, the ringleader of the group, did everything he could to threaten rangers "without pointing [his] gun."[8] In December 1948, rangers broke up a melee over shrimping privileges that rangers labeled the "Battle of Slagel's Ditch." In the course of this fight, someone was "hit over the head with a gasoline lantern," another participant received a black eye, and at least one shrimper "began carrying a gun."[9] In January 1950, another altercation ended in "in a wild chase through the park" involving at least three cars and eight residents, one of whom was taken to a local hospital for a broken jaw.[10]

The park's creation meant the destruction of Flamingo. The park service would acquire these lands, force all residents out of the region, and outlaw the economic livelihood of Flamingoites. They in turn rebelled against the park's creation. Throughout the twenty-year campaign for the park, Flamingo residents had never been consulted by park advocates or the NPS. While Seminoles, landowners, oil companies, sportsmen, commercial fishers, and county politicians had all been involved in the park's creation, the Gladesmen had been ignored almost entirely. They had no real political power and no ability to influence the park's creation.

Their actions, which Beard dismissed as irrational acts of violence, were protests against the extension of the environmental regulatory state and their own removal from the Everglades. These protests were consistent with the class dynamics of preservation throughout American history. Elites preserved nature for their use, while poor populations who lived off the land were removed to make way for parks and preserves. Often, like in the case of the Adirondacks and the Appalachians, parks removed people whose families had been using these lands for generations or even centuries. Sometimes, these groups, in particular Native Americans, were effective stewards of the land.[11]

Yet, in the Everglades nothing was simple. The region's wetland nature twisted historical precedents and impacted the region's history. Residences in the Glades were precarious and often temporary. Hurricanes especially impacted these coastal settlements. Storms in the 1920s, the Labor Day hurricane in 1935, and storms in the late 1940s damaged Flamingo and other homesites throughout the islands. Other natural hazards, like heat, humidity, and mosquitoes, made these regions inhospitable to humans. As a consequence, Flamingo's population was highly itinerant. A handful of families with deep roots in the Glades were still living in the region in the late 1940s and early 1950s, but many of the residents removed from the park were actually recent transplants.

The 1940 federal census found 141 people living in the coastal regions and islands of the Everglades. The census certainly did not count every single resident, but it did surprisingly capture populations on isolated islands like Rabbit Key, Mormon Key, and along Lostman's River. Out of these 141 people on the Glades' coast, 62 lived in the area around Flamingo. 48 of these were adults, while just 27 were listed as household heads. Out of these 27, only 12 had lived in the Everglades in 1930. Out of the total Flamingo population, only 7 were still living in the village in 1945, according to the state's 1945 census, which found only 39 total residents at Flamingo.[12]

Hurricanes, not the NPS, removed most of these people from the Everglades, although the agency certainly prevented anyone from moving back in. Everglades old-timers were bitterly angry with the agency, which destroyed their livelihoods and forced them off their ancestral lands. Marjory Stoneman Douglas gave voice to this discontent in a young-adult novel published in 1958. *Alligator Crossing* celebrated Everglades National Park and its biocentric purposes, but it also sympathetically gave voice to Gladesmen whose hunting and fishing destroyed so much of the region's flora and fauna. Douglas's fictional Artie Dillon was removed from Flamingo by the agency. He explains that "they kicked us out. . . . They tore down our houses." "They took ever'thing away from us—our houses, the plume birds, the alligators. Why, you couldn't even shoot you a deer."[13]

In June 1950, all squatters on park lands were ordered to vacate by December 1, 1950, and by December, all private lands at Flamingo had been acquired by the NPS. Those formers owners were ordered to vacate by February 4, 1951, although many commercial fish companies still had facilities at Flamingo until May 1951.

Likewise, squatters did not honor their deadline, which the NPS extended to June 1, 1951. Three residents engaged in one final act of defiance. Drunk on local moonshine, they "decided to rip down the park's sign." They were taken to Miami for a talk with the U.S. Attorney, but no charges were filed.[14] After their June 1951 eviction, many Flamingo's residents converted their boats to houseboats and anchored this "flotilla of craft defying all description" near Joe Kemp Key, which lay just off Flamingo.[15] Many of these houseboats were still present as late as 1953, and rangers still policed this population.[16]

Commercial fishing regulations were another front in the ENP's struggle to protect the Everglades. This issue was entwined with the fate of Flamingo's population and had been a controversial topic for the NPS as far back as the 1930s. Commercial fishers and the Monroe County Commission opposed the park in that decade because they believed the NPS would ban commercial fishing in the park. Although the NPS had consistently pledged it would not interfere with fishing in the Everglades, it had in fact, banned commercial fishing at Dry Tortugas National Monument on its creation in 1935. Arno Cammerer explained that fishers there had "landed on the Keys, captured turtles, took turtles' eggs and birds' eggs, [and] destroyed coral."[17] To appease these powerful interests, Cammerer lifted that ban in March 1937 and reiterated that commercial fishing would not be restricted in the ENP.

Beard, however, had a different attitude. Even before the park's creation, he was concerned about commercial fishing's negative biological impacts. In 1946 he explained how "commercial fisherman have just about ruined Florida Bay" through overfishing, the destruction of bay bottoms, and bycatch. Commercial fishers were also hurting the profitable recreational sportfishing industry in the state. Beard singled out the use of dragnets, which destroyed the seabed and resulted in bycatch. He argued that regulations were needed to protect the ecology of the park's marine areas but admitted he was unsure what form those regulations would take. In contrast to the terrestrial biota in the Everglades, Beard noted that there was "practically no data at all" on the area's marine life.[18]

Beard continued to focus on commercial fishing after the park's creation. He commonly heard complaints from sportfishing groups blaming the decline of game fish species on commercial fishing practices. Beard noted in March 1949 that "the drums began to beat for a better program of salt water fisheries conservation" due to the activity of sportfishers, whose industry in 1947 was valued at $625 million.[19] Pressure to rein in commercial fishers mounted throughout 1949 and 1950. In November 1950, the NPS held a public meeting on proposed regulations. The NPS pledged to allow fishing on "a sustained yield basis" and addressed specific abuses by fishers such as the "use of large drag seines," the taking of shrimp for bait, the decline in Florida lobster populations, and the destruction of sea turtles and their nests. Some commercial fishers opposed the proposed ban on drag seines, but opinion at this meeting was largely in favor of these regulations.[20] In June 1950, Beard closed all inland waters to nets and seines, an emergency measure directly aimed at Flamingo fishers.[21] By March 1951, drag seines were banned in the entire Florida Bay.[22] No further fishing regulations were posted in the ENP until 1965, when all fishers were required to obtain no-fee permits and report all catches.[23] In 1980, further regulations pertaining to bag limits and the closing of sanctuary areas to commercial fishing followed. Finally, in 1985, all commercial fishing was banned in the ENP.[24]

All these efforts—the policing of boundaries, the eviction of squatters, and fishing regulations—helped the park fulfill its park's primary purpose: protecting the Everglades' biota. With this goal in mind, park staff surveyed park flora and fauna, conducted biological research, and engaged in some preliminary restoration activities. In his monthly reports, Beard paid particular attention to the success or failure of major bird rookeries and to the status of the alligator population. He reported on any significant or unusual species found in the park and wrote about interesting animal behaviors, as well. For example, in December 1952, Beard noted that "from 200 to 250 Swainson's hawks were seen," as well as an "immature American brant," an "old squaw duck," a long-billed curlew, and "a flamingo" at Lake Ingraham that was "off and on all month."[25] In July 1951 Beard noted several surprising predation events, including "two alligators eating a full grown otter at Seven Mile Tower," and a "bobcat catching birds in full daylight at Nine Mile Bend."[26] Beard even occasionally commented on specific animals, like Mable, "the venerable manatee of Pearl Bay," and Bozo, the alligator of Coot Pond Bay.[27] Joseph C. Moore, the ENP chief biologist from 1949 to 1955, studied the area's species and informed park policy. He often published his results in scientific journals and from 1953 to 1955 edited *Everglades Natural History*, a scientific journal published by the Everglades Natural History Association.[28]

The ecological restoration of the Everglades was a priority for Beard and his staff. In 1948 Beard celebrated the "noteworthy ecological change" that occurred once the park had stopped hunters from setting fires along the Shark River. Now, orchids were flowering, custard apples were blossoming and bearing fruit, and red mangroves were "coming back in 'thicker than hair on a dog's back.'" These areas were once again becoming "the best alligator habitats" in the state.[29]

Yet Beard quickly found that ecological restoration was not so simple a concept. Rather than simply allowing the ecosystem to rejuvenate on its own, park staff found they sometimes needed to intervene in nature to create the outcomes they desired. Protecting and restoring bird rookeries was a high priority for ENP staff, but in 1946 and 1947 the Shark River rookery, the largest in Florida, failed due to predation by vultures and crows. Beard requested permission from the

NPS to control "black vultures, crows, and turkey vultures" at this site by shooting them with "high powered air rifles or .22 rifles with silencers." Beard was wary of this action, and although he noted his discomfort with these methods of "population control," he argued that this was "an emergency situation" and drastic measures needed to be taken.[30] Beard's supervisor, T. J. Allen, found the request unusual but approved it. He noted that "there is an unequal balance" in the ENP but that "action by us may assist in eventually restoring normal balances."[31] Although this action was approved, it is unclear if rangers went through with their predation control, as the Shark River rookery failed to form in 1948.[32]

Although biological protection was the park's primary mission, Beard probably spent more time preparing the park to receive tourists. As a wildlife biologist, Beard knew how treacherous this task could be and tried to limit development and construction in the new park. He urged that overnight accommodations in the ENP be kept to a minimum, as he hoped most visitors would be day-trippers staying outside the park. Due to this, concessions could be kept to a minimum and could be limited to a gas station, a small store, and a few minimal dining areas. Beard believed that "the only way to see the Everglades is by boat," and he stressed the need for boat rentals and charters. Boat tourism would allow the service to more easily control the tourist population. It limited tourism's biological impact and alleviated the need to build roads and other infrastructure.[33] NPS officials mostly agreed with Beard's suggestions, although they eventually caved to pressure to allow overnight accommodations in the park in 1957.[34]

When the park opened in 1947, there were no accommodations for tourists, no interpretive activities, and few rangers or interpretive staff able to guide tourists through the Everglades. The National Audubon Society conducted two-day birding tours in the Everglades into the 1950s, but these were specialized tours, unsuited for the general public. Throughout the first several years of the park's existence, tourists commonly complained about the lack of facilities in the park. Beard noted "the very general, bitter complaint that there is 'nothing to see,'" although he explained that personal contact with rangers alleviated that complaint.[35] As Ernest Coe and Beard had both understood, the beauty of the Everglades was subtle. Beard understood that making the ecological beauty of the Everglades evident to the public would build support for the park, so he worked to build interpretive facilities in the ENP. In January 1949, park staff created a "self-guiding nature trail" at Paradise Key (the site of the former Royal Palm State Park) and posted "interpretive personnel" at the site.[36] By December 1949, staff rebuilt and renamed the Taylor Slough Trail at Paradise Key. Now called Anhinga Trail, Beard anticipated it would become "an outstanding interpretive facility." Today it is one of the most popular sites for wildlife viewing in the park.[37] Guided tours of the Anhinga and Gumbo Limbo Trails (also located at Paradise Key) began in January 1950, and by November 1951 the construction of a "contact-comfort" ranger station was completed at the site.[38] Beard also directed the construction of temporary concession buildings at Coot Bay in 1950; a store, snack bar, and restroom opened that December.[39] Before 1950, the only public toilet facility in the park was the infamous "powder room" at Coot Bay, consisting of a wooden shack and a hole in the ground.[40]

The NPS also rebuilt the Ingraham Highway, as it had longed pledged. However, much of the original road ran through the Hole in the Doughnut, which could not be acquired as long as that land was used for farming. The NPS needed a usable road to Flamingo and so diverted the road's course north. A case could be made that this constituted new road construction and violated the 1934 law authorizing the park. This road was completed in 1957.

These minimal facilities were later supplemented by Mission 66, a major NPS initiative that began in 1955 and sought to update and outfit the national parks with new facilities in preparation of the agency's fiftieth anniversary in 1966. Congress appropriated $700 million over ten years for Mission 66, and increased the NPS budget by about $300 million over that period, as well.[41] Mission 66 completed remade Flamingo as a center of park tourism. The NPS constructed concessions, overnight accommodations, a visitor center, and an updated harbor at Flamingo. Additional construction in the park included a visitor center at the park's entrance near Homestead, more employee housing at Pine Island, campgrounds at Long Pine Key, and the retrofitting of the fire road and fire tower off Tamiami Trail at Shark Valley into a sightseeing road and observation tower.[42]

In 1958 Daniel Beard was transferred to Olympic National Park in Washington, bringing to an end his time in the Everglades. He later served as the director of the NPS Southwest Region and retired from the agency in 1967. His work in the Everglades was tremendous. He made important studies of the Everglades' biota and served as an important park advocate before 1947. As superintendent, he kept the tradition of wildlife biology alive in the park service, restrained development in the ENP, built a professional and competent ranger force, and worked to keep tourists and other important constituencies happy. In short, Beard's tenure as superintendent was an enormous success. Ernest Coe was the "papa" of the ENP. Holland, Caldwell, and Pennekamp made the park a reality. Daniel Beard took a set of boundaries drawn on a map and an abstract legislative mandate and created a functioning national park.

CONCLUSION

Since its creation in 1947, Everglades National Park has protected the southern section of the Everglades. It has attracted millions of tourists to the area and inspired many of them to rethink their relationship with the environment. It has also contributed to Florida's economic modernization and growth. Parks are important for obvious reasons: they can protect nature, biota, and habitats; they bring economic benefits to their regions; and they can build support for environmental causes. The ENP, though, has had an even larger impact on Florida's environment. This park facilitated Everglades restoration and prompted the further preservation of Florida's nature.

The park's existence, the political power it wields within the federal bureaucracy, and the infrastructure of ideas that undergirded its creation facilitated the restoration of the larger Everglades watershed. Today, most of the concerns about the Everglades revolve around the important questions of water flow and water quality. The historic flow of water south from Lake Okeechobee through the Everglades' sloughs has now been marked by almost 140 years of human alteration. That flow of water is central to the health of all life in the Everglades. Without it, the Everglades will dry out and die. Both drainage and flood control efforts diverted that water to agricultural and urban areas, but the fix is not as simple as pumping more water south. Rather, the Everglades is marked by wet and dry periods, and many species are dependent on both the absence of water and a surfeit of it. Timing is crucial, and water needs to be delivered during the historical wet season, or else, for example, bird nesting and breeding patterns are disrupted, leading to species decline. Water quality is another central issue today. The Everglades needs clean water. The water that rightfully belongs to the Glades is used by sugar and other agricultural interests that pollute this water with phosphates, nitrates, and other agricultural runoff. Although this water is supposed to be diverted to water conservation areas so that it can be filtered and cleaned, much of these excess nutrients end up in the Everglades and alter the area's biological makeup.

The issues of water quantity and quality dominate political discussions about the Everglades today but were almost totally absent from the conversation prior the park's creation. Marjory Stoneman Douglas's 1947 *The Everglades: River of Grass* brought the issues to the public's attention, but only in the 1960s did threats to water flow became apparent and dire. Today there is a widespread acknowledgment that the Everglades is under siege and that large-scale corrective action is needed to restore the region's water flow.

When seen in the context of these larger hydrological questions, the park can seem almost like an afterthought or an appendage. The ENP is an easy target of criticism from scholars and activists who note that the park does not protect the entire Everglades or its hydrological system. Rather, it encompasses a partial and artificial boundary hastily thrown up around the southern section of the Everglades. While the lower Glades has been protected, the upper Glades—which is the source of all the Everglades water—has been intensively developed and altered. It is easy to scoff at this national park, thrown up around the southern Glades, cut off from its water flow, and inadequate to the task of protecting the Everglades.

Yet these criticisms are both ahistorical, and they misunderstand the complex hydro-politics in the Everglades. The park was created before the Everglades' water flow was well understood and before the current water control regime was constructed. Creating a park that encompassed the entire Everglades would have been politically impossible—even Ernest Coe's expansive boundaries were too controversial and expensive. Creating an even larger park that took in the farmlands in the upper Glades was a financial and political impossibility.

More importantly, the park administration has never been a passive spectator in these conversations about water control. Rather, ENP and NPS administrators influenced the state and federal governments' water control efforts and worked to ensure waterflow to the park. Just as the park was created in 1947, massive flooding inundated all of South Florida. In response, Florida politicians and the USACE began studying a new comprehensive water control project for the entire Kissimmee River–Lake Okeechobee–Everglades watershed.[1] Unlike previous efforts that sought to drain the Everglades, the KOE project sought to prevent flooding and to provide agricultural areas and urban populations with water. These plans also gave lip service to the idea of providing water to the park. Many Everglades advocates, including Marjory Stoneman Douglas and Daniel Beard, praised the plan and assumed it would protect the Everglades water supply. Congress passed the Flood Control Act of 1948 and approved the C&SF Project. This plan, in the words of journalist Michael Grunwald would turn the "Kissimmee River into a ditch, Lake Okeechobee and the central Glades into reservoirs, the northern Glades into farms, and the eastern Glades into suburbs."[2] The southern Glades were still protected as Everglades National Park, and although the initial plan pledged to deliver water to the park, the state of Florida and the USACE saw the park's needs as a distant third priority behind the desires of agricultural and suburban interests.

Throughout the 1950s, the NPS complained about the USACE's lackadaisical attitude toward the park and the dearth of water they sent south. In the 1960s, the ENP experienced a dire water crisis. The urban population of South Florida was exploding, the sugar industry in the northern Everglades was booming, water flow south had been cut off by the construction of new levees and water conservation areas, and a drought struck the area. Friction between the NPS and the USACE erupted into bitter disagreement. Journalists, environmentalists, and local politicians highlighted the crisis in the Glades, and the public became aware of the detrimental impacts of these flood control projects. Throughout the 1960s, the NPS, the state of Florida, and the USACE debated how much water the park would receive from the C&SF Project. This crisis led to Congress passing the 1970 federal law that mandated that the ENP receive either 315,000 acre-feet annually or at least 16.5 percent of the total water flow handled by the C&SF Project. This law was the first milestone in protecting the Everglades' water flow and only came about due to the park's status within the federal government and the NPS's willingness to stand up to the USACE. Without the park, the southern Glades could have easily lay parched and forgotten.

In 1989, the federal government again acted to secure water flow to the ENP with the Everglades National Park Protection and Expansion Act of 1989. This law expanded the park northeast by over 100,000 acres. This expansion encompassed the Shark River Slough, an important source of water into the park, and included much of the northeastern areas eliminated from the park in 1958. This law also ordered the USACE to modify the C&SF Project to restore a more natural water flow to the park. The USACE Modified Water Deliveries Project aimed to imitate the Everglades' historic sheet flow by delivering more water into the park through the Shark River Slough. As of this writing, these actions were probably the most significant in terms of their actual impact on the hydrological health of the Everglades, and they were explicitly seen as a way to improve the health of the ENP ecosystems.

Although the 1989 law probably had the largest impact on Everglades hydrology, the Comprehensive Everglades Restoration Plan (CERP), approved by the federal government in 2000, has been more heralded. This ambitious plan aimed to "restore, preserve, and protect the south Florida ecosystem while providing for other water-related needs of the region, including water supply and flood protection."[3] CERP's impact has been mixed at best. CERP is a huge array of sixty-eight individual projects, many of which address water flow into the park, yet much of the program has remained unfunded and unrealized. Like previous water control projects, CERP has often been criticized for prioritizing the water needs of urban and agricultural interests, but part of its goals do include improved water flow and water quality in Everglades National Park. The NPS and the DOI played major roles in the creation and implementation of CERP and have worked to ensure that the Everglades' needs remain central to the project.

Indeed, the ENP has been central to the fight over the Everglades' water. Whenever Everglades advocates talk about restoring waterflow to the Everglades, they are, in fact, actually talking about restoring water to Everglades National Park. The park in turn, has made much of this restoration possible. The park's very existence, its supporters in the environmentalist and business communities, its continued support from Florida politicians, and the place it occupies in the federal bureaucracy all exert an enormous amount of political power. That power has been used to force the USACE to deliver more water to the ENP. The park, in effect, has become the Everglades for which environmentalists fight. While other sections of the Glades have been turned into subdivisions and corporate farms, the ENP preserves the last great bastion of the Everglades' biological integrity.

The creation of the ENP also prompted further preservation throughout South Florida. Ernest Coe advocated for enormous park boundaries that protected the southern Everglades, a large cross-section of Key Largo and the Key's offshore reefs, and cypress swamps north of the Tamiami Trail. While impractical, Coe's vision set an agenda for Florida preservationists. Additionally, the park itself proved that protecting Florida's nature was possible. Even its reduced 1958 boundaries protected an enormous swath of Florida's nature and inspired future generations of Florida environmentalists. Finally, its rationales for preservation, especially its emphasis on flora and on marine ecosystems, provided an intellectual foundation for future preservationist efforts.

The ENP was the first major effort in U.S. history to protect marine and estuarine ecosystems. The park does not just protect sawgrass marshes; it includes extensive mangrove swamps, saltwater marshes, and vast marine areas, including the Florida Bay, Whitewater Bay, and the waters around the Ten Thousand Islands. Coe prioritized the protection of these marine ecosystems, making them central to his redefinition of the Everglades. In doing so, he offered future activists positive ideas about the identities of these aquatic areas and justifications for their preservation. This emphasis on marine preservation laid the groundwork for the protection of other aquatic areas in Florida.

In the late 1940s, Ernest Coe had obsessed over including Key Largo's coral reefs in the park. Their inclusion was too politically controversial and the NPS excluded these areas from the park's boundaries. After the ENP's creation, however, John Pennekamp worked to protect these reefs. He solicited donations from landowners and worked with the state to establish a state park in 1959. Pennekamp continued to work with landowners and economic elites to expand this park's boundaries after that date. This park, named John Pennekamp Coral Reef State Park, was billed as the world's first underwater park. Due to his involvement with the ENP, Pennekamp became an environmentalist and a powerful advocate for Florida's state park system. He served as chair of the Florida Board of Parks and Historic Memorials from 1953 to 1976, and he worked to expand and fund the state park system.

As coastal areas were threatened by the development in the 1960s, environmentalists mobilized to protect Florida's coastal and marine ecosystems. Activists in Miami fought against a proposed oil refinery off Biscayne Bay and major developments on Elliot Key in the bay. These individuals, many of whom were members of the Izaak Walton League, formed the Safe Progress Association and eventually succeeded in protecting these aquatic regions and islands as Biscayne National Monument in 1969. This monument was expanded in 1978 and made a national park in 1980. Other fights over marine waters in the state led the creation of Estero Bay Aquatic Preserve, Rookery Bay National Estuarine Research Reserve, the enlargement of Pelican Island National Wildlife Reserve, and eventually a state system of aquatic preserves.

The ENP, John Pennekamp State Park, Biscayne National Park, and the state's system of aquatic preserves were individual puzzle pieces that fit together to preserve Florida's marine ecosystems. Other pieces that adjoined or connected these protected areas were added in subsequent years, creating a patchwork of connected marine preserves. For example, Key Largo Marine Sanctuary, a federal preserve created to further protect Key Largo's reefs and waters was created in 1975. This preserve protected 103 square miles of federal waters on the eastern border of John Pennekamp Coral Reef State Park. In 1989 that sanctuary, as well as Looe Key National Marine Sanctuary, was incorporated into the much larger Florida Keys National Marine Sanctuary. The state of Florida created Bill Baggs Cape Florida State Park, which borders Biscayne National Park to the north, and two aquatic preserves in Biscayne Bay. Other protected areas in the Florida Keys also sought to preserve marine ecosystems. State parks in the Keys, like Bahia Honda and Lignumvitae Key, and national wildlife refuges, like the Great White Heron and the Key West National Wildlife Refuges, all protected significant marine resources.

The ENP also prioritized the protection of the state's native flora. Preserves created to the north and west of the park helped protect sensitive flora populations. The creation of Big Cypress National Preserve in 1974 was directly tied to the ENP. Large sections of this preserve had been part of the ENP's original proposed boundaries but had been eliminated early in the campaign. These lands would be expensive to acquire and were politically controversial, both to sport hunters and to wilderness advocates like Robert Sterling Yard, who wanted to keep the Tamiami Trail out of the park. The protection of these areas in the 1970s was a reaction to a proposed jetport in Big Cypress. In 1968, work began on a thirty-nine-acre jetport located just six miles north of the ENP. This facility, with six runways, would have been the largest airport in the world and would have been connected to the east and west coasts of Florida by a 1,000-foot-wide highway. A new generation of Everglades advocates like Nat Reed and Joe Browder were joined by Marjory Stoneman Douglas to fight this development. They argued it would cause immense damage to the ENP and would further degrade water flow to the park. They successfully used the park to protect the larger Everglades watershed. Construction on the jetport was halted in 1970; Big Cypress National Preserve was created in 1974 to permanently protect these ecosystems.

Big Cypress National Preserve also prioritized the protection of flora. It protected huge tracts of the finest old-growth and second-growth cypress forests in Florida. The desire to protect Florida's flora also manifested itself in the creation of Fakahatchee Strand Preserve State Park, which borders both Big Cypress and the ENP. This region, also called the orchid swamp, is known for its magnificent orchids and old-growth cypress. Other preserves in this region that protected flora include Picayune Strand State Forest, Collier-Seminole State Park, and the Ten Thousand Islands National Wildlife Refuge. These preserves created a patchwork of preservation that spread out from the ENP to protect larger sections of South Florida's nature.

The ENP was thus a nucleus of preservation that, like a mangrove, slowly spread over the years. Those parks and preserves were one important thrust in a broader environmental campaign toward finding a healthy and sustainable relationship with nature. Although simply preserving a few areas as wilderness cannot solve the world's myriad environmental problems, parks and preserves are important tools that protect nature. They wield political power as legal entities supported by federal and state laws, and they create economic benefits that build constituencies that support diverse environmental causes. Most importantly, parks are publicly accessible and visible symbols of nature. They are the best advertisement for the power and promise of environmentalism. Parks inspire humans with a love of nature and challenge us to rethink our actions as members of ecological communities.

Everglades National Park is not perfect. Its boundaries are arbitrary, its water flow is polluted and inadequate, and it is beset on all sides by threats, including that of global climate change. But the perfect cannot be the enemy of the good, and there is so much good about Everglades National Park.

NOTES

Abbreviations

David Sholtz Papers	David Sholtz Papers, SAF
DF	David Fairchild
DF Papers	David Fairchild Papers, Fairchild Tropical Garden Archives, Miami, Florida
EC	Ernest Coe
EC Papers	Ernest Coe Papers, South Florida Collections Management Center, Everglades National Park
ENP	Everglades National Park
MMA	Mary McDougal Axelson
MMA Papers	Mary McDougal Axelson Papers, Richter Library, Special Collections, University of Miami, Miami, Florida
Peterson Papers	J. Hardin Peterson Papers, P. K. Younge Library, University of Florida, Gainesville, Florida
NPS Records	Records of the NPS, National Archives, College Park, Md.
SAF	State Archives of Florida, Tallahassee
SH	Spessard Holland
SH Papers-UF	Spessard Holland Papers, P. K. Younge Library, University of Florida, Gainesville
SH Papers-SAF	Spessard Holland Papers, State Archives of Florida, Tallahassee
SMR	File Unit 002: Monthly Narrative Reports, 1947–1967, series II: Correspondence and Reports; subseries B: Superintendent's Monthly Reports, 1947–1967, Records of the Superintendent's Office, EVER 22965, South Florida Collections Management Center, Everglades National Park
UM	University of Miami

Foreword

1. *Everglades National Park*, produced by the U.S. Department of the Interior, 1937; William Roy Shelton, *Land of the Everglades: Tropical Southern Florida* (Tallahassee: Florida Department of Agriculture, 1957), 10–11.

Introduction

1. William M. Rigdon, "Log of the President's Third Visit to Key West, December 3–8, 1947," President Truman's Travel Logs, Harry S. Truman Library website, www.trumanlibrary .org/calendar/travel_log/.

2. ENP Dedication Ceremony Program, 6 December 1947, EC Papers. For other accounts of this ceremony, see Jack Davis, *Everglades Providence*, 392–94; Grunwald, *Swamp*, 214–15.

3. ENP Dedication Ceremony Program.

4. On the transitional nature of the interwar period and the 1950s, see Maher, *Nature's New Deal*; Sutter, *Driven Wild*; Sarah Phillips, *This Land, This Nation*; Beeman and Pritchard, *Green and Permanent Land*; Sellars, *Preserving Nature*; Way, *Conserving Southern Longleaf*; Worster, *Dust Bowl*; Dunlap, *Saving America's Wildlife*; Mighetto, *Wild Animals*; Sutter, "Terra Incognita"; Harvey, *Symbol of Wilderness*; Rome, *Bulldozer in the Countryside*. On biocentric ethics, see Dunlap, *Saving America's Wildlife*; Mighetto, *Wild Animals*; Barrow, *Nature's Ghosts*; E. O. Wilson, *Biodiversity*; E. O. Wilson, *Biophilia*; Aldo Leopold, *Sand County Almanac*; Meine, *Aldo Leopold*; Flader, *Thinking like a Mountain*; Callicot, *In Defense*; Callicot, *Beyond the Land Ethic*; Callicot, "Non-Anthropocentric Value Theory"; Roderick Nash, *Rights of Nature*. On the history of ecology, see Hagen, *Entangled Bank*; Golley, *History of the Ecosystem Concept*; Worster, *Nature's Economy*; Kricher, *Balance of Nature*; Kingsland, *Modeling Nature*; Kingsland, *Evolution of American Ecology*; Bocking, *Ecologists and Environmental Politics*.

5. The most comprehensive histories of the Everglades include Grunwald, *Swamp*; Jack Davis, *Everglades Providence*. Other histories that focus on the Everglades' water include Blake, *Land into Water*; Godfrey and Catton, *River of Interests*; Hanna and Hanna, *Lake Okeechobee*; McCally, *Everglades*; Douglas, *Everglades*. Also see Tebeau, *Man in the Everglades*; McIver, *Death in the Everglades*; and Derr, *Some Kind of Paradise*.

6. The two most important histories on national parks are Runte, *National Parks*; and Sellars, *Preserving Nature*. Other histories of the NPS or of parks in general include Shankland, *Steve Mather*; Ise, *Our National Park Policy*; Swain, *Federal Conservation Policy*; Swain, *Wilderness Defender*; Swain, "National Park Service"; Swain, "Passage"; Tilden, *National Parks*; Wirth, *Parks, Politics, and the People*; Miles, *Guardians of the Parks*; Miles, *Wilderness in National Parks*; Mengak, *Reshaping Our National Parks*; Louter, *Windshield Wilderness*; Rothman, *Blazing Heritage*; Rothman, *Preserving Different Pasts*; Rothman, "Regular Ding-Dong Fight"; Spence, *Dispossessing the Wilderness*; Frome, *Regreening the National Parks*; Lowry, *Repairing Paradise*; Foresta, *America's National Parks*; Hampton, *How the U.S. Calvary Saved*; Hampton, "Opposition to National Parks"; Jacoby, *Crimes against Nature*; Kaufman, *National Parks*; Keller and Turek, *American Indians and National Parks*; Spence, *Dispossessing the Wilderness*; Gerald Wright, *Wildlife Research and Management*; Roderick Nash, "American Invention of National Parks"; Mackintosh, "Harold L. Ickes"; Kupper, "Science and the National Parks"; Righter, "National Monuments to National Parks." On park design, see McClelland, *Building the National Parks*; Ethan Carr, *Wilderness by Design*; and Ethan Carr, *Mission 66*. Many histories have been written on individual parks, as well. Few focus exclusively on the creation of parks but rather tell broader stories about parks and the landscapes they protect. These include Righter, *Crucible of Conservation*; Runte, *Yosemite*; Magoc, *Yellowstone*; Bartlett, *Yellowstone*; Schullery and Whittlesey, *Myth and History*; Frank, *Making Rocky Mountain National Park*; Buchholtz, *Rocky Mountain National Park*; Rawson, *Changing Tracks*; Margaret Brown, *Wild East*; Rothman and Miller, *Death Valley National Park*; Smith, *Mesa Verde National Park*; Catton, *National Park*; Jameson, *Story of Big Bend*; Richardson, "Olympic National Park"; Dilsaver and Strong, "Sequoia and Kings Canyon"; Simmons, "Conservation, Cooperation, and Controversy"; Whisnant, *Super-Scenic Motorway*; Harper, "Conceiving Nature." The *George Wright Forum* publishes interdisciplinary articles on the national parks, many of which are of interest to historians. See particularly their NPS centennial essay series. The NPS, in coordination

with the Organization of American Historians, commissions administrative histories of various units in the NPS. These are often written by public historians or by NPS employees and contain a plethora of valuable information. Two useful general administrative histories are NPS, *Shaping the System*; and Unrau and Williss, *Administrative History: Expansion*. A list of all administrative histories can be found at www.nps.gov/parkhistory/hisnps/NPSHistory/adminhistory .htm and at www.nps.gov/parkhistory/parkhistories.htm. For more on the administrative histories, see www.nps.gov/parkhistory/hisnps/NPSHistory/guide.pdf. Also see the excellent resources on npshistory.com. An administrative history of the Everglades is currently being written by Robert Blythe. On history within the NPS, also see Whisnant et al., *Imperiled Promise*.

7. On parks as cultural creations, see especially Reich, "Re-creating the Wilderness." Wilderness in the parks is explored in Louter, *Windshield Wilderness*; Turner, *Promise of Wilderness*; Miles, *Wilderness in National Parks*. Works on Native removal include Keller and Turek, *American Indians and National Parks*; Spence, *Dispossessing the Wilderness*.

8. See note 14 on wetlands. On marine environmental history, see Bolster, "Opportunities in Marine Environmental History"; Rozwadowski, *Fathoming the Ocean*; Rozwadowski, *Vast Expanses*; Philip E. Steinberg, *Social Construction of the Ocean*; Mack, *Sea*; Rozwadowski and van Keuren, *Machine in Neptune's Garden*; Deacon, *Scientists and the Sea*. On deserts, see, for example, Rothman and Miller, *Death Valley National Park*.

9. Overviews of the field include Graham, "Again the Backward Region?"; Morris, "More Southern Environmental History"; Matt Stewart, "Southern Environmental History"; Sutter, "No More the Backward Region."

10. Many southern environmental histories are either explicitly agricultural or tell stories that are entwined with agriculture: Sutter, *Let Us Now Praise Famous Gullies*; Matt Stewart, *What Nature Suffers to Groe*; Hersey, *My Work*; Worster, *Dust Bowl*; Giesen, *Boll Weevil Blues*; Mauldin, *Unredeemed Land*; Lynn Nelson, *Pharsalia*; Gisolfi, *Takeover*; Daniel, *Toxic Drift*; Strom, *Making Catfish Bait*; Edelson, *Plantation Enterprise*.

11. On Appalachia, see Margaret Brown, *Wild East*; Silver, *Mount Mitchell*; Newfont, *Blue Ridge Commons*; Pierce, *Great Smokies*; Donald Davis, *Where There Are Mountains*. Gregg, *Managing the Mountains*. On the South's forests, see Boyd, *Slain Wood*; Walker, *Southern Forest*; Way, *Conserving Southern Longleaf*. Southern forestry can also be seen as a subsection of agriculture, as many forests are managed to create timber. On water in the South, see Manganiello, *Southern Water, Southern Power*; Kelman, *River and Its City*. Both forestry and water have been major fields of study in American environmental history. A surprisingly large number of works on southern wetlands have been published though, pointing to the centrality of wetlands in the South.

12. Works that have examined environmental politics, state building, and environmental activism in the South include Bruce Stewart and Manganiello, "Watershed Democracy"; Newfont, *Blue Ridge Commons*; Gregg, *Managing the Mountains*. Adam Rome, *Genius of Earth Day*, includes brief accounts of Earth Day in Miami and Birmingham (126–35). Although the South has often been seen as a place without strong conservationist leanings, recent work have shown that there was a significant conservationist presence in the South, even beyond agricultural reformers. See, for example, Jack Davis, *Everglades Providence*; Way, *Conserving Southern Longleaf*; Hersey, *My Work*.

13. On cultural attitudes toward wetlands in American history, see David Miller, *Dark Eden*; Hurd, *Stirring the Mud*; Vileisis, *Discovering the Unknown Landscape*; Siry, *Marshes of the Ocean Shore*; Megan Nelson, *Trembling Earth*; Kirby, *Poquosin*; Ogden, *Swamplife*;

Anthony Wilson, *Shadow and Shelter*; Meindl, "Past Perceptions"; Meindl, "Southerners and Their Swamps"; Zwieg and Wiley, "Semiglades"; Colten, *Unnatural Metropolis*; Sawyer, *America's Wetland*; Ray, *Pinhook*.

14. The term "wetland" has a positive connotation today, whereas Americans before the era of modern environmentalism used the word swamp as an epithet. Some Americans, like Donald Trump with his calls to "drain the swamp," still use the term in that way. Scientifically speaking, a swamp is a tree-dominated wetland. A marsh is a plant-dominated wetland. A wetland is merely an ecosystem regularly inundated with water. I am using these terms here not in their scientific sense, but according to their popular usage.

15. On Progressive Era conservation and preservation, see Hays, *Conservation* ; Reiger, *American Sportsmen*; Roderick Nash, *Wilderness and the American Mind*; Fox, *American Conservation Movement*; Cohen, *Pathless Way*; Char Miller, *Gifford Pinchot*; Righter, *Battle over Hetch Hetchy*.

16. On modern environmentalism, see Hays, *Beauty, Health, and Permanence*; Shabecoff, *Fierce Green Fire*; Gottlieb, *Forcing the Spring*; Rothman, *Greening of a Nation?*; Rome, *Genius of Earth Day*.

17. Runte, *National Parks*; Sears, *Sacred Places*.

18. The literature on the sublime in nature, not to mention the philosophical and literary concept of the sublime, is immense. For an introduction, see Cronon, "Trouble with Wilderness," 71–75; Emerson, "Method of Nature"; Burke, *Philosophical Enquiry*; Novak, *Nature and Culture*; Dunaway, *Natural Visions*; McKinsey, *Niagara Falls*.

19. On wilderness, tourism, and development in the national parks, see Miles, *Wilderness in National Parks*; Louter, *Windshield Wilderness*; Ethan Carr, *Wilderness by Design*; Ethan Carr, *Mission 66*. On wilderness, see Sutter, *Driven Wild*; Roderick Nash, *Wilderness and the American Mind*; Turner, *Promise of Wilderness*; Harvey, *Wilderness Forever*; Frome, *Battle for the Wilderness*; Scott, *Enduring Wilderness*; Callicot and Nelson, *Great New Wilderness Debate*; Callicot and Nelson, *Wilderness Debate Rages On*.

20. Sellars, *Preserving Nature*. Also see Dunlap, "Wildlife, Science"; Shafer, "Conservation Biology Trailblazers"; Duncan, "George Melendez Wright"; Runte, "Joseph Grinnell and Yosemite"; Rawson, *Changing Tracks*; Pritchard, *Preserving Yellowstone's Natural Conditions*; Kupper, "Science and the National Parks." Alfred Runte makes similar points in *National Parks*, when he argues that the ENP was the first park to embody what he called "complete conservation" (128–37).

21. On biocentric wilderness, see Sutter, *Driven Wild*, 13–15; Roderick Nash, *Wilderness and the American Mind*, 425–29; Hendee and Stankey, "Biocentricity in Wilderness Management"; Noss, "Building a Wilderness Recovery Network"; Foreman, *Rewilding North America*; Callicot and Nelson, *Great New Wilderness Debate*. On George Wright and early biocentric ideas about wilderness, see Callicot and Nelson, *Wilderness Debate Rages On*, 21–188.

22. On the impact of World War II on the South, see Cobb, *South and America*; McMillen, *Remaking Dixie*; Bartley, *New South*; Schulman, *From Cotton Belt to Sunbelt*; Kirby, *Rural Worlds Lost*; Gavin Wright, *Old South, New South*.

23. On the Sunbelt South, see Cobb, *Selling of the South*; Schulman, *From Cotton Belt to Sunbelt*; Cobb, *Industrialization and Southern Society*; Mohl, *Searching for the Sunbelt*; Abbott, *The New Urban America*; Bartley, *New South*; Bernard and Rice, *Sunbelt Cities*.

24. On tourism in the United States, see Rothman, *Devil's Bargains*; Sears, *Sacred Places*; Jakle, *Tourist*; Mooney-Melvin, "Harnessing the Romance." On tourism in national parks, see Shaffer, *See America First*; Runte, *National Parks*; Runte, *Trains of Discovery*; Starnes, *Creating*

the Land. On tourism in the South, see Hillyer, *Designing Dixie*; Karen Cox, *Destination Dixie*; Yuhl, *Golden Haze of Memory*; Stanonis, *Creating the Big Easy*; Stanonis, *Dixie Emporium*; Aron, *Working at Play*; Way, *Conserving Southern Longleaf*, 19–55; Matt Stewart, *What Nature Suffers to Groe*, 216–24. On tourism in Florida, see Mormino, *Land of Sunshine*, 76–122; Derr, *Some Kind of Paradise*, 37–60; Fogelson, *Married to the Mouse*; Noll, "Steamboats, Cypress, and Tourism"; George, "Passage to the New Eden"; Dave Nelson, "When Modern Tourism Was Born"; Rogers, "Florida in World War II"; Mormino, "Midas Returns"; Dawson, "Travel Strengthens America?"; Evans, "Weathering the Storm," 143–50. Holland's ideas about tourism foreshadowed ecotourism, see Honey, *Ecotourism and Sustainable Development*. On tourism in the Sunbelt South, see Kahrl, *Land Was Ours*; Stanonis, *Creating the Big Easy*. Most studies of Sunbelt tourism focus on the U.S. West, and especially on Las Vegas. See Rothman, *Neon Metropolis*.

25. On southern identity, see Woodward, *Burden of Southern History*; Cash, *Mind of the South*; Cobb, *Redefining Southern Culture*; Cobb, *Away Down South*; Reed, *Enduring South*. Landscape and identity have played a major role in many southern histories, most notably in Phillips, *Life and Labor in the Old South*, yet southern environmental histories have made few explicit connections between their works and Southern identity. Also see Koeniger, "Climate and Southern Distinctiveness"; Sutter, *Let Us Now Praise Famous Gullies*. Hillyer's *Designing Dixie* examines how post–Civil War New South boosters used tourism to both reconstruct the South's postwar identity and bring economic growth to the area. Florida boosters after World War II sought the same things. On Florida's identity, see Whitfield, "Florida's Fudged Identity"; Mormino, *Land of Sunshine*; Chambliss and Cummings, "Florida"; Parker, "Is South Florida"; Rowe, *Idea of Florida*; Nicole Cox, "Selling Seduction; Noll and Tegeder, *Ditch of Dreams*.

26. Works on the emergence of modern conservativism in the Sunbelt include Kruse, *White Flight*; Shermer, *Sunbelt Capitalism*; McGirr, *Suburban Warriors*; Lassiter, *Silent Majority*; Crespino, *In Search of Another Country*; Lassiter and Crespino, *Myth of Southern Exceptionalism*; Lowndes, *From the New Deal*; Fredrickson, *Dixiecrat Revolt*. For a more complete analysis of the literature on modern conservativism, see Kim Phillips-Fein, "Conservatism."

27. Phillips-Fein argues that historical studies of conservativism show that the movement's legacy is "conflicted and contingent" ("Conservatism," 742). The same can be said for conservative views of nature. On modern conservative views of the environment, see Drake, *Loving Nature*; Turner, "Specter of Environmentalism'; Flippen, *Conservative Conservationist*; Flippen, *Nixon and the Environment*.

28. Turner, "Specter of Environmentalism"; Switzer, *Green Backlash*; Helvarg, *War against the Greens*; Cawley, *Federal Land, Western Anger*; Mueller, *DeVoto's West*; Thomas, *Country in the Mind*; Robbins and Foster, *Land in the American West*.

29. On nature's agency in the history of natural disasters, see Ted Steinberg, *Acts of God*; Worster, *Dust Bowl*. Hurricanes had no official names before 1954; see www.nhc.noaa.gov /aboutnames_history.shtml.

Chapter 1. The Everglades and a New England Nurseryman

1. Douglas, *Everglades*, 5.

2. This section on the Everglades' ecosystems and biota relies on a number of synthetic texts that provide overviews of the Everglades. The most useful to nonscientific audiences include Lodge, *Everglades Handbook*; Steven M. Davis and Ogden, *Everglades*; Myers and Ewel, *Ecosystems of Florida*; McPherson et al., *Environment of South Florida*; and McCally, *Everglades*.

3. On sheet flow, see "Sheet-Flow Velocities."

4. Gleason and Stone, "Age, Origin, and Landscape Evolution."

5. Lodge, *Everglades Handbook*, 15–16.

6. Douglas, *Everglades*, 10.

7. John Kunkel Small, "Proposed Everglades National Park," 264.

8. Wylie, *Crunch and Des*; Grey, *Tales of Southern Rivers*.

9. Vileisis, *Discovering the Unknown Landscape*; Siry, *Marshes of the Ocean Shore*.

10. Motte, *Journey into Wilderness*, 232.

11. Buckingham Smith, "Report of Buckingham Smith on his Reconnaissance of the Everglades, submitted to R. J. Walker, Secretary of the Treasury, 1 June 1848," in *Everglades of Florida*, 46–54, 52, 54.

12. William T. Hornday to John Kunkel Small, ca. 1931; Robert Sterling Yard to Henry Isaac Ward, 4 February 1929; Horace Albright to Ray Lyman Wilbur, 10 May 1930, all in NPS Records.

13. On Progressive reform, see Wiebe, *Search for Order*; Hofstadter, *Age of Reform*; Weinstein, *Corporate Ideal*; Kolko, *Triumph of Conservatism*; McCormick, "Discovery that Business Corrupts Politics."

14. On Progressive Era conservation and preservation, see Hays, *Conservation*; Reiger, *American Sportsmen and the Origins of Conservation*; Roderick Nash, *Wilderness and the American Mind*; Fox, *American Conservation Movement*; Cohen, *Pathless Way*; Char Miller, *Gifford Pinchot*; Righter, *Battle over Hetch Hetchy*; Worster, *Passion for Nature*.

15. The next few paragraphs rely on the excellent secondary literature on Everglades drainage. See Blake, *Land into Water*; Godfrey and Catton, *River of Interests*; Hanna and Hanna, *Lake Okeechobee*; McCally, *Everglades*; Grunwald, *Swamp*, 57–97, 130–50; Jack Davis, *Everglades Providence*, 55–69, 81–89, 115–26, 138–52.

16. Jack Davis, *Everglades Providence*, 113–26; McCally, *Everglades*, 130–40.

17. Jack Davis, *Everglades Providence*, 144–47; McCally, *Everglades*, 94–105; Meindl, Alderman, and Waylen, "On the Importance."

18. McCally, *Everglades*, 109–15, 131–37; Grunwald, *Swamp*, 160–63.

19. Florida rebuilt the dike around Lake Okeechobee and deepened the St. Lucie Canal and Caloosahatchee River. These projects were aimed at flood control.

20. The following works examine the Everglades and criticize drainage but do not reflect a scientific understanding of the Everglades' sheet flow: Small, *From Eden to Sahara*; Simpson, *In Lower Florida Wilds*; Bailey, *Birds of Florida*.

21. On Douglas's views, see Jack Davis, *Everglades Providence*, 497–98.

22. McIver, *Death in the Everglades*, 5.

23. Jack Davis, "Alligators and Plume Birds," 246.

24. McIver, *Death in the Everglades*; Poole, "Women"; Derr, *Some Kind of Paradise*, 135–50.

25. Derr, *Some Kind of Paradise*, 141.

26. An obituary for Anna Coe stated that her concern for orchids being taken out of the Everglades contributed to EC's desire to protect the Everglades. See *Miami Herald*, July 1940, undated clipping, attached to SH to EC, 26 July 1940, SH Papers-UF.

27. Various U.S. Census records taken between 1880 and 1930 list EC's birth year as each of the years between 1867 and 1870. According to all other sources, he was born in 1867. See EC, Passport Application, National Archives and Records Administration, Washington, D.C.; *Passport Applications, January 2, 1906–March 31, 1925*, collection number ARC identifier 583830, MLR number A1 534; NARA series M1490, roll 100.

28. Pratt, "Papa."

29. EC, "insert with federal application employment form," 28 June 1949, EC Papers; U.S., School Catalogs, 1765–1935, Ancestry.com, 2012. EC did not hold a degree from Yale, as Marjory Stoneman Douglas claimed in "The Forgotten Father." Historians have repeated this incorrect claim.

30. U.S. City Directories, 1821–1989, Ancestry.com, 2012. Established in 1892, Elm City Nursery was owned by C. P. Lines & Co.

31. Advertisement for Elm City Nursery, *Proceedings*, Annual Convention American Association of Nurserymen, American Association of Nurserymen, 1893, 77; *American Florist*, 26 December 1914, 1196; *National Nurseryman* 20, no. 6 (June 1912): 218; *Elm City Nursery, 1901 Catalog*, New York Botanical Garden Special Collections. For more on EC, see Jack Davis, *Everglades Providence*; Grunwald, *Swamp*. The only exploration of EC's early life is Woodside, "Father of the Everglades."

32. *National Nurseryman* 4, no. 10 (November 1896): 129.

33. *National Nurseryman* 13 (1905).

34. *American Fruits* 21 (January 1915): 28; *National Nurseryman* 23, no. 2 (February 1915): 58; *National Nurseryman* 29, no. 1 (January 1921): 34; *Elm City Nursery, 1916 Catalog*, New York Botanical Garden Special Collections.

35. *National Nurseryman* 16, no. 4 (April 1908): 129.

36. *Elm City Nursery, 1916 Catalog*, New York Botanical Garden Special Collections.

37. *National Nurseryman* 19, no. 4 (April 1911): 145; *National Nurseryman* 18, no. 2 (February 1910): 486.

38. *Elm City Nursery, 1901 Catalog*.

39. *Elm City Nursery, 1907 Catalog*, New York Botanical Garden Special Collections.

40. The box-barberry was a Japanese dwarf hedge, while the ibolium privet was a hybrid of a Japanese ibota privet and the Californian ovalifolium privet (*Garden Magazine*, March 1921, 73). Other periodicals containing advertisements for both plants include *National Nurseryman*, *Field Illustrated*, *Park and Cemetery and Landscape Gardening*, and *Guide to Nature*.

41. Elias, *History*; Coe, "Keeping Japanese Picture Plants." Also see the museum's history page (https://www.bbg.org/about/history/).

42. Pauley, *Biologists*, 71–92. On DF, see DF, *World Was My Garden*; Daniel Stone, *Food Explorer*; and Harris, *Fruits of Eden*.

43. EC participated in landscape architecture organizations only after his move to Miami in 1925.

44. *American Fruits* 23, no. 3 (March 1916): 66; *American Fruits*, April 1915, 95; *American Fruits*, March 1914, 76. These papers included "Varieties of Ornamental Trees, Shrubs and Vines Best Adapted to Different Geographical Section of New England," "Effects of the European War," and "Local Retail Nursery and Sales Grounds."

45. *National Nurseryman* 22, no. 3 (March 1914): 107; *American Fruits*, May 1914, 124; *Proceedings*, Annual Convention American Association of Nurserymen, vols. 39–45, 1914–20. These papers included "Varieties of Ornamental Trees, Shrubs and Vines Best Adapted to Different Geographical Section of New England," "Effects of the European War," and "Local Retail Nursery and Sales Grounds."

46. Coe, "Nursery Condition"; EC, "Horticulture in Japan."

47. *Elm City Catalog, 1906*, New York Botanical Gardens Archives.

48. *Elm City Catalog, 1916*.

49. *Elm City Catalog, 1906*.

50. Elias, *History*, 31.

51. Coe, "Keeping Japanese Picture Plants."

52. On the 1920s Florida land boom and bust, see Nolan, *Fifty Feet in Paradise*; Jarvis, "Secrecy Has No Excuse"; George, "Brokers, Binders, and Builders"; Frazer and Guthrie, *Florida Land Boom*.

53. George, "Brokers, Binders, and Builders."

54. Most other accounts of the park's creation do not examine EC's past life in New England and hence buy into EC's mythmaking about his own life.

55. Orville Rigby to the *Miami Herald*, December 3, 1947, EC Papers. Harold H. Bailey, an ornithologist and member of the Florida Society of Natural History, also claimed to have first taken EC into the Everglades. Harold H. Bailey, letter to editor, *Miami Herald*, 30 November 1947.

56. Pratt, "Papa," 32, 46, 47; Douglas, "Forgotten Man."; Pratt, "Papa," 32.

57. EC to Arno Cammerer, 15 April 1930, NPS Records.

58. DF, "The Unique Everglades," 20 December 1933, EC Papers.

59. Fred Foster, "Fish Life in the Proposed Everglades National Park," 22 March 1930, NPS Records.

60. Donald Worster (*Dust Bowl*), Ted Steinberg (*Acts of God*), and other historians have shown that humans are complicit in the destruction caused by natural disasters.

61. McCally, *Everglades*, 133–35; Grunwald, *Swamp*, 186–96; Jack Davis, *Everglades Providence*, 294–309; Mykle, *Killer 'Cane*. Zora Neal Hurston's *Their Eyes Were Watching God* is an excellent fictional account of this hurricanes effects on the migrant farm workers around the dike.

62. This is another central argument in Ted Steinberg, *Acts of God*.

63. EC to Arno Cammerer, 15 April 1930, NPS Records.

64. Subsequent chapters examine these individuals and their contributions to the park's creation in more detail.

65. Other books that examine the interwar period and the connections between Progressive Era conservation movements and modern environmentalism include Sutter, *Driven Wild*; Maher, *Nature's New Deal*; Sarah Phillips, *This Land, This Nation*; Beeman and Pritchard, *A Green and Permanent Land*.

66. On the history of ecology, see Hagen, *Entangled Bank*; Golley, *History of the Ecosystem Concept*; Worster, *Nature's Economy*; Kricher, *Balance of Nature*; Kingsland, *Modeling Nature*; Kingsland, *Evolution of American Ecology*.

67. Hagen, *Entangled Bank*, 26; Clements, *Plant Succession*, 99, from Hagen, *Entangled Bank*, 26.

68. Kricher, *Balance of Nature*, 1.

69. Although the science of ecology influenced EC's ideas about the Everglades, popular ideas about the Everglades' nature would not be similarly influenced by ecological notions until the 1947 publication of Marjory Stoneman Douglas's *Everglades*. EC was not a popularizer of ecological ideas as was Douglas or the more widely known Rachel Carson. See Douglas, *Everglades*; Jack Davis, *Everglades Providence*; Lear, *Rachel Carson*; Lytle, *Gentle Subversive*.

70. EC to Edward Pou, 16 February 1933, Peterson Papers.

71. EC to Harold Bryant, 16 April 1936, EC Papers.

72. EC to Arno Cammerer, 9 November 1933, NPS Records.

73. EC to George Wright, 31 January 1935, NPS Records.

74. On attitudes toward fire, see Pyne, *Fire in America*; Way, *Conserving Southern Longleaf*. On attitudes toward predators and wildlife in the 1930s, see Dunlap, *Saving America's Wildlife*; Mighetto, *Wild Animals*.

75. Sellars, *Preserving Nature*, 74–75, 98, 119–121; Dunlap, *Saving America's Wildlife*.

76. EC to Arno Cammerer, 9 November 1933, B921, NPS Records.

77. Drye, *Storm of the Century*; Knowles, *Category 5*.

78. EC, "Notes on the Influence of the Storm of September 2, 1935," 5 October 1935, David Sholtz Papers; EC, "Further Notes. The Influences of the September 2, 1935 Hurricane on the Everglades National Park Project Area," 5 February 1936, NPS Records; EC, "Notes on the Influence of the Storm"; EC to Arthur Demaray, 14 October 1935, NPS Records.

79. EC, "Notes on the Influence of the Storm."

80. Ibid.

81. Worster, "Ecology of Order and Chaos."

82. EC to NPS director, 25 April 1931, NPS Records.

83. EC to Roger Toll, 14 May 1930, B232, NPS Records.

84. EC to John Kunkel Small, 6 May 1932, NPS Records.

85. Beard, "Let "er Burn?," 2.

86. EC to Robert T. Morris, 8 July 1932, NPS Records.

87. Jack Davis, *Everglades Providence*, 354–59, McCally, *Everglades*, 146–47, Douglas, *Everglades*.

88. Simpson, *In Lower Florida Wilds*; Bailey, *Birds of Florida*; John Kunkel Small, *From Eden to Sahara*.

89. EC, Suggestions, 1 March 1930, NPS Records.

90. EC to NPS director, 25 April 1931, NPS Records.

91. EC to NPS, 13 November 1934, NPS Records.

92. EC to Newton Drury, 14 February 1949, NPS Records. On these water conservation areas, see McCally, *Everglades*, 147–53; Godfrey and Catton, *River of Interests*; Grunwald, *Swamp*, 216–36, 315–70; Jack Davis, *Everglades Providence*, 387–91, 594–601.

93. Newton Drury to EC, 25 February 1949, NPS Records.

94. Douglas, "Forgotten Man."

95. Grunwald, *Swamp*, 206–7.

Chapter 2. Redefining National Parks, Redefining the Everglades

1. Runte, *National Parks*, 82–105; National Park Service, *Shaping the System*; Hampton, *How the U.S. Calvary Saved*.

2. Parks created via federal fiat and carved out of federal lands include Yellowstone, Rocky Mountain, Sequoia, King's Canyon, Grand Canyon, Zion, Glacier, Lassen Volcanic, Mount Rainier, Crater Lake, and Olympic National Parks. See Runte, *National Parks*; Ise, *Our National Park Policy*; Runte, *Yosemite*; Magoc, *Yellowstone*; Bartlett, *Yellowstone*; Schullery and Whittlesey, *Myth and History*; Frank, *Making Rocky Mountain National Park*; Buchholtz, *Rocky Mountain National Park*; Harper, "Conceiving Nature"; Dilsaver and Strong, "Sequoia and Kings Canyon"; Krahe and Catton, *Little Gem of the Cascades*; Catton, *National Park*; Unrau and Stephan, *Administrative History: Crater Lake*; Louter, *Windshield Wilderness*; National Park Service, *Olympic National Park*; Schene, Only the Squeal"; Richardson, "Olympic National Park." Many of these parks were first established as national monuments and then

later made national parks. See Righter, "National Monuments to National Parks." The creation of Grand Teton National Park followed a much more complicated route. See Righter, *Crucible of Conservation.*

3. On parks and the railroads, see Runte, *Trains of Discovery.* On Stephen Mather, see Shankland, *Steve Mather.* On the 1916 Organic Act, see Winks, "National Park Service Act"; Swain, "Passage."

4. Albright, *Birth of the National Park Service;* Albright and Schenck, *Creating the National Park Service.*

5. Runte, *National Parks,* 219–20; Unrau and Williss, *Administrative History: Expansion;* National Park Service, *Shaping the System.*

6. See Runte, *National Parks,* 112–37; Ise, *Our National Park Policy,* 248–270; Swain, *Federal Conservation Policy,* 123–43; Unrau and Williss, *Administrative History: Expansion.*

7. After these parks were created, the federal government did often expand the boundaries of these parks using federal appropriations.

8. Runte, *National Parks,* 114–15; Duncan and Burns, *National Parks,* 189–95.

9. Wood, *Beautiful Land;* Reich, "Re-creating the Wilderness."

10. Lambert, *Undying Past of Shenandoah;* Reich, "Re-creating the Wilderness"; Dennis Simmons, "Conservation, Cooperation, and Controversy." The creation of Shenandoah National Park, like all others, entailed the forced removal of people from these lands. Western parks were built on the removal of Native Americans, while in eastern parks, state governments often used eminent domain to purchase needed lands from property owners.

11. Margaret Brown, *Wild East,* 78–103, 120–21.

12. Miles, *Wilderness in National Parks,* 67–70, 88–91.

13. Jameson, *Story of Big Bend;* Welsh, *Landscape of Ghosts.*

14. Little, *Island Wilderness.*

15. National Park Service Organic Act, 1916 (39 Stat. 535); Winks, "National Park Service Act"; Swain, "Passage"; Sutter, *Driven Wild,* 116–20; Runte, *National Parks,* 209–18.

16. "National Park Standards: A Declaration of Policy," Campfire Club of America, 1929, in Dilsaver, *America's National Park System;* Riordan, "Development and Implementation."

17. Douglas, *Everglades,* 6.

18. Vileisis, *Discovering the Unknown Landscape,* and Siry, *Marshes of the Ocean Shore,* examine both these older negative ideas about wetlands and the reconsideration of wetlands in the 1930s. Also see David Miller, *Dark Eden;* Hurd, *Stirring the Mud;* Megan Nelson, *Trembling Earth;* Kirby, *Poquosin;* Ogden, *Swamplife;* Anthony Wilson, *Shadow and Shelter;* Ray, *Pinhook;* Meindl, "Past Perceptions."

19. See, for example, EC, ENPA bulletin, 25 October 1934, David Sholtz Papers.

20. On the social construction of nature, see, for example, Cronon, *Uncommon Ground;* Soule and Lease, *Reinventing Nature?,* Bird, "Social Construction of Nature"; Demeritt, "What Is the 'Social Construction'"; Haraway, *Simians, Cyborgs and Women.*

21. Austin et al., *Florida of John Kunkel Small;* Wilhelm, "Pragmatism, Seminoles, and Science."

22. Barnhart, *Bibliography of John Kunkel Small.*

23. Small, *Flora.*

24. Small, *From Eden to Sahara,* 112, 114.

25. EC to John Kunkel Small, 6 November 1929, UM Presidential Archives, Richter Library, Special Collections, UM.

26. EC to John Kunkel Small, 6 May 1932, NPS Records.

27. EC to John Kunkel Small, 9 March 1932, NPS Records.

28. EC bulletin, n.d., Doyle Carlton Papers.

29. EC, 20 May 1933, John D. Pennekamp Papers, PKYL, UF.

30. EC, "America's Only Tropics," lecture at the Cosmos Club, 28 October 1929, UM Presidential Archives.

31. Schrepfer, *Fight to Save the Redwoods*; Hays, *Wars in the Woods*; Hays, *American People*; Char Miller, *Gifford Pinchot*.

32. Mighetto, *Wild Animals*; Dunlap, *Saving America's Wildlife*.

33. EC to John Merriam, 13 December 1929, NPS Records.

34. EC, "Is It a Tragedy?," 6 July 1931, DF Papers.

35. EC radio address, 11 April 1931, NPS Records.

36. *Elm City Nursery, 1907 Catalog*, New York Botanical Garden Special Collections.

37. On tropicality, see Arnold, "Illusory Riches"; Driver and Martins, *Tropical Visions*; Driver, "Imagining the Tropics"; Martins, "Naturalist's Vision"; Stepan, *Picturing Tropical Nature*; Sutter, "Nature's Agents"; Sutter, "Tropics."

38. Humboldt, *Personal Narrative*.

39. Humboldt, *Cosmos*; Wulf, *Invention of Nature*; Sachs, *Humboldt Current*.

40. Stepan, *Picturing Tropical Nature*, 25.

41. Martins, "Naturalist's Vision"; David Taylor, "Biogeographer's Construction of Tropical Lands."

42. Pauley, *Fruits and Plains*; Harris, *Fruits of Eden*; DF, *World Was My Garden*.

43. DF, *Proposed National Park*.

44. EC to NPS director, 1 August 1934, DF Papers. Although the park and the ENPA had the word "tropic" attached to them between 1928 and 1931, for the sake of clarity I have referred to the park as the Everglades National Park and EC's organization as the Everglades National Park Association throughout this book. EC periodically reinserted the world "tropic" into both these names after 1931, causing additional confusion.

45. ENPA bulletin, EC, 10 April 1929, Doyle Carlton Papers, SAF; EC, press release, May 1934, DF Papers; EC, ca. 1929–31, "Outlining some of the Benefits the State of Florida will enjoy . . . ," Doyle Carlton Papers.

46. EC, "Everglades National Park," *All Florida Magazine*, June 1931; EC, "National Park in Everglades Asked," address before the Annual Convention of the American Institute of Park Executive and American Park Society, ca. 1929–31, both in NPS Records.

47. EC to DF, 13 August 1929, DF Papers; EC general letter, 5 June 1928, DF Papers; EC, "America's Only Tropics"; EC, "National Park in Everglades Asked," address before the Annual Convention of the American Institute of Park Executive and American Park Society, ca. 1929–31, NPS Records; EC.

48. EC, ENPA Action Plan, 6 December 1928, EC Papers; EC press release, May 1934, DF Papers.

49. EC, Submitted Suggestions, 1 March 1930, NPS Records; Charles Burke, 8 January 1929, DF Papers; EC to David Sholtz, 7 June 1935, David Sholtz Papers.

50. Simpson, *In Lower Florida Wilds*.

51. La Plante, "Sage of Biscayne Bay; Rothra, *Florida's Pioneer Naturalist*.

52. Simpson, *In Lower Florida Wilds*, 110.

53. Ibid., 59, 109–10.

54. EC, speech at Simpson Park dedication, 1 April 1932, NPS Records.

55. EC, "America's Only Tropics."

56. On the sublime in nature, see Cronon, "Trouble with Wilderness"; Emerson, "Method of Nature"; Burke, *Philosophical Enquiry*; Novak, *Nature and Culture*; Dunaway, *Natural Visions*; McKinsey, *Niagara Falls*. This belief that natural landscapes possess an exalted and supernatural sense of grandeur is often connected to Progressive conservation, but it has remained an important element of environmental views of nature as well. Historians focused on defining modern environmentalism have rightly identified rising standards of living, new scientific views of the natural world, and reactions against the degradation of local environments as important elements of modern environmentalism. See Hays, *Beauty, Health, and Permanence*; Shabecoff, *Fierce Green Fire*; Gottlieb, *Forcing the Spring*; Rothman, *Greening of a Nation?*; Rome, *Genius of Earth Day*. Modern environmentalists, though, particularly adherents of deep ecology, have often touted the beauty and spiritual power of nature.

57. EC, 5 June 1928, UM Presidential Archives.

58. EC, "America's Only Tropics."

59. EC, "Submitted Suggestions."

60. EC to Roger Toll, 14 May 1930, NPS Records.

61. Douglas, *Everglades*.

62. David McCally offers similar criticisms of the ways Douglas's phrase has been misused (*Everglades*, 179–80).

63. George Wright, Dixon, and Thompson, *Fauna*, 1. A. Starker Leopold's *Wildlife Management in the National Parks*, more commonly known as the Leopold Report, made the same point in its declaration that parks should "represent a vignette of primitive America" (3). Historians have paid great attention to the Leopold Report, while giving less credit to George Wright's *Fauna*.

64. On the removal of humans from national parks and other protected spaces, see Spence, *Dispossessing the Wilderness*; Catton, *Inhabited Wilderness*; Jacoby, *Crimes against Nature*; Keller and Turek, *American Indians and National Parks*. On national parks as human landscapes that create wilderness, see Sellars, *Preserving Nature*; Reich, "Re-creating the Wilderness,"

65. Milanich, *Florida Indians*; Covington, *Seminoles of Florida*; West, *Enduring Seminoles*. Also see the works of Harry Kersey, who published nine books and over seventy articles, many on the Seminoles' history.

66. Tebeau, *Man in the Everglades*; Ogden, *Swamplife*. The history of Ed Watson was adapted by Peter Matthiessen into a series of novels. His award-winning trilogy was later reworked into a single volume, *Shadow Country*. That work of fiction reflects a great deal of historical research. On Matthiessen's historical research, see Watson, "Man Writing."

67. Griffin, *Archaeology of the Everglades*.

68. EC, "Submitted Suggestions."

69. EC, "Speech at the Ladies Night of the Cosmos Club," 28 October 1929, UM Presidential Papers. Other features at the Cape likewise belied Coe's claims of primitiveness. By the 1920s, settlers and road construction companies employed by the Model Land Company cut at least eight canals in the vicinity of Cape Sable. See Wanless and Vlaswinkel, *Coastal Landscape*; Will, *Dredgeman of Cape Sable*; Will, "Digging the Cape Sable Canal." Noted New York and Miami conservationist Augustus Houghton, who helped evaluate the Everglades for the NPS, toured the region in 1932 and reported on these canals. According to Houghton, they were "a

great detriment" to the Cape's composition and bird populations. Canals altered the salinity and water levels of Whitewater Bay and Alligator Lake, "resulting in the killing of many acres of black mangrove trees and the lowering of the water level" (Augustus Houghton, "Unofficial Report," 4 March 1932, Auguston Seymour Houghton Papers, Richter Library, Special Collections, UM). EC, ENP advocates, and NPS officials avoided all mention of these canals.

Chapter 3. Promoting the Park

1. Harold Bailey, "Historian Tells Version of How Park Idea Started," 30 November 1947, *Miami Herald*; EC, "Preliminary Considerations for Everglades National Park," 1928, NPS Records.

2. EC, "Preliminary Considerations for Everglades National Park." The park standards EC referenced in this report were outlined in Yard, *Glimpses of Our National Parks*, 4.

3. NPS memo, 24 February 1930, NPS Records.

4. EC, Progressive Sequence of Action, 6 December 1928, DF Papers.

5. Ibid.

6. DF to Henry Ward, 3 February 1929, DF Papers.

7. DF to EC, 26 September 1930, DF Papers.

8. EC, "Story of the Everglades National Park Project," unpublished manuscript, 1 December 1950, EC Papers.

9. ENPA meeting, 27 January 1933, DF Papers.

10. Clifford Bourne to ENPA, finance report, 23 June 1932, DF Papers; ENPA report on the $5,000 fund, n.d., DF papers.

11. EC to ENPA Executive Council, 24 March 1933, DF Papers.

12. On the organization structure of Progressive Conservationist organizations, see Fox, *American Conservation Movement*. On the importance of popular publicity methods to modern environmentalism, see Harvey, *Symbol of Wilderness*.

13. Other historians also noted EC's prolific letter-writing campaigns. See Grunwald, *The Swamp*, 206–7; Jack Davis, *Everglades Providence*, 332–37.

14. EC, "Is It a Tragedy?," miscellaneous mailing, 6 July 1931, DF Papers.

15. EC to ENPA and ENPC Executive Council, 28 June 1935, EC Papers.

16. EC Papers; EC to Governor Sholtz, 4 May 1936, EC Papers.

17. Douglas, "Forgotten Man."

18. EC, 10 April 1929, Doyle Carlton Papers, SAF; EC, 11 April 1929, DF Papers. The EC Papers held at the South Florida Collections Management Center in ENP only cover EC's activities in the ENPC from 1935 to 1937 and his correspondence in the late 1940s. Much of EC's correspondence, however, can be found in other archival collections. His bulletins especially can easily be found in most of the collections listed in the bibliography.

19. Jay N. Darling to EC, 7 October 1943, UM Presidential Archives, Richter Library, Special Collections, UM; Harlan P. Kelsey to EC, 23 October 1943, UM Presidential Archives; EC to John Kunkel Small, 6 November 1929, UM Presidential Archives; V. E. Shelford to EC, 20 October 1943, UM Presidential Archives; George M. Wright to EC, 9 October 1931, David Carlton Papers; Ales Hrdlicka to EC, 8 December 1932, SH Papers-SAF.

20. Douglas and Rothchild, *Marjory Stoneman Douglas*, 135; Henry Ward to Robert T. Morris, 12 February 1931, NACP. ENPC meeting, 2 December 1936, EC Papers. Although the quantity of EC's letters was impressive, many of his letters were poorly written and confusing.

Much of his correspondence seemed hurried and confused, as if he was dictating a stream-of-consciousness rant to an overwhelmed secretary. See, for example, EC to David Sholtz, 23 June 1935, DF Papers.

21. Meindl, "Frank Stoneman"; Jack Davis, *Everglades Providence*, 117–18; Wilhelm, "Pragmatism, Seminoles, and Science."

22. EC bulletin, 20 September 1940, SH Papers-UF; *Miami Herald*, 23 September 1940.

23. *Miami Herald*, 2 December 1930, 1; 16 December 1930, 1, 20; 17 December 193, 1; 24 December 1930, 13; 28 December 1930, 1, 33; 28 December 1930, 4; 29 December 1930, 1, 7; 30 December 1930, 1, 3; and 31 December 1930, 1, 3.

24. Douglas wrote four long articles on this trip, which was her first lengthy journey into the ecosystems she would later write about in *The Everglades: River of Grass*. These articles later served as the basis of much of Douglas's 1959 children's book, *Alligator Crossing*, and had a powerful influence on Douglas's perceptions of the Everglades. See *Miami Herald*, 12 February 1930, 2; 14 February 1930, 39; and 16 February 1930, 26–27.

25. Jack Davis, *Everglades Providence*, 335.

26. Ibid., 335–37; Douglas, "Plumes"; Douglas, "Wings"; Douglas, *Alligator Crossing*.

27. Hester Scott to D. Graham Copeland, 15 December 1936, EC Papers; Hester Scott, "Analysis of ENP Publicity," 28 January 1937, DF Paper.

28. ENPA mailing, transcript of EC's WIOD radio address, 13 April 1931, UM Presidential Archives; EC, excerpt from WQAM commentator, 11 December 1937, Fred Cone Papers, SAF; EC, excerpt from WQAM commentator, 1 February 1941, SH Papers-SAF.

29. Press release, ca. 1928–31, DF Papers; Douglas, "Forgotten Man."

30. La Gorce, "Florida," 26, 35; O'Reilly, "South Florida's Amazing Everglades."

31. EC to Arthur Pack, 23 October 1935, David Sholtz Papers; *Nature Magazine*, 7 July 1934, 21; Small, "Proposed Everglades National Park," 264; Morrison, "America's Last Frontier"; Cahalane, "Everglades."

32. On the environmental politics of the interwar period, see Maher, *Nature's New Deal*; Sutter, *Driven Wild*; Sarah Phillips, *This Land, This Nation*; Beeman and Pritchard, *Green and Permanent Land*; Sellars, *Preserving Nature*; Way, *Conserving Southern Longleaf*. Mighetto, *Wild Animals*. Dunlap, *Saving America's Wildlife*, also focused explicitly on the issue of biocentric ethics.

33. Mighetto, *Wild Animals*; Dunlap, *Saving America's Wildlife*.

34. Dunlap, *Saving America's Wildlife*; Way, *Conserving Southern Longleaf*; Flader, *Thinking Like a Mountain*; Meine, *Aldo Leopold*; Sellars, *Preserving Nature*.

35. George Wright's ideas and the ways they impacted EC's thinking about park boundaries are further examined in chapter 4.

36. On commodification in the Everglades and more generally, see Cronon, *Nature's Metropolis*; Derr, *Some Kind of Paradise*; Poole, "Women"; Jack Davis, "Alligators and Plume Birds"; Hornaday, *Our Vanishing Wild Life*.

37. EC, ENPA plan, 6 February 1937, DF Papers.

38. EC to Edward Pou, 16 February 1933, Peterson Papers.

39. Alagona, "What Is Habitat?," 434.

40. Ibid.; Block and Brennan, "Habitat Concept in Ornithology."

41. EC to Henry Ward, 4 February 1929, NPS Records.

42. Robert T. Morris to T. Gilbert Pearson, 17 January 1931, NPS Records.

43. John Baker to Arthur Demaray, 7 August 1936, NPS Records.

44. Pritchard, *Preserving Yellowstone's Natural Conditions*, 50, 52, 118–20. Also see the NPS biography of Bryant at www.nps.gov/parkhistory/online_books/sontag/bryant.htm.

45. Sellars, *Preserving Nature*, 55; Pritchard, *Preserving Yellowstone's Natural Conditions*, 96–97, 145. Also see the NPS biography of Roger Toll at www.nps.gov/parkhistory/online _books/sontag/toll.htm. Toll allowed the destruction of predators earlier in his career.

46. Bryant-Toll Report to the director, NPS, 14 January 1935, SH Papers-UF.

47. Ibid.

48. Beard, *Wildlife Reconnaissance*. Daniel Beard was the son of Daniel Carter "Uncle Dan" Beard, one of the founders of modern scouting.

49. Beard, Wildlife Reconnaissance, 1.

50. Ibid., 58, 59, 61.

51. Barrow, "Dragons in Distress"; Barrow, "Alligator's Allure."

52. Beard, Wildlife Reconnaissance, 50, original emphasis.

53. Ibid., 85–87.

54. The centrality of tourism to the national parks is examined in Runte, *National Parks*; Sellars, *Preserving Nature*; Miles, *Wilderness in National Parks*; Shaffer, *See America First*; Runte, *Trains of Discovery*; Starnes, *Creating the Land*.

55. EC, "Annual Meeting of the ENPA," 17 January 1935, DF Papers. Also see EC, 5 July 1934, DF Papers; EC, "Florida Wants the Everglades National Park," 1938, DF Papers; EC, "Something Every Candidate for Office in Florida Can Well Ponder Over and Stand for in His Platform," 26 March 1936, EC Papers.

56. Form letter for fund-raising, on the back of Thomas J. Pancoast to Dr. Bowman Ashe, 4 March 1938, UM Presidential Archives.

57. EC, ENPA bulletin, 16 February 1932, DF Papers.

58. EC "Something Every Candidate for Office." Also see EC, ENPA bulletin, ca. 1929, David Sholtz Papers.

59. EC to Governor David Sholtz, 4 May 1936.

60. EC, "Something Every Candidate for Office."

61. EC, ENPA bulletin, 13 June 1930, DF Papers.

62. EC, ENPA bulletin, ca. 1929, Doyle Carlton Papers, SAF.

63. These ideas are addressed more fully in chapter 6.

64. EC, ENPA bulletin, 13 June 1930, Doyle Carlton Papers. Not all park advocates believed EC's claims about tourism in the park. For example, DF explained to T. Gilbert Pearson of the National Audubon Society that "Coe in his talks to the Clubs gives them the idea that the Park will bring millions to Florida." DF thought this dubious, though, in part because "the area will never be adapted to camping out parties as in the Yellowstone or the Glacier of the Yosemite National Park." He wrote that "there is nothing on earth for the boys and girls to do in the evening and I am sure that the Park Service will have the dickins [*sic*] of a time inventing pastimes for these people which would compete with the dance halls and palaces of pleasure of Miami" (DF to Gilbert Pearson, 23 January 1931, DF Papers). Despite DF's reservations, the ENP eventually attracted large numbers of tourists and probably had an even larger nontangible impact on Florida's economy and identity. Since 1965 the park has typically attracted around a million tourists a year. The NPS estimates that an additional half a million visitors enter the park by boat every year. Park visitation statistics for all parks are at https://irma.nps.gov/Stats/Reports /Park/. Also see Cullinane, Huber, and Koontz, *2014 National Park Visitor Spending Effects*. The NPS estimates that an additional half a million visitors enter the park via boat every year.

65. T. J. Brooks to EC, 2 June 1931, Doyle Carlton Papers.

66. EC to Miss Harlean James, 18 March 1931; EC to Frederick Law Olmsted, 3 February 1931, both in Doyle Carlton Papers.

67. EC, "America's Only Tropics," lecture, 28 October 1929, UM Presidential Archives.

68. EC, ENPA bulletin, ca. 1929, Doyle Carlton Papers.

69. Other accounts of this controversy are in Runte, *National Parks*, 133; Sutter, *Driven Wild*, 130–35; Jack Davis, *Everglades Providence*, 366–71.

70. EC to Robert Morris, 3 August 1931, DF Papers.

71. [EC and DF], form letter beginning "A movement has been started," ca. late 1928 or early 1929, DF Papers; ENPA bulletin, 18 March 1932, EC Papers.

72. Robert Sterling Yard to DF, 18 January 1929, DF Papers.

73. Robert Sterling Yard to Ray Lyman Wilbur, 7 January 1931, NPS Records.

74. Robert Sterling Yard to Henry Ward, 29 January 1929, DF Papers, original emphasis.

75. Robert Sterling Yard, letter, 6 January 1931, NPS Records.

76. Robert Sterling Yard, statement at the hearing on the Everglades National Park Bill, 15 December 1930, NPS Records. In fact, this did come to pass. SH and John Pennekamp, both of whom supported the park for economic reasons, applied significant pressure to the NPS to develop the park for tourism and to construct overnight housing for tourists.

77. Yard, statement at the hearing.

78. Robert Sterling Yard to Horace Albright, 10 January 1931, NPS Records.

79. Henry Ward to DF, 28 January 1929; George Pratt to DF, 14 January 1929, both in DF Papers.

80. Olmsted and Wharton, "Proposed Everglades National Park"; Olmsted and Wharton, "Florida Everglades." Also see Runte, *National Parks*, 128–37.

81. Olmsted and Wharton, "Florida Everglades," 142.

82. Runte, *National Parks*, 133–37.

83. Olmsted and Wharton, "Florida Everglades."

84. Sutter, *Driven Wild*, 130–35.

Chapter 4. Authorizing a Wilderness Park

1. EC to Doyle Carlton, 12 November 1930, Doyle Carlton Papers, SAF; *General Acts and Resolutions Adopted by the Legislature of Florida*, 1929, 701–5, chapter 13887 (323).

2. Vance, *May Mann Jennings*.

3. May Mann Jennings to EC, 16 May 1931, Doyle Carlton Papers.

4. Vance, *May Mann Jennings*.

5. EC to David Sholtz, 7 May 1935, David Sholtz Papers. Also see EC to William C. Hodges, 20 and 21 May 1935, David Sholtz Papers.

6. *General Acts and Resolutions*, 1935, 829–31, chapter 17131 (300); *General Acts and Resolutions*, 1935, 505–8, chapter 16996 (225).

7. *General Acts and Resolutions*, 1935, 508–9, chapter 16997 (226).

8. ENPA report, ca. 1929–30, DF Papers; Senate Committee on Public Lands and Surveys Report, "Tropic Everglades National Park," 71st Cong., 3rd Sess., Washington, D.C.: Government Printing Office, 1930, Doyle Carlton Papers.

9. EC, "Story of the Everglades National Park Project," unpublished manuscript, 1 December 1950, EC Papers, 46; quote from ENPA meeting, 27 January 1933, DF Papers.

10. *Hearings before the Committee on Public Lands*, House of Representatives, 71st Cong., 3rd Sess., on HR 12381.

11. Vickers, *Life of Ruth Bryan Owen*.

12. *Hearings before the Committee on Public Lands*; quote is from the *Lincoln (NE) Journal Star*, (night ed.) 22 December 1930, 1. Also see *Miami Herald*, 17 December 1930, 1, 11.

13. 71 Cong. Rec. S4493–95 (10 February 1931); 72 Cong. Rec. S2238–40 (19 January 1932); 73 Cong. Rec. S2970–71 (8 May 1933). In 1931, the Senate briefly debated the rights of the Seminoles in connection to the ENP's creation before passing the bill.

14. Horace Albright to EC, 20 March 1931, NPS Records.

15. 71 Cong. Rec. H5644–49 (21 February 1931).

16. Horace Albright to DF, 25 March 1931, DF Papers.

17. EC to Ruth Bryan Owen, 11 June 1932, UM Presidential Archives, Richter Library, Special Collections, UM.

18. EC, "Submitted Suggestions," 1 March 1930, NPS Records. This report was first used by EC in March 1930 but was recirculated throughout that year as part of EC's work in lobbying for the federal authorization of the park. Apparently Robert Sterling Yard did not see this document until late 1930 or early 1931, at which point the EC-Yard controversy re-erupted.

19. On the history of this road, see Epperson, *Roads through the Everglades*. The current park road does not quite conform to the Old Ingraham Highway, as much of the road was not in the park's 1947 boundaries when this reconstruction project began. See the epilogue for details on that road's construction.

20. Epperson, *Roads through the Everglades*, 83–84.

21. EC, "Submitted Suggestions."

22. Ibid.

23. Ibid.

24. Ibid. On biocentric wilderness, see Sutter, *Driven Wild*, 13–15; Roderick Nash, *Wilderness and the American Mind*, 425–29; Hendee and Stankey, "Biocentricity in Wilderness Management"; Noss, "Building a Wilderness Recovery Network"; Foreman, *Rewilding North America*; Callicot and Nelson, *Great New Wilderness Debate*. On Wright and early biocentric ideas about wilderness, see Callicot and Nelson, *Wilderness Debate Rages On*, 21–188.

25. Robert Sterling Yard to NPS, 6 January 1931, NPS Records.

26. Robert Sterling Yard to Horace Albright, 10 January 1931, NPS Records.

27. Cronon, "Foreword," xii.

28. On wilderness see Sutter, *Driven Wild*; Roderick Nash, *Wilderness and the American Mind*; Turner, *Promise of Wilderness*; Harvey, *Wilderness Forever*; Frome, *Battle for the Wilderness*; Scott, *Enduring Wilderness*; Callicot and Nelson, *Great New Wilderness Debate*; Callicot and Nelson, *Wilderness Debate Rages On*.

29. Robert Sterling Yard to Ray Lyman Wilbur, 7 January 1931, NPS Records.

30. Ibid., original emphasis; Henry Ward to EC, 18 April 1932, NPS Records.

31. Horace Albright to Henry Ward, 24 January 1931, NPS Records.

32. Horace Albright to Henry Ward, 30 January 1931, NPS Records.

33. Horace Albright to EC, 25 March 1931, DF Papers. EC would advocate for the construction of this highway one other time. In 1935 EC briefly promoted the construction of this road in correspondence with Governor David Sholtz. See EC to David Sholtz, 14 June 1935, David Sholtz Papers; EC to David Sholtz, 23 June 1935, DF Papers.

34. Robert Sterling Yard to Ray Lyman Wilbur, 10 February 1931, NPS Records.

35. *Palm Beach Post Times*, 4 February 1956, 1 and 2; *Palm Beach Post Times*, 5 February 1956, 4.

36. EC, ENPA Summary for 1934, 1 November 1934, DF Papers; EC to Members of Congress, 25 March 1934, Augustus Seymour Houghton Papers, Richter Library, Special Collections, UM.

37. EC, press release, May 1934, DF Papers.

38. 73rd Cong. Rec. H9494–516, H9495 (24 May 1934).

39. 73rd Cong. Rec. H9497, H9503, H9500–9501 (24 May 1934).

40. 73rd Cong. Rec. H9497 (24 May 1934).

41. 73rd Cong. Rec. H9494–516 (24 May 1934). Interestingly, most of these attacks were more extreme versions of Robert Sterling Yard's criticisms of the ENP. Yard's opposition to the park is detailed in chapter 4.

42. 73rd Cong. Rec. H9496 (24 May 1934).

43. 73rd Cong. Rec. H9504 (24 May 1934).

44. Ibid.

45. Ibid.

46. On these wilderness parks, see Miles, *Wilderness in National Parks*, 67–136; Louter, *Windshield Wilderness*, 68–104; Sellars, *Preserving Nature*, 187–94, 213–14; Turner, *Promise of Wilderness*, 58–61.

47. EC, press release, May 1934, DF Papers.

48. EC, speech, 8 March 1935, NPS Records.

49. EC to Aldo Leopold, 14 October 1941, NPS Records.

50. Horace Albright to Robert Sterling Yard, 5 January 1931; Horace Albright to Robert Sterling Yard, 24 January 1931, both in NPS Records.

51. Arno Cammerer to William P. Wharton, 8 January 1935, NPS Records.

52. Bryant report to the director of the NPS, 14 January 1935, SH Papers-UF.

53. Beard, "Diversity," 25.

54. Beard, *Wildlife Reconnaissance*, 100.

55. Ibid., 101, 1; Daniel Beard to the NPS, memo, 12 May 1942, NPS Records, original emphasis.

56. Douglas, *Everglades*, 10. On attitudes toward wetlands and their contradictory qualities, see David Miller, *Dark Eden*; Hurd, *Stirring the Mud*; Vilesis, *Discovering the Unknown Landscape*; Siry, *Marshes of the Ocean Shore*; Megan Nelson, *Trembling Earth*; Kirby, *Poquosin*; Ogden, *Swamplife*; Anthony Wilson, *Shadow and Shelter*; Ray, *Pinhook*; Meindl, "Past Perceptions."

57. Thoreau, *Walden*, 345.

58. EC to Duncan Fletcher, 2 April 1929, NPS Records.

59. EC to Arno Cammerer, 7 June 1935, David Sholtz Papers.

60. George Wright to EC, 9 October 1931, NPS Records. EC used this letter as a ENPA bulletin. Some of these ideas about roads in the park were similar to those discussed in Louter, *Windshield Wilderness*, 68–104. These ideas show that the NPS was perhaps not as dedicated to roadless wilderness as they would have liked observers and wilderness advocates to believe.

61. Beard, *Wildlife Reconnaissance*, 100, 2.

62. Marine protection did not become a major impetus for environmentalists and conservation biologists until the 1970s, yet conservationists and environmentalists in South Florida understood much earlier the need to protect these marine systems and to conserve fish species. The ENP set major precedents for the protection of marine areas and prompted further

marine preservation in Florida. On marine environmental history, see Bolster, "Opportunities in Marine Environmental History"; Rozwadowski, *Fathoming the Ocean*; Philip E. Steinberg, *Social Construction of the Ocean*; Mack, *Sea*; Rozwadowski and van Keuren, *Machine in Neptune's Garden*; Deacon, *Scientists and the Sea*. Historians have not written much on the history of marine protected areas in the United states, although conservation biologists have written extensively on the topic. An excellent starting point is Sloan, "History and Application." Also see Safina, *Song for the Blue Ocean*; Gary Davis, "Designing Ocean Parks"; Lubchenco et al., "Plugging a Hole"; Carlton, "Apostrophe to the Ocean"; McCloskey, "Protected Areas on the High Seas"; Barr and Lindholm, "Conservation of the Sea." The history of fisheries is extensive; see McEvoy, *Fisherman's Problem*; Pope, *Fish into Wine*; Joseph E. Taylor, *Making Salmon*.

63. Sloan, "History and Application," does not discuss roadlessness in the context of marine areas but does examine more recent biocentric ideas about wilderness in the context of protected marine areas. See also Harvey, "Sound Politics." These areas are officially part of the Marjory Stoneman Douglas Wilderness as well. The Marjory Stoneman Douglas Wilderness was designated in 1978 in accordance with the 1964 Wilderness Act.

64. For more on these ideas, see Wilhelm, "For the Birds."

65. EC, "Submitted Suggestions."

66. ENPA bulletin, 13 June 1930, DF Papers.

67. George Wright, Dixon, and Thompson, *Fauna*, 136–37.

68. Runte, "Joseph Grinnell and Yosemite."

69. George Wright, Dixon, and Thompson, *Fauna*. On George Wright and these NPS wildlife biologists, see Sellars, *Preserving Nature*, 91–148; Shafer, "Conservation Biology Trailblazers"; Dunlap, "Wildlife, Science"; Duncan, "George Melendez Wright"; Gerald Wright, *Wildlife Research and Management*, 14–20; Pritchard, *Preserving Yellowstone's Natural Conditions*, 75–146; Kupper, "Science and the National Parks." Also see various articles in the *George Wright Forum*, the publication of the George Wright Society.

70. Sellars, *Preserving Nature*, 96, 91.

71. George Wright, Dixon, and Thompson *Fauna*, 19.

72. Ibid., 19, 38.

73. Ibid., 71.

74. George Wright receives a great deal of attention in Sellars, *Preserving Nature*. However, no biography or monograph is devoted to Wright, and he appears infrequently in synthetic and larger works in U.S. environmental history. A. Starker Leopold, *Wildlife Management*.

75. George Wright to EC, 9 October 1931, NPS Records.

76. George Wright to EC 14 July 1932, NPS Records.

77. Because the NPS never formally endorsed EC's vision, they never calculated the acreage. The 1934 Bryant-Toll report endorsed EC's substantial boundaries as the maximum possible park boundaries but likewise never calculated the total park acreage. The park's initial boundaries in 1947 amounted to 1,228,488 acres. Today the park encompasses about 1.5 million acres. See Bryant-Toll Report to the director, NPS, 14 January 1935, SH Papers-UF; map 1944 boundary, n.d., NPS Records; map accompanying Arthur Demaray memo, 1 April 1947, NPS Records.

78. Miles, *Wilderness in National Parks*, 77–81; Ethan Carr, *Wilderness by Design*, 194–97.

79. See, for example, EC to Arthur Pack, 7 January 1936, EC Papers; EC to David Sholtz, 23 June 1935, DF Papers.

80. EC, "Why Monroe County interests will be greatly benefited by the Everglades National Park project," unpublished article, 22 September 1936, NPS Records.

Chapter 5. The ENPC and the New Deal in Florida

1. Standard texts on the New Deal include Rauch, *History of the New Deal*; Leuchtenburg, *Franklin D. Roosevelt*; Schlesinger, *Age of Roosevelt*; Freidel, *Franklin D. Roosevelt*; Hofstadter, *Age of Reform*. On the New Deal's impact on the South, see Tindall, *Emergence of the New South*; Schulman, *From Cotton Belt to Sunbelt*; Cobb, *Selling of the South*; Kirby, *Rural Worlds Lost*; Gavin Wright, *Old South, New South*; Daniel, *Breaking the Land*; Cobb and Namorato, *New Deal and the South*.

2. The phrase "new conservation" is from Philips, *This Land, This Nation*. On conservation and the New Deal, also see Worster, *Dust Bowl*; Owen, *Conservation under F.D.R.*; Cutler, *Public Landscape*; Beeman and Pritchard, *Green and Permanent Land*; Henderson and Woolner, *FDR and the Environment*; Maher, *Nature's New Deal*; Sutter, *Let Us Now Praise Famous Gullies*.

3. Swain, "National Park Service"; Sutter, *Driven Wild*; Maher, *Nature's New Deal*.

4. See Maher, *Nature's New Deal*.

5. Swain, "National Park Service," 317–18.

6. See ENP vertical file, Franklin Delano Roosevelt (FDR) Presidential Library, Hyde Park, N.Y.; memo, 23 September 1938, Presidents Personal File 24, FDR Presidential Library; Marguerite LeHand to EC, 3 December 1932, Box 230, NPS Records.

7. EC to Sholtz, 6 February 1934; EC to Sholtz, 16 February 1934, both in David Sholtz Papers.

8. Grace Lyman to FDR, 26 March 1934, Official File 6P, Box 14; EC to Grace Lyman, 27 March 1934, Official File 6P, Box 14, both in FDR Presidential Library.

9. "Withdrawal of Public Lands for National Park Classification," 22 October 1934, Exec. Order No. 6883, accessed at www.fdrlibrary.marist.edu/_resources/images/eo/e00024.pdf.

10. Note attached to Harold Ickes to FDR, 29 March 1934, Official File 6P, Box 14, FDR Presidential Library.

11. Jackson, *Pioneer of Tropical Landscape Architecture*; Dave Nelson, "Florida Crackers and Yankee Tourists," 95–97, 111; Vance, *May Mann Jennings*.

12. May Mann Jennings to Fred Cone, 6 June 1937; EC to Ruth B. Owen, 9 May 1937; EC to Julius Stone, 20 April 1935; EC, Works Progress Administration Project Proposal, 21 August 1935, all in EC Papers.

13. EC to George M. Wright, 23 March 1935, David Sholtz Papers.

14. EC to William L. Wilson, Florida WPA, 6 September 1935, EC Papers. Although EC's efforts did produce these abstracts, which were then maintained by subsequent iterations of the ENPC, they were never used in the land acquisition process.

15. EC mailing, 24 August 1937; EC to G. O. Palmer, 19 August 1937, both in EC Papers.

16. On these subdivisions, see A. B. Manly, "Statement by A.B. Manly Concerning the Lands in Northwestern Monroe County within Compromise Boundaries Described in House Bills 6641 & 6653," DF Papers.

17. For example, see McElvaine, *Down and Out*; Green, *Looking for the New Deal*.

18. Mrs. Raphie Adams to EC, 22 April 1935; Mrs. G. A. Ginger to EC, 29 July 1937; Mrs. J. H. Hill to EC, 10 December 1936; Dr. Ella X. Quinn to David Sholtz, 21 September 1935; EC to T. H. Russell, 25 January 1937, all in EC Papers.

19. Ivar Axelson, memorandum on Tropic Everglades National Park, 5 March 1934, MMA Papers. On the family laying out Pinecrest, see MMA to Charlton Tebeau, 4 February 1959, MMA Papers.

20. Harold Bryant, memorandum to the director, NPS, 3 January 1935, NPS Records.

21. Vilesis, *Discovering the Unknown Landscape*, 5–7.

22. This apocryphal quote was recently attributed to an unknown landowner in 110 Cong. Rec. V153 Pt 9, S11961 (10 to 21 May 2007).

23. On property rights regimes and their implications for use and protection, see Hardin, "Tragedy of the Commons"; Feeny et al., "Tragedy of the Commons"; Berkes et al., "Benefits of the Commons."

24. Spence, *Dispossessing the Wilderness*; Catton, *Inhabited Wilderness*; Jacoby, *Crimes against Nature*; Keller and Turek, *American Indians and National Parks*.

25. On the history of Seminoles, see Milanich, *Florida Indians*; Covington, *Seminoles of Florida*; West, *Enduring Seminoles*. Also see the works of Harry Kersey, of which the most relevant to this section are *Pelts, Plumes, and Hides*; *Florida Seminoles*; "New Red Atlantis."

26. Covington, *Seminoles of Florida*.

27. Ch. 285.01, Florida Statues.

28. Kersey, *Florida Seminoles*, 89.

29. Kersey, *Pelts, Plumes, and Hides*; Kersey, *Florida Seminoles*.

30. Graham D. Taylor, *New Deal*; Hauptman, *Iroquois and the New Deal*; Kelly, "Indian Reorganization Act"; Blackman, *Oklahoma's Indian New Deal*.

31. Daily, *Battle for the BIA*; Schwartz, "Red Atlantis Revisited"; Rusco, "John Collier."

32. Collier, "Red Atlantis."

33. Collier, "With Secretary Ickes."

34. Kersey, "New Red Atlantis."

35. EC to Lucian Spencer, 18 October 1929, Doyle Carlton Papers, SAF. On Seminole souvenirs and broader Seminoles tourism, see West, *Enduring Seminoles*.

36. EC to John Collier, 3 April 1934, DF Papers.

37. Kersey, *Florida Seminoles*, 88–108.

38. Ibid., 172, 21.

39. Kersey, "New Red Atlantis," 133.

40. Kersey, *Florida Seminoles*, 75–80; Collier, "With Secretary Ickes."

41. Kersey, *Florida Seminoles*, 110.

42. *St. Petersburg Times*, 23 February 1936.

43. David Sholtz to Harold Ickes, 28 February 1936, David Sholtz Papers.

44. Harold Ickes to David Sholtz, 20 March 1936, David Sholtz Papers.

45. Kersey, *Florida Seminoles*, 95; Ch. 285.04, 285.05, and 285.06, Florida Statues.

46. Harold Ickes to Burton Wheeler, 23 March 1934, David Sholtz Papers.

47. Kersey, *Florida Seminoles*, 75–80; Collier, "With Secretary Ickes."

48. Kersey, "New Red Atlantis," 149.

49. Kersey, *Florida Seminoles*, 96–97.

50. Daniel Beard to James Silver, 30 May 1947, NPS Records.

51. Merlin Cox, "David Sholtz"; Dave Nelson, "Florida Crackers and Yankee Tourists."

52. Ch. 13887 (no. 323), Florida Statutes.

53. Although much early work on the New Deal was overly laudatory, early works that critically examined the New Deal's conservativism and pro-business leanings include Leuchtenburg, *Franklin D. Roosevelt*, and Hawley, *New Deal*. For a more radical critique, see Bernstein, "Conservative Achievement." Both these moderate works and Bernstein's New Left critique caused historians to reexamine the New Deal. Subsequent historians had a more nuanced perspective of the Roosevelt's achievements and of the New Deal's relationship to capitalism and

American businesses. See Badger, *New Deal*; Schwarz, *New Dealers*; Brinkley, *End of Reform*; Skocpol and Finegold, *State and Party in America's New Deal*.

54. EC to Governor Sholtz, 13 August 1934; EC to Governor Sholtz, 20 March 1935, both in David Sholtz Papers.

55. Scott Loftin to Governor Sholtz, 26 March 1935; Thomas Pancoast to Governor Sholtz, 15 August 1934, both in David Sholtz Papers.

56. Governor Sholtz, undated memo, David Sholtz Papers; minutes of the ENPC meeting, 15 January 1936, EC Papers.

57. Arno Cammerer to EC, 28 June 1934; EC to David Sholtz, 27 July 1934, both in David Sholtz Papers.

58. Lorenzo Wilson to Governor Sholtz, 1 May 1935; J. W. Hoffman to Governor Sholtz, 22 June 1935; May Mann Jennings to Governor Sholtz, 2 October 1936, all in David Sholtz Papers.

59. Minutes of the ENPC meeting, 15 January 1936, EC Papers.

60. May Mann Jennings to Governor Sholtz, 2 October 1936, David Sholtz Papers.

61. Harold Bryant report to the director of the NPS, 14 January 1935, SH Papers-UF. This report is also discussed in chapter 2.

62. George Wright, memorandum to the director, 4 February 1935, NPS Papers.

63. EC to Arno Cammerer, 19 June 1936, EC Papers.

64. Minutes of the meeting of the Lands and Boundaries Committee, ENPC, 27 June 1936, EC Papers.

65. Ibid.

66. Ibid.

67. ENPC minutes, 2 December 1936, EC Papers.

68. ENPC lands and boundaries report, SH Papers-SAF.

69. John Shares to D. Graham Copeland, 18 February 1937, EC Papers.

70. John Shares to D. Graham Copeland, 15 March 1937, EC Papers.

71. ENPC minutes, 11 January 1937, EC Papers.

72. ENPC minutes, 3 April 1937, EC Papers.

73. May Mann Jennings to EC, 17 May 1937, EC Papers.

74. D. Graham Copeland to EC, 31 May 1937, EC Papers.

75. May Mann Jennings to Thomas Pancoast, 6 June 1937, EC Papers.

76. EC to J. W. Hoffman, 2 June 1936, EC Papers.

77. EC to John Shares, 1 March 1937, EC Papers.

78. Augustus Houghton to Arno Cammerer, 25 October 1937, NPS Records.

79. On Fred Cone, see Dave Nelson, "New Deal for Welfare"; Colburn and DeHaven-Smith, *Government in the Sunshine State*; Colburn and Scher, *Florida's Gubernatorial Politics*.

80. Dave Nelson, "New Deal for Welfare"; Jennings to Pancoast.

81. May Mann Jennings to EC, 30 May 1937, EC Papers.

82. Dave Nelson, "New Deal for Welfare."

83. Between July and November, EC continued to act as the commission's executive chairman and argued that although he had resigned, since no appointments had been made he was still the acting chairman. See EC, ENPA bulletin, "Important Events during the Year of 1937," 27 January 1938; EC to Fred Cone, 18 June 1939, both in Fred Cone Papers, SAF. EC later asked to be paid for that period of work, and in fact another ENPC employee, Ben Axelroad, sued the state of Florida and received his back pay. See State, Ex Rel. v. Lee, Supreme Court of Florida, 132 Fla 512–15 (Fla. 1938). By 1940 EC's back salary was ready to be paid and only awaited Governor Cone's approval. EC begged Cone for this money, appealing to Cone's sense of decency

and morality. EC explained that his wife had been "hopelessly paralyzed" for two years and noted the many sacrifices he had made for the park. See EC to Fred Cone, 24 January 1940, Fred Cone Papers, SAF.

84. EC to Arno Cammerer, 9 June 1937, EC Papers.

85. Fred Cone to G. O. Palmer, 28 July 1937, Fred Cone Papers, SAF.

86. See, for example, G. O. Palmer to Fred Cone, 14 July 1937, Fred Cone Papers, SAF.

87. G. O. Palmer to Fred Cone, 24 November 1937, Fred Cone Papers, SAF.

88. Governor Cone to G. O. Palmer, 28 July 1937, Fred Cone Papers, SAF; G. O. Palmer to Gilbert Leach, 15 March 1945, SH Papers-SAF.

89. Daniel Beard, *Wildlife Reconnaissance*, 46–51.

90. Arthur Demaray to Abel Wolman, 12 June 1939, NPS Records.

91. C. B. Taylor memorandum, 18 July 1939, NPS Records. On Garald Parker, see Jack Davis, *Everglades Providence*, 355–59.

Chapter 6. The Creation of Everglades National Park

1. Despite Holland's importance to Florida politics, little has been written on his career. See Evans, "Weathering the Storm"; Evans, "Origins"; Colburn and Scher, *Florida's Gubernatorial Politics*, esp. 36–44, 72, 195, 201, 223, 282; Spessard Stone, "Extraordinary Floridian"; Grunwald, *Swamp*, 210–15.

2. On World War II's impacts on the South, see Cobb, *South and America*; McMillen, *Remaking Dixie*; Bartley, *New South*; Schulman, *From Cotton Belt to Sunbelt*; Kirby, *Rural Worlds Lost*; Gavin Wright, *Old South, New South*. On World War II's specific impact on Florida, see Mormino, "World War II."

3. "Intercensal Estimates of the Total Resident Population of States: 1940–1949," in *Population Distribution Branch*, U.S. Census, 1996; Mormino, "World War II."

4. On the Sunbelt South, see Cobb, *Selling of the South*; Schulman, *From Cotton Belt to Sunbelt*; Cobb, *Industrialization and Southern Society*; Mohl, *Searching for the Sunbelt*; Abbott, *New Urban America*; Bartley, *New South*; Bernard and Rice, *Sunbelt Cities*.

5. "Intercensal Estimates."

6. Evans, "Origins"; Spessard Stone, "Extraordinary Floridian."

7. EC, "Attached to Letters to Candidates for Nomination for Governor of Florida," 21 March 1940, SH Papers-UF.

8. EC bulletin, 10 January 1943, NPS Records.

9. SH, quoted by EC in Chamber of Commerce Speech, 13 June 1940, SH Papers-UF.

10. ENPC meeting, 21 October 1946, EC Papers.

11. Ibid.

12. On ornithology and birding in the United States, see Barrow, *Passion for Birds*.

13. Everglades National Park Commission Executive Meeting, 21 October 1946, EC Papers.

14. Shaffer, *See America First*. Holland's correspondence on the park was generally concerned with practical issues concerning the park's creation, and he very rarely discussed his rationale for supporting the park. He often mentioned it would be visited by millions of tourists but rarely discussed the park's benefits in more detail. Even his speech at the park's dedication was primarily concerned with the practicalities of the park's creation. See Everglades National Park Dedication, 6 December 1947, EC Papers.

15. EC, "Attached to Letters."

16. G. O. Palmer report to the Internal Improvement Fund, 15 June 1938, SH Papers-SAF.

17. John D. Pennekamp speech at the Florida State Retailers Association, 29 October 1947, John D. Pennekamp Papers, PYKL, UF.

18. Vileisis, *Discovering the Unknown Landscapes*; Siry, *Marshes of the Ocean Shore*.

19. Mormino, *Land of Sunshine*, 2.

20. On pre–World War II tourism in Florida, see Hollis, *Dixie before Disney*; Revels, *Sunshine Paradise*; Noll, "Steamboats, Cypress, and Tourism"; Dave Nelson, "When Modern Tourism Was Born"; George, "Passage to the New Eden." On tourism in the U.S. South, see Starnes, *Creating the Land*; Barbour, *Florida for Tourists*; Way, *Conserving Southern Longleaf*, 19–55; Matt Stewart, *What Nature Suffers to Groe*, 216–24; Hillyer, *Designing Dixie*; Karen Cox, *Destination Dixie*; Yuhl, *Golden Haze of Memory*; Stanonis, *Creating the Big Easy*; Stanonis, *Dixie Emporium*; Aron, *Working at Play*. Much of the literature on tourism in the United States has focused on the West. On tourism in the United States, see Rothman, *Devil's Bargains*; Shaffer, *See America First*; Runte, *Trains of Discovery*.

21. On wartime and post–World War II tourism, see Mormino, *Land of Sunshine*, 76–122; Derr, *Some Kind of Paradise*, 37–60; George, "Passage to the New Eden"; Fogelson, *Married to the Mouse*; Rogers, "Florida in World War II"; Mormino, "Midas Returns"; Dawson, "Travel Strengthens America?"; Evans, "Weathering the Storm," 143–50.

22. Hillyer's *Designing Dixie* examines how post–Civil War New South boosters used tourism to both reconstruct the South's postwar identity and bring economic growth to the area. Sunbelt boosters like Holland employed tourism in a similar fashion. On boosterism in the South, see Ayers, *Promise of the New South*; Woodward, *Origins of the New South*; Gavin Wright, *Old South, New South*; Bartley, *New South*.

23. Runte, *National Parks*; Sears, *Sacred Places*.

24. On tourism's centrality to the NPS, see Runte, *National Parks*. In *Preserving Nature in the National Parks*, Sellars shows how this focus on tourism was challenged by wildlife biologists in the 1930s. Other works on postwar park tourism include Runte, *Trains of Discovery*; Miles, *Wilderness in National Parks*; Louter, *Windshield Wilderness*; Ethan Carr, *Mission 66*. Carr's work examines Mission 66 in detail but is more focused on park planning and landscape architecture in the context of that initiative.

25. Everglades National Park Commission Executive Meeting, 21 October 1946, EC Papers. Although it may have seemed unreasonable to assume that a wetland wilderness park would attract tourists, the ENP's actual economic benefits have been enormous. In typical years, the park attracts between 800,000 and 1 million tourists. This is significantly fewer tourists than the very popular Yellowstone and Yosemite. In 2014 it saw 1,110,900 tourists who spent $104,477,000 in Florida. The vast majority of those tourists (991,282) were from outside the local area. Additionally, those numbers do not include visitors who enter the park via boat and are not counted by the NPS. While the construction of new roads and facilities is barred in ENP, the federal government has appropriated millions to improve the roads and facilities that existed prior to the park's creation. The park's intangible benefits are harder to assess, but tourism certainly remains central to both Florida's economy and identity. Park visitation statistics for all parks can be found at https://irma.nps.gov/Stats/Reports/Park/. The specific statistics for 2014 are from Cullinane, Huber, and Koontz, *2014 National Park Visitor Spending Effects*. The NPS estimates that an additional half a million visitors enter ENP by boat every year.

26. The relationship between tourism and Florida's postwar identity is examined in detail in Mormino, *Land of Sunshine*. Mormino largely ignores the park's contributions to these processes, though, in part because his study begins in 1950. When he does discuss the park, it is

only to note that it attracted only a million tourists a year, but, as seen here, the park's economic impact was the perhaps least important way it contributed to the state's modernization.

27. For examples, see Jack Davis, *Everglades Providence*; Way, *Conserving Southern Longleaf*; Hersey, *My Work*; Fredrick Davis, *Man Who Saved Sea Turtles*.

28. The state of Florida owned half the mineral rights on all the lands owned by the MLC. The state therefore could allow or veto oil drilling on those lands.

29. "Relative to the Proposed Everglades National Park," meeting minutes, 10 March 1941, NPS Records.

30. Ibid.

31. Memorandum on conference at Tallahassee, 4 June 1942, SH Papers-SAF.

32. William E. Brown and Hudson, "Henry Flagler."

33. Memorandum covering conference with C. R. Vinten, 12 August 1942, SH Papers, SAF.

34. Newton Drury to SH, 1 April 1943, SH Papers-SAF.

35. Drury memo to the Secretary, 27 September 1943, NPS Records.

36. Newton Drury to SH, 2 December 1943, SH Papers-SAF.

37. Ray Vinten, "Memorandum for the Director," 5 January 1944, NPS Records.

38. Ibid.

39. Newton Drury to SH, 15 February 1944, NPS Records.

40. SH to J. Hardin Peterson, 10 August 1944, NPS Records.

41. Vinten, "Memorandum for the Director," 5 January 1944.

42. SH to J. Hardin Peterson, 10 August 1944 NPS Records.

43. Ray Vinten, "Memorandum for the Director," 18 December 1944, NPS Records.

44. SH, ENP meeting minutes, 13 December 1944, SH Papers-UF.

45. Ray Vinten, "Memorandum for the Director," 16 December 1944, NPS Records.

46. "Conference Re: Everglades National Park," 13 December 1944, SH Papers-UF.

47. Vinten, "Memorandum for the Director," 16 December 1944.

48. "Conference Re: Everglades National Park," 13 December 1944, Box 343, SH Papers-UF.

49. Ralph Davis to Harold Colee, 26 February 1943, SH Papers-SAF.

50. Fitzgerald, *Seaweed Rebellion*, 33.

51. Raymond Parker to Charley Johns, 8 January 1954, Daniel McCarty/Charley Johns Papers, SAF.

52. Colburn and Scher, *Florida's Gubernatorial Politics*, esp. 36–44, 73, 119–22, 195, 201, 244–50.

53. Ray Vinten, "Memorandum for the Director," 24 May 1945, NPS Records.

54. Ray Vinten memo, 21 April 1945, NPS Records.

55. These lands included both hiatus lands (physical lands that lay between surveyor lines and resulted from errors in the surveying process) and sovereignty lands (lands below mean high tide). The MLC claimed to own these sovereignty lands, while a state study concluded that Florida never had the authority to deed these lands to private owners.

56. SH to EC, 25 May 1945, NPS Records.

57. Gilbert Leach to Millard Caldwell, 25 May 1945, Millard Caldwell Papers, SAF.

58. "Caldwell Wants More Local Support for 'Glades Park," *St. Petersburg Times*, 23 May 1945.

59. Ray Vinten memo, 14 February 1946, NPS Records. EC was not permanently gone, however. Over the next five years, EC would periodically reactivate the ENPA to mail letters and publicity materials.

60. Twigg, "Editor John D. Pennekamp"; Nixon Smiley, "Poker Game Helped Found Everglades Park," *Miami Herald*, 3 December 1967; Smiley, *Knights of the Fourth Estate*, 61–63, 219–27, 284–89.

61. Twigg, "Editor John D. Pennekamp," 29, 28.

62. Smiley, "Poker Game."

63. John Pennekamp to Millard Caldwell, 1 November 1945, NPS Records.

64. Ray Vinten, "Memorandum for the Director," 14 November 1945, NPS Records. The commission was still maintaining land abstracts records in the park area. EC attended this meeting as well, despite not being invited.

65. Ray Vinten, "Memorandum for the Director," 30 October 1945, NPS Records.

66. Ray Vinten, "Memorandum for the Director," 14 December 1945, NPS Records; Harold Ickes to Millard Caldwell, 8 January 1946, Peterson Papers.

67. John Pennekamp to Millard Caldwell, 4 January 1946; John Pennekamp to Millard Caldwell, 14 February 1946, both in NPS Records.

68. Burghard, *Half a Century in Florida*.

69. ENPC meeting minutes, 25 April 1946, NPS Records.

70. Ibid.

71. August Burghard to Millard Caldwell, 3 May 1946, Millard Caldwell Papers.

72. ENPC meeting minutes, 25 April 1946, NPS Records.

73. Ray Vinten memo, 14 May 1946, NPS Records; Will Preston to the ENPC, 21 May 1946, Millard Caldwell Papers; Will Preston to August Burghard, 27 May 1946, Millard Caldwell Papers.

74. ENPC meeting minutes, 25 April 1946, NPS Records.

75. ENPC to property owners within the Everglades National Park area, 19 July 1946, Millard Caldwell Papers.

76. Gilbert Leach to Ed Straughn, 5 November 1946, Box 25, Millard Caldwell Papers.

77. Blake, *Land into Water*, 175.

78. Godfrey and Catton, *River of Interests*.

79. Daniel Beard, "Notes on the Everglades National Park Project," 7 February 1947, NPS Records.

80. August Burghard to Millard Caldwell, 31 October 1946, Millard Caldwell Papers.

81. Gilbert Leach, "Report on the Activities . . .," 27 February 1947, Millard Caldwell Papers. The MLC eventually sold 210,000 acres and half the mineral rights for 295,000 acres in 1948 and 1949. See Carl Hawkins to John Pennekamp, 19 February 1949, SH Papers-UF.

82. *The Administration of Millard F. Caldwell as Governor of Florida, 1945–49* (Tallahassee, Fla., 1949), government publication in the general collection at State Library of Florida.

83. Ray Vinten memo, 21 January 1947, NPS Records.

84. "40 Million Dollar Map Presented to Governor," *Miami Herald*, 16 March 1947, in NPS Records.

85. Thomas Allen memo, 10 March 1947, NPS Records.

86. Gilbert Leach to Ed Straughn, 19 March 1947, Box 26, Millard Caldwell Papers.

87. Colburn and DeHaven-Smith, *Government in the Sunshine State*, 28–42.

88. Smiley, "Poker Game"; Smiley, *Knights of the Fourth Estate*, 223–25.

89. *Journal of the Senate*, 31st reg. sess., 8 April through 6 June 1947; *Journal of the House of Representatives*, 31st reg. sess., 3 April through 6 June 1947. Caldwell also retracted the $500,000 he had advanced the park from the post–World War II fund he controlled. Originally, park

advocates had sought only a $1.5 million appropriation to add to that amount from the governor. The legislature was more generous than they had thought possible.

90. Millard Caldwell to Newton Drury, 8 January 1946,; Newton Drury to Millard Caldwell, 10 January 1946, both in Millard Caldwell Papers, FSA.

91. Arthur Demaray to the Secretary, 1 April 1947, NPS Records; "Three Point Agreement of April, 1947," George Smathers Papers, PKYL, UF; J. A. Krug to Millard Caldwell, 2 April 1947, NPS Records.

92. Demaray to the Secretary.

93. "Three Point Agreement of April, 1947."

94. Thomas Allen to Fred Elliot, 17 June 1947, Millard Caldwell Papers.

95. Arthur Demaray to John Pennekamp, 20 June 1947; Deveraux Butcher, National Park Association press release, 26 June 1947, both in Millard Caldwell Papers.

96. Map 1944 boundary, n.d.; map accompanying Arthur Demaray memo, 1 April 1947, both in NPS Records.

97. Colburn and Scher, *Florida's Gubernatorial Politics*, 124.

98. As a member of the Florida cabinet, Watson was also a member of the Board of Trustees of Florida's IIF, which owned those mineral rights.

99. J. Tom Watson to the IIF Board, 13 June 1947, SH Papers-SAF—two documents with identical names and dates.

100. J. Tom Watson statement, 20 June 1947, Peterson Papers.

101. John Pennekamp to Millard Caldwell, 28 June 1947, NPS Records.

102. Watson v. Larson, 33 So. 2d 155, 159 Fla. 860.

103. Editorial, "Are We All Out of Step—But Tom?," *Miami Herald*, 19 June 1947.

104. Quote is from *Miami Herald*, 22 October 1947. See speeches in the John D. Pennekamp Papers, especially Pennekamp speech at the Florida Retailers Association, 29 October 1947; Pennekamp speech to Florida Press Association, 4 November 1950; Pennekamp statement at the U.S. Senate Insular Affairs Committee Meeting, 11 June 1957; and other undated speeches. The *Miami Herald* often reported on the speeches from their local section and published Pennekamp's editorials in the late 1940s and 1950s.

105. J. Tom Watson to John Pennekamp, 6 May 1948, John D. Pennekamp Papers.

106. Demaray to Pennekamp; Butcher, National Park Association press release.

107. ENPC meeting minutes, 15 January 1936, EC Papers.

108. Herman Shuptrine to Millard Caldwell, 5 December 1947; Herman Shuptrine to Millard Caldwell, 12 December 1947, both in Millard Caldwell Papers.

109. Herbert Mills to Millard Caldwell, 3 January 1948, Millard Caldwell Papers.

110. Daniel Beard to Herman Shuptrine, 30 December 1947, NPS Records.

Chapter 7. Finalizing the Park's Boundaries

1. Epperson, *Roads through the Everglades*, 107–8, 123–24, 169, 176–77, 185, and 201–4.

2. Hoder-Salmon, "Myrtle Archer McDougal," 333. On the Chevelier company, see Epperson, *Roads through the Everglades*, 107–8.

3. Hoder-Salmon, "Myrtle Archer McDougal"; Hoder-Salmon, "Intimate Agony," 55.

4. Ivar died in 1972, and Mary was tragically murdered the next year by their daughter, Mary Ivonne Axelson. Mary was eighty-two years old, suffering from leukemia and anemia, and bedridden in the hospital. Mary Ivonne, who had been working as a dancer in New York, was

visiting her mother in the hospital when she attacked her. Mary died twenty-two hours later of a cerebral hemorrhage; the daughter was later found not guilty of murder by reason of insanity. Hoder-Salmon, "Oklahoma Mary"; "Miami Police Hold Daughter in Slaying of Mother, a Writer," *New York Times*, 4 December 1973, 29.

5. MMA to Hopkins, 17 March 1961; MMA to Charlton Tebeau, 4 February 1959, both in MMA Papers. On the history of oil in Florida, see Hughes, *Oil in the Deep South*; Cockrell, *Drilling Ahead*; Gerald Nash, *United States Oil Policy*; Paige and Van Horn, *Ethnohistory of Big Cypress*; Lane, *Florida Geological Survey*. The family's insistence that these valuable lands should be excluded from the park is consistent with the worthless-land thesis in Runte, *National Parks*.

6. D. A. McDougal, statement at hearing on HR 1254, February 1948; MMA to Joel Hopkins, 17 March 1961, both in MMA Papers.

7. MMA to Ivar Axelson, 9 May 1949, MMA Papers.

8. Ivar Axelson mass mailing, ca. 1950; UM Jones Land sales advertisement, ca. 1954, both in MMA Papers.

9. Ivar Axelson statement on HR 3378, 14 July 1947; Ivar Axelson to Hugh Butler, 27 March 1954, both in MMA Papers.

10. Lester Velie, "They Kicked Us Off Our Land II," *Collier's*, 9 August 1947, 21, reprinted in Switzer, *Green Backlash*, 42; Switzer, *Green Backlash*, 41–42; Cawley, *Federal Land, Western Anger*, 72–74; Muller, *DeVoto's West*; Robbins and Foster, *Land in the American West*; Thomas, *Country in the Mind*; DeVoto, "Western Land Grab."

11. DeVoto, "Two-Gun Desmond Is Back"; Cooke, "Drafting the 1952 Platforms"; 1952 Republican Party Platform, 7 July 1952, www.presidency.ucsb.edu/documents/republican-party-platform-1952; DeVoto, "One Way Partnership Derailed."

12. DeVoto, "Western Land Grab"; Crespino, *In Search of Another Country*; Lassiter, *Silent Majority*; Kruse, *White Flight*, 8.

13. Works on the emergence of modern conservativism in the Sunbelt include Kevin Kruse, *White Flight*; Shermer, *Sunbelt Capitalism*; McGirr, *Suburban Warriors*; Lassiter, *Silent Majority*; Crespino, *In Search of Another Country*; Lassiter and Crespino, *Myth of Southern Exceptionalism*; Lowndes, *From the New Deal*; Fredrickson, *Dixiecrat Revolt*. For a more complete analysis of the literature on modern conservativism, see Phillips-Fein, "Conservatism." On conservative attitudes toward nature, see Drake, *Loving Nature*; Turner, "Specter of Environmentalism"; Flippen, *Conservative Conservationist*; Flippen, *Nixon and the Environment*; Switzer, *Green Backlash*; Helvarg, *War against the Greens*.

14. Worster, *Dust Bowl*, 6.

15. Turner, "Specter of Environmentalism," 137.

16. Ibid. Also see Cawley, *Federal Land, Western Anger*; Spitzer, *Green Backlash*.

17. Lang, "Titles Must Be Perfect"; Eller, *Miners, Millhands*; Gates, *History of Public Land Law Development*, 495–531.

18. Vilesis, *Discovering the Unknown Landscape*, 5–6; see also note 23 in ch. 5.

19. In May and June 1947, the NPS had established a procedure and process for using the $2 million appropriation for land acquisition within the 1944 boundaries. The NPS established a land acquisition office in Miami, appointed appropriate personnel, and created policies governing negotiations with landowners and the initiation of condemnation proceedings in coordination with the U.S. Justice Department. See Newton Drury to the Secretary of the DOI, 19 May 1947; Arthur Demaray memo, 9 July 1947, both in NPS Records.

20. A. B. Manly to SH, 5 November 1948, SH Papers-UF. For additional details on this land sale, see Carl Hawkins to John Pennekamp, 19 February 1949, Peterson Papers; Newton Drury

to John Baker, 18 November 1948, NPS Records. On the MLC, see William E. Brown and Hudson, "Henry Flagler"; Dovell, "Railroads and the Public Lands." On Florida's sovereignty lands, see MacGrady, "Florida's Sovereignty Submerged Lands." Because these lands had not been surveyed, the mean high water line had never been determined in the area. That line is the official boundary between sovereignty lands, which lie below the mean high water line, and privately owned lands. The MLC and the NPS not only disagreed about the status of sovereignty lands, but because the mean high water line had not been determined, the two parties could not determine how much of this property was below that line.

21. Newton Drury to John Baker, 18 November 1948.

22. Manly to SH, 5 November 1948.

23. John Baker to Newton Drury, 12 November 1948, NPS Records; Newton Drury to John Baker, 18 November 1948.

24. Newton Drury to John Baker, 18 November 1948; Carl Hawkins to John Pennekamp, 19 February 1949, EC Papers.

25. Unit 2 was located around Snake Bight, while unit 3 was located east of the bight.

26. Donald Lee memo, 8 February 1949, NPS Records; Carl Hawkins to John Pennekamp, 19 February 1949, EC Papers, and in SH Papers-UF; DOI press release, 20 November 1956, SH Papers-UF. On the reconstruction of the road to Flamingo, see Daniel Beard to J. Lee Cuddy, 12 February 1957, LeRoy Collins Papers, SAF. E. C. Lunsford, an ENPC member and Miami dentist, erected an airplane landing strip and other structures at Cape Sable in anticipation of the construction of a resort at the cape. The NPS had to pay for those structures and others hastily erected at Flamingo by the residents of that fishing village. See Daniel Beard memo, 26 May 1947, NPS Records; Daniel Beard to Augustus Burghard, 7 February 1949, NPS Records; Daniel Beard to regional director, 13 June 1949, Peterson Papers.

27. Carl Hawkins to Donald Lee, 5 February 1949, NPS Records.

28. On Pennekamp's efforts, see John Pennekamp to Thomas Allen, 19 April 1948, Peterson Papers; Julius Krug to J. Hardin Peterson, 20 April 1949, Peterson Papers. On landowner's efforts in 1947, see C. Ray Vinten memo, ca. 1947, NPS Records; C. Ray Vinten memo, 16 June 1947, NPS Records; D. A. McDougal to Ivar Axelson, 17 June 1947, MMA Papers; SH to Ben Shepard, 16 June 1947, MMA Papers; John Pennekamp to Joe. E. Hendricks, 2 July 1947, SH Papers-SAF. On landowner's efforts in 1948, see D. A. McDougal statement on HR 1254, ca. February 1948; Arthur Klipstein statement on HR 1254, ca. February 1948; Ivar Axelson report on HR 3378, 24 April 1948, all in MMA Papers. Quotes are from J. Hardin Peterson to John Pennekamp, 28 April 1948, Peterson Papers; John Pennekamp to Thomas Allen, 19 April 1948, Peterson Papers.

29. Julius Krug to J. Hardin Peterson, 20 April 1949, Peterson Papers; Carl Hawkins to Ivar Axelson, 18 February 1949, MMA Papers.

30. Ivar Axelson, minutes of meeting of landowners of the Everglades Park Area, 18 December 1947, MMA Papers; D. A. McDougal statement before the Senate Committee on Interior and Insular Affairs, 12 August 1949, MMA Papers; Ivar Axelson statement on HR 4025, ca. 1949, Peterson Papers.

31. Letter to landowners, 1948; McDougal statement before the Senate Committee, both in MMA Papers.

32. Quote about the group's purpose is from: Minutes of Meeting of Landowners of the Everglades Park Area, 18 December 1947, MMA Papers; Gloria M. Laswell to William Dawson, 2 April 1948, MMA Papers, emphasis in original; Ralph T. Folwell to John R. Murdock, 21 February 1949, MMA Papers. Also see Everglades National Park Landowners Association form

letter, 2 April 1948, MMA Papers. The organization was usually in debt, and the McDougal-Axelsons paid most of the group's expenses. See ENPLA fund-raising letter, April 1949,MMA Papers; MMA to Simonhoff, April 1949, MMA Papers.

33. SH to John Pennekamp, 9 August 1949, Peterson Papers.

34. SH to D. A. McDougal, 9 April 1948, Peterson Papers; U.S. Code 410e, 10 October 1949, Ch. 659, 63 Stat. 733; DOI press release, 5 November 1949, EC Papers.

35. On the deed's acceptance, see SH to Newton Drury, 6 November 1948, SH Papers-UF. This state park was owned and run by the Florida Federation of Women's Clubs. May Mann Jennings, the former president of that organization and a longtime member of the ENPC, had been instrumental in that park's creation in 1916. See Vance, *May Mann Jennings*." Although the Royal Palm State Park had been offered to the proposed ENP in the early 1930s, the park had also been significantly altered, most notably by the CCC. The area today remains a center of tourism and interpretation in the park and contains the popular Anhinga Trail. On CCC actions in Royal Palm State Park, see Jackson, *Pioneer of Tropical Landscape Architecture*. Acreage data is from Daniel Beard to SH, 11 September 1950, SH Papers-UF.

36. Acreage data from 1950 is from Beard to SH, 11 September 1950. On the Klipstein case, see DOI press release, 5 March 1950, EC Papers. On the condemnation proceedings, see DOI press release, 9 May 1950, EC Papers; Beard to SH, 11 September 1950; United States, Plaintiff, v. Certain Lands in Dade and Monroe County, Florida, Henry Booker Jr., et al., Defendants, no. 3378-M Civil; Albert Manly memo, October 1958, MMA Papers. The Ivar Axelson lawsuit was a "friendly" condemnation according to Daniel Beard and was due to the questionable legal status of some lands. Axelson and the NPS did agree on a sale price. On the park's boundaries as of 1953, see DOI to Governor McCarty, 10 April 1953, SH Papers-UF.

37. Thomas Allen memo, 26 February 1948, NPS Records; Newton Drury memo, 14 January 1948, NPS Records; Daniel Beard memo, 30 January 1948, NPS Records; DOI to Dan McCarty, 10 April 1953, SH Papers-UF.

38. On the initial agreement to expand this boundary, see Daniel Beard to Fuller Warren, 7 June 1951; Dorothy MacMaster to A. E. Demaray, 27 June 1951, both in Fuller Warren Papers, SAF. Quote from IIF is from *Minutes of the Trustees*, 1950–52, 353–54. On the Collier lands and Warren's approval for future land acquisition, see ENP meeting minutes, 22 March 1954, attached to Daniel Beard to NPS director, 4 August 1954; SH to Nathan Mayo, 26 February 1954, both in SH Papers-UF. On the Patton Tract, see DOI to Governor McCarty, 10 April 1953; SH to Nathan Mayo, 26 February 1954; SH and James Franklin telephone call transcript, 2 June 1953, all in SH Papers-UF. On the additional lands needed for this acquisition, see DOI to Governor McCarty, 10 April 1953; SH to Nathan Mayo, 26 February 1954, both in SH Papers-UF.

39. Colburn and Scher, *Florida's Gubernatorial Politics*, 103. Other reasons for Florida's weak governor include strict term limits (other cabinet positions had none), the unwieldy and decentralized administrative agencies in the state government that the governor had little control over, the disparate and divided geography and demography of the state that gave most governors no stable or established base of political support, and a powerful legislature that often ignored or rejected the governor's agenda. On Florida politics and the nature of the Florida cabinet, see Key, *Southern Politics*; Colburn and DeHaven-Smith, *Government in the Sunshine State*; Colburn and Scher, *Florida's Gubernatorial Politics*.

40. *Minutes of the Trustees*, 7 May 1952, 803–4; *Minutes of the Trustees*, 12 August 1952, 47–49.

41. *Minutes of the Trustees*, 19 August 1952, 55–60.

42. *Minutes of the Trustees*, 27 January 1953, 210–12.

43. Quote is from May 1953, SMR. On this bill's passage, see Ivar Axelson to Arthur Klipstein, 8 June 1953, MMA Papers; *Florida Journal of the House of Representatives*, 22 May 1953, 892; *Florida Journal of the Senate*, 4 June 1953, 1213; *Miami News*, 10 May 1953, 7-D. On Bernie Papy, see *Miami News*, 11 August 1964, 1. The title of this bill was long and curious: "A bill to be entitled An Act to prohibit the sale, conveyance, exchanging or other disposition of land in any county in the State of Florida having a population of 29,957 according to the United States Census of 1950, owned, managed or controlled by the Trustees of the Internal Improvement Fund, the State Board of Education, or any other state board or agency of the State of Florida, which would have the effect of, or tend to have the effect of enlarging the boundaries of the Everglades National Park as those boundaries are set forth in that certain deed numbered 19035, executed December 28, 1944 by the Trustees of the Internal Improvement Fund of the State of Florida to the United States of America: repealing all laws in conflict therewith and providing that same shall become effective immediately." *Florida Journal of the House of Representatives*, 22 May 1953, 892.

44. James Franklin to SH, 27 May 1953; James Franklin and SH phone conversation transcript, 2 June 1953, both in SH Papers-UF.

45. On McCarty's veto, see Administrative Assistant to A. E. Surdam, 19 June 1953, Daniel McCarty/Charley Johns Papers, SAF. McCarty suffered a heart attack in February 1958 and then later died of pneumonia. On Johns, see Schnur, "Cold Warriors"; Star, "McCarthyism in Florida"; ENP meeting minutes, 22 March 1954, attached to Daniel Beard to NPS director, 4 August 1954, SH Papers-UF. Quote on Johns is from Colburn and Scher, *Florida's Gubernatorial Politics*, 142.

46. *Minutes of the Trustees*, 1952–54, 556–57, 557; Ivar Axelson to Charley Johns, 25 January 1954, Daniel McCarty/Charley Johns Papers, SAF.

47. *Minutes of the Trustees*, 1952–54, 609–28.

48. Gunter, *Exploration for Oil and Gas, 1954 Supplement*; Gunter, *Exploration for Oil and Gas, 1955 Supplement*.

49. Ivar Axelson to Courtney Campbell, 2 February 1954, MMA Papers. Also see "Truth of Miami Herald's Statements . . . ," Association of the Best Use of Florida Lands circular, attached to Ivar Axelson to Charley Johns, 23 February 1954, Daniel McCarty/Charley Johns Papers, SAF.

50. MMA to Jock Murray, 17 February 1954, MMA Papers; Arthur Klipstein to Orme Lewis, 3 March 1954, Daniel McCarty/Charley Johns Papers, SAF.

51. E. C. Lunsford to Millard Caldwell, 1 October 1945, Millard Caldwell Papers, SAF. Also see John Baker to Millard Caldwell, 9 October 1945, Millard Caldwell Papers.

52. E. C. Lunsford to SH, 9 January 1952, SH Papers-UF; E. C. Lunsford to SH, 12 March 1952, SH Papers-UF; E. C. Lunsford statement, House hearing, 11 July 1957, LeRoy Collins Papers.

53. List of fifteen organizations to Charley Johns, telegram, 15 March 1954, Daniel McCarty/Charley Johns Papers, SAF; Ivar Axelson to Hugh Butler, 27 March 1954, Daniel McCarty/Charley Johns Papers, SAF. This letter was also used as a Association of the Best Use of Florida Lands mailing, found in MMA Papers.

54. ASSOCIATION FOR THE BEST USE OF FLORIDA LANDS mailing, "Why the Secretarial Order adding 271,000 acres . . ." ca. 1954, MMA Papers; MMA to LeRoy Collins, 4 April 1955, LeRoy Collins Papers. These arguments were also connected to the historian Alfred Runte's worthless-lands thesis. Runte argued that parks were typically only composed of lands

deemed worthless. Land that had economic value were typically excluded from parks. Axelson here sought to show that these lands were in fact not worthless. See Runte, *National Parks*; Sellars, "National Parks."

55. Unknown author to George Smathers, 12 April 1954, MMA Papers.

56. Ivar Axelson to Douglas McKay, 20 April 1953, MMA Papers. On Douglas McKay's conservation record, see Richardson, "Interior Secretary."

57. On capitalism and the commodification of nature, see Donald Worster, *Dust Bowl*; Cronon, *Nature's Metropolis*.

58. Ivar Axelson to W. L. C. Clements, 14 April 1954; [Ivar Axelson?], "First Memo on Washington Memo," 15 July 1955; MMA to Jock Murray, 18 February 1954, all in MMA Papers.

59. Daniel Beard memo, 30 January 1948, NPS Records; Daniel Beard memo, 27 June 1949, NPS Records; "Statements made by Dan Beard," 12 February 1953, MMA Papers; Daniel Beard to LeRoy Collins, 19 October 1956, SH Papers-UF.

60. Daniel Beard to Fuller Warren, 7 June 1951, Fuller Warren Papers, SAF; Daniel Beard to SH, 19 July 1955, SH Papers-UF.

61. *Miami Daily News*, 5 March 1957, MMA Papers; "Will the U.S. Government Respect the Request of the State of Florida?," mass mailing, January 1956, MMA Papers; William Neblett to LeRoy Collins, 24 January 1956, LeRoy Collins Papers; "Bernie C. Papy Statement to the Congressional Subcommittees on Public Lands Re: The Everglades National Park (H.R. 6641, H.R. 6653, and S. 1790)," 12 July 1957, MMA Papers. Also see Association of the Best Use of Florida Lands, "The So-Called 40,000 Acre 'Vital Zone,'" MMA Papers.

62. Connie Wirth to LeRoy Collins, 25 February 1955, LeRoy Collins Papers; *Minutes of the Trustees*, 2 April 1955, 225–33; *Minutes of the Trustees*, 1954–56.

63. *Minutes of the Trustees*, 9 May 1955, 264–69; *Minutes of the Trustees*, 1955–56.

64. Connie Wirth to LeRoy Collins, 7 June 1955, LeRoy Collins Papers. On Collins's attitudes, see: LeRoy Collins to Connie Wirth, 10 June 1955; LeRoy Collins to SH, 10 June 1955, both in LeRoy Collins Papers. On the park as a hot potato, see *Miami Daily News*, 5 March 1957, MMA Papers.

65. On SH and Pennekamp's efforts, see SH to Baker, 21 June 1948, SH Papers-UF; SH to Newton Drury, 4 June 1948, SH Papers-UF; SH to Newton Drury, 29 June 1948, SH Papers-UF; Daniel Beard to LeRoy Collins, 22 October 1956, LeRoy Collins Papers. On the NPS's biological views of the park's boundaries, see Connie Wirth to Richard Ervin, 30 January 1956, LeRoy Collins Papers.

66. John Pennekamp to George Smathers, 7 January 1957, LeRoy Collins Papers. Pennekamp's list of excuses is in John Pennekamp to George Smathers, 15 January 1957, LeRoy Collins Papers. Collins's quote is from John Pennekamp to Redford Mobley, 28 September 1956, LeRoy Collins Papers. On the broader issue of Flamingo's tourist facilities, see Ethan Carr, *Mission 66*, 97–100.

67. John Pennekamp to LeRoy Collins, 23 October 1956, LeRoy Collins Papers; Ethan Carr, *Mission 66*, 100; LeRoy Collins to Connie Wirth, 22 February 1957, LeRoy Collins Papers. Also see *Minutes of the Trustees*, 1954–56, 13 March 1956, 572–75.

68. "Action of Trustees of Internal Improvement Fund," 26 March 1957; LeRoy Collins to SH, 4 April 1957, both in LeRoy Collins Papers. Also see Richard Ervin to SH, 22 February 1957, LeRoy Collins Papers.

69. Dante Fascell, who served in the U.S. House of Representatives from 1955 to 1993, would later be instrumental in the creation of Biscayne National Park.

70. John Pennekamp statement, 11 July 1957, LeRoy Collins Papers; Kathryn Hanna statement, 11 July 1957, LeRoy Collins Papers; E. C. Lunsford statement, 11 July 1957, LeRoy Collins Papers; Ivar Axelson to J. L. McCord, 6 July 1957, MMA Papers; Ivar Axelson to Arthur Klipstein, 15 April 1957, MMA Papers; Bernie Papy statement, 12 July 1957, MMA Papers.

71. 72 Stat. 280 (2 July 1958); Holland quote is from 85th Cong. Rec. S11918 (23 June 1958). On the bill's passage, see 85th Cong. Rec. S11915–19 (23 June 1958); 85th Cong. Rec. H11958–66 (23 June 1958); Connie Wirth to LeRoy Collins, 17 March 1959, LeRoy Collins Papers.

Epilogue. Managing the Everglades

1. Daniel Beard, November 1947; Daniel Beard, February 1949; Daniel Beard, January 1950, all in SMR.

2. Daniel Beard, February 1950, SMR.

3. Tebeau, *Man in the Everglades*, 161; Will, *Dredgeman of Cape Sable*; Will, "Digging the Cape Sable Canal"; Epperson, *Roads through the Everglades*, 69–71.

4. Daniel Beard, April 1949; Daniel Beard, May 1949, both in SMR.

5. Daniel Beard, June 1951, SMR.

6. For examples, see Daniel Beard memo, 20 August 1947, NPS Records; M. B. Parker statement, 16 February 1950, SH Papers-UF; Earl Semingson to Daniel Beard, 18 February 1950, SH Papers-UF.

7. Beard, June 1951.

8. Daniel Beard, June 1948, SMR.

9. Daniel Beard, December 1948, SMR.

10. Beard, January 1950, SMR.

11. On the class dynamics of preservation, see Spence, *Dispossessing the Wilderness*; Catton, *Inhabited Wilderness*; Jacoby, *Crimes against Nature*; Keller and Turek, *American Indians and National Parks*.

12. 1940 U.S. Census, 1945 state of Florida census. Mormon Key was not on the 1940 census but was listed on the 1930 U.S. Census.

13. Douglas, *Alligator Crossing*, 52, 55. Also see Simmons and Ogden, *Gladesmen*.

14. Beard, June 1951. Only one individual, Arthur Leslie Darwin, was allowed to remain a resident in the park. He lived on Possum Key, on the west coast of Florida.

15. Beard, June 1951.

16. Daniel Beard, April 1953, SMR.

17. Arno Cammerer memo, 10 March 1937, EC Papers.

18. Daniel Beard to Ray Vinten, 6 June 1946, NPS Records.

19. Daniel Beard, March 1949, SMR.

20. Beard, November 1950, SMR.

21. Beard, June 1950, SMR.

22. Daniel Beard, March 1951, SMR.

23. Gary Davis and Thue, *Fishery Data Management Handbook*.

24. Organized Fishermen of Florida, Herbert Z. Marvin, Victor H. Markley, and Clyde R. Raffield, Plaintiffs-appellants, v. Donald P. Hodel, Secretary, U.S. Department of the Interior, Russell Dickensen, Director of the National Park Service, Bob Baker, Regional Director of the Southeast Regional office of the National Park Service, and John Morehead, Superintendent of Everglades National Park, U.S. Department of the Interior, the National Park Service, and Ever-

glades National Park, Defendants-appellees, Everglades Protection Association, Inc., & World Wide Sportsmen, Inc., Intervenors, 775 F.2d 1544 (U.S. Court of Appeals for the Eleventh Circuit November 15, 1985).

25. Daniel Beard, December 1952, SMR.

26. Daniel Beard, July 1951, SMR.

27. Daniel Beard, July 1948; Daniel Beard, August 1948, both in SMR.

28. Beard, May 1949; Moore, "Status of the Manatee"; Moore, Stimson, and Robertson, "Observations of the Short-Tailed Hawk"; Moore, "Crocodile in the Everglades."

29. Daniel Beard, May 1948, SMR.

30. Daniel Beard memo, 12 December 1947, NPS Records.

31. Thomas Allen memo, 15 December 1947, NPS Records.

32. Daniel Beard, January 1948, SMR.

33. Daniel Beard report on concessions, 1 July 1948, NPS Records.

34. Thomas Allen memo, 14 July 1948, NPS Records.

35. Beard, December 1948, SMR.

36. Daniel Beard, January 1949, SMR.

37. Daniel Beard, December 1949, SMR.

38. Beard, January 1950; Daniel Beard, November 1951, SMR.

39. Beard, June 1950, SMR.

40. Daniel Beard, December 1950, SMR.

41. Ethan Carr, *Mission 66*, 10.

42. Blythe, *Wilderness on the Edge*, 176–212.

Conclusion

1. On flood control efforts since 1947, see Grunwald, *Swamp*, 316–66; Godfrey and Catton, *River of Interests*; Jack Davis, *Everglades Providence*; CERP reports, accessed at www.everglades restoration.gov.

2. Grunwald, *Swamp*, 226.

3. Water Resource Development Act of 2000, Pub. L. No. 106-541, 11 December 2000.

BIBLIOGRAPHY

Manuscript Collections

Fairchild Tropical Garden Archives, Miami, Fla.
David Fairchild Papers

Franklin Delano Roosevelt Presidential Library, Hyde Park, N.Y.

National Archives, College Park, Maryland
Records of the National Park Service, RG79

New York Botanical Garden Special Collections

P. K. Younge Library, University of Florida, Gainesville, Florida
Spessard Holland Papers
John D. Pennekamp Papers

J. Hardin Peterson Papers
George Smathers Papers

Richter Library Special Collections, University of Miami, Miami, Florida
Mary McDougal Axelson Papers
August Seymour Houghton Papers

University of Miami Presidential Archives

South Florida Collections Management Center, Everglades National Park, Florida
Ernest Coe Papers
File Unit 002: Monthly Narrative Reports, 1947–1967. Series II: Correspondence and Reports; subseries B: Superintendent's Monthly Reports, 1947–1967. Records of the Superintendent's Office, EVER 22965.

State Archives of Florida, Tallahassee, Florida
Doyle Carlton Papers
David Sholtz Papers
Fred Cone Papers
Spessard Holland Papers

Millard Caldwell Papers
Fuller Warren Papers
Daniel McCarty/Charley Johns Papers
LeRoy Collins Papers

Periodicals

All Florida Magazine
American Florist
American Fruits
American Forests

American Heritage
Audubon Magazine
Forest and Stream
Garden Magazine

George Wright Forum
Landscape Architecture
Lincoln (NE) Journal Star
Miami Herald
Miami Daily News
National Nurseryman

National Geographic
Nature Magazine
New York Times
Palm Beach Post Times
Saturday Evening Post
Tequesta

Other Works

Abbott, Carl. *The New Urban America: Growth and Politics in Sunbelt Cities*. Durham: University of North Carolina Press, 1981.

Alagona, Peter S. "What Is Habitat?" *Environmental History* 16 (July 2011): 433–38.

Albright, Horace. *The Birth of the National Park Service: The Founding Years, 1913–1933*. Salt Lake City: Howe Brothers, 1985.

Albright, Horace, and Marian Albright Schenck. *Creating the National Park Service: The Missing Years*. Norman: University of Oklahoma Press, 1999.

Arnold, David. "Illusory Riches: Representations of the Tropical World, 1840–1950." *Singapore Journal of Tropical Geography* 21 (March 2000): 6–18.

Aron, Cindy S. *Working at Play: A History of Vacations in the United States*. New York: Oxford University Press, 1999.

Austin, Daniel F., with assistance of Anita F. Cholewa, Rita B. Lassiter, and Bruce F. Hansen. *The Florida of John Kunkel Small: His Species and Types, Collecting Localities, Bibliography, and Selected Reprinted Works*. New York: New York Botanical Garden, 1987.

Ayers, Edward L. *The Promise of the New South: Life after Reconstruction*. New York: Oxford University Press, 1992.

Badger, Anthony J. *The New Deal: The Depression Years, 1933–40*. New York: Macmillan, 1989.

Bailey, Harold. *The Birds of Florida*. Baltimore: William & Wilkins, 1925.

Barbour, George. *Florida for Tourists, Invalids, and Settlers*. Rev. ed. New York: D. Appleton and Company, 1881.

Barnhart, John Hendley. *Bibliography of John Kunkel Small*. [New York?], 1935.

Barr, Bradley W., and James Lindholm. "Conservation of the Sea: Using Lessons from the Land." *George Wright Forum* 17 (2000): 77–85.

Barrow, Mark, Jr. "The Alligator's Allure." In *Beastly Natures: Animals, Humans, and the Study of History*, edited by Dorotee Brantz, 127–52. Charlottesville: University of Virginia Press, 2010.

———. "Dragons in Distress: Naturalists as Bioactivists in the Campaign to Save the American Alligator." *Journal of the History of Biology* 2 (2009): 267–88.

———. *Nature's Ghosts: Confronting Extinction from the Age of Jefferson to the Age of Ecology*. Chicago: University of Chicago Press, 2009.

———. *A Passion for Birds: American Ornithology after Audubon*. Princeton, N.J.: Princeton University Press, 2000.

Bartlett, Richard A. *Yellowstone: A Wilderness Besieged*. Tucson: University of Arizona Press, 1985.

Bartley, Numan V. *The New South, 1945–1980: The Story of the South's Modernization*. Baton Rouge: Louisiana State University Press, 1995.

Beard, Daniel. "Diversity in the Everglades." *Regional Review* 1 (August 1938): 23–25.

———. "Let 'er Burn?" *Everglades Natural History Journal* 2 (March 1954): 2–8.

———. *Wildlife Reconnaissance: Everglades National Park Project*. NPS, Department of the Interior, 1938.

Beeman, Randal S., and James A. Pritchard. *A Green and Permanent Land: Ecology and Agriculture in the Twentieth Century*. Lawrence: University of Kansas Press, 2001.

Berkes, Fikret, David Feeny, Bonnie J. McCay, and James Acheson. "The Benefits of the Commons." *Nature* 340 (13 July 1989): 91–93.

Bernard, Richard M., and Bradley R. Rice, eds. *Sunbelt Cities: Politics and Growth since World War II*. Austin: University of Texas Press, 1983.

Bernstein, Barton J. "The New Deal: The Conservative Achievement of New Deal Reform." In *Towards a New Past: Dissenting Essays in American History*, edited by Barton J. Bernstein, 263–88. New York: Pantheon, 1968.

Bird, Elizabeth Ann R. "The Social Construction of Nature: Theoretical Approaches to the History of Environmental Problems." *Environmental History* 11 (Winter 1987): 255–64.

Blackman, John S. *Oklahoma's Indian New Deal*. Norman: University of Oklahoma Press, 2013.

Blake, Nelson, with updated content by Christopher F. Meindl, Steven Noll, and David Tegeder. *Land into Water/Water into Land: A History of Water Management in Florida*. 1980; rpt., Tallahassee: University Presses of Florida, 2010.

Block, William, and Leonard A. Brennan. "The Habitat Concept in Ornithology: Theory and Applications." *Current Ornithology* 11 (1993): 35–91.

Bocking, Stephen. *Ecologists and Environmental Politics: A History of Contemporary Ecology*. New Haven, Conn.: Yale University Press, 1997.

Bolster, W. Jeffrey. "Opportunities in Marine Environmental History." *Environmental History* 11 (July 2006): 567–97.

Boyd, William. *The Slain Wood: Papermaking and Its Environmental Consequences in the American South*. Baltimore: John Hopkins University Press, 2015.

Brinkley, Alan. *The End of Reform: New Deal Liberalism in Recession and War*. New York: Alfred A. Knopf, 1995.

Brown, Margaret. *The Wild East: A Biography of the Great Smoky Mountains*. Gainesville: University Press of Florida, 2000.

Brown, William E., Jr., and Karen Hudson. "Henry Flagler and the Model Land Company." *Tequesta*, 1996, 46–78.

Buchholtz, C. W. *Rocky Mountain National Park: A History*. Boulder: Colorado Associated University Press, 1983.

Burghard, August. *Half a Century in Florida: Land of Matters Unforgot*. Fort Lauderdale, Fla.: Manatee Books, 1982.

Burke, Edmund. *A Philosophical Enquiry into the Origin of Our Ideas of the Sublime and Beautiful*. London: Printed for R. and J. Dodsley, 1757.

Cahalane, Victor H. "The Everglades—Yesterday, Today, and Tomorrow." *Nature Magazine*, December 1947, 512–17.

Callicot, J. Baird. *Beyond the Land Ethic: More Essays in Environmental Philosophy*. Albany: State University of New York Press, 1999.

———. *In Defense of the Land Ethic: Essays in Environmental Philosophy*. Albany: State University of New York Press, 1989.

———. "Non-Anthropocentric Value Theory and Environmental Ethics." *American Philosophical Quarterly* 12 (October 1984): 299–309.

Callicot, J. Baird, and Michael Nelson. *The Great New Wilderness Debate: An Expansive Collection of Writings Defining Wilderness from John Muir to Gary Snyder*. Athens: University of Georgia Press, 1998.

Callicot, J. Baird, and Michael Nelson. *The Wilderness Debate Rages On: Continuing the Great New Wilderness Debate*. Athens: University of Georgia Press, 2008.

Carlton, James T. "Apostrophe to the Ocean." *Conservation Biology* 12 (December 1998): 1165–67.

Carr, Ethan. *Mission 66: Modernism and the National Park Dilemma*. Amherst: University of Massachusetts Press, 2007.

———. *Wilderness by Design: Landscape Architecture and the National Park Service*. Lincoln: University of Nebraska Press, 1998.

Cash, W. J. *The Mind of the South*. Garden City, N.J.: Doubleday, 1954.

Catton, Theodore. *Inhabited Wilderness: Indians, Eskimos, and National Parks in Alaska*. Albuquerque: University of New Mexico Press, 1997.

———. *National Park, City Playground: Mount Rainier in the Twentieth Century*. Seattle: University of Washington Press, 2006.

Cawley, R. McGreggor. *Federal Land, Western Anger: The Sagebrush Rebellion and Environmental Politics*. Lawrence: University Press of Kansas, 1993.

Chambliss, Julian C., and Denise K. Cummings. "Florida: The Mediated State." *Florida Historical Quarterly* 90 (Winter 2012): 275–85.

Clements, Frederic E. *Plant Succession: An Analysis of the Development of Vegetation*. Washington, D.C.: Carnegie Institution of Washington, 1916.

Cobb, James C. *Away Down South: A History of Southern Identity*. New York: Oxford University Press, 2005.

———. *Industrialization and Southern Society, 1877–1984*. Lexington: University Press of Kentucky, 1984.

———. *Redefining Southern Culture: Mind and Identity in the Modern South*. Athens: University of Georgia Press, 1999.

———. *The Selling of the South: The Southern Crusade for Industrial Development 1936–1980*. Baton Rouge: Louisiana State University Press, 1982

———. *The South and America since World War II*. New York: Oxford University Press, 2011.

Cobb, James C., and Michael V. Namorato, eds. *The New Deal and the South*. Jackson: University Press of Mississippi, 1984.

Cockrell, Alan. *Drilling Ahead: The Quest for Oil in the Deep South, 1945–2005*. Jackson: University Press of Mississippi, 2005.

Coe, Ernest [Francis]. "Horticulture in Japan, as Seen by an American Nurseryman." *National Nurseryman* 19, no. 4 (April 1911): 142.

———. "Keeping Japanese Picture Plants Alive." *Garden Magazine* 37 (1923): 331–32.

———. "Nursery Condition in Northwest—Fall Drought Affected Planting." *American Fruits*, November 1914, 113.

Cohen, Michael. *The Pathless Way: John Muir and American Wilderness*. Madison: University of Wisconsin Press, 1984.

Colburn, David R., and Lance DeHaven-Smith. *Government in the Sunshine State: Florida Since Statehood*. Gainesville: University Press of Florida 1999.

Colburn, David R., and Richard K. Scher. *Florida's Gubernatorial Politics in the Twentieth Century*. Gainesville: University Press of Florida 1980.

Collier, John. "The Red Atlantis." *Survey* 49 (October 1922).

———. "With Secretary Ickes and the Seminoles." *Indians at Work* 2 (1 April 1935): 1–6.

Colten, Craig E. *An Unnatural Metropolis: Wresting New Orleans from Nature.* Baton Rouge: Louisiana State University Press, 2005.

Cooke, Edward F. "Drafting the 1952 Platforms." *Political Research Quarterly* 9 (September 1956): 699–712.

Covington, James W. *The Seminoles of Florida.* Gainesville: University Press of Florida, 1993.

Cox, Karen, ed. *Destination Dixie: Tourism and Southern History.* Gainesville: University Press of Florida, 2012.

Cox, Merlin G. "David Sholtz: New Deal Governor of Florida." *Florida Historical Quarterly* 43 (October 1964): 142–52.

Cox, Nicole C. "Selling Seduction: Women and Feminine Nature in 1920s Florida Advertising." *Florida Historical Quarterly* 89 (Fall 2010): 186–209.

Crespino, Joseph. *In Search of Another Country: Mississippi and the Conservative Counterrevolution.* Princeton, N.J.: Princeton University Press, 2007.

Cronon, William. "Foreword: Why Worry about Roads." In *Driven Wild: How the Fight against Automobiles Launched the Modern Wilderness Movement,* by Paul S. Sutter, vii–xii. Seattle: University of Washington Press, 2002

———. *Nature's Metropolis: Chicago and the Great West.* New York: W. W. Norton, 1991.

———. "The Trouble with Wilderness." In *Uncommon Ground: Toward Reinventing Nature,* edited by William Cronon, 69–90. New York: W. W. Norton, 1995.

———. *Uncommon Ground: Toward Reinventing Nature.* New York: W. W. Norton, 1995.

Cullinane Thomas, Catherine, Christopher Huber, and Lynne Koontz. *2014 National Park Visitor Spending Effects: Economic Contributions to Local Communities, States, and the Nation.* Natural Resource Report NPS/NRSS/EQD/NRR—2015/947. Washington, D.C.: National Park Service, 2015. https://pubs.er.usgs.gov/publication/70148496.

Cutler, Phoebe. *The Public Landscape of the New Deal.* New Haven, Conn.: Yale University Press, 1985.

Daily, David W. *The Battle for the BIA: G. E. E. Lindquist and the Missionary Crusade against John Collier.* Tucson: University of Arizona Press, 2004.

Daniel, Pete. *Breaking the Land: The Transformation of Cotton, Tobacco, and Rice Cultures since 1880.* Urbana: University of Illinois Press, 1985.

———. *Toxic Drift: Pesticides and Health in the Post–World War II South.* Baton Rouge: University of Louisiana Press, 2005.

Davis, Donald Edward Davis. *Where There Are Mountains: An Environmental History of the Southern Appalachians.* Athens: University of Georgia Press, 2000.

Davis, Fredrick Rowe. *The Man Who Saved Sea Turtles: Archie Carr and the Origins of Conservation Biology.* New York: Oxford University Press, 2007.

Davis, Gary E. "Designing Ocean Parks for the Next Century." *George Wright Forum* 25 (2008): 7–22.

Davis, Gary E., and Edith B. Thue. *Fishery Data Management Handbook, Everglades National Park.* Homestead: South Florida Research Center, 1979.

Davis, Jack E. "Alligators and Plume Birds: The Despoliation of Florida's Living Aesthetic." In *Paradise Lost?: The Environmental History of Florida,* edited by Jack E. Davis and Raymond Arensault, 235–59. Gainesville: University Press of Florida, 2005.

————. *An Everglades Providence: Marjory Stoneman Douglas and the Environmental Century*. Athens: University of Georgia Press, 2009.

Davis, Steven M., and John C. Ogden, eds. *Everglades: The Ecosystem and Its Restoration*. Delray Beach, Fla.: St. Lucie Press, 1994.

Dawson, Michael. "'Travel Strengthens America'? Tourism Promotion in the United Stated During the Second World War." *Journal of Tourism History* 3 (November 2011): 217–36.

Deacon, Margaret. *Scientists and the Sea, 1650–1900: A Study of Marine Science*. 1971. Brookfield, Vt.: Ashgate, 1997.

Demeritt, David. "What Is the 'Social Construction of Nature'? A Typology and Sympathetic Critique." *Progress in Human Geography* 26 (2002): 766–89.

Derr, Mark. *Some Kind of Paradise: A Chronicle of Man and the Land in Florida*. Gainesville: University Press of Florida, 1998.

————. "One Way Partnership Derailed." *Harper's Magazine*, 210 (May 1955).

DeVoto, Bernard. "Two-Gun Desmond Is Back." *Harper's Magazine*, 202 (March 1951): 48–51.

————. "The Western Land Grab." *Harper's Magazine, 140* (June 1947): 120–35.

Dislaver, Lary M. *America's National Park System: The Critical Documents*. Lanham, Md.: Rowman & Littlefield, 1994.

Dilsaver, Lary M., and Douglas H. Strong. "Sequoia and Kings Canyon National Parks: One Hundred Years of Preservation and Resource Management." *California History* 69 (Summer 1990): 98–117.

Douglas, Marjory Stoneman. *Alligator Crossing*. 1959; rpt. Minneapolis: Milkweed Editions, 2003.

————. *The Everglades: River of Grass*. New York: Rinehart, 1947.

————. "The Forgotten Man Who Saved the Everglades." *Audubon* 73 (September 1971): 79–96.

————. "Plumes." *Saturday Evening Post*, 14 June 1930, 8–9, 112, 114, 117–18, 121.

————. "Wings." *Saturday Evening Post*, 14 March 1931, 10–11, 74, 77–78.

Douglas, Marjory Stoneman, and John Rothchild. *Marjory Stoneman Douglas: Voice of the River, an Autobiography*. Englewood, Fla.: Pineapple Press, 1987.

Dovell, J. E. "The Railroads and the Public Lands of Florida, 1879–1905." *Florida Historical Quarterly*, January 1956, 236–58.

Drake, Brian Allen. *Loving Nature, Fearing the State: Environmentalism and Antigovernment Politics before Reagan*. Seattle: University of Washington Press, 2013.

Driver, Felix. "Imagining the Tropics: Views and Visions of the Tropical World." *Singapore Journal of Tropical Geography* 25 (March 2004): 1–17.

Driver, Felix, and Luciana Martins, eds. *Tropical Visions in an Age of Empire*. Chicago: University of Chicago Press 2005.

Drye, Willie, *Storm of the Century: The Labor Day Hurricane of 1935*. Washington, D.C.: National Geographic Society, 2002.

Dunaway, Finis. *Natural Visions: The Power of Images in American Environmental Reform*. Chicago: University of Chicago Press, 2005.

Duncan, Dayton. "George Melendez Wright and the National Park Idea." *George Wright Forum* 26 (2009): 1–13:

Duncan, Dayton, and Ken Burns. *The National Parks: America's Best Idea*. New York: Alfred A. Knopf, 2009.

Dunlap, Thomas R. *Saving America's Wildlife: Ecology and the American Mind, 1850–1990*. Princeton, N.J.: Princeton University Press 1988.

———. "Wildlife, Science, and the National Parks, 1920–1940." *Pacific Historical Review* 59 (May 1990): 187–202.

Edelson, S. Max. *Plantation Enterprise in Colonial South Carolina*. Cambridge, Mass.: Harvard University Press, 2011.

Elias, Thomas S. *History of the Introduction and Establishment of Bonsai in the Western World.* Accessed at https://citeseerx.ist.psu.edu/viewdoc/summary?doi=10.1.1.543.8959.

Eller, Ronald D. *Miners, Millhands, and Mountaineers: Industrialization of the Appalachian South, 1880–1930*. Knoxville: University of Tennessee Press, 1982.

Emerson, Ralph Waldo. "The Method of Nature." 1841. Accessed at American Transcendentalism Web, https://archive.vcu.edu/english/engweb/transcendentalism/authors/emerson/essays/method.html.

Epperson, Bruce D. *Roads through the Everglades: The Building of the Ingraham Highway, the Tamiami Trail, and Conners Highway, 1914–1931*. Jefferson, N.C.: McFarland, 2016.

Evans, Jon S. "The Origins of Tallahassee's Racial Disturbance Plan: Segregation, Racial Tensions, and Violence during World War II." *Florida Historical Quarterly* 79 (Winter 2001): 346–64.

———. "Weathering the Storm: Florida Politics during the Administration of Spessard L. Holland in World War II." PhD diss., Florida State University, 2011.

Everglades of Florida: Acts Reports and Other Papers, State and National, Relating to the Everglades of the State of Florida and their Reclamation. Washington, D.C.: Government Printing Office, 1911.

Everhart, William. *The National Park Service*. New York: Praeger, 1983.

Fairchild, David. *The Proposed National Park in Southern Everglades of Florida*. Department of Agriculture, State of Florida, 1929.

———. *The World Was My Garden: Travels of a Plant Explorer*. New York: Charles Scribner's Sons, 1938.

Feeny, David, Fikret Berkes, Bonnie J. McCay, and James Acheson. "The Tragedy of the Commons: Twenty-Two Years Later." *Human Ecology* 18, no. 1 (1990): 1–19.

Fitzgerald, Edward A. *The Seaweed Rebellion: Federal-State Conflicts over Offshore Energy Development*. Lanham, Md.: Lexington Books, 2001.

Flader, Susan L. *Thinking like a Mountain: Aldo Leopold and the Evolution of an Ecological Attitude toward Deer, Wolves, and Forests*. Columbia: University of Missouri Press, 1974.

Flippen, J. Brooks. *Conservative Conservationist: Russell E. Train and the Emergence of American Environmentalism*. Baton Rouge: Louisiana State University Press, 2006.

———. *Nixon and the Environment*. Albuquerque: University of New Mexico Press, 2000.

Fogelson, Richard E. *Married to the Mouse: Walt Disney World and Orlando*. New Haven, Conn.: Yale University Press: 2001.

Foltz, Richard C. "Does Nature Have Historical Agency? World History, Environmental History, and How Historians Can Help Save the Planet." *History Teacher* 37 (November 2003): 9–28.

Foresta, Ronald. *America's National Parks and Their Keepers*. Washington, D.C.: Resources for the Future, 1984.

Forman, David. *Rewilding North America: A Vision for Conservation in the 21st Century*. Washington, D.C.: Island Press 2004.

Fox, Stephen. *The American Conservation Movement: John Muir and His Legacy*. Madison: University of Wisconsin Press, 1985.

Frank, Jerry J. *Making Rocky Mountain National Park: The Environmental History of an American Treasure*. Lawrence: University Press of Kansas, 2013.

Frazer, William, and John J. Guthrie Jr. *The Florida Land Boom: Speculation, Money and the Banks*. Westport, Conn: Quorum, 1995.

Fredrickson, Kari. *The Dixiecrat Revolt and the End of the Solid South, 1932–1968*. Chapel Hill: University of North Carolina Press, 2001.

Freidel, Frank. *Franklin D. Roosevelt: A Rendezvous with Destiny*. Boston: Little, Brown, 1990.

Frome, Michael. *Battle for the Wilderness*. New York: Praeger, 1974.

———. *Regreening the National Parks*. Tucson: University of Arizona Press, 1992.

Gates, Paul W. *History of Public Land Law Development*. Washington, D.C.: Government Printing Office, 1968.

George, Paul S. "Brokers, Binders, and Builders: Greater Miami's Boom of the Mid-1920s." *Florida Historical Quarterly* 65 (July 1986): 27–51.

———. "Passage to the New Eden: Tourism in Miami from Flagler through Everest G. Sewell." *Florida Historical Quarterly* 59 (April 1981): 440–63.

Giesen, James C. *Boll Weevil Blues: Cotton, Myth, and Power in the American South*. Chicago: University of Chicago Press, 2011.

Gisolfi, Monica R. *The Takeover: Chicken Farming and the Roots of American Agribusiness*. Athens: University of Georgia Press, 2017.

Gleason, Patrick J., and Peter Stone. "Age, Origin, and Landscape Evolution of the Everglades Peatland." In *Everglades: The Ecosystem and Its Restoration*, edited by Steven M. Davis and John C. Ogden, 149–97. Delray Beach, Fla.: St. Lucie Press, 1994.

Godfrey, Matthew C., and Theodore Catton. *River of Interests: Water Management in South Florida and the Everglades, 1948–2010*. Washington, D.C.: Department of the Army, 2011.

Golley, Frank B. *A History of the Ecosystem Concept in Ecology: More than the Sum of its Parts*. New Haven, Conn.: Yale University Press, 1993.

Gottleib, Robert. *Forcing the Spring: The Transformation of the American Environmental Movement*. Washington, D.C.: Island Press, 1993.

Graham, Otis L. "Again the Backward Region?" *Southern Cultures*, Summer 2000, 50–72.

Green, Elna, ed. *Looking for the New Deal: Florida Women's Letters during the Great Depression*. Columbia: University of South Carolina Press, 2007.

Gregg, Sara M. *Managing the Mountains: Land Use Planning, the New Deal, and the Creation of a Federal Landscape in Appalachia*. New Haven, Conn.: Yale University Press, 2010.

Grey, Zane. *Tales of Southern Rivers*. New York: Harper and Brothers, 1924.

Griffin, John W. *Archaeology of the Everglades*. Edited by Jerald T. Milanichv and James J. Miller. Gainesville: University Press of Florida, 2002.

Grunwald, Michael. *The Swamp: The Everglades, Florida and the Politics of Paradise*. New York: Simon & Schuster Paperbacks, 2006.

Gunter, Herman. *Exploration for Oil and Gas in Florida, 1954 Supplement to Information Circular No. 1*. Tallahassee: Florida Geological Survey, 1955. https://ufdc.ufl.edu/UF00081126/00007.

———. *Exploration for Oil and Gas in Florida, 1955 Supplement to Information Circular No. 1*. Tallahassee: Florida Geological Survey, 1956. https://ufdc.ufl.edu/UF00081126/00009.

Hagen, Joel B. *An Entangled Bank: The Origins of Ecosystem Ecology*. New Brunswick, N.J.: Rutgers University Press, 1992.

Hampton, H. Duane. *How the U.S. Cavalry Saved Our National Parks*. Bloomington: Indiana University Press, 1971.

————. "Opposition to National Parks." *Journal of Forest History* 25 (January 1981): 36–45.

Hanna, Alfred Jackson, and Kathryn Abbey Hanna. *Lake Okeechobee: Wellspring of the Everglades*. Indianapolis: Bobbs-Merrill, 1948.

Haraway, Donna J. *Simians, Cyborgs, and Women: The Reinvention of Nature*. New York: Routledge, 1991.

Hardin, Garrett. "The Tragedy of the Commons." *Science* 162 (3859): 1243–48.

Harper, Andrew C. "Conceiving Nature: The Creation of Montana's Glacier National Park." *Montana: The Magazine of Western History* 60 (Summer 2010): 3–24, 91–94.

Harris, Amanda. *Fruits of Eden: David Fairchild and America's Plant Hunters*. Gainesville: University Press of Florida, 2015.

Harvey, Mark. "Sound Politics: Wilderness, Recreation, and Motors in the Boundary Waters, 1945–1964." *Minnesota History* 58, no. 3 (Fall 2002): 130–45.

————. *A Symbol of Wilderness: Echo Park and the American Conservation Movement*: Albuquerque: University of New Mexico Press, 1994.

————. *Wilderness Forever: Howard Zahniser and the Path to the Wilderness Act*. Seattle: University of Washington Press, 2005.

Hauptman, Laurence. *Iroquois and the New Deal*. Syracuse, N.Y.: Syracuse University Press 1981.

Hawley, Ellis. *The New Deal and the Problem of Monopoly: A Study in Economic Ambivalence*. Princeton, N.J.: Princeton University Press, 1966.

Hays, Samuel P. *The American People and the National Forests: The First Century of the U.S. Forest Service*. Pittsburgh: University of Pittsburgh Press, 2009.

————. *Beauty, Health, and Permanence: Environmental Politics in the United States, 1955–1985*. New York: Cambridge University Press, 1987.

————. *Conservation and the Gospel of Efficiency: The Progressive Conservation Movement, 1890–1920*. Cambridge, Mass.: Harvard University Press 1959.

————. *Wars in the Woods: The Rise of Ecological Forestry in America*. Pittsburgh: University of Pittsburgh Press 2007.

Helvarg, David. *The War against the Greens: The "Wise-Use" Movement, the New Right, and the Browning of America*. Rev. and updated, Boulder, Colo.: Johnson Books, 2004.

Hendee, John C., and George H. Stankey. "Biocentricity in Wilderness Management." *BioScience* 23, no. 9 (1973): 535–38.

Henderson, Henry L., and David B. Woolner, eds. *FDR and the Environment*. New York: Palgrave Macmillan, 2005.

Hersey, Mark D. *My Work Is That of Conservation: An Environmental Biography of George Washington Carver*. Athens: University of Georgia Press, 2011.

Hillyer, Reiko. *Designing Dixie: Tourism, Memory and Urban Space in the New South*. Charlottesville: University of Virginia Press, 2014.

Hoder-Salmon, Marilyn. "The Intimate Agony of Mary McDougal Axelson's Life Begins." *American Studies* 18 (Fall 1977): 55–69.

————. "Myrtle Archer McDougal: Leader of Oklahoma's 'Timid Sisters.'" *Chronicles of Oklahoma* 60 (Fall 1982): 332–43.

————. "'Oklahoma Mary:' Mary McDougal Axelson, the Activist Years, 1916–1922." PhD diss., University of Miami, 1976.

Hofstadter, Richard. *The Age of Reform: From Bryan to F.D.R.* New York: Alfred A. Knopf, 1955.

Hollis, Tim. *Dixie before Disney: 100 Years of Roadside Fun*. Jackson: University Press of Mississippi, 1999.

Honey, Martha. *Ecotourism and Sustainable Development: Who Owns Paradise?* 2nd ed. Washington, D.C.: Island Press, 2008.

Hornaday, William T. *Our Vanishing Wild Life: Its Extermination and Preservation*. New York: C. Scribner and Sons, 1913.

Hughes, Dudley J. *Oil in the Deep South: A History of the Oil Business in Mississippi, Alabama, and Florida, 1859–1945*. Jackson: University Press of Mississippi, 1993.

Humboldt, Alexander von. *Cosmos: A Survey of the General Physical History of the Universe*. 5 vols. New York: Harper & Brothers, 1845–62.

——— . *Personal Narrative of Travels to the Equinoctial Regions of America, During the Years 1799–1804*. 7 vols. 1849–29.

Hurd, Barbara. *Stirring the Mud: On Swamps, Bogs, and Human Imagination*. Athens: University of Georgia Press, 2008.

Hurston, Zora Neale. *Their Eyes Were Watching God*. Philadelphia: J. B. Lippincott, 1937.

Ise, John. *Our National Park Policy: A Critical History*. Baltimore: Johns Hopkins University Press, 1961.

Jackson, Faith. *Pioneer of Tropical Landscape Architecture: William Lyman Phillips in Florida*. Gainesville: University Press of Florida, 1997.

Jacoby, Karl. *Crimes against Nature: Squatters, Poaches, Thieves and the Hidden History of American Conservation*. Berkeley: University of California Press, 2001.

Jakle, John. *The Tourist: Travel in Twentieth-Century North America*. Lincoln: University of Nebraska Press, 1985.

Jameson, John. *The Story of Big Bend National Park*. Austin: University of Texas Press: 1996.

Jarvis, Eric. "'Secrecy Has No Excuse': The Florida Land Boom, Tourism, and the 1926 Smallpox Epidemic in Tampa and Miami." *Florida Historical Quarterly* 89 (Winter 2011): 320–46.

Kahrl, Andrew. *The Land Was Ours: African American Beaches from Jim Crow to the Sunbelt South*. Cambridge, Mass.: Harvard University Press, 2012.

Kaufman, Polly Welts. *National Parks and the Woman's Voice: A History*. Albuquerque: University of New Mexico Press, 2006.

Keller, Robert H., and Michael F. Turek. *American Indians and National Parks*. Tucson: University of Arizona Press, 1998.

Kelly, Lawrence C. "The Indian Reorganization Act: The Dream and the Reality." *Pacific Historical Review* 44 (August 1975): 291–312.

Kelman, Ari. *The River and Its City: The Nature of Landscape in New Orleans*. Berkeley: University of California Press, 2003.

Kersey, Harry, Jr. *The Florida Seminoles and the New Deal, 1933–1942*. Boca Raton: Florida Atlantic University Press, 1989.

——— . "A 'New Red Atlantis:' John Collier's Encounter with the Florida Seminoles in 1935." *Florida Historical Quarterly* 66 (October 1987): 131–51.

——— . *Pelts, Plumes, and Hides: White Traders among the Seminoles Indians 1870–1930*. Gainesville: University Press of Florida, 1975.

Key, V. O. *Southern Politics in State and Nation*. New York: A. A. Knopf, 1949.

Kingsland, Sharon. *The Evolution of American Ecology: 1890–2000*. Baltimore: John Hopkins University Press, 2005.

——— . *Modeling Nature: Episodes in the History of Population Ecology*. Chicago: University of Chicago Press, 1985.

Kirby, Jack Temple. *Poquosin: A Study of Rural Landscape and Society*. Chapel Hill: University of North Carolina Press, 1995.

————. *Rural Worlds Lost: The American South, 1920–1960*. Baton Rouge: Louisiana State University Press 1987.

Knowles, Thomas. *Category 5: The 1935 Labor Day Hurricane*. Gainesville: University Presses of Florida, 2009.

Koeniger, A. Cash. "Climate and Southern Distinctiveness," In *Journal of Southern History* 54 (February 1988): 21–44.

Kolko, Gabriel. *The Triumph of Conservatism: A Re-interpretation of American History, 1900–1916*. New York: Free Press of Glencoe, 1963.

Krahe, Diane L., and Theodore Catton. *Little Gem of the Cascades: An Administrative History of Lassen Volcanic National Park*. 2010. Accessed at National Park Service History Electronic Library, http://npshistory.com/publications/lavo/adhi.pdf.

Kricher, John. *The Balance of Nature: Ecology's Enduring Myth*. Princeton, N.J.: Princeton University Press, 2009.

Kruse, Kevin. *White Flight: Atlanta and the Making of Modern Conservatism*. Princeton, N.J.: Princeton University Press, 2007.

Kupper, Patrick. "Science and the National Parks: A Transatlantic Perspective on the Interwar Years." *Environmental History* 14 (January 2009): 58–81.

La Gorce, Oliver. "Florida—The Fountain of Youth." *National Geographic*, January 1930, 1–93.

La Plante, Leah. "The Sage of Biscayne Bay: Charles Torrey Simpson's Love Affair with South Florida." *Tequesta* 55 (1995): 61–81.

Lambert, Darwin. *The Undying Past of Shenandoah National Park*. Boulder, Colo.: Roberts Rinehart, 1989.

Lane, Ed. *The Florida Geological Survey—An Illustrated Chronicle and Brief History*. Tallahassee: Florida Geological Survey, 1998.

Lang, Stephanie M. "'Titles Must Be Perfect': The Broad Form Deed, Politics, and Landownership in Eastern Kentucky at the Turn of the Century." *Register of the Kentucky Historical Society*, Winter 2015, 27–57.

Lassiter, Matthew D. *The Silent Majority: Suburban Politics in the Sunbelt South*. Princeton, N.J.: Princeton University Press, 2006.

Lassiter, Matthew D., and Joseph Crespino, eds. *The Myth of Southern Exceptionalism*. New York: Oxford University Press, 2010.

Lear, Linda. *Rachel Carson: Witness for Nature*. New York: Henry Holt, 1997.

Leopold, Aldo. *Sand County Almanac*. New York: Oxford University Press, 1949.

Leopold, A. Starker. *Wildlife Management in the National Parks*. Washington, D.C.: U.S. Government Printing Office, 1963. Accessed at National Park Service History Electronic Library, http://npshistory.com/publications/leopold_report.pdf.

Leuchtenburg, William E. *Franklin D. Roosevelt and the New Deal*. New York: Harper & Row, 1963.

Little, John J. "Island Wilderness: A History of Isle Royale National Park." PhD diss., University of Toledo, 1978.

Lodge, Thomas E. *The Everglades Handbook: Understanding the Ecosystem*. Boca Raton, Fla.: St. Lucie Press, 1998.

Louter, David. *Windshield Wilderness: Cars, Roads, and Nature in Washington's National Parks*. Seattle: University of Washington Press, 2006.

Lowndes, Joseph E. *From the New Deal to the New Right: Race and the Southern Origins of Modern Conservatism*. New Haven, Conn.: Yale University Press, 2008.

Lowry, William R. *Repairing Paradise: The Restoration of Nature in America's National Parks.* Washington, D.C.: Brookings Institution Press, 2009.

Lubchenco, Jane, Stephen R. Palumbi, Steven D. Gaines, and Sandy Andleman. "Plugging a Hole in the Ocean: The Emerging Science of Marine Reserves." *Ecological Applications* 13 (Supplement, 2003): S3–S7.

Lytle, Mark H. *The Gentle Subversive: Rachel Carson,* Silent Spring *and the Rise of the Environmental Movement.* New York: Oxford University Press, 2007.

MacGrady, Glenn J. "Florida's Sovereignty Submerged Lands: What Are They, Who Owns Them, and Where Is the Boundary?" *Florida State University Law Review* (Fall 1973): 596–644.

Mack, John. *The Sea: A Cultural History.* London: Reaktion Press, 2011.

Mackintosh, Barry. "Harold L. Ickes and the National Park Service." *Journal of Forest History* 29 (April 1985): 78–84.

Magoc, Chris J. *Yellowstone: The Creation and Selling of an American Landscape, 1870–1903.* Albuquerque: University of New Mexico Press, 1999.

Maher, Neil. *Nature's New Deal: The Civilian Conservation Corps and the Roots of the American Environmental Movement.* New York: Oxford University Press, 2008.

Manganiello, Christopher J. *Southern Water, Southern Power: How the Politics of Cheap Energy and Water Scarcity Shaped a Region.* Chapel Hill: University of North Carolina Press, 2017.

Martins, Luciana. "A Naturalist's Vision of the Tropics: Charles Darwin and the Brazilian Landscape." *Singapore Journal of Tropical Geography* 21 (March 2000): 19–33.

Matthiessen, Peter. *Shadow Country: A New Rendering of the Watson Legend.* New York: Modern Library, 2008.

Mauldin, Erin. *Unredeemed Land: An Environmental History of Civil War and Emancipation in the Cotton South.* New York: Oxford University Press, 2018.

McCally, David. *The Everglades: An Environmental History.* Gainesville: University Press of Florida, 1999.

McClelland, Linda Flint. *Building the National Parks: Historic Landscape Design and Construction.* Baltimore: John Hopkins University Press, 1997.

McCloskey, Maxine. "Protected Areas on the High Seas and the Case for Marine Wilderness." *Wild Earth* 86 (Spring 1997): 87–92.

McCormick, Richard L. "The Discovery that Business Corrupts Politics: A Reappraisal of the Origins of Progressivism." *American Historical Review* 86 (April 1981): 247–74.

McElvaine, Robert S., ed. *Down and Out in the Great Depression: Letters from the Forgotten Man.* Chapel Hill: University of North Carolina Press, 1983.

McEvoy, Arthur F. *The Fisherman's Problem: Ecology and Law in the California Fisheries, 1850–1980.* New York: Cambridge University Press, 1986.

McGirr, Lisa. *Suburban Warriors: The Origins of the New American Right.* Princeton, N.J.: Princeton University Press, 2002.

McIver, Stuart B. *Death in the Everglades: The Murder of Guy Bradley, America's First Martyr to Environmentalism.* Gainesville: University Press of Florida, 2003.

McKinsey, Elizabeth R. *Niagara Falls: Icon of the American Sublime.* New York: Cambridge University Press, 1985.

McMillen, Neil R., ed. *Remaking Dixie: The Impact of World War II on the American South.* Jackson: University of Mississippi Press, 1997.

McPherson, Benjamin F., et al. *The Environment of South Florida: A Summary Report: A*

Description of the Ecosystem and Changes Resulting from Man's Activity. Washington, D.C.: U.S. Government Printing Office, 1976.

Meindl, Christopher F. "Frank Stoneman and the Florida Everglades during the Early 20th Century." *Florida Geographer* 29 (1998): 44–54.

———. "Past Perceptions of the Great American Wetland: Florida's Everglades During the Early Twentieth Century." *Environmental History* 5, no. 3 (2000): 378–95.

———. "Southerners and Their Swamps: The View from Middle Georgia." *Southeastern Geographer* 44 (2004): 74–89.

Meindl, Christopher F., Derek H. Alderman, and Peter Waylen. "On the Importance of Environmental Claims-Making: The Role of James O. Wright in Promoting the Drainage of the Florida Everglades in the Early Twentieth Century." *Annals of the Association of American Geographers* 92 (December 2002): 682–701.

Meine, Curt. *Aldo Leopold: His Life and Work.* Madison: University of Wisconsin Press, 1988.

Mengak, Kathy. *Reshaping Our National Parks and Their Guardians: The Legacy of George B. Hartzog Jr.* Albuquerque: University of New Mexico Press, 2012.

Mighetto, Lisa. *Wild Animals and American Environmental Ethics.* Tucson: University of Arizona Press, 1991.

Milanich, Jerald T. *Florida Indians and the Invasion from Europe.* Gainesville: University of Florida Press, 1995.

Miles, John C. *Guardians of the Parks: A History of the National Parks and Conservation Association.* Washington, D.C.: Taylor & Francis, 1995.

———. *Wilderness in National Parks: Playground or Preserve.* Seattle: University of Washington Press, 2009.

Miller, Char. *Gifford Pinchot and the Making of Modern Environmentalism.* Washington, D.C.: Island Press, 2001.

Miller, David C. *Dark Eden: The Swamp in Nineteenth-Century American Culture.* New York: Cambridge University Press, 1989.

Minutes of the Trustees of the Internal Improvement Fund. Tallahassee, Fla., 1935–60. Accessed at Digital Collections Center, Florida International University, http://digitalcollections.fiu.edu/iif/about.htm.

Mohl, Raymond, ed. *Searching for the Sunbelt: Historical Perspectives on a Region.* Athens: University of Georgia Press, 1993.

Mooney-Melvin, Patricia. "Harnessing the Romance of the Past: Preservation, Tourism, and History." *Public Historian* 13 (Spring 1991): 35–48.

Moore, Joseph C. "The Crocodile in the Everglades National Park." *Copeia* 1 (1953): 54–59.

———. "The Status of the Manatee in the Everglades National Park, with Notes on Its Natural History." *Journal of Mammalogy*, February 1951, 22–36.

Moore, Joseph C., Louis A. Stimson, and W. Robertson. "Observations of the Short-Tailed Hawk in Florida." *Auk* 70, no. 4 (October, 1953): 470–78.

Mormino, Gary. *Land of Sunshine, State of Dreams: A Social History of Modern Florida.* Gainesville: University Press of Florida, 2008.

———. "Midas Returns: Miami Goes to War, 1941–1945." *Tequesta* 57 (1997): 5–52.

———. "World War II." In *The New History of Florida*, edited by Michael Gannon, 323–44. Gainesville: University Press of Florida, 1996.

Morris, Christopher. "A More Southern Environmental History." *Journal of Southern History* 75 (August 2009): 581–98.

Morrison, Kenneth D. "America's Last Frontier." *Nature Magazine*, December 1941, 570–78.

Motte, Jacob. *Journey into Wilderness: An Army Surgeon's Account of Life in Camp and Field during the Creek and Seminole Wars, 1836–1838*. Gainesville: University of Florida Press, 1953.

Mueller, Edward K., ed. *DeVoto's West: History, Conservation, and the Public Good*. Athens, Ohio: Swallow Press, 2005.

Myers, Ronald L., and John J. Ewel, eds. *Ecosystems of Florida*. Orlando: University of Central Florida Press, 1990.

Mykle, Robert. *Killer 'Cane: The Deadly Hurricane of 1928*. New York: Cooper Square Press, 2002.

Nash, Gerald D. *United States Oil Policy, 1890–1964: Business and Government in Twentieth Century America*. Westport, Conn.: Greenwood, 1968.

Nash, Roderick. "The American Invention of National Parks." *American Quarterly* 22 (Fall 1970): 726–35.

———. *The Rights of Nature: A History of Environmentalist Ethics*. Madison: University of Wisconsin Press, 1989.

———. *Wilderness and the American Mind*. New Haven, Conn.: Yale University Press, 1967.

National Park Service. *Olympic National Park: Administrative History*. U.S. Government Printing Office, 1992.

———. *Shaping the System*. U.S. Department of the Interior, 2005.

Nelson, Dave. "Florida Crackers and Yankee Tourists. The Civilian Conservation Corps, the Florida Park Service, and the Emergence of Modern Florida Tourism." PhD diss., Florida State University, 2008.

———. "A New Deal for Welfare: Governor Fred Cone and the Florida State Welfare Board." *Florida Historical Quarterly* 84 (Fall 2005): 185–204.

———. "When Modern Tourism Was Born: Florida at the World Fairs and on the World State in the 1930s." *Florida Historical Quarterly* 88 (Spring 2010): 435–68.

Nelson, Lynn A. *Pharsalia: An Environmental Biography of a Southern Plantation, 1780–1880*. Athens: University of Georgia Press, 2007.

Nelson, Megan Kate. *Trembling Earth: A Cultural History of the Okefenokee Swamp*. Athens: University of Georgia Press. 2009.

Newfont, Kathryn. *Blue Ridge Commons: Environmental Activism and Forest History in Western North Carolina*. Athens: University of Georgia Press, 2012.

Nolan, David. *Fifty Feet in Paradise: The Booming of Florida*. San Diego: Harcourt, Brace, Jovanovich, 1984.

Noll, Steven. "Steamboats, Cypress, and Tourism: An Ecological History of the Ocklawaha Valley in the Late Nineteenth Century." *Florida Historical Quarterly* 83 (Summer 2004): 6–23.

Noll, Steven, and David Tegeder. *Ditch of Dreams: The Cross-Florida Barge Canal and the Fight for Florida's Future*. Gainesville: University Press of Florida, 2009.

Noss, Reed. "Building a Wilderness Recovery Network." *George Wright Forum* 11 (1994): 17–40.

Novak, Barbara. *Nature and Culture: American Landscape and Painting, 1835–1875*. 1980; 3rd ed., New York: Oxford University Press, 2007.

Ogden, Laura A. *Swamplife: People, Gators, and Mangroves Entangled in the Everglades*. Minneapolis: University of Minnesota Press, 2011.

Olmsted, Frederick Law, Jr., and William P. Wharton. "The Florida Everglades." *American Forests* 38 (1932): 142–47.

Olmsted, Frederick Law, Jr., and William P. Wharton. "The Proposed Everglades National Park." 72nd Cong., 1st Sess., document no. 54, 22 January 1932. Washington, D.C., 1932.

O'Reilly, John. "South Florida's Amazing Everglades." *National Geographic*, January 1940, 115–42.

Owen, A. L. Riesch. *Conservation under F.D.R.* New York: Praeger, 1983.

Paige, John C., and Lawrence F. Van Horn. *An Ethnohistory of Big Cypress National Preserve, Florida*. Washington, D.C., 1982.

Parker, David M. "Is South Florida the New Southern California? Carl Hiaasen's Dystopian Paradise." *Florida Historical Quarterly* 90 (Winter 2012): 306–23.

Pauley, Philip. *Biologists and the Promise of American Life: From Meriwether Lewis to Alfred Kinsey*. Princeton, N.J.: Princeton University Press, 2000.

———. *Fruits and Plains: The Horticultural Transformation of America*. Cambridge, Mass.: Harvard University Press, 2007.

Phillips, Sarah. *This Land, This Nation: Conservation, Rural American and the New Deal*. New York: Cambridge University Press, 2007.

Phillips, Ulrich Bonnell. *Life and Labor in the Old South*. Boston: Little, Brown, 1929.

Phillips-Fein, Kim. "Conservatism: A State of the Field." *Journal of American History* 98 (December 2011): 723–43.

Pierce, Daniel S. *The Great Smokies: From Natural Habitat to National Park*. Knoxville: University of Tennessee Press, 2000.

Poole, Leslie Kemp. "The Women of the Early Florida Audubon Society." *Florida Historical Quarterly* 85, no. 3 (2007): 297–323.

Pope, Peter E. *Fish into Wine: The Newfoundland Plantation in the Seventeenth Century*. Chapel Hill: University of North Carolina Press 2004.

Pratt, Theodore. "Papa of the Everglades National Park." *Saturday Evening Post*, 9 August 1947.

Pritchard, James A. *Preserving Yellowstone's Natural Conditions: Science and the Perception of Nature*. Lincoln: University of Nebraska Press, 1999.

Pyne, Stephen J. *Fire in America: A Cultural History of Wildland and Rural Fire*. Princeton, N.J.: Princeton University Press, 1982.

Rauch, Basil. *The History of the New Deal, 1933–1938*. New York: Creative Age 1944.

Rawson, Timothy. *Changing Tracks: Predators and Politics in Mt. McKinley National Park*. Fairbanks: University of Alaska Press 2001.

Ray, Janisse. *Pinhook: Finding Wholeness in a Fragmented Land*. White River Junction, Vt.: Chelsea Green, 2005.

Reed, John Shelton. *The Enduring South: Subcultural Persistence in Mass Society*. 1972; new ed., Chapel Hill: University of North Carolina Press, 1986.

Reich, Justin. "Re-creating the Wilderness: Shaping Narratives and Landscapes in Shenandoah National Park." *Environmental History* 6 (January 2001) 95–117.

Reiger, John. *American Sportsmen and the Origins of Conservation*. New York: Winchester Press, 1975.

Revels, Tracy J. *Sunshine Paradise: A History of Florida Tourism*. Gainesville: University Press of Florida, 2011.

Richardson, Elmo R. "The Interior Secretary as Conservation Villain: The Notorious Case of Douglas 'Giveaway' McKay." *Pacific Historical Review* 41 (August 1972): 333–45.

———. "Olympic National Park: Twenty Years of Controversy." *Forest History Newsletter* 12 (April 1969): 6–15.

Righter, Robert. *The Battle over Hetch Hetchy: America's Most Controversial Dam and the Birth of Modern Environmentalism.* New York: Oxford University Press, 2005.

———. *Crucible of Conservation: The Creation of Grand Teton National Park.* Boulder: Colorado Associated University Press, 1982.

———. "National Monuments to National Parks: The Use of the Antiquities Act of 1906." *Western Historical Quarterly* 20 (August 1989): 281–301.

Riordan, Craig Nicholas. "The Development and Implementation of National Park Standards." PhD diss., University of Maine, August 2000.

Robbins, William G., and James C. Foster. *Land in the American West: Private Claims and the Common Good.* Seattle: University of Washington Press, 2000.

Robertson, William B., Jr. *Everglades: The Park Story.* Coral Gables: University of Miami Press, 1959.

Rogers, Benjamin F. "Florida in World War II: Tourists and Citrus." *Florida Historical Quarterly* 39 (July 1960): 34–41.

Rome, Adam. *The Bulldozer in the Countryside: Suburban Sprawl and the Rise of American Environmentalism.* New York: Cambridge University Press, 2001.

———. *The Genius of Earth Day: How a 1970 Teach-In Unexpectedly Made the First Green Generation.* New York: Hill & Wang, 2014.

Rothman, Hal. *Blazing Heritage: A History of Wildland Fire in the National Parks.* New York: Oxford University Press, 2007.

———. *Devil's Bargains: Tourism in the Twentieth-Century American West.* Lawrence: University Press of Kansas, 1998.

———. *The Greening of a Nation? Environmentalism in the United States since 1945.* Fort Worth, Tex.: Harcourt Brace College, 1998.

———. *Neon Metropolis: How Las Vegas Started the Twenty-First Century.* New York: Routledge 2002.

———. *Preserving Different Pasts: The American National Monuments.* Urbana: University of Illinois Press, 1989.

———. "'A Regular Ding-Dong Fight': Agency Culture and Evolution in the NPS-USFS Dispute, 1916–1937." *Western Historical Quarterly* 20 (May 1989): 141–61.

Rothman, Hal, and Char Miller. *Death Valley National Park: A History.* Reno: University of Nevada Press, 2013.

Rothra, Elizabeth Ogren. *Florida's Pioneer Naturalist: The Life of Charles Torrey Simpson.* Gainesville: University Press of Florida,1995.

Rowe, Anne. *The Idea of Florida in the American Literary Imagination.* Baton Rogue: Louisiana State University Press, 1986.

Rozwadowski, Helen M. *Fathoming the Ocean: The Discovery and Exploration of the Deep Sea.* Cambridge, Mass.: Belknap Press of Harvard University Press, 2005.

———. *Vast Expanses: A History of the Oceans.* Chicago: University of Chicago Press, 2019.

Rozwadowski, Helen M., and David K. van Keuren, eds. *The Machine in Neptune's Garden: Historical Perspectives on Technology and the Marine Environment.* Sagamore Beach, Mass.: Science History Publications, 2004.

Runte, Alfred. "Joseph Grinnell and Yosemite: Rediscovering the Legacy of a California Conservationist." *California History* 69 (Summer 1990): 170–81.

———. *National Parks: The American Experience.* Lincoln: University of Nebraska Press, 1979.

————. *Trains of Discovery: Railroads and the Legacy of Our National Parks.* 5th ed. Lanham, Md.: Roberts Rinehart, 2011.

————. *Yosemite: The Embattled Wilderness.* Lincoln: University of Nebraska Press, 1990.

Rusco, Elmer R. "John Collier: Architect of Sovereignty or Assimilation?" *American Indian Quarterly* 15 (Winter 1991): 49–54.

Sachs, Aaron. *The Humboldt Current: Nineteenth-Century Exploration and the Roots of American Environmentalism.* New York: Viking, 2006,

Safina, Carl. *Song for the Blue Ocean: Encounters Along the World's Coast and Beneath the Seas.* New York: Henry Holt, 1998.

Sawyer, Roy T. *America's Wetland: An Environmental and Cultural History of Tidewater Virginia and North Carolina.* Charlottesville: University of Virginia Press, 2010.

Schene, Michael G. "Only the Squeal Is Left: Conflict over Establishing Olympic National Park." *Pacific Historian* 27 (Fall 1983): 53–61.

Schrepfer, Susan R. *The Fight to Save the Redwoods: A History of Environmental Reform, 1917–1978.* Madison: University of Wisconsin Press, 1983.

Schlesinger, Arthur M., Jr. *The Age of Roosevelt.* 3 vols. Boston: Houghton Mifflin, 1956–60.

Schnur, James Anthony. "Cold Warriors in the Hot Sunshine: The Johns Committee's Assault on Civil Liberties in Florida, 1956–1965." Master's thesis, University of South Florida, 1995.

Schullery, Paul, and Lee Whittlesey. *Myth and History in the Creation of Yellowstone National Park.* Lincoln: University of Nebraska Press, 2003.

Schulman, Bruce J. *From Cotton Belt to Sunbelt: Federal Policy, Economic Development, and the Transformation of the South, 1938–1990.* Durham, N.C.: Duke University Press, 1994.

Schwartz, E. A. "Red Atlantis Revisited: Community and Culture in the Writings of John Collier." *American Indian Quarterly* 18 (Autumn 1994): 507–31.

Schwarz, Jordan A. *The New Dealers: Power Politics in the Age of Roosevelt.* New York: Knopf, 1993.

Scott, Doug. *The Enduring Wilderness.* Golden, Colo.: Fulcrum, 2004.

Sears, Richard. *Sacred Places: American Tourist Attractions in the Nineteenth Century.* New York: Oxford University Press, 1989.

Sellars, Richard. "The National Parks: A Forum on the 'Worthless Lands' Thesis." *Journal of Forest History* 27 (July 1983): 130–45.

————. *Preserving Nature in the National Parks: A History.* New Haven, Conn.: Yale University Press, 1997.

Shabecoff, Philip. *A Fierce Green Fire: The American Environmental Movement.* New York: Hill & Wang, 1993.

Shafer, Craig L. "Conservation Biology Trailblazers: George Wright, Ben Thompson, and Joseph Dixon." *Conservation Biology* 15 (April 2001): 332–44.

Shaffer, Marguerite. *See America First: Tourism and National Identity 1880–1940.* Washington, D.C.: Smithsonian Books, 2001.

Shankland, Robert. *Steve Mather of the National Parks.* New York: Knopf, 1951.

"Sheet-Flow Velocities and Factors Affecting Sheet-Flow Behavior of Importance to Restoration of the Florida Everglades." U.S. Geological Survey. Fact sheet 2004-3123. November 2004. https://pubs.usgs.gov/fs/2004/3123/.

Shermer, Elizabeth. *Sunbelt Capitalism: Phoenix and the Transformation of American Politics.* Philadelphia: University of Pennsylvania Press, 2013.

Silver, Timothy. *Mount Mitchell and the Black Mountains: An Environmental History of the Highest Peaks in Eastern America.* Chapel Hill: University of North Carolina Press, 2003.

Simmons, Dennis E. "Conservation, Cooperation, and Controversy: The Establishment of Shenandoah National Park, 1924–1936." *Virginia Magazine of History and Biography* 89 (October 1981): 387–404.

Simmons, Glen, and Laura Ogden. *Gladesmen: Gator Hunters, Moonshiners, and Skiffers.* Gainesville: University Press of Florida, 1998.

Simpson, Charles Torrey. *In Lower Florida Wilds: A Naturalist's Observations on the Life, Physical Geography and Geology of the More Tropical Part of the State.* New York: G. P. Putnam's Sons, 1920.

Siry, Joseph V. *Marshes of the Ocean Shore: Development of an Ecological Ethic.* College Station: Texas A&M University Press, 1984.

Skocpol, Theda, and Kenneth Finegold. *State and Party in America's New Deal.* Madison: University of Wisconsin Press, 1995.

Sloan, N. A. "History and Application of the Wilderness Concept in Marine Conservation." *Conservation Biology* 16 (April 2002): 294–305.

Small, John Kunkel. *Flora of the Southeastern United States.* New York: The Author, 1903, revised 1913, 1933.

———. *From Eden to Sahara: Florida's Tragedy.* Lancaster, Pa.: Science Press Printing Agency, 1929.

———. "The Proposed Everglades National Park, USA." *Nature Magazine*, 14 August 1937, 263–64.

Smiley, Nixon. *Knights of the Fourth Estate: The Story of the Miami Herald.* Miami: E. A. Seeman, 1974.

Smith, Duane A. *Mesa Verde National Park: Shadows of the Centuries.* Boulder: University Press of Colorado, 2002, rev. ed.

Soule, Michael, and Gary Lease, eds. *Reinventing Nature? Responses to Postmodern Deconstruction.* Washington, D.C.: Island Press, 1995.

Spence, Mark David. *Dispossessing the Wilderness: Indian Removal and the Making of the National Parks.* New York: Oxford University Press, 1999.

Stanonis, Anthony J. *Creating the Big Easy: New Orleans and the Emergence of Modern Tourism, 1918–1945.* Athens: University of Georgia Press, 2006.

———, ed. *Dixie Emporium: Tourism, Foodways, and Consumer Culture in the American South.* Athens: University of Georgia Press, 2008.

Star, Bonnie. "McCarthyism in Florida: Charley Johns and the Florida legislative investigation committee, July 1956 to July 1965." Master's thesis, University of South Florida, 1985.

Starnes, Richard D. *Creating the Land of the Sky: Tourism and Society in Western North Carolina.* Tuscaloosa: University of Alabama Press, 2005.

Steinberg, Philip E. *The Social Construction of the Ocean.* Cambridge, 2001.

Steinberg, Ted. *Acts of God: The Unnatural History of Natural Disasters in America.* New York: Oxford University Press, 2000.

———. *Down to Earth: Nature's Role in American History.* New York: Oxford University Press, 2013.

Stepan, Nancy Leys. *Picturing Tropical Nature.* Ithaca, N.Y.: Cornell University Press, 2001.

Stewart, Bruce E., and Christopher J. Manganiello. "Watershed Democracy: Rural Environmentalism and the Battle against the TVA in Western North Carolina, 1965–1972." *Environmental History* 23 (October 2018): 748–73.

Stewart, Mart A. "Southern Environmental History." In *A Companion to the American South*, edited by John B. Boles, 409–43. Malden, Mass.: Blackwell, 2002.

———. *"What Nature Suffers to Groe": Life, Labor, and Landscape on the Georgia Coast, 1680–1920*. Athens: University of Georgia Press, 1996.

Stone, Daniel. *The Food Explorer: The True Adventures of the Globe-Trotting Botanist Who Transformed What American Eats*. New York: Dutton, 2018.

Stone, Spessard. "An Extraordinary Floridian: A Profile of Spessard Lindsey Holland." *Sunland Tribune* 28, article 8 (2002): 69–76.

Strom, Claire. *Making Catfish Bait out of Government Boys: The Fight against Cattle Ticks and the Transformation of the Yeoman South*. Athens: University of Georgia Press, 2009.

Sutter, Paul S. *Driven Wild: How the Fight against Automobiles Launched the Modern Wilderness Movement*. Seattle: University of Washington Press, 2002.

———. *Let Us Now Praise Famous Gullies: Providence Canyon and the Soils of the South*. Athens: University of Georgia Press, 2015.

———. "Nature's Agents or Agents of Empire? Entomological Workers and Environmental Change during the Construction of the Panama Canal." *Isis* 98 (December 2007): 724–54.

———. "No More the Backward Region." In *Environmental History and the American South: A Reader*, edited by Paul S. Sutter and Christopher J. Manganiello, 1–24. Athens: University of Georgia Press, 2009.

———. "Terra Incognita: The Neglected History of Interwar Environmental Thought and Politics." *Reviews in American History* 29 (June 2001): 289–97.

———. "The Tropics: A Brief History of an Environmental Imaginary." In *The Oxford Handbook of Environmental History*, edited by Andrew C. Isenburg, 178–204. New York: Oxford University Press, 2014.

Swain, Donald C. *Federal Conservation Policy: 1921–1933*. Berkeley: University of California Press, 1963.

———. "The National Park Service and the New Deal, 1933–1940." *Pacific Historical Review* 41 (August 1972): 312–32.

———. "The Passage of the National Park Service Act of 1916." *Wisconsin Magazine of History* 50 (Autumn 1966): 4–17.

———. *Wilderness Defender: Horace M. Albright and Conservation*. Chicago: University of Chicago Press, 1970.

Switzer, Jacqueline Vaughn. *Green Backlash: The History and Politics of Environmental Opposition in the U.S.* Boulder, Colo.: Lynne Rienner, 1997.

Taylor, David. "A Biogeographer's Construction of Tropical Lands: A. R. Wallace, Biogeographical Method and the Malay Archipelago." *Singapore Journal of Tropical Geography* 21 (March 200): 63–75.

Taylor, Graham D. *The New Deal and American Indian Tribalism: The Administration of the Indian Reorganization Act, 1934–45*. Lincoln: University of Nebraska Press, 1980.

Taylor, Joseph E., III. *Making Salmon: An Environmental History of the Northwest Fisheries Crisis*. Seattle: University of Washington Press, 1999.

Tebeau, Charlton W. *Man in the Everglades: 2000 Years of Human History in the Everglades National Park*. Coral Gables: University of Miami Press, 2nd rev. ed., 1968.

Thomas, John L. *A Country in the Mind: Wallace Stegner, Bernard DeVoto, History, and the American Land*. New York: Routledge, 2000.

Thoreau, Henry David. *Walden and Other Writings*. New York: Bantam Books, 1962.

Tilden, Freeman. *The National Parks*. New York: Alfred A. Knopf, 1968.

Tindall, George. *The Emergence of the New South, 1913–1945*. Baton Rouge: Louisiana State University Press, 1967.

Turner, James Morton. *The Promise of Wilderness: American Environmental Politics Since 1964.* Seattle: University of Washington Press, 2012.

———. "'The Specter of Environmentalism': Wilderness, Environmental Politics, and the Evolution of the New Right." *Journal of American History* 96 (June 2009): 123–48.

Twigg, Cornelia Mae, "Editor John D. Pennekamp: Herald of Change." Master's thesis, University of Florida, 1977.

Unrau, Harlan, and Mark Stephan. *Administrative History: Crater Lake National Park.* Washington, D.C., 1987, 1991.

Unrau, Harlan D., and G. Frank Williss. *Administrative History: Expansion of the National Park Service in the 1930s.* [Denver:] Denver Service Center, 1983.

Vance, Linda D. *May Mann Jennings: Florida's Genteel Activist.* Gainesville: University Presses of Florida, 1985.

Vickers, Sally. *The Life of Ruth Bryan Owen: Florida's First Congresswoman and America's First Woman Diplomat.* Tallahassee: Sentry, 2009.

Vileisis, Ann. *Discovering the Unknown Landscape: A History of American Wetlands.* Washington, D.C.: Island Press, 1997.

Walker, Laurence C. *The Southern Forest: A Chronicle.* University of Texas Press, 2014.

Wanless, Harold R., and Brigitte M. Viaswinkel. *Coastal Landscape and Channel Evolution Affecting Critical Habitats at Cape Sable, Everglades National Park.* Report to the U.S. Department of Interior, CESI Research Project 02-1, 2005. Accessed at "Everglades," National Park Service, www.nps.gov/ever/learn/nature/cesires02-1.htm.

Watson, James G. "Man Writing: The Watson Trilogy: Peter Matthiessen in the Archive." *Texas Studies in Literature and Language* 46 (June 2004): 245–70.

Way, Albert G. *Conserving Southern Longleaf: Herbert Stoddard and the Rise of*

Weinstein, James. *The Corporate Ideal In the Liberal State, 1900–1918.* Boston: Beacon, 1968.

Welsh, Michael. *Landscape of Ghosts, River of Dreams: A History of Big Bend National Park.* U.S. Government Printing Office, 2002. www.nps.gov/parkhistory/online_books/bibe/adhi/adhi.htm.

West, Patsy. *The Enduring Seminoles: From Alligator Wrestling to Ecotourism.* Gainesville: University Press of Florida, 1998.

Whisnant, Anne Mitchell. *Super-Scenic Motorway: A Blue Ridge Parkway History.* Chapel Hill: University of North Carolina Press, 2006.

Whisnant, Anne Mitchell, Marla R. Miller, Gary B. Nash, and David Thelen. *Imperiled Promise: The State of History in the National Park Service.* Bloomington: Organization of American Historians, 2011.

Whitfield, Stephen J. "Florida's Fudged Identity." *Florida Historical Quarterly* 71 (April 1993): 413–35.

Wiebe, Robert. *The Search for Order: 1870–1920.* New York: Hill and Wang, 1968.

Wilhelm, Chris. "For the Birds: Challenging Wilderness in the Everglades." *Journal of Environmental Studies and Sciences* 3 (June 2013): 153–66.

———. "Pragmatism, Seminoles, and Science: Opposition to Progressive Everglades Drainage." *Florida Historical Quarterly* 90 (Spring 2012): 426–52.

Will, Lawrence E. "Digging the Cape Sable Canal." *Tequesta* 19 (1959): 29–63.

———. *A Dredgeman of Cape Sable.* St. Petersburg, Fla.: Great Outdoors, 1967.

Wilson, Anthony. *Shadow and Shelter: The Swamp in Southern Culture.* Jackson: University of Mississippi Press, 2006.

Wilson, E. O. *Biophilia.* Cambridge, Mass.: Harvard University Press, 1984, rev. ed.

————, ed. *Biodiversity*. Washington, D.C.: National Academy Press, 1988.

Winks, Robin M. "The National Park Service Act of 1916: 'A Contradictory Mandate'?" *Denver University Law Review* 74 (1997): 575–623.

Wirth, Conrad. *Parks, Politics, and the People*. Norman: University of Oklahoma Press, 1980.

Wood, Loren M. *Beautiful Land of the Sky: John Muir's Forgotten Eastern Counterpart, Harlan P. Kelsey*. Bloomington, Ind.: iUniverse, 2013.

Woodside, Christine. "Father of the Everglades." *Connecticut Woodlands* 77 (Fall 2012): 6–9.

Woodward. C. Vann. *The Burden of Southern History*. Updated 3rd ed. Baton Rouge: Louisiana State University Press, 2008.

Woodward, C. Vann. *Origins of the New South, 1877–1913: A History of the South*. Baton Rouge: Louisiana State University Press 1951.

Worster, Donald. *The Dust Bowl: The Southern Plains in the 1930s*. New York: Oxford University Press, 1979.

————. "The Ecology of Order and Chaos." *Environmental History Review* 14 (Spring–Summer 1990): 1–18.

————. *Nature's Economy: A History of Ecological Ideas*. New York: Cambridge University Press, 1994.

————. *A Passion for Nature: The Life of John Muir*. New York: Oxford University Press, 2008.

Wright, Gavin. *Old South, New South: Revolutions in the Southern Economy since the Civil War*. New York: Basic Books, 1986.

Wright, George M., Thomas Dixon, and Ben Thompson. *Fauna of the National Parks of the United States*. U.S. Government Printing Office, 1933.

Wright, Gerald. *Wildlife Research and Management in the National Parks*. Urbana: University of Illinois Press, 1992.

Wulf, Andrea. *Invention of Nature: Alexander von Humboldt's New World*. New York: Vintage Books, 2015.

Wylie, Philip. *Crunch and Des: Stories of Florida Fishing*. New York: Rinehart, 1948.

Yard, Robert Sterling, *Glimpses of our National Parks*. Washington, D.C.: Government Printing Office, 1920.

Yuhl, Stephanie E. *A Golden Haze of Memory: The Making of Historic Charleston*. Chapel Hill: University of North Carolina Press, 2005.

Zweig, Christa L., and M. Kitchens Wiley. "The Semiglades: The Collision of Restoration, Social Values, and the Ecosystem Concept." *Restoration Ecology* 18 (March 2010): 138–42.

INDEX

Acadia National Park, 37–38
Albright, Horace, 18, 36, 45, 72–74, 81
Antienvironmentalism, 9, 138–40, 151–54
Axelson, Ivar, 92–93, 135, 146, 148–54, 158

Bailey, Harold H., 27, 29, 34, 57
Baker, John, 60, 115, 125, 143
Beard, Daniel, 32, 34, 61–63, 82–84, 98–99, 108–9, 127, 131–32, 153–55, 159–66, 168
Big Bend National Park, 38
Big Cypress National Preserve, 11, 171–72
Biocentrism, 9, 59–63, 80–86, 104, 131–32
Biscayne National Park, 84, 171
Bryant, Harold, 61, 81–82, 106
Bryant-Toll report, 61, 103
Burghard, Augustus, 126

Caldwell, Millard, 123–31
Cammerer, Arno, 30, 81, 106–7
Chevelier Land Company, 134–35
Civilian Conservation Corp, 91–92
Coe, Ernest, x, 7, 12; assessment of accomplishments, 110; biocentric vision for preservation, 12–13, 28–29, 59–60, 75, 131–32; boundaries, ideas about, 86–89, 102–3, 105, 124, 131; changing ideas about nature, 26–29; controversies, involved in, 65–68, 71–74, 76–77, 101–6; early life, 23; ecological ideas of, 29–34; efforts to build new rationales for preservation, 59–60; efforts to catalog and acquire park lands, 91–93, 100–110; efforts to pass legislation and influence politicians, 70–74, 77–80, 91–92; efforts to redefine the Everglades, 12–13, 35, 40–51; ENPC, tenure on, 100–110; environmentalism of, 28–29, 34; Everglades drainage, ideas about, 33–34; initial efforts in park fight, 52–54; Key Largo, Coe's desire for inclusion in park, 88, 102–4, 124, 170; love of exotic plants, 23–25; move to Miami, 26; nursery in New England, 22–24; personal life, 106–7, 109–10; publicity efforts, 54–59, 108;

pushed out of park matters, 124–25; Seminoles, relationships and views of, 50, 96–97; tourism, used to promote the park, 63–66, 74–75, 83, 88, 114–15; wilderness, ideas about, 74–75, 80–81
Collier, John, 94–99
Collins, LeRoy, 155–57
Cone, Fred, 90, 99, 106–8
Conservatism, 8–9, 113–14, 133
Copeland, D. Graham, 56, 100, 102–6, 119, 125

DDT, 131–32
DeVoto, Bernard, 138–39
Douglas, Marjory Stoneman, 13–14, 21, 27, 34, 46, 49, 56–58, 108, 162, 168, 172
Drury, Newton, 34, 119–20, 142–43

Ecology, science of, 29–30, 32, 59, 61–63
Environmental regulatory state, 3–4, 7–9, 39, 90–91, 111, 139–40, 161
Everglades: agriculture in, 20, 50; destruction of flora and fauna, 21–22, 59–60, 62–63; drainage, 4, 9–10, 12, 17–20, 32–34, 108–9; flood control, 9–10, 12, 20–21, 127, 168–70; flora and fauna, 13–17, 21–22, 41–43, 45, 55, 72–73, 115–16; human use, 49–51, 90, 94–99, 161–63, 184–85n69; identity of, 12, 14, 35, 40–51; natural features, ix, 3, 4–5, 12, 13–17, 27, 50; oil drilling in, 8–9, 118–21, 130, 133, 136–37, 147–50; private property ownership in, 92–94; rationales for preservation, 5, 22, 52, 59–63; real estate in, 20, 25–26, 94, 102, 134–36 (see also Florida land boom); restoration, 10–11, 167–70; spiritual and inspirational values, 48, 65; water flow, 11–16, 21, 33–34, 108–9, 167–70; water quality, 167
Everglades National Park: biological justification for preservation, 52, 58–63, 85–86, 131–32; boating and tourism in, 75, 84–85, 165; boundaries, discussions of and proposals, 7, 59–61, 74–76, 81, 87–90, 102–6, 119, 121–22, 125–26, 129; boundary expansions, 133, 146–50,

ENVIRONMENTAL HISTORY AND
THE AMERICAN SOUTH